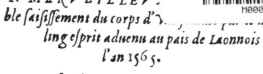

PRODIGIE

VN MERVEILLEV:

ble saisissement du corps d'〤...〤...........par le mau

ling esprit aduenu au pais de Laonnois

l'an 1565.

Chapitre   XLI.

A 2

Engraving from Jean Boulaese, *Le Miracle de Laon en Lannoys*, ed. A. H. Chaubard, Lyon: Sauvegarde Historique, 1955, (from an original in Pierre Boaistuau, *Histories prodigieuses*, 1575). © Bibliothèque Nationale de France

Demonic Possession and Exorcism
in Early Modern France

This is a highly original study of demon possession and the ritual of exorcism, both of which were rife in early modern times, and which reached epidemic proportions in France.

Catholics at the time believed that the devil was everywhere present, in the rise of the heretics, in the activities of witches, and even in the bodies of pious young women. The rite of exorcism was intended to heal the possessed and show the power of the Church – but it generated as many problems as it resolved. Possessed women endured frequently violent exorcisms, exorcists were suspected of conjuring devils, and possession itself came to be seen as a form of holiness, elevating several women to the status of living saints.

Looking towards the present day, the book also argues that early modern conflicts over the devil still carry an unexpected force and significance for Western Christianity.

Sarah Ferber is Lecturer in History at the University of Queensland, Australia. She teaches early modern history, and the history of modern bioethics. She is a co-editor of *Beasts of Suburbia: Reinterpreting Cultures in Australian Suburbs*.

Demonic Possession and Exorcism
in Early Modern France

Sarah Ferber

Routledge
Taylor & Francis Group

LONDON AND NEW YORK

First published 2004
by Routledge
11 New Fetter Lane, London EC4P 4EE

Simultaneously published in the USA and Canada
by Routledge
29 West 35th Street, New York, NY 10001

Routledge is an imprint of the Taylor & Francis Group

Typeset in Goudy by
Keystroke, Jacaranda Lodge, Wolverhampton
Printed and bound in Great Britain by
MPG Books Ltd, Bodmin

British Library Cataloguing in Publication Data
A catalogue record for this book is available from the British Library

Library of Congress Cataloging in Publication Data
Ferber, Sarah, 1957–
    Demonic possession and exorcism in early modern France / Sarah Ferber.
        p.   cm.
    Includes bibliographical references.
    1. Demoniac possession–France–History. 2. Exorcism–
France–History. I. Title.
    BF1517.F5F47 2004
    235′.4′0944–dc22

                                        2003025879

ISBN 0–415–21264–2 (hbk)
ISBN 0–415–21265–0 (pbk)

For my family, and in memory of my brother and my father

Contents

Acknowledgements

I wish to thank Kevin Carney, Rebecca Carter, Margaret Keys and Alison Stewart from the inter-library loan service at the University of Queensland for all their help. In Paris, Caroline Leckenby and Julia McLaren at CPEDERF provided important research materials, and staff at the Bibliothèque Nationale and Bibliothèque Sainte-Geneviève were patient and resourceful. (Certain individual librarians and archivists are mentioned in endnotes.) I am grateful for a semester's teaching relief provided by the Centre for Critical and Cultural Studies at the University of Queensland in 2001. Emily Wilson provided valuable research assistance at a critical time. At Routledge, Vicky Peters and Jane Blackwell were generous editors, while Robin Briggs and Lyndal Roper wrote encouraging and constructive readers' reports. Wolfgang Behringer, Denis Crouzet, Cristina Dessi, Nicole Jacques-Chaquin, Éva Pócs and Alison Weber kindly provided me with copies of their work.

The generosity of my friends, family and colleagues has been incalculable: none can be fully repaid. I mention in particular Albrecht Burkardt, Stuart Clark, Christian Renoux and Alfred Soman, each of whom also provided me with essential references. Jenny Ferber, Constant Mews, the late Ian Robertson and Charles Zika helped me with translations. I thank also Robyn Adams, Carmel Bird, Sue Broomhall, Trish Crawford, Mark Cryle, Georgia Dacakis, Leigh Dale, Joy Damousi, Simon Devereaux, Marion Diamond, Kate Eckstein, Nick Eckstein, Raymond Evans, David Ferber, Helen Ferber, Francis Goodfellow, Lynne Hillier, Johanna Hough, Adrian Howe, Sandy Jeffs, the Lewenhagen family, Andrea McKenzie, Dolly MacKinnon, Bernadette McNevin, Philippa Maddern, John Moorhead, Felicity Nottingham, Helen Pausacker, Kate Reeves, Kay Saunders, Alison Sayers, the late Bob Scribner, Diane Simmons, Chips Sowerwine, Jane Washington-Smith, Helen Weder and Stasia Zika. Special thanks are due to Katie McConnel. The book could not have been completed without them. However, any mistakes are mine.

Parts of Chapter 8 appeared as 'Possession sanctified: the case of Marie des Vallées', in Jürgen Beyer, Albrecht Burkardt, Fred van Lieburg and Marc Wingens, eds, *Confessional Sanctity, (c. 1550–c.1800)*, Veröffentlichungen Des Instituts Für Europäische Geschichte Mainz, Abteilung Abendländische Religionsgeschichte, Beiheft 51, Herausgegeben von Gerhard May), (Mainz: Verlag Philipp von Zabern, 2003), 259–70. Reproduced by kind permission.

Engraving by Thomas Belot, from Jean Boulaese, *Le Thrésor et entière histoire de la triomphante victoire du corps de Dieu sur l'esprit maling Beelzebub, obtenuë à Laon l'an 1566*, Paris: N. Chesneau, 1578. © Bibliothèque Nationale de France

Introduction

In 1993 in the state of Victoria, Australia, four people went on trial for the manslaughter of a woman, Joan Vollmer. The four accused said she had died during their attempts to control and expel violent devils, which they claimed had taken over her body. To defend this use of force against 'demonic' resistance, the counsel for the accused referred the court to a seventeenth-century account of authorised Catholic exorcisms in France. The account was written in 1635 by a young English Anglican playwright, Thomas Killigrew, who had travelled to France with a Catholic friend to visit the town of Loudun, in Poitou.[1] This is some of what he saw:

> Upon Thursday morning last . . . we went . . . to the Monastory of the Nunns that were possest . . . upon our first entry we heard nothing but praying to which the possest were as attentive as any . . . but on a suddaine two of them grew unruly . . . [one] tooke her Preist by the Throte, & Struke him, & then got from him & ran roring & talking to the Preist that was saying Masse, where she committed some extravigances before the Frier could take her away. . . . The Preist then desired us to come aftter dinner . . . to the Churches . . . and [we] were noe sooner entered but were drawne by a greate Noyse & Crye to a little Chappell in the Church, where we saw a Frier & one of the possest at Exorcisme, when we came we found her in her fitt, layed upon the ground raging Madd. . . . The Preist . . . stood treading on her brest, & holding the Host over her commaunding the Devill to worship it calling him Dog, Serpent, & other names but I saw in her noe obedience, for I was driven away with the variety of Strange noyse to an other Chapell where there was one possest & in her fitt; when I came I found the Preist holding the Sanctified strings in his hand, by which they lead the possest, she lay upon her Back her heeles under her Breech, & her Head as she lay thus turn'd backward. . . . And in this posture houling & talking & ever as the Preiste strucke her with a Brush and Holy-water, she roared as if she felt new tortures . . . the Preist set his foote upon her Throate, & commaunded the devill to tell him why he lay in that strange posture, but the Stubborne Villaine would not obey till he had Charm'd him by the truth of the Romaine Catholike Church, by the present Bodye & Blood of our Saviour that was resident in the Box which he held over him.[2]

Events such as those Killigrew described were quite common in early modern France, and indeed across western Europe. As D.P. Walker suggests, exorcism of the possessed was exceptional enough to arouse comment, but routine enough to be formulaic: predictably unpredictable.[3] For Catholics, the aim of such displays was to reinforce the shaky foundations of their church's authority in a time of religious upheaval, by demonstrating demons' willingness to yield to an armoury of holy objects and rites deployed by exorcists. Hence Killigrew's description of exorcists using holy water, the Host, and even 'sanctified strings' – leads blessed by priests – to bring the possessed to heel.

Two questions suggest themselves: 'How could such things have happened then? And how could they be seen as acceptable now?' In addressing the first question in depth, this book will seek to provide ways in which the second question might be answered. Modern 'common sense' might suggest that a practice such as exorcism would have been by now relegated to oblivion, yet it is alive and well and being defended at the elite level, even in its extreme forms, as in the case of the manslaughter of Joan Vollmer. This recent example might give pause to reflect on the limitations of 'common sense' understandings of the relationship of past and present religious behaviours: why assume a practice such as exorcism is archaic, or that religious practices are automatically subject over time to a progressive refinement, spiritualisation or rationalisation? And, when considering those who believe in exorcism, why imagine that the type of person most likely to believe in the reality of possession and the power of exorcism would be uneducated or socially marginal? In the early modern period it was common for critics of public exorcism to say that the uneducated, 'the vulgar', were the practitioners and the public to whom the rite appealed. In practice this was simply not the case: exorcism was performed and patronised at the highest social and intellectual levels. Thomas Killigrew, for example, was an educated man visiting an elite convent of nuns, where the reality of possession and the validity of exorcisms had been endorsed by, among others, members of King Louis XIII's family, and the master of realpolitik, the *premier ministre* Cardinal Richelieu. In the modern era, the defence barrister in the 1993 Vollmer trial who cited Killigrew's letter was an eminent Queen's Counsel. In this case, even the presiding judge did not explicitly refute the possibility of demonic possession, thereby legitimating exorcism from within the heart of the judicial system in a professedly secular nation.[4] That is not to say that the uneducated might not be historically a prime audience for public exorcism, nor to deny that sceptical views have more often been articulated among the educated classes. But to assume a socially differentiated view of exorcism a priori would be a fundamental misapprehension about the historical and present realities of this Christian rite.

The status of exorcism as a religious 'fringe' phenomenon also needs to be examined, or, to use a formulation from Natalie Zemon Davis, public exorcism needs to be understood as relating 'less to the pathological than to the normal'.[5] Stuart Clark's paradigm-changing *Thinking with Demons* establishes irrefutably the 'mainstream' position of early modern demonology, notably in the spheres of language, science, history, religion and politics. The present book seeks to address some of the social and institutional processes through which this status for exorcism was created. For exorcism was not a unique form of religious extremism, but one among a range of manifestations of religiosity in early modern France which entailed either actual or symbolic violence, and which touched the lives of countless people, not just a rabid minority.[6] What needs to be investigated, then, are the belief systems and social conditions which permitted scenes such as the one Killigrew described, not simply to take place, but to form a significant part of Catholic proselytism. In examining several cases of possession, this book will argue that the distance between 'mainstream' and 'fringe' in the early modern era, and what constituted each, cannot be assumed on the basis of factors such as education, or scientific knowledge, or position within or outside the social or church hierarchy. Rather, I will suggest that an understanding of the role of tradition in Catholicism and the social and political landscape in which cases of possession arose shows that very little can be assumed about who was likely to believe in demonic possession and miraculous exorcism, or their significance in French society. The arguments I will explore ultimately have implications for understanding how a text such as Thomas Killigrew's might become evidence at a manslaughter trial in late twentieth-century Australia.

Fear of the devil's power was one of the dominant forces in early modern Europe.[7] The first hundred years following the Protestant schism of the sixteenth century was a time of intense theological, political, military and social conflict, and in this context public displays of battles with Satanic forces became a showcase for rival strands of Christianity. Exorcism – the ritual invocation and controlling of possessing demons, using prayer, sacred texts and exhortation – took place among every western Christian group, to varying degrees, in Europe and in its colonies. In Christianity, the presence of a demonic spirit in the body is believed effectively to override the physical humanity of the possessed, and to control their every move. Such an erasure of the human identity of the possessed made it possible for the body of a human being – usually a woman, in the early modern period – to become a *tabula rasa*, upon which religious conflict and claims for religious authority were made visible.[8] A sense that the devil was truly present implicated all parties: as Killigrew's nonchalant tone suggests, not only exorcists but onlookers were complicit in the erasure of the humanity of the devil's human hosts. Rather than being concerned solely with the well-being of the individual, exorcism was also a way of displaying God's willingness to grant an individual exorcist, whether a Catholic priest or a freelance Puritan, the power of the apostles to cast out demons in Christ's name.[9] Each exorcism was a proving ground for faith, legitimising the authority of the individual who performed it and the church they claimed to represent. And while it was not new for the possessed to serve the purposes of proselytism, the scale of possession and exorcism in this period was.

The degree to which the more extreme manifestations of exorcism were practised and accepted varied from place to place, and within each religious group, with a somewhat greater prevalence among Catholics; all had in common a sense of the urgent need for the resolution of religious uncertainty. This was a time characterised by a seemingly universal desire to fix truth, to resolve ambiguity and to reinforce a sense of authority. At the same time – and to those same ends – people appear to have felt a significantly increased need for a sense of God's presence and responsiveness to urgent human pleas. The paradoxical reaction to this crisis was a positive surfeit of certainty, of verified and verifying manifestations of divine power, in the form of visions, ecstasies and prophecies, as well as demonic possession and its miraculous containment through the rite of exorcism. In turn, a situation arose where the need for differentiation between one claim and another became urgent. For there was no preordained limit on the number of miracles available – or rather, there was a destabilising lack of consensus on where the limits lay to the credibility of claims of divine intervention. For Catholic exorcism, such a situation was both permitted and exacerbated by certain structural features unique to Catholicism. This book will argue that in France, home of the most intense and enduring scandals of possession, competing and equally valid claims of spiritual authority allowed at times for seemingly limitless expansion in uses of the rite of exorcism.[10] And it will show that the possibilities of possession and exorcism were exploited to further aspirations at the interpersonal, institutional, social and political levels.

There were three principal 'predisposing conditions' for the expanded use of exorcism in early modern France: religious war, witch trials, and new forms of affective spirituality, all of which were underpinned by, and articulated, a fear of the devil.[11] In the remainder of this introduction I will briefly outline these three sets of circumstances, and then consider the rules and traditions within which exorcism took place in Catholicism. Together these sections will provide the interpretive framework for the book, the basis upon which we can consider how individual cases of possession and exorcism unfolded, and the ways in which each case built upon the example of others. The book itself is divided into three parts, each headed by an introductory essay providing background for the case studies which follow.

Religious war

The schism in Western Christendom which followed the sixteenth-century rise of Protestant evangelicalism began a period of endemic religious war, lasting until the mid-seventeenth century. A system of religious authority that had claimed supreme religious authority, Catholicism, suddenly confronted an alternative Christianity on its own turf. The effects on France were devastating: it is hard to estimate how deeply this fracturing of religious authority affected people's psychological structures, except perhaps by reference to the kind of violence they were prepared to inflict upon each other, which was immense. In exploring this violence, Denis Crouzet has emphasised that the French Wars of Religion need to be understood primarily as being about religion in its own terms, implicitly not a function of other aspects of social life.[12] With this in mind, we need look no further than the opening salvo of Protestant disputation in France, to see how central theological issues were to this period. The so-called 'affair of the placards' was the foundation moment in the rise of schismatic tendencies in France. On the Sunday morning of 18 October 1534, in several cities in northern France, including Paris, supporters of Calvinism hammered up placards in public places decrying what the evangelical writer, Antoine Marcourt, saw as the church magic of the doctrine of the Real Presence.[13]

This central Catholic doctrine holds that the body of Christ is miraculously made present in the hands of the priest at the moment of consecration in the Mass. For French Calvinists – later known as Huguenots – this doctrine was the index of both the ceremonialism and materialism of Catholic tradition, and evidence of a misplaced reliance on an overweening Catholic priesthood as dispensers of papist magic. This focus on the church magic of Catholicism resonated throughout the period in which religious civil war took hold, from 1560 to 1629, and beyond. For while the doctrinal issue of priestly magic could be a soft target for ridicule, it also remained an impressive feature of Catholic proselytism, as Catholics used not only military weapons against Huguenots, but also ceremonial and symbolic force.

It might be hard for some moderns to credit that a street procession in which the Host was borne aloft could truly inspire awe and devotion, or that a hell-fire preacher could induce rage in Catholics or recantation in Huguenots, or that stories of miracles might reclaim Huguenots to the Catholic fold and reinforce the choice of those who had remained loyal to Catholicism.[14] Yet such public and affective displays were crucial features of the religious wars, and the periods of uneasy peace between them. It was as one among a range of such devotional displays that public exorcism of the possessed came to the fore as a way for Catholics to show divine approval for their side, visibly and repeatedly. When Catholic exorcists were presented with sufferers whose bodies were said to be totally taken over by demons, they were given an opportunity to show the miraculous power of the panoply of Catholic devotional forms. They used the Host and other holy objects, such as saints' relics, to deliver the possessed of their demons. And when the 'devils' put up a fight and refused to depart, exorcists conducted mock battles with them, making the 'devils' speak and even to testify to the power of the Church's spiritual weapons. It was this kind of battle which Thomas Killigrew described as taking place between exorcists and the possessed at Loudun: each of the implements used by the priests was made sacred through priestly blessings, and then marshalled to fight the devil.

Theologically speaking, these battles with the devil could not be 'real', as the devil is always subject to God, and is therefore not only unable to defeat God in a confrontation in the body of the possessed, but cannot act at all except by His permission. But in allowing the devil 'air-time', ostensibly under command from exorcists, militant Catholics believed that God was giving His church a chance to show its unique capacity to humble Satan and his heretical agents, the Huguenots. Many other Catholics objected to this kind of display, calling it superstitious, and urged the immediate expulsion of possessing demons. But the pressures of war and confessional rivalry provided nourishment for more extreme forms of exorcism.

Part I will trace the fortunes of exorcism in the second half of the sixteenth century, starting with an account of probably the most famous continental possession case of the century, the story of the 16-year-old Nicole Obry, dispossessed in the 'Miracle of Laon' of 1566. People high up the intellectual, ecclesiastical and social scale gave Obry's miraculous exorcisms their blessing, by endorsing them both at the time and later in vast and numerous written accounts. Notoriously, her exorcists forced Obry's 'devils' to speak at length, in support of the Catholic church. For while it is the role of the exorcist to bring a devil to heel (with the aim of expelling him), the temptation to adjure 'him' to speak and show his obedience to God proved irresistible. This practice exposed ambiguities in the rite of exorcism. Such displays left the Church open to criticism from within its own ranks and, more pointedly, from Huguenots: what better way for the devil to gain the hearts and minds of the faithful than to show them supposedly divine cures, which were really only tricks played by a self-seeking or simply foolish exorcist, duped by, or even working in cahoots with, the devil? The discussion of the Obry case will argue that, notwithstanding a rise in Catholic scepticism in the late fifteenth and early sixteenth century, and in spite of the risk of ridicule and anti-Huguenot violence, the case lent the rite of exorcism a new high profile and respectability, becoming the model for a wave of exorcisms in the second half of the century. The last of these led to a dramatic division among Catholics in Paris, at a moment of high political tension. In 1599, Henri IV was trying to instate a new peace with the Huguenots (the Edict of Nantes), when supporters of the by-then defunct militant Holy Catholic League brought a quasi-'professional' demoniac named Marthe Brossier to Paris with the aim of obstructing the peace. Catholic critics of the possession – moderate *politiques* supporting the king – drew on the tradition of Catholic scepticism to argue that Brossier's possession was invalid, while militant supporters of her public exorcisms elevated it as a sign of divine endorsement for their party.[15] Thus by the end of the century, the status of exorcism among the educated had come to embrace a broad spectrum of vigorously contested, but equally authoritative, views.

Witchcraft

The late sixteenth and early seventeenth centuries saw the peak of witch trials in France, and, in the same period, most of the classic French demonology texts appeared, including those by Jean Bodin, Pierre de Lancre, Henri Boguet and Nicolas Rémy.[16] Witch trials only rarely occurred as a direct result of people reading demonological literature; however, the production of multiple editions of major texts and of many minor works – from pamphlets to accounts of trials – shows the existence of a literate class preoccupied with the power of the devil, and attentive to calls to rid the world of witches. The devil was thus being fought on many fronts: in witch trials; in literature; through public exorcism, and (in the view of Catholics) through direct conflict with the Huguenots.

In several infamous seventeenth-century French possession cases, the possessed accused high-profile figures – notably priests and senior female religious – of using witchcraft to send devils into their bodies. These *causes célèbres* produced a voluminous polemical literature, which further contributed to possession and exorcism being subjects of intense debate. A pervasive fear of the devil's capacity for trickery meant that exorcism itself was sometimes seen as a form of witchcraft, of diabolical conjuring. This became a particularly pressing problem when the possessed, speaking as devils under exorcism, accused priests of causing the possession through witchcraft. Who had more credibility: an exorcist getting a demoniac to reveal a hidden act of priestly witchcraft, or an ordained minister of the Church, claiming to be a victim of an exorcist's potentially diabolical fraud? For the Catholic church, public exorcisms and accusations of witchcraft under-scored at once the vulnerability and the power of its priesthood.

Part II will address this problematic status of the Catholic priesthood, in a time when Huguenots reviled priests for being magicians, and the Catholic church itself, after the Council of Trent, sought increasingly to purify its ministry, and to reinforce its divinely ordained and socially separate identity. We will consider two major cases of possession which had implications for the role of the Catholic priesthood. A case of possession among Ursuline nuns in Aix-en-Provence (1609–11) was the first in a series of seventeenth-century convent possessions from which later cases, most notably the 1630s story of Fr Urbain Grandier and the 'devils of Loudun' (described in Part III, Chapter 8), took their cue. At Aix two young possessed nuns, Louise Capeau and Madeleine Demandols, accused a parish priest, Louis Gaufridy, of witchcraft and debauchery. After a prolonged series of exorcisms, in which the possessed elaborated on their accusations, Gaufridy was executed. One of the chief exorcists, Sébastien Michaelis, wrote about the case in order to publicise what he saw as a triumph for the reforming Catholic church, but also to defend the potentially suspect actions of exorcists and their unseemly zeal in prosecuting a brother priest. In another convent possession, at Louviers in Normandy in the 1640s, Hospitaller nuns alleged that two priests – by then deceased – had corrupted the convent by allowing nuns to imagine themselves recipients of holy ecstasies, which exorcists later alleged to be diabolical frauds. Another priest, Thomas Boullé, became ensnared in the nuns' accusations during exorcisms conducted over a period of years, and was executed in 1647. The case became a vehicle for arguments among Catholics about the authenticity of possession and exorcism, and about the risks of a more affective, potentially diabolical, form of religiosity. This type of spirituality was widespread in the seventeenth century, and was, in different ways, central to several further episodes of possession.

Mystical and affective spirituality

Personal sanctity and direct communication with God came to the fore in late medieval and early modern religiosity. From around the late fourteenth century, individuals in increasing numbers sought direct contact with God, through devotional techniques such as prayer, contemplation and asceticism. In return, God might show His grace by granting the devotee ecstasies, visions, spiritual illumination, or the power of prophecy. Some of these people came to be known as 'living saints'.[17] In Spain and Italy in the fifteenth and sixteenth centuries this movement flourished, particularly among women. In France, the religious wars slowed up the potential for such development, but around the turn of the seventeenth century, when Catholicism began to reinforce its gains under Henri IV, there began an unprecedented period of efflorescence in devotional life. The first half of the seventeenth century has been called the 'century of saints', a time when mystical aspirations achieved prominence in the work of the so-called French School, and the inspirational lives of figures such as Madame Barbe Acarie, founder of the Discalced Carmelites, and the eminent theologian Cardinal Pierre de Bérulle.[18]

The sixteenth-century Spanish saint Teresa of Avila loomed large in the French spiritual landscape of the seventeenth century, and the idea of emulating such a great figure and possibly gaining for oneself a reputation for sanctity held a potent attraction for many women. For several aspiring holy women and their male sponsors, demonic possession came to be seen as a kind of praiseworthy suffering, an opportunity to display the martyrdom to which many female devotees aspired in this era.[19] Diabolical torture of the bodies of the possessed, sometimes through inner (especially sexual) temptations, or violent actions such as the devil throwing the possessed to the ground, were seen to be as valid as other forms of asceticism, such as fasting or self-flagellation. In these cases possession by demons lies on a continuum with ecstatic spirituality and other forms of spiritual endowment.[20] Possession of the body by a devil or devils was also held to endow the possessed with the same powers of natural magic to which devils, as fallen angels, are heir. Thus the possessed, speaking as their demons, not only preached under the pressure of successful exorcism and made accusations of witchcraft, but they also (slightly ironically) worked as visionaries, telling people's fortunes.

Yet inevitably this kind of 'positive possession'[21] brought with it the risks attendant on any claim for divine favour in individuals. In a climate of acute anxiety about the true sources of apparently divine inspiration, how was it possible to tell if God were really granting the possessed the opportunity for spiritual advancement, or if the devil were simply duping the possessed, and in turn having the possessed dupe the public by drawing them into the unreliable realm of the senses for proof of God's might? In an era troubled by fear of women's witchcraft and of the devil's incursions, a too-close female affinity with the devil, even through a supposedly blameless possession, led to suspicion that the possessed might themselves be witches. Part III argues that there existed a scale of authenticity, which separated divinely endowed ecstatic spirituality, potentially suspect demonic possession, and outright witchcraft. It considers the lives of two prominent possessed women from this era: Marie des Vallées in Normandy, and Jeanne des Anges, superior of the Ursuline convent at Loudun. It shows that the status of these women as living saints, while endorsed by several influential sponsors, led each woman to become the subject of intense suspicion and scrutiny.

Change and innovation in a sacramental religion

War, witchcraft and affective spirituality were sources of anxiety that led people to identify the presence of evil in different ways. The process was dialectical, however, for while outbreaks of possession and their resolution through exorcism were responses to a changing religious climate, these displays themselves led to further anxiety about the presence of the devil. Thus, fear of the devil's presence led both to the proliferation of the use of exorcism and to challenges to its use, because of the perceived risk of fraud and collaboration with demons. Exorcism practices thus both responded and contributed to the malleability of the foundations of religious authority in early modern France. In the remainder of this introduction, therefore, we need to consider how Catholic authorities understood and dealt with those ritual practices that had the potential to draw the Church as a whole into disrepute.

Manifestations of sacred power and the divine presence were especially complex matters for the early modern Catholic church, which held (as indeed the Church still holds) that inanimate objects, times, places and human bodies could potentially mediate God's power.[22] This feature of Catholicism is referred to variously as belief in religious immanence,[23] sacramental religiosity,[24] and, in reference to manifestations in the human body, 'embodied' religiosity.[25] The central ritual manifestation of this belief was in the Mass. However, there was a wide array of other rites and observances, known as 'sacramentals', through which religious immanence was also experienced. These included, for example, the cult of saints honoured through pilgrimage, prayer, supplication, and observance of feast days, and the use of blessings and weather magic, employing objects such as saints' relics, holy water, or the Host. All rely on the notion that God seeks actively to be praised and that He will, to some extent, reward faith and devotion by ad hoc displays of His power. The sacramentals can be distinguished from the seven sacraments, as they do not result in grace, which is essential to salvation. Their function within the Church, rather, is to draw believers closer to God, through the worship of His power. As one French historian puts it: 'times and places are not matters of indifference to the Creator. [Miracles] do not occur just wherever or whenever, but at fixed times, and at specific places. The power of God, who chose these times and these places, desires that they be consecrated, and that this choice be honoured by men'.[26] But while miracles which occur following the observation of sacramental practices are to some extent a reward for human devotion, they come, of necessity, with no guarantee of authenticity. The phenomenon of demonic possession itself is also an endorsement of the idea that divine action can manifest in a physical form, and exorcism of those possessed by demons is a sacramental, which in this period became controversial because of the sheer volume of cases, and because of the extreme forms it took.

As historical debates about the proliferation and forms of exorcism imply, this capacity for divine power to be displayed in sacramental forms has always been of mixed value for the Church. It allows for the penetration of holiness into daily life, in holy places, objects, rituals, persons living and dead, and at special times. Yet the very diffusion of this form of religiosity is also a risk to authority in the Church, because it allows for a degree of innovation to take place at the local level, or within specific interest groups. Nevertheless, if religious passions and vigour emerge from far-flung places or in innovative practices these can ultimately serve the interests of central authority, too, by promoting cohesion and allegiance among believers, or indeed, by generating revenue. For the sake of institutional continuity, there is a need to balance the tensions between innovation – or rather, the identification of new signs of God's grace – and tradition. Sacramental forms provided innovative sources of allegiance to the Church as a whole, at the same time as the disputation they aroused exposed the weaknesses in institutional Catholicism.

From the point of view of church authorities, whose historical task it was to assess competing claims of divine action, nothing was given about the distinction between a true and a false claim to immanent holiness. Rather, the need for judgement implied the constant (re-)creation of a hierarchy of rites, people and objects. Authorities representing the Church as an institution judged certain claims to be above others, (for example, in distinguishing a claimed piece of the True Cross from an ordinary piece of wood). However, problems arose when sources of authority disagreed. For while an office-bearer in the secular hierarchy, such as a bishop, was the usual source of such an imprimatur, another advocate of comparable authority, such as a university theologian or a papal nuncio, might nonetheless take an opposing view. Such differences could expose the individuality at work in the assertion of institutional authority, and selectivity in the processes of authentication. And there were also competing hierarchies: a local bishop may not have had access to support in Rome, for example, in the way a provincial of a religious order might; thus, opposing views could become enmeshed in jurisdictional rivalries.

Apart from official human sources of judgement, there also existed since the medieval era constantly evolving, notionally objective criteria whereby licit claims were distinguished from illicit. Ideas such as excessive veneration (superstition or 'vain observance'[27]), the use of designated criteria for telling genuine inspiration from diabolic,[28] the rejection of 'curiosity' (that is, of desire for knowledge for its own sake, rather than for godly ends), and the idea of 'abuse' (either an uninformed or deliberately manipulative attitude to potentially holy rituals) all provided guides for authorities. But there comes a point when a proliferation of available criteria and competing historical precedents can create a range of conflicting authority sources, paradoxically returning the act of judgement to individuals. The complexity of this situation was intensified when individuals claimed a divine gift of the power to discern the authenticity of claims. This power lay potentially outside of the priestly hierarchy, being notably (if infrequently) attributed to women, and it could introduce a 'wild card' of spiritual authority that was potentially threatening to institutional hierarchies. Social hierarchy, too, played a part: the support of people of high social standing often lent weight to claims of immanence, particularly as sacramental forms mediated God's action in the physical world, and were thus sometimes regarded as intrinsically the province of the uneducated or 'the vulgar', who lacked spiritual refinement.[29]

Crucially, both critics and practitioners of exorcism in this period found justification for their views in orthodox Catholic sources of authority. These sources of authority could be written, such as the Bible, saints' lives or other canonical texts, or they could be institutional authorities, such as senior figures in the religious hierarchy. To assume that Church hierarchy was inherently resistant to expanding the practice of exorcism, and simply had trouble controlling growing numbers of 'rogue' exorcists, would therefore be to misconstrue entirely the nature of authority in Catholicism. Holiness can manifest in unexpected ways, and openness to claims of divine manifestations is as much a part of clerical duty as is the need to reject fakes. If change and innovation are to occur in a sacramental religion, there must necessarily be a process for the determination of authentic divine intervention. At the top of this ladder of authenticity lie true miracles, and at the bottom are the dubious areas of human fraud, or worse, diabolical imitations of God's works, which, fatally, can lead the faithful astray. The existence of such a scale of possible determinations in cases of dispute is what endows the 'pure' manifestations with their credibility. But how to know whose holiness is real, and whose is merely apparent, possibly the result of vainglory? The need for the so-called discernment of spirits (*discretio spirituum*) to determine true from false claims to personal holiness was an ancient one, but in the early modern era such discernment became especially critical because of the pressure of many competing claims.

At stake in the negotiation of these competing claims was not only the authority of individual members of the Church hierarchy, but the definition of what might broadly be called the identity of French Catholicism. For much of the early modern period, this complex identity was negotiated in part within the strongly contested spheres of sacramental religiosity, and of affective and charismatic spirituality. Specifically, cases of demonic possession and exorcism highlighted in a dramatic and public way the instability and contingency of the many sources of religious authority. To use a perhaps overused metaphor, the sacramental system provided a set of spaces in which change was negotiated in and by the Church, for it was in disputes over interpretation that French Catholic reform and revival took on different and sometimes conflicting attributes.

The use of new or expanded forms of officially sanctioned exorcism reached levels in this period which had not been seen before and have not been seen since.

Yet in a revealed religion like Catholicism innovation is not, strictly speaking, legitimate, because all actions must be justifiable within a tradition of authority traceable to Christ and the Apostles, the saints, canon law, official liturgy, and other authorised and authorising texts. Multiple authoritative traditions in Catholicism allow therefore for a somewhat cyclical understanding of its history. That is not to say that Catholicism, by virtue of these multiple traditions, is in some way untouched by the historical moment: on the contrary, the wide range of potential readings available for any given phenomenon – or indeed the shaping of any phenomenon in the first place – is open to the exigencies of that moment, because of the spectrum of available authoritative sources. This tradition provides the rules within which change can occur. Thus, while sacramental forms require hierarchy to retain their value, the number of things which can drift into the 'accepted' category, through practice, is virtually limitless. To use an inelegant metaphor, this system presents the possibility of a 'bulge' in the history of exorcism practice, such as occurred in the early modern period. This happened notwithstanding published attempts to corral exorcist enthusiasm, such as the papal *Rituale Romanum* of 1614, and the many exorcism manuals which stressed caution, notably in regard to public performances and especially in the interrogation of demons. For even these texts tended to leave loopholes, and indeed, the very existence of these new and detailed 'how-to' works, had at best a mixed value.

What Roy Porter has called the 'agonizing ambiguities' for Catholicism in the early modern period were these somewhat perennial ones, albeit writ large in a time of desperation – or perceived desperation – where some thought extreme measures were advisable, and others thought that they only made problems worse. The stakes grew higher in the context of war and witchcraft accusations, in particular, and this intensification helped to drive a wedge into the differences within Catholicism that were there all along, each new drama reinforcing scepticism and belief, by turns. Thus sacramental religiosity provided the openings for innovation, but also the risk of exposure of its own sometimes frail hold on credibility. At the heart of debates about the authenticity of specific cases of possession and exorcism lay this conundrum: successful exorcism displayed the authority of the Church over demons, but all sacramental and charismatic forms, including or especially 'positive' possession and exorcism, were suspect by reference to their own potentially diabolical origins. And in an era which placed especially high value on direct gifts from God, and in which there were tensions between competing hierarchies – institutional and spiritual – the question of whose authority was to prevail was raised afresh by each incident of possession. Questions such as this were indeed 'agonising' for the Church as a whole, but importantly, they were not generally experienced as such by parties to debate. On the contrary, seeing issues in black and white was a characteristic feature of this period: the religiosity of Catholic reform and renewal was frequently one of proof, of signs, of struggle, and of punishment. There was rarely room for the middle ground.[30]

Historical work in possession and exorcism has examined these phenomena within the context of numerous histories, notably those of witch-hunting, medicine and psychology, confessional division, eschatology, demonology, spirituality, sexuality and female religiosity. Most research has appeared in the form of case studies, and chapters or articles. This book aims to synthesise many of these authors' insights while providing an extended analysis of the complexities of possession and exorcism for the history of Christianity, and Catholicism in particular. (Particular analyses are addressed in the relevant text and notes, but see especially Introduction, n. 3). In writing this book I have had to remind myself that it deals with the frequently horrific stories of people seeking power over others. It is sometimes easy for historians to forget this human factor when we write. Polishing a phrase, refining an argument can easily become ends in themselves. A colleague once commented at a witchcraft conference, during morning tea break, on the bizarre contrast she once felt sitting in a beautiful comfortable room in an archive, with the sun coming through the high windows, while reading the records of an inquisition. One imperative I have felt in writing this book is to give voice to those silenced in the past, and in so doing to see a way into the violence at the heart of actions and self-images that are, I suggest, intrinsic to the operation of the dominant religious institution in early modern France.

Part I

Chapter 1

Scepticism and Catholic reform

Introductory remarks

Around 1530, the Spanish Franciscan reformer Pedro Ciruelo wrote: 'In order to create greater confusion, the devil has invented certain exorcisms quite similar to those used by the Holy Catholic Church against demons who are reluctant to abandon human bodies.'[1] This observation encapsulates the problem of exorcism for the early modern Catholic church: the devil was the Ape of God, and could hold sway when untutored observation allowed him the opportunity to imitate holiness. Ciruelo's comment is a disarmingly frank admission of the difficulty of discerning licit from illicit exorcism, a statement indicative of the troubled mood of educated Catholic sentiment in the late fifteenth and early sixteenth centuries. The ability to know when the devil was at work was the most pressing of a range of aspects of Catholic sacramental religiosity which preoccupied reformers, and it underpinned many other anxieties. Reformers targeted the problem of reliance on physical appearances as against spiritual realities – the evidence of the flesh taken over that of the spirit – and feared that for many believers the physical effects of sacramental practices were consistently elevated over the spiritual. The risk of over-reliance on the physical realm was seen as inhering in the magical practices of the unlettered – especially practices associated with healing and fertility – and in flamboyant clerical healing rituals, of which exorcism of the possessed, especially in public, was one of the most troubling.

These critiques also convey a sense that there existed a considerable 'hinterland' of exorcism practices (to use Clark's word), which were carried on with relatively little written publicity.[2] In the absence of a triumphal literature of exorcism, which was to emerge only later in the sixteenth century, these texts give us a clue as to what practising exorcists were actually doing. They suggest that exorcism at the local pastoral level was taking place everywhere. Clerics like Ciruelo feared the devil lurked in such activities, eager to capitalise on the gullibility of laity and uneducated clergy alike. They portrayed the uneducated and those bent on material and physical benefits alone as the permeable points through which the devil's destructive power was able to seep into the body of the Church.

Several other Catholic commentators from this period, with otherwise divergent agendas, wrote hostile accounts of apparently widespread exorcism practices. The Dominican witch-hunters and authors of the *Malleus Maleficarum*, Heinrich

Krämer (Institoris) and Jakob Sprenger, along with the humanist Desiderius Erasmus, and another Spanish cleric, Manuel de Castañega, levelled criticisms that in some ways prefigured – or later, paralleled – emergent evangelical Protestant views; they also reflected a long historical anxiety about sacramentals in the Catholic church. These authors wanted to streamline Catholic practice, without abandoning its central tenets regarding sacramental forms. It is important to realise that scepticism and credulity in this context were not naturally at odds.[3] Rather, achieving certainty in sacramental practices always required a degree of scepticism. Scepticism itself was not new, having been present in the Church since late antiquity; indeed it could be said that a measure of scepticism had been essential to the Church's institutional survival. What was new in this early reform era was the relative unanimity with which scepticism was expressed. Where Protestants on the Continent largely denied the need for physical proofs of divine action, the preoccupying theme of Catholic reformist writing in this period was the need for discernment between otherwise indistinguishable divine, human, and diabolical causes of events.

In the face of growing anxiety about the powers of the devil an almost uniformly critical view of the ancient rite of exorcism was emerging, part of an ongoing critique of so-called superstitions. This tendency had been escalating since the late fourteenth century, and coincided with the intellectualist reforms of the Conciliar era and attendant anxiety about flourishing popular practices. Learned critiques imposed an imperative of distinction, or hierarchy, between ritual objects and forms. The hope was to eradicate excess, 'vanity', reliance on external signs and, in the worst case, diabolism among exorcists themselves.[4] There was an effort to centralise and prescribe ritual, to prevent the proliferation of highly localised forms of practice. Catholic reformers sought to distinguish licit from illicit in order (at least implicitly) to preserve as valid the inner core of an inherently labile set of beliefs. Ciruelo's treatise and other works aimed to educate readers – presumably the theologically uncertain lower clergy – in how to make just such necessary distinctions, teasing out holy from unholy exorcisms.[5] Yet almost every feature of exorcism practice seemed to expose some kind of thorny theological dilemma.

As Ciruelo indicated, the mixing of holy and unholy in the practice of exorcism put even potentially licit exorcisms in jeopardy. Ciruelo continued his critique, saying: 'In these diabolical exorcisms, gross expressions as well as superstitious formulas are mixed with holy and pious words.'[6] Manuel de Castañega likewise deplored the mixing of holy and unholy, and forbad the use of otherwise licit amulets in tandem with 'suspicious and superstitious words and figures.'[7] The authors of the *Malleus* sought to separate holy from profane usages. They stipulated, for example, that charms should contain no 'written characters beyond the sign of the Cross'.[8] They also urged practitioners to focus on the meaning of the holy words they uttered, thereby joining together theology and performance, and implicitly challenging the magical element of practices whose very mystique could derive from the incomprehension of healers, or more, especially, their clients. Reinforcing this concern to purge practices which relied on method over meaning,

Institoris and Sprenger required that exorcists place 'no faith in the method' of blessing itself, but rather in God's will, as the source of any success they achieved.[9] It cannot be stressed enough that these anxieties were not new. As early as the fourth century, at the Council of Carthage, church officials had warned exorcists not to devise their own rites: the Council proclaimed that the choice of formulae to be used by an exorcist should not be 'abandoned to the liberty of particular exorcists'; to prevent exorcists from making up the rite as they went along, the Council instructed them to receive the formula of exorcism 'from the hands of the bishop' and to commit it to memory.[10]

Exorcists letting possessing 'devils' speak, or even preach, under the authority of the exorcist, presented perhaps the stickiest commingling of holy and unholy. The devil could potentially have access to accurate knowledge through his own heightened powers of learning, and he could even know theological truths. Critically, though, he was also likely make his own blend, unannounced, and in that way steal ground from the Church and lead souls to perdition. Ciruelo therefore rejected the practice of interrogating demons, in which exorcists held 'a prolonged discussion with the devil' and performed 'other actions that resemble a lawsuit or a trial'.[11] He argued that the devil 'desires greatly to preach and speak publicly to men, because then, like a dragon, he can inject much poison into the hearts of his listeners, which poison will lead to their damnation'.[12] Yet it is also important to recall that there was a measure of credible historical support for such practices. In the gospels the devil correctly identifies Christ as the son of God.[13] Similarly, as part of early Christian proselytism, Gregory of Tours showed relics to the 'devils' of the possessed outside a temple, pointing to their reaction as proof to the pagans of the relics' authenticity and power.[14] Thus demonstrations of diabolic presence paradoxically offered proof of God's presence and authority.[15]

Other evidence suggested the acceptance of such practices if they served some holy purpose. The abbot Caesarius of Heisterbach, writing in the thirteenth century, told the story of a cleric who conjured the devil at the behest of his bishop, in order to reveal the secret means whereby heretics seemed resistant to injury.[16] Caesarius made no comment on the use of an evil force to bring about good ends, a practice generally condemned by the Church and repeatedly opposed in the early modern era. An example of the persistence of such forbearance may be found, however, in a large c. 1500 tapestry from the Cathedral of Auxerre, now housed in the Cluny Museum, depicting a tale from the medieval *Golden Legend* of Jacob of Voragine. It illustrates the story of Eudoxia, a possessed woman whose demons prophesied.[17] The panels show that devils, acting on divine instruction, refused to leave Eudoxia's body until God's will had been fulfilled, through the burial of St Laurent and St Denis in Rome. Eudoxia in this legend was both host and hostage to the devil.[18] Most importantly, the image of her demons helping to fulfil their own prophecy by departing was commissioned by a bishop, Jean III Baillet, and on full display – apparently uncontroversially – in a cathedral. How to account for this? Perhaps even in the early stages of an era when theologically oriented works were critical of exorcism, artistic and fabulous representations at the elite level may have remained relatively unaffected. Clearly, any imputation that either Eudoxia or her exorcists were collaborating with the devil was not seen as important, yet such a preoccupation appears to have coloured most of the views articulated in the era 1480–1550.

The exorcist-as-impresario was especially dangerous not only if he were fooled by the devil, but worse, if he were in league with him. Ciruelo and Castañega explicitly accused exorcists of sorcery. Ciruelo referred to any exorcist who conducts dialogues with devils as an 'evil and superstitious sorcerer,'[19] while Castañega said: 'The devil himself will also aid in an exorcism by leaving the premises in order to contract a discipleship with that exorcist or sorcerer, who would be more daring to gain a foothold in similar businesses, seeing that his exorcisms worked so well.'[20] Castañega condemned the practice whereby devils left the bodies of the possessed 'with license to return to the same body the next day',[21] saying that this could only result from 'an express diabolical pact'.[22] However, this kind of 'exorcism by postponement' appears to have been a recognised practice. Caesarius tells the story of a woman whose devil, when adjured to leave her, said: 'It is not yet the will of the Most High.'[23] When an abbot adjured the demon to depart, the demon said: '"The Most High does not yet will it; for two years longer I shall dwell in her; after that time she will be delivered from me . . ." which indeed actually came to pass'.[24] Caesarius, whose writings were sources of only the mildest religious instruction, made no comment on the validity of such an exorcism, an absence which might seem to underscore the shift suggested by the anxieties of writers in the fifteenth- and sixteenth-century reforming era. It is worth recalling, however, that Christ's own conjurations (Mark 3:22) had led him to be accused of using demons to cast out demons.[25] This accusation posed a profound problem, only surmountable by faith in Christ's own defence of his claim to be the son of God. While the gospels portrayed this accusation as unjust, the slur nonetheless articulated a suspicion which formed a major part of the Church's ongoing internal critiques of exorcisms: the perception that exorcists practised magic.

The possibility that exorcists were conjurors is of course one which found echoes in Protestant critiques of the Catholic priesthood, especially in relation to the Mass. It is an accusation which highlights more generally the problems of church magic, a field of operation whose limits historically, and increasingly in this period, were seen as needing to be patrolled. Yet because this was an area of theological and historical ambiguity, the Catholic project of discernment in these matters was almost certain to derail. Inconsistencies between the assertions of the authors of the late fifteenth and early sixteenth century, for example, belie the radical and authoritative image they were trying to promote. Let us consider a few examples. The authors of the *Malleus* at one point sought to distinguish the practice of exorcists rounding up infesting serpents into a pit to destroy them from the ritual expulsion of serpents 'for a useful purpose, such as driving them away from men's houses'.[26] While the distinction seems to relate to private over public ritual, the authors do not say this, and in asserting such a distinction, they might fairly be said to have been toiling with their logic. And Ciruelo refutes altogether the use of exorcisms against animals.[27]

A comparison between Erasmus and Castañega is more revealing. In his 1524 colloquy, 'Exorcism', Erasmus rehearsed the things which amused and irritated him about what he saw as superstitious exorcist bumbling:

> A large vessel filled with holy water was brought. In addition, a sacred stole (as it's called), with the opening verses of St John's Gospel hanging from it, was draped over Faunus' shoulders. In his pockets he had a waxen image of the kind blessed annually by the pope and known as an Agnus Dei. Long ago – before a Franciscan cowl became so formidable – people used to protect themselves by this armor against harmful demons.[28]

Erasmus's mention of St John's gospel refers to one of the most common practices of exorcists and an element of church magic much favoured since at least the eleventh century: the recitation of the words of St John. These words refer to the Incarnation, an especially apt evocation it would seem, in the struggle against habitation of the body by demons. Yet Castañega, scathing of exorcists in so many ways, nonetheless prescribes reading out the gospel of St John (1:1) '*In principio erat verbum* with much faith' among the licit means of exorcism. Castañega adds that the exorcist 'should reverently kneel with much devotion at the phrase *Verbum caro factum* [John 1:14], kissing the earth with much humility in memory of the son of God, who to free us from the devil and his power descended from heaven to earth, taking our nature in the virginal womb of Our Lady the Virgin Mary'.[29] He describes as licit other behaviours and rituals which would seem to be ruled out by the anti-materialism of someone like Erasmus, recommending, for example, that the exorcist wear 'some true relics around his neck with the Gospel of *In principio*'.[30] In so doing, Castañega appears to see as acceptable the kind of paraphernalia which Erasmus cites as objectionable.

It seems that what we are seeing here was not so much a consensus on reliable categories and uniformly consistent criteria of practice, as simply a mood or a climate which privileged the need for discernment, or perhaps simply a need for the statement of imperatives. These inconsistencies do not reflect a failing on the part of authors or of a system; they simply identify an institution trying to grapple with and within its own historically given tensions. Ultimately, the agenda central to each of these reformers could be seen as not so much the defence of categories of practice, as it was the definition of categories of person, in order, paternalistically, to protect those who were unable to discern the presence of the devil from being misled.[31] The imperative which informed these critiques was thus both theological and social. It makes sense, then, that when the social situation changed, priorities concerning exorcism might also change. For just as suspicion of exorcism had predated the late medieval rise in scepticism, exorcism as proselytism always remained an option for elites to take up. Biblical and other valid historical precedents allowed for it, and ongoing 'popular' practices still apparently displayed the kind of virtuosity which writers of the fifteenth and earlier sixteenth centuries had rejected. But a crucial shift took place when, confronted by the Protestant threat, Catholicism ceased, in some ways, to have the luxury of introspection.

Western European Catholicism spent the sixteenth century facing the twin threats of the time: schism and Satan. The French situation in many ways typifies the extremes of this. The institution of the Church shuddered under the strain of two such powerful and, it was often held, profoundly related threats, and the question of exorcism became a source of explicit and sustained division between Catholic authors. Catholics feared and despised their confessional enemies – members of the Protestant and Reformed Churches – and they also increasingly feared Satan, in part at least because the fragmentation of Christendom betokened for them the end of the world and the beginning of Satan's rule. Witchcraft, too, began to feature more consistently as a concern from the mid-sixteenth century. Yet there was less and less consensus about how to counter these threats.

Exorcism offered cures for those directly affected by witches, the devil's agents, while public exorcism, in particular, showed the power of the Church to defeat the devil, a vivid image of Catholic miracles at work. In this period, practices which seem to have been present at the local level – the ones earlier Catholic reformers objected to – were finding their way into print, as exorcists and their increasing number of elite patrons began to portray exorcism as a panacea for the ills of the age. Yet the risk that the exorcist was either a fool, a conjuror, or the devil's dupe continued to inform views on the rite. No single view was characteristic of a type of person or school of thought, however. It was, for example, a humanist, Pierre de Bérulle, who became the most ardent and articulate defender of exorcism.[32] Increasing divisions around exorcism in times of acute anxiety about the devil came to accentuate the contrasting views of the rite, views which the Church had inherited through centuries of shifting attitudes and contradictory doctrines.

Chapter 2

'Into the realm of the senses'
Nicole Obry and the Miracle of Laon

In 1578 Jean Boulaese, the Hebraist and priest, published a compendious 800-page collection of works by several authors, each one describing just one miracle of exorcism from 1566, the story of Nicole Obry of Vervins. The title page of *Le Thresor et entiere histoire de la triomphante victoire du corps de Dieu sur l'esprit maling Beelzebub* announces what Boulaese saw as the authorities who proved the truth of the miracle. Title pages in this period were quite likely to be lengthy, but this one states succinctly, for our purposes, the author's preoccupation with the ways religious authority for Catholics was to be established. It reads:

> The Treasury and Entire History of the Triumphant Victory of the Body of God over the Evil Spirit Beelzebub obtained at Laon in the year 1566 . . . collected from the works and public acts specified hereafter, from word to word entirely couched by this Notary; by impugned heretics; and publicly averred by the sight, hearing and touch of more than one hundred and fifty thousand people; and according to faith; and according to the fact of the double letter-patent and the double public seal, authenticated as a real instrument of public faith, whose judgements are to be believed. Thus presented to the pope, to the king, to the chancellor of France, and to the first president [of the Parlement of Paris], and printed according to their will by Jean Boulaese, priest, professor of Holy Hebrew Letters.[1]

The title demonstrates the contemporary concern with proof and authority, but its very length alerts us to the complex, layered and unpredictable nature of this authority. The first to be mentioned are the heretics, the Huguenots who converted when Obry was successfully exorcised. Their conversion is itself a miracle, and therefore their testimony is valued seemingly above all. They represent those human beings closest to the devil, the triumph over his works in them mirroring the triumph over the devil in the body of the possessed.[2] What is also striking is the fact that the human senses are cited as an almost free-standing authority in themselves. Dependence on personal faith and on the body, then, come first, followed by the more commonly cited public authorities of church and state. The Paris Faculty of Theology has provided a letter-patent, and the secular and religious leaders, to whom the work has been offered for personal approval, follow. The author's acceding to their manifold wishes, in publishing the work, takes its modest place in the sun. In the following pages, we shall trace the social and theological paths along which the mysterious affliction of Nicole Obry travelled, an affliction which came to be diagnosed as possession by demons and whose treatment through exorcism came to be an index of the preoccupations of a Catholic church at war, in the sixteenth century.

On 3 November 1565, the day after All Souls' Day, Nicole Obry, a recently married woman of sixteen, went to pray for her deceased grandfather Joachim Vuillot at his tomb in the village church of Vervins, in the diocese of Laon, in north-eastern France. As Obry prayed, a vision of a man appeared before her, draped in white cloth, saying it was her grandfather. Shortly after, the spirit pursued her and 'entered into her' (a curiously matter-of-fact verb in the circumstances).[3] As a result of this incursion, Obry became ill, so ill that she had to receive extreme unction.[4] While she was ill, the spirit spoke to her inwardly, and also appeared to her, asking for Masses to be said for his soul, and for pilgrimages to be undertaken on his account, wishes that her family (acting on the Catholic doctrine of merit, where one person can in effect do another's good deed) undertook to fulfil.[5] They did not make a pilgrimage to St James of Compostella which she had requested, however, and the possession continued. Obry herself then began to speak as the possessing spirit, reporting 'in the open mouth of Nicole' that it came from God, was her grandfather, and was his soul and good angel.[6]

For ghosts of the dead to appear before their relatives was not an entirely unexpected occurrence among Europeans in the early modern era, and it was a belief which found some qualified learned support. Even a kind of possession, such as Obry experienced, although generally discredited as demonic by church authorities, was believed to be within the sphere of potential interactions between the world of the living and that of the dead.[7] A visitation by the dead usually occurred when a person had died suddenly, as Vuillot had, without making a general confession or without having fulfilled a vow made in life. Tormented souls thus sought ways to have the living help them resolve their spiritual debt and speed their passage through purgatory. It was often believed that the dead, to communicate their desperation, were able to transfer their spiritual torment into the physical torment of the living, a communication after death said to come from a 'personal purgatory'.[8] This is what happened in the most dramatic – and theologically more dubious – way to Nicole Obry. After appearing before her, then speaking to her, the ghost then inflicted on her an array of debilitating conditions, including making her deaf, dumb, blind and unnaturally stiff and heavy of limb. Obry's parents had begun to doubt that Obry was possessed by her grandfather's ghost, and sought help from two of the local clergy, who tried to expel the spirit by conjuring it.[9] When this failed the local churchmen called in a Dominican father, Pierre de la Motte, to assess the case.

On 27 November, la Motte performed a 'probative exorcism' on Obry, that is, an exorcism designed to elicit the true source of her torment, to see if it were indeed the grandfather's ghost causing the problem, or something more sinister.[10] Such a test in this case entailed la Motte interrogating Obry (or rather, the 'devil' possibly afflicting her) in Latin. Tests like this were generally seen as a crucial step in the process of establishing possession by demons, as a key sign of possession was the ability to understand languages unknown to the sufferer, where the 'real' speaker was therefore held to be the demon. In this case, however, when the demon showed a much less decisive preference for French, la Motte remained undeterred. (And indeed, in many possession cases in the decades which followed, 'demons' chose to answer Latin questions in French.) La Motte also splashed Obry's face with holy water, which caused her to shrink away and pull a face, showing, it was perceived, her demon's revulsion in the presence of a holy object.[11] Up until this point the conjurations of the priests appear to have been of a fairly ambit kind, targeting whatever spirit was there, but the tests by la Motte introduced the critical distinction between a ghostly possession and a demonic one as they aimed to show the spirit responding in ways that were distinctively demonic. The demon's revulsion on contact with holy water showed 'his' fear in the face of holy things, and a grudging recognition of the power of God to challenge his presence in Obry's body. Decisively, la Motte succeeded in making the devil admit his name. Obry said that her voice was really that of Beelzebub, biblical Prince of Demons and Lord of the Flies.[12] This was a watershed moment which drew on the ancient pre-Christian idea of the power of names to control demons, the demon's reluctant response a chink in his armour, and an early hint of the exorcist triumphs to follow.[13]

Let us pause for a moment to consider the causes and symptoms of possession and some of its forms in this era. Possession was seen as demonic seizure of a person's body, and not, generally, of their soul,[14] although at least one author writing about this case appears to have been unaware of this distinction.[15] Another commentator described possession as a 'commotion of flesh, blood and members, by vital spirits', brought about by demons.[16] Possession was sometimes distinguished from a condition known as 'obsession', a somewhat less severe form of demonic incursion compared to assault from without, for example in visions and visitations, rather than manipulation and torture from within.[17] The possible causes of possession were multiple, ranging from the sins of the possessed themselves to the curses and witchcraft of outsiders. Possession associated with the gift of prophecy and with ecstasy was found more often in possessed girls and women, and to a lesser extent little boys. Mass possessions in female convents became the hallmark of the early modern period, whereas mass possessions outside convents – also quite common in this era – tended to be more sexually mixed. One male religious house also faced an outbreak of bewitchment.[18] (Possession of men on their own was, however, quite rare.) Indeed there seem to have been almost as many types of possession as there were possessed people: witches themselves might even be exorcised as possessed.[19] According to Caesarius of Heisterbach, the medieval abbot, possession occurred when the demonic spirit 'shoots in its wickedness like an arrow, by suggesting evil and fashioning the mind to vice'.[20] In this way, the fate of the soul was put at risk by a bodily disposition such as lust, for example. Another consequence of a demonic attack was an emotional or physical incapacity to participate in devotional life. In this way too, possession compromised the fate of the soul. This manifestation of possession was one of the most common in an era in which Catholics were increasingly expected to fulfil their devotional obligations.

New testament accounts, the lives of saints, as well as medical manuals and demonological texts, provided the wide range of symptoms of possession. The principal symptoms were displays of physical convulsion; rigidity; extraordinary facial or bodily contortions or levitation; exceptional strength; knowledge of languages hitherto unknown by the sufferer; meaningless babbling or impenetrable silence; speaking in altered voices, notably in the case female demoniacs speaking as their male demons; a knowledge of distant or future events or secrets, including holy mysteries; and knowledge of the fate of souls in purgatory or details of the unconfessed sins of other people. Sudden loss of the power of the senses and falling 'as if dead' – in a state resembling ecstasy – were also signs.[21] The Ambrosian Francesco Maria Guazzo's 1608 *Compendium Maleficarum* lists around fifty symptoms.[22] The failure of all previous attempts to cure an illness over a prolonged period could also suggest possession. Certain incongruities between symptoms or the absence of changes to the body following some violent episode were also taken as signs: a normal pulse rate after a violent convulsion or no indication of pain in response to pricking with a needle, for example, could point to the conclusion that the sufferer's body was totally subject to the devil's powers. Displays of revulsion by the possessed in the presence of sacred objects such as the Host, or of holy persons, signalled the presence of the devil and his fear in the face of sacred power.

Critically, whatever the symptoms, a diagnosis of possession did not mean very much except in relation to its potential to be cured by exorcism. Possession required exorcism, in a sense, to prove its reality: its incursions could only be truly countered by spiritual weapons. Because the symptoms of possession can be roughly divided into those which were purely physical and those which concerned the religious aspect of possession – such as rejection of the Host – the exorcist's actions could be decisive in determining a true possession, even before he tried to expel the demon. As one physician, Barthélemy Pardoux, remarked, a doctor cannot 'bring on' the symptoms of illness by his tests, whereas in the case of possession, it is common for the actions of the exorcist to alter decisively the behaviour of the possessed.[23] Since exorcists could show their power simply by conjuring demons, it is important to understand the somewhat confusing notion that exorcism was still 'working', even when it did not expel the demon. An exorcism which elicited a measure of obedience from a demon, without fully controlling him through expulsion, was nonetheless a successful priestly act.

Pierre de la Motte in this case was the pivotal figure. To the point where la Motte had diagnosed possession, his probative exorcisms were uncontroversial and well within the sphere of accepted ritual practice. Even though their purpose was diagnostic, the knowledge supplied by the demon, such as his name, helped the exorcist to know how ultimately to expel him. But in more elaborate forms, exorcisms which did not immediately expel the demon were potentially very controversial. It was just such elaborate performances – in which the possessing 'devil' berated and harangued observers – for which Nicole Obry became famous. And la Motte, after 'exposing' the demonic nature of the spirit afflicting Obry at home, became Obry's principal exorcist and later, in effect, her personal tour manager. For Obry, this new relationship with an outsider to Vervins was the basis of a matrix of patronage which sustained the credibility of her public possession. La Motte's intervention provided the foundation for the case to cross from a self-diagnosed affliction, to a demonised version of possession acceptable to the Church hierarchy. Obry's possession catapulted her, or at least her name, to local and indeed national and international fame. Over a relatively short but intense period of ten months, from November 1565 to August 1566, Obry went from being a young woman of no account, to being renowned, manhandled, reviled, imprisoned, and interviewed by royalty, only to return again, by and large, to the life of a home-maker and, later, a mother.[24]

Vervins

After exposing the demon to his satisfaction, Pierre de la Motte took Obry to the church of Vervins to attempt to deliver her. By then, her physical symptoms had become exaggerated and grotesque, more clear evidence of the devil supplanting a possibly less malevolent, more enigmatic spirit. Obry had become too strong for her husband and two other men to control, as she thrashed around at home on her bed. Her writhing was the result of the demon being tormented, we are told, by the prayers of the local curé, as he prayed for her release. When she was thirsty, her grandmother suggested she be given some water and wine mixed with holy water. This was done, apparently without Obry knowing, prompting another violent reaction in the percipient demon, who again detected an attempt to remove it using something holy. Obry's body went into violent contortions. As the glass touched her mouth, her 'first deformity' arose:

> suddenly her neck and the head were thrown back, and her throat and stomach swelled up . . . [H]er face was suddenly long, large, of a red colour . . . becoming like the crest of a Turkey cock . . . Her eyes were forced back in her head, then, horrible to see, they started right out of it. The tongue was long, large and thick, now red, now purplish black, now of diverse other colours, sticking out as far as her chin, sometimes longer, sometimes less so.[25]

The demon also spoke through Obry's mouth to the people who gathered around her. Without moving her mouth or lips, Obry, or the demon, as it was held, revealed to some of those present 'the things they took to be most secret' about themselves – though mixing these with untruths – and reproached their vices.

And 'he' said, moreover, that 'the Huguenots were his and that they did his commandments well'.[26] This polemic aspect of the possession was what la Motte appears to have wanted to promote, for if the devil himself said that the Huguenots were his, this was a new and potentially powerful propaganda weapon in a time of intense hostility between French Catholics and the Calvinist Huguenots.

By 1565, there had already been one in the series of six tragic religious wars which were to wrack France for the next sixty years. The Edict of Amboise of 19 March 1563, which ended the first war, had guaranteed freedom of conscience to the Huguenots. Profound tensions remained: many Catholics felt that this compromise would allow the devil's agents to live in their midst, a kind of national state of demonic possession.[27] Others, notably Catholics in positions of secular authority who wanted to keep public order, were more inclined to moderation. The Obry case brought these and other differences between Catholics to the fore. As we have seen, even before the Protestant schism, Catholic reformers feared public exorcism because of anxieties about exciting 'popular' appetites. Yet creating a stir appears to have been exactly what la Motte, and possibly Obry, sought to do. It seems this had been la Motte's plan all along: he had arrived in Vervins only after first passing through Laon, the local episcopal see, to secure 'the orders and powers' of the dean of the cathedral of Laon, Christofle de Héricourt, apparently to permit him to exorcise Obry.[28] And when la Motte took Obry to the church in Vervins to exorcise her, he saw to the erection of a scaffold in the church, to enable crowds to see the exorcism. Nicole Obry must have seemed to la Motte to be the ideal candidate for public exorcism, a pious young married woman deceived only by her desire to save the soul of her grandfather. Erecting a stage for better viewing in a culture where churches and ritual already catered amply for the sense of sight was far from routine, but it suggests that la Motte (and possibly Obry or her family) anticipated that the exorcisms would not be over quickly. If so, they were right. Exorcisms at Vervins took place nearly every day from late November 1565 to early January 1566.

At Vervins, Beelzebub's control over Obry's senses prevented her confessing and receiving the Host.[29] He also hurled her into the snow. La Motte used baptism manuals as his guide in how to exorcise Obry, as these contain the ritual words of expulsion of the devil from the newborn child: 'I exorcise thee, unclean spirit . . . accursed one, damned and to be damned'.[30] This use of baptism manuals seems to be an indication of the scarcity of specialist exorcism manuals, a literary and liturgical form which spread across western Europe only later in the century. La Motte, with the help of other priests and townsfolk from Vervins and beyond, also conducted processions and prayers for Obry's deliverance.[31] Catholic prayer relied on the individual holiness of each bystander to effect a transfer of merit to the possessed, via divine intercession. In that sense, there was here a devolution of priestly power which allowed onlookers to participate in a sacramental, but it was also a public and communal action, overseen and stage-managed by priests, and mediated by the possessed. When la Motte touched Obry with the crucifix, she recovered her senses, confessed, and took Communion. Indeed she took the Host, the 'only victorious remedy of our Creator' several times in one hour, her receptivity seen as evidence of the Church's dominance over the demon, though, of course, the mere repetition of the remedy could equally be seen as weakness and failure.[32] For this was only a partial victory. Beelzebub was still there, and, having taken refuge 'in one of her legs, then in her left arm', he proceeded to call in twenty-nine more devils as reinforcements.[33] On 4 January 1566, the Church's own reinforcements arrived, in the person of the Bishop of Laon, Jean de Bours. Upping the ante, and underlining the importance of an ascent through the Church hierarchy to the progress of the story, 'Beelzebub' said he would only leave Obry's body for the bishop, adding that he would not do so at Vervins.[34] The group therefore left Vervins, to go first to the famous shrine of Our Lady of Liesse, where Obry prayed to the Virgin, and later twenty-six of the devils were expelled when la Motte administered the Host to her. The group then went to Pierrepont, where Obry was freed of the demon Legio (the name evoking the biblical 'Legion', who, as the multiple devils of the Gadarene demoniac, entered the herd of swine, who pitched themselves into the sea).[35] Finally, they headed towards the cathedral city of Laon, in the hope of expelling the three remaining demons, Beelzebub the lion, Cerberus the dog and Astaroth the pig.[36] Thus, in making a clear hierarchical transition to the bishop's seat of power, as well as showing to believers – or more importantly to doubters – the power of specific holy places and objects, Obry and her exorcists found a geographical and social path to dignify the evidence of the senses, in defence of Catholicism. At the Cathedral at Laon the exorcisms of Nicole Obry entered legend.

It is not clear that Obry had sought the identity of a demoniac. Certainly there was no talk of demons in her earliest displays. We cannot know how much her intentions, conscious or unconscious, played a part in what she later did as a demon. Such a lack of evidence of motive is a daily lament for historians seeking the voices of the obscure, and especially those of women. Yet some speculation seems legitimate. Obry was in the first three months of marriage when the possession took hold. Perhaps, as Crouzet has implied, her marriage was too agreeable, possibly prompting guilt.[37] Or, perhaps the marriage, which was quite likely to have been arranged, had not proven agreeable to her, and she sought some kind of escape. It is quite possible that her visit to her grandfather's grave reopened a seam of grief within her which proved unbearable, and led to some kind of traumatised reaction. Was Obry ambitious? Did she know it was possible to be something like a 'living saint'? Even as early as when she spoke as her grandfather, Obry sought to go on pilgrimage. Did she just want to travel? Or was this the only way she could fulfil her own desire for holiness?

Once Obry adopted – or was assigned – the identity of a demon, she continued to seek travel, and with more success. Yet can we impute a conscious desire for worldly pleasures like travel, and escape from domesticity, when such desires might imply clear fraud? Is it not possible Obry sought principally to pursue holy deeds, even if she were perhaps overplaying her hand? To be chosen to be a vehicle of divine action could be seen as an honour. In a region like Picardy, known for its deep traditions of piety, she would be unspectacular in seeking pious aims. On the other hand, how can we assume a young woman secretly wanted to leave her possibly quite safe and pleasant home and go on the road with a group of religious fanatics? Perhaps she was a conscript, trying all the while to find some escape from the role the Church had assigned to her, never mind escaping the role of a wife? Would polemicists endorsing the case tell us of any resistance on the part of the possessed? It is unlikely. In any event, such resistance could easily be seen as resistance by the devil. And could the possessed woman grasp the full implications of being possessed in such a public way, before it had happened? Certainly, there is little evidence that exorcisms on quite the scale of Obry's took place regularly. Public exorcism was not unknown, of course, as we have seen. The French political theorist and writer on witchcraft, Jean Bodin, reported that as close in time as 1552, a French woman was publicly exorcised in Paris before 'an infinity of people'.[38] But Obry's experience (or her practice) as a demoniac would have been very physically and emotionally taxing. Even beyond the physical exertion of her exorcisms, there was at one point, we are told, an attempt on her life.[39] In a social climate with an ever-present undercurrent of religious violence, would a young woman want to put herself forward in such a public way? Perhaps we can assume she was no more sure than we can be. Erik Midelfort has appositely suggested for a similar case, a possession such as this might give a young woman the opportunity to express the 'violently contradictory' ways she felt about Catholicism and her place in it.[40]

It is possibly more important to canvas these questions about Obry's motivations, I think, than to pretend to be able to answer them. Only one thing is certain: if la Motte had not explored the possibility of demonic possession in Obry and given his diagnosis, the first critical gender, class and lay/clerical line would not have been crossed, and the case could not have been one of possession, at least not in any public forum. A 'real' possession, to be brought into existence, needed to be confirmed by a member of the religious hierarchy. And, more to the point, religious authorities were more likely to see, for their own reasons, a demonic possession than a homegrown haunting, and to see in a time of confessional tension its potential for polemic. The very scale of the story's success may nonetheless have contributed to increasing scepticism among Catholics about the limits of the good to be achieved through such means.

Laon

Obry entered the city of Laon in triumphal style on 24 January 1566, in procession with an entourage of priests and family, and was met by the bishop, Jean de Bours.[41] Again a scaffold had been constructed, in the cathedral, to permit the crowds (it was said, of 20,000 people) to witness the bishop's exorcisms. By this point, it was clear that Obry's chief functions were to attack the Huguenots by aligning them with the devil, and to defend the Catholic church, most notably by displaying the triumph of the Host as a means of exorcism. Obry's performances heightened the centrality of the doctrine of the Real Presence when the devil Beelzebub jeered at the Host. A large and extraordinary engraving by Thomas Belot depicting the exorcisms at Laon, and printed in 1569, is accompanied by a legend which quotes a dialogue between Bishop de Bours and Obry's devil Beelzebub. The images (see p. x; cf. frontispiece) show a sequence of events as she was brought into church on a litter, her face puffed up and her tongue out, men struggling to control her superhuman strength and people saying prayers for her, while demons fly out of the cathedral after the successful exorcism. This text, alongside the pictorial account of the sequence of events at Laon, was published both in books and as a placard. Most sentences in it were preceded by a letter of the alphabet, which corresponded to a letter in the image, allowing a reader quickly to locate the event described. The use of the present tense here is therefore of special interest, suggesting the kind of breathlessness that might accompany someone reading out loud to enthralled non-readers.

The text reads in part:

> At Laon, then, the demoniac is taken to the Church and in procession, after which there is preaching by a good Cordelier [friar]. Then the Bishop says the Mass, after which he does the conjuration.
>
> To which Beelzebub responds: I entered here by the commandment of God, for the sins of the people, to show that I am a devil here to convert or harden my Huguenots, and to make all one or all the other, and by the blood Bod [sic; 'Bieu' for the French 'Dieu', meaning God[42]], I have to do my task and my office. I will make them all one.
>
> To which the bishop says: it will be Jesus who will make them all one, in one sole religion. . . . You must show [who is] your master, [he] who will make you leave.
>
> Beelzebub responds: Who? Your John the white? [Jean le blanc: referring to the presence of God in the bread of the Host]
>
> The bishop says to him: that is why he is pursuing you.
>
> Beelzebub responds: Ha, ha, I am constrained by it, there is the Hoc there, there is the Hoc [referring to the words of consecration 'Hoc est corpus meum' – 'this is my body']. This he repeats several times, at which those present marvelled greatly.
>
> The bishop then elevates the precious Body of God, saying: Look, here is the precious Body of our Saviour Jesus Christ your master. You will say not one more word now. I command you in the name and in the virtue of the precious body of our Saviour and Lord Jesus Christ, true God and man, here present, that now you will leave directly the body of this creature of God, without harming anyone, and will go the depths of hell, to be tormented there, and that you will not come back here. Get out evil spirit, get out, here is your master, get out.
>
> Before which the demoniac, having the face of a great devil, levitates six feet up in the air, and cries very horribly. . . . The people filled the Church,

the pulpit, and the . . . vaults, seeing this and hearing it, and redoubling their cries to God of 'mercy'.

Then . . . hard, stiff, mute, blind, deaf, without any movement or feeling, she is shown to the view of all, as a statue of wood, which was also ascertained by the experience of touching her.[43]

This encounter was the last major appearance of Beelzebub, whose powers receded in Obry's body each day, after she received the Host. On 8 February 1566, at three in the afternoon, Beelzebub, who had been chased into her left arm, exited her body. This was to be the date commemorated as the 'Miracle of Laon', a feast observed until the French Revolution.[44]

Such, in any event, is the triumphalist version of the story. Once senior church figures, notably Bishop Jean de Bours, identified themselves with the case, this type of narrative would be almost certain to emerge from official accounts. As Erik Midelfort says, one searches fruitlessly for certified Catholic narratives of exorcism where exorcism has not worked.[45] And, as 'Beelzebub' let it be known at one point, the outcome was always foregone, the battle between God and him not a real battle but only one which occurred with the permission of God to instruct Huguenots in the true faith. Yet interwoven into the story of triumph are elements of resistance which in retrospect serve to heighten the drama, but which in reality threatened regularly to undermine the exorcisms. Obry and the promoters of her exorcisms encountered intense scrutiny, anxiety and hostility. Indeed, some of this opposition was violent, albeit intended to prevent outbreaks of religious violence and the possibility of reignited civil war. Predictably, Huguenots, as the devil's targets, claimed Obry was a fraud and opposed the exorcisms, but there was also considerable wariness among Catholics about letting the public displays get out of hand.

As early as the exorcisms in the Church at Vervins, Huguenots attempted to exorcise Obry themselves, to deflate claims that any successes were triumphs for the Catholic side. (Successful exorcism can technically be achieved without the presence of a priest: that is why, for example, Jean de Bours asked his congregation to pray for Obry.) It is not clear what Huguenots did in their attempts to exorcise Obry, but it is likely that they too prayed for her, possibly laying their hands on her. One of the early accounts of the case, written by Jean Boulaese, makes clear to readers that although both Huguenots and Catholics were trying to exorcise, only the Catholics succeeded. It appears as if Huguenots may have claimed at the time, however, that it was they who had gained success, showing the superiority of their belief system, for Boulaese rejoins tartly: 'Beelzebub [was] constrained by the presence of [Christ in the Host], (and not by all the sovereign efforts of the members of supposed reformed religion, who presented themselves here).'[46] History might have been different: we might have been reading the story of a Calvinist triumph over the devil.

When Huguenots were not trying to exorcise Obry – which suggests that some believed the possession to be real – they were accusing her and her Catholic exorcists of perpetrating fraud. They insisted that their physicians be permitted to test her, and so doctors from both sides of the confessional divide assessed her condition. This entailed pricking Obry with needles to see if devils really had rendered her insensitive – a 'standard' test – and Jean Boulaese, admittedly for his own polemical purposes, referred to 'the pain of the prickings . . . of her poor body'.[47] (This is not to suggest that sceptical Catholic doctors were not themselves capable of performing equally aggressive 'scientific' experiments. They did, but Boulaese's story is unusual in referring at all to the injuries such tests inflicted, especially as his mention of pain actually undermines claims of demon-inflicted anaesthesia.[48] Yet unblushingly, he also states: 'no amount of pain or violence brought her feeling back, only the Mass said in her presence'.[49]) It is reported that one group of Huguenots in Laon imprisoned Obry and had a Huguenot doctor try to kill her using 'a smelly and very suspect drink',[50] which only failed because her possessed body was divinely protected.[51] We are told that Huguenots tried to murder Pierre de la Motte,[52] while the Huguenot Prince of Condé, Louis de Bourbon, the Governor of Picardy, attempted to 'de-programme' Obry's Catholicism by having a Huguenot theologian dispute with her, then imprisoned her for six weeks. While these events were taking place her father solicited the 16-year-old King Charles IX, who was at that time touring France with his mother Catherine de Médicis. That Obry had been seen worthy of imprisonment by Condé, together with the public notoriety the exorcisms had already attained, may have motivated Charles to become involved. He intervened and issued an *arrêt* to have Obry released in early June 1566.[53]

In their campaign to discredit Obry Huguenots also accused Obry's mother and her priests of causing the possession through witchcraft, but it did not stick.[54] This supports the view that some Huguenots saw the possession as in some sense real, but the product nonetheless of human malice, not the work of God. Interestingly, Obry herself also made three witchcraft accusations, alleging spells and curses (including one by her mother) as the cause of the possession, but these too carried little force.[55] It seems significant that Obry's own claims were ignored, in the light of later cases where witchcraft was the most compelling element of possession. It is also perhaps most remarkable, given the polemic aspect of the case, that Obry did not accuse Huguenots themselves of having caused the possession through witchcraft. Identifying Huguenots and the devil as closely as she did would seem to beg for such a connection to be made. Perhaps Obry did make an accusation and it was hushed up out of fear of a mass panic or possible lynchings: we cannot know. For it is clear that fear of violence motivated Catholic authorities to restrict the amount of public display, even as 'Beelzebub' carolled that God's work 'should not be hidden'.[56] In Laon on 29 January 1566, following the processional entry of the group into the city, the Catholic Duc de Montmorency, governor of Île-de-France, fearing riots, stopped processions taking place in the street and restricted them to the cathedral itself.[57]

Perhaps it is not a coincidence that soon after, on 31 January, a royal notary began to take an official record of the miraculous proceedings.[58] These developments show cracks emerging in the Catholic ranks, the note-taking representing the start of a second phase of the story's history. For if ecclesiastical authorities sensed suspicion from either secular or other church authorities about ritual displays, then the next best thing was to document the miracle with a view not only to publication – a somewhat more peaceful and more legal form of propaganda – but also as a first step to having the miracle authenticated higher up the hierarchical ladder. Such a move could and in this case did go as high as Rome, for example, lending support which would in turn give any publications that much more credibility. It is important to recognise that this kind of strategy did not represent a defensive action by those actors who perhaps secretly doubted the truth of their cause. Rather, this was simply how things were done when the process of authentication had to be activated in the face of suspicion, either from Huguenots or Catholics. It was how the system of miracles and sacramentals worked, and seeing its workings allows us to see into the tensions and complexities even in official Catholic attitudes at this time.

Bishop Jean de Bours, for example, while himself a prime means of ascent of the exorcisms into public view, did not rely solely on his own status as a prelate to underwrite their legitimacy. He was clearly aware of the possibility that there would be challenges to his position, and so ordered that signatures be collected from 200 eyewitnesses to the exorcisms.[59] And indeed his personal style had itself encountered scepticism, apparently even among Catholics. The bishop used fifteen exorcisms over eight days to exorcise Obry, evidently placing some spiritual value in the number and times involved. Guillaume Postel, the mathematician and mystic, records that some saw this as resembling the behaviour of a naive 'rustic'.[60] This was a significant reflection of the assumption that outward signs of spiritual activity were inherently the province of persons other than senior clerics, and of the difficulty of some Catholics in coming to terms with the novelties of a major public exorcism. Yet there was nothing inherently superficial about the rite to make a prelate shun it. On the contrary, there is a need to distinguish the desire to assign exorcism rhetorically to the realm of the superficial from the fact of its actual social status, which in this period was high and rising. As D.P. Walker noted succinctly, by the time Jean Boulaese published his 1578 account of the story he had secured 'the approval of two Popes and two French kings, Charles IX and Henri III, and an *imprimatur* from the Sorbonne', testament to the high standing of the miracle.[61]

Even if the move to record events was a response to initial fears of conflict or disbelief, it was the miracle's life in print in the second half of the sixteenth century that entrenched it in learned consciousness. The king himself appears to have been pivotal in this process. When Charles IX responded to Obry's father's request to have her released from the hands of Condé, he also quietly slipped Obry's husband Pierre ten *écus*, to ensure the family went home to Vervins.[62] This seems to have been a move to get the family out of the public view. Nonetheless, the king also ordered that the dean of the cathedral chapter of Laon, Christofle de Héricourt – the person who had first approved la Motte's ventures the previous

year – write the story of the miracle.[63] Thus in moving to end public displays
which threatened the peace, the king also appears to have seen to the continued
influence of the Catholic version of the miracle as propaganda. Publications sealed
respectability which events had already attained, while the imprimatur of elites
on published accounts of the miracle gave the case a life well beyond Picardy.

Jean Boulaese, a theologian and Hebraist, generated several of the foundational
texts describing the miracle. He was present at some of the exorcisms, and in
August 1566, in the wake of the royal visit, published a pamphlet entitled *Le
Miracle de Laon en Lannoys*, in Latin, French, Spanish, German and Italian.
Soliciting patronage, he dedicated one version to the king of Spain and another
to the pope, both of whom he trekked to in person. He collaborated with
Guillaume Postel to produce another account in Latin, around the same time.[64]
In 1578 he assembled the eye-witness accounts of the dean, Christofle de
Héricourt, a canon, Nicolas Despinoys, and the royal notary, Guillaume Gorret
and published these, along with other accounts and documents, in his *Thresor*. In
the interim, in 1571, Boulaese's friend, the Paris *parlementaire* Barthélemy Faye
published a Latin treatise, *Energumenicus*.[65] The publication of works on the
miracle in Latin, in particular, signalled their appeal (in both senses of the word)
to social elites. In short, men of substance gave the miracle credibility. It entered
the literature and its veracity became, to some extent, a given: it also made regular
cameo appearances in marvel stories and demonological texts.[66]

The high profile of this case suggests the possibility of reflection on its
significance for the identity of Catholicism as a whole in this period. References
in Boulaese's texts to the importance of the senses in verifying the reality of the
possession and the exorcisms can be read as indices of a sea change in Catholicism
at a time of religious schism and war. Boulaese states explicitly what the whole
story of Obry implies. He speaks of Catholics being assured of their faith 'by sight,
by hearing and by touch'[67] and says 'by the most certain senses of sight, hearing
and touch . . . the precious body of our saviour and lord Jesus Christ destroys all
the effects of our common enemy Beelzebub and chases him away'.[68] The exorcists
at Laon, we recall, invited the congregation to touch Obry, to feel her stiffness.[69]
Another text by Boulaese similarly invoked the idea that the reality of Obry's
possession was closely bound up with the sensory perception of observers:
Beelzebub, he said, rendered the patient 'hideously horrible to see, terrible to hear
and incredibly hard and stiff to touch'.[70] Indeed, Beelzebub had also affected Obry's
own senses, making her deaf, mute, blind and insensate. These were traditional
signs of possession, to be sure, but symptoms whose alleviation nonetheless became
in this case a matter of urgency for public authorities.

It is an index of the anxieties and defeats which Catholicism was facing in this
period, perhaps even an indication of something like institutional shock, that
Obry's story sprang as rapidly as it did from being a personal story of familial
grief and illness to become public property, not only as it occurred, but with
reverberations for decades to come. Through this case, the identity of French
Catholicism became contested in ways which early sixteenth-century Catholicism,

characterised by anti-enthusiastic reforming impulses, would not have anticipated. The story reinforced Catholic material religiosity, in focusing on the body of the possessed as the index of the efficacy of its priestly rituals, and on the object of Host.[71] The scale of the Obry story in performance and print places assumptions about the essential extremism of her promoters in doubt.[72] Rather, Catholic practice was found to be malleable within this historical moment, arguably showing extremism to be a relative concept, able to be reduced in its explanatory value when the 'extremes' came to predominate, or hold public attention on a large scale, as they did here.

After Obry

In the late 1570s there emerged a political split within French Catholicism between royalist forces, known as 'politiques', who wanted to unite France as Catholic in a slow and deliberate fashion using compromise when necessary, and the nascent Catholic associations – notably the Holy Catholic League of 1584–93 – who were identified with Spain, and sought to destroy the Huguenots outright 'by blood and by fire', to enforce a militant and uncompromising vision of Catholicism.[73] This political split came to mirror and amplify in some ways the inherent ambivalence of Catholicism about possession and public exorcism, and these phenomena came to be associated with the vehement public proselytism and ritual aggression of Catholic militants.[74] Denis Crouzet has suggested that the Miracle of Laon itself can even be seen as a model for the style which Holy Catholic League religiosity took in the 1580s and 1590s, notable for its vigorous preaching and provocative and intimidatory religious processions.[75]

From 1566, for the duration of the sixteenth century (and indeed beyond), exorcism became a staple of anti-Huguenot propaganda.[76] And while some exorcisms did not take place primarily for the purposes of propaganda, most entailed an element of it nonetheless. The geographical location of most of these incidents also shows an association of exorcism with Holy Catholic League activity, such as in Paris and in the north-east (drawing in the Spanish Netherlands), or with places of intense confessional rivalry, such as Lyon. The Franciscan Jean Benedicti reported numerous exorcisms which he conducted in the confessionally divided city.[77] Natalie Davis sees his exorcisms as part of a fight for the confessional geography of Lyon during the wars, a means of taking back the streets for Catholicism. Other outbreaks occurred at Annonay in 1581, Soissons in 1582 and Rouergue in 1587.[78] Pierre Crespet reported in 1590 that the Celestine friars had in 1588 housed two possessed women in their convents, during the rise of the League, and that one had been exorcised in front of 'hundreds of people'.[79] An (admittedly royalist) account of the exorcisms of Françoise Fontaine in Louviers in 1591 describes Catholic exorcisms which hinted at the ecumenical possibilities of such a performance, saying that Catholics and Huguenots alike fell to their knees praying for Fontaine's well-being.[80] The story of the exorcisms of the nun Jeanne Féry in the Spanish Low Countries was also propaganda for French consumption, being published in Paris in 1586, when League power was on the ascendant.[81] Most cases featured a lone woman, and there were two major group possessions (Soissons and Annonay), the latter of which also came to focus on a particular woman.[82]

It is significant that, just as the story of Obry emerged in a time of official peace, none of these cases arose during a time of official war. This suggests that militant Catholics saw exorcism as a form of war pursued by other means.[83] Claimed possessions did not go entirely unchallenged, however. As in the Obry case, some Catholics were sceptical, rejecting some cases of claimed possession, and putting up obstacles to public exorcism. In the League town of Amiens in Picardy in 1585, a royal surgeon, Pierre Pigray, reported that a possession claimed by a 27-year-old woman and her parents was thwarted when the bishop whipped her and made her admit her fraud.[84] In 1583, at Reims, a militant Catholic stronghold, a national synod issued a ritual clearly intended to reduce the likelihood of public exorcism taking place.[85] Scepticism of a derisive kind could exist even amongst promoters of exorcism. For example, Fr Gerard Grudius, otherwise an enthusiastic believer, relates with relish the attempt of a young woman and her family to promote a suspect possession for financial gain, which resulted in the exorcist Fr Jean Benedicti threatening the girl with a whip and her parents with prison. Grudius says: 'I think that gave them all a good exorcism.'[86]

If the performances of exorcists and the possessed were to have the capacity to convert, however, we have to assume that even sceptics could change their views about them, not necessarily on the basis of pre-given religio-political choices, but on the basis of the performances themselves. This kind of genuine openness needs to be borne in mind, lest we become tempted to reduce the significance of such events to their state-political dimensions.[87] Such reductiveness can risk misrepresenting the depth of ambivalence within Catholicism itself, real individual ambivalence, and the historical power of displays that to many modern readers might seem farcical (as they did to many contemporaries). The exceptional violence of the displays could itself be persuasive, just as it was at times menacing. This was an era when religious conversion – which could mean conversion from a former confession but also simply the reinforcement of belief in a new more militant mould of Catholicism – was alluring to contemplate and satisfying to relate. The jurist Florimond de Raemond, for example, told of his conversion under the inspiration of the Laon miracle.[88] This new reliance on public and affective religiosity heightens the paradox of the role of the human body and the human senses. The body of the possessed and the sensory perceptions of onlookers became a source of proof of the central truth, that God had chosen the Catholic church as the vehicle to display publicly his glory. Yet at the core of the sceptical tradition regarding sacramental forms is the view that the feelings and dispositions of the body are also the most likely to deceive, most likely to veil the moral and spiritual truth in the service of which institutional Christianity exists.

Notwithstanding this ambivalence about the body and rituals, or perhaps in the face of it, the Church came in the context of war to be identified for many

Catholics with its sacramental paraphernalia. This was, I suggest, a volte-face from the late fifteenth and early sixteenth century, when the move was to expunge from Catholicism anything which might identify it too closely with 'superstition'. Perhaps the most conspicuous exponent of this emerging view was the Jesuit Louis Richeome who in 1597 'reinvented' Catholic history in the light of its exorcisms. He presented an account which began with Christ's exorcisms, moved through the lives of the saints and arrived at the present time, an unbroken line of precedent and hence of justification for current practices. For Richeome, exorcism, rather than being an embarrassment – arguably a concern of early sixteenth-century reformers – is what makes Christianity and hence Catholicism special. He was making a virtue of a necessity: if Protestants and Calvinists were prepared to junk wholesale the virtues of Catholic paraphernalia, then that left Catholics with a vast repertoire of devotional artillery to which their enemies no longer had access, or for whom access was denied by God, because of their heresy. He related a story of Luther attempting to exorcise a woman and failing.[89] Richeome made explicit what was implied throughout the period of increasing deployment of exorcism: that exorcism had the power to save not only individual possessed but the Catholic church as a whole.[90]

For once Catholicism had become isolated as one church among several, its exorcisms began to be an identifier of distinctly Catholic forms. While the miracle of the Mass and its production of the consecrated Host was the rhetorical focus of the Obry case, it was a miracle whose value was mediated by the sacramental of exorcism. This seems to show Catholicism, now an institution on the defensive, being presented to believers as more of a 'package', with the miracles which could flow from sacramental forms (and be channelled from the more ordinary miracle of the Eucharist) becoming indices of the Catholic church as a whole. This needs to be qualified somewhat: there was, of course a long history of miraculous uses of the Host and also specifically of the Host in exorcism. And it was not only Catholics who used exorcism: both Lutherans and Puritans did. This testifies to a broader search for direct divine intervention in this period as well as an awareness of the perceived need publicly to display each confession's superiority, in what was still something of a 'buyer's market'.

The possibility of mixed messages being sent by exorcists to a Catholic public hungry for miracles was something of which even exorcists who promoted the rite were aware. Thus while the first exorcism literature to emerge in France was largely polemical, the rite's growing popularity Europe-wide came to be accompanied by the publication of several new, authorised, exorcism manuals.[91] These texts presented something of a conundrum. The works of the Italian Franciscan exorcist Girolamo Menghi, for example, featured heavily in accounts of exorcisms, with the ironic result that even exorcists accused of charlatanism were now able to hold up his books in court as proof of the legitimacy of their rites.[92] Even though Menghi himself had cautioned against excessive and inappropriate uses of exorcism, the paradox of publishing in multiple editions books of rites whose uses were meant to be strictly limited could not fail to leave the Church open to derision. The new

Rituale Romanum of 1614 similarly embodied this mixed view of exorcism: designed to restrict exorcisms, it nonetheless allowed for interrogation as to the reason why devils had entered a person's body.[93] Exorcism manuals were at least implicitly 'how-to' manuals, which promoted the virtues of exorcism. (Protestant sceptics, tellingly, called Menghi 'the Devill master'.[94]) Few if any exorcism manuals originated in France; however, Menghi's work – the bulk of it published in Latin – was widely cited there. Illicit rites, too, continued to circulate widely, to the consternation of reformers.[95] The Jesuit writer Martín Del Rio echoed reformers of the turn of the previous century, warning darkly of collaboration between the exorcist and the devil. He said that those exorcists who had 'personalised formulas and ceremonies' were to be suspected of having made a 'convention with the demons' to make them appear to flee at his exorcisms.[96] Del Rio's demonology emphasised the threat of the devil in exorcism, paralleling it to witchcraft, just as Ciruelo and Castañega had done.

By the turn of the seventeenth century the spectre of the devil impinged on people across western Europe, and combat against him took many forms: witch-hunting; the production of witch-hunting manuals; vigorous public exorcisms and their accompanying accounts; and an emerging genre of exorcism manuals. Each of these means was not always consistent with the others; rather, for exorcism, the scope and preoccupations of demonological literature had fanned out to encompass a broad spectrum of equally authoritative views, from the almost uncritical promotion of exorcism to angry scepticism voicing fears about fraud or collusion between exorcists and devils. For Catholics writing on exorcism, what also had changed was the intensity of speculation and reflection on the power of the devil. In the case that follows, this intense conflict coincided with a crucial moment in the Wars of Religion.

Chapter 3

Marthe Brossier

At the end of the sixteenth century the Wars of Religion were moving into a phase which led to the gradual ascendancy of Catholicism. The eighth and longest civil war, lasting from 1584 to 1598, saw the rise of the Paris-based Holy Catholic League, its nine-year stranglehold on the country, the assassination of Henri III in 1589, the decisive conversion of Henri IV to Catholicism in 1593, and the ensuing royalist defeat of the League as a military force.[1] Yet the militancy of the years of League power, 1584–93, had etched with acid the sentiments of Leaguer sympathisers, and as Henri IV formalised the 1598 Edict of Nantes with the Huguenots, opponents of the compromises embodied in the edict reached for their spiritual weapons. March 1599 was a delicate political moment: the king had just registered the peace with a circumspect Paris Parlement, and Catholic preaching and Huguenot polemic still resounded through Paris. For Huguenots and for radical Catholics, the peace was unsatisfactory: it gave too much ground to the opposition and too much authority to the king. In Paris, the Catholic opponents of the edict included prominent clerics and theologians who had been supporters of the Holy Catholic League. They saw the edict as a threat to the authority of the Church in religious affairs, as it gave royal guarantee to limited rights of worship for Huguenots in France, and for them, nothing short of a total national conversion was enough: 'Better the city of Paris and all the bridges be swallowed up than one soul be lost!' was the battle cry of a leading Capuchin priest, Jean Brûlart.[2] Into this environment, Leaguer-style Catholics took the chance of sponsoring a possessed woman, Marthe Brossier, an 'experienced' demoniac from the provinces. The arrival of the Brossier family in Paris from the Loire Valley seems to have been an action carefully planned by militant Catholics to add to the city's political and confessional tensions. And indeed, Brossier's possession by demons – and her ultimately failed role as a mouthpiece of Catholic opposition to the edict – came to be portrayed by royalists as leading to something close to a national crisis.

All we know of the life of 26-year-old Marthe Brossier prior to her arrival at centre stage in Parisian politics comes from a letter addressed to the Bishop of Paris, Henri de Gondi, in mid-March 1599, on the eve of Brossier's arrival in the capital. The unknown author claims to be writing, in the first person, as a woman named Anne Chevriou, a neighbour of Brossier's, who begged the bishop not to 'believe too lightly' in the reality of Brossier's possession. Chevriou had good reason to caution the bishop: Brossier had accused her of witchcraft during an exorcism a year before and she was incarcerated in Romorantin, Brossier's home town.[3] In her view, Brossier had over the previous two or three years become a demoniac to escape the miserable life of an unmarried daughter, a life from which she had already tried to escape more than once. She said that Brossier despaired of finding a husband and had become 'quite frenetic'.[4] Her temperament, Chevriou said, had earlier led Brossier to run away from home, wearing her father's clothes and with her hair cropped, only to be brought back to Romorantin, where she hid her head for shame.[5] Brossier had also sought to join an order of nuns, but without success.[6] She then began to display symptoms of possession: to 'do the demoniac',[7] leading her family to call in the local clergy. According to Anne Chevriou, Brossier was a fraud. She said that Brossier had decided to act possessed following an outbreak of possessions and a witch trial in the region of Romorantin, and that she copied the animal-like sounds of the demoniacs she had seen, 'behaving as a dog, a pig or a frog'. Notably, she also said that Brossier and her exorcists used a book about Nicole Obry as a manual of instruction, on how to act and what questions to ask.[8] These few insights are all we have to fill out the image of Marthe Brossier the person, for over time she became little more than a cypher for the religious conflicts of the day. As Anita M. Walker and Edmund H. Dickerman put it, by the end of her brief 'career', she had been 'scrutinized, prodded, and pricked', reduced by authorities from all sides, each of which had found their own uses for her.[9]

The Brossier case can be seen as a watershed. It was the last story of possession to relate in such an immediate way to the politics of the day. Later cases involved Catholic–Huguenot tensions to a considerable extent, but none came so close to the heart of affairs of state. Indeed, an indicator of this is that it was the first and the last major scandal of possession in Paris. The case was also the first to introduce a mystical understanding of possession, a development which reflected the influence of so-called League piety. In this context the events associated with Marthe Brossier's possession introduced in a highly controversial way some of the key figures of seventeenth-century French Catholicism: among them were Pierre de Bérulle, André Duval and Benet of Canfield (or Canfeld; born William Fitch). The Brossier story also appears to have initiated something like a new polemical genre of pamphlet disputation about cases of possession, a format which remained a literary vogue for at least the next fifty years.

The documentation from the case allows us to gain insight into the ways in which possession was understood increasingly as a continuous state – something which suited the needs of militant exorcists keen to display the possessed, but which was also portrayed as having a theological significance – and, as with the Obry case, we are able to see here the workings of authentication in a controversial case. We will focus here on two related bodies of literature that emerged from the Brossier story. The first is a rich repository of copied manuscript certificates, which religious and other authorities provided to Marthe Brossier and her family and exorcists between 1598 and 1599, in order to avoid (in the words of a certificate given to her father) 'the calumny that might befall him for want of good and sufficient witness of the possession'.[10] These certificates give us a singular insight into the way in which a case of possession became legitimated, showing in close-up the process of authentication and counter-challenge which could occur. The fact that these certificates testify repeatedly to Brossier's possession as ongoing, rather than something which could be removed by exorcism, raises further questions about whether possession was understood as a condition which defined a person for good and all, or as one which could be dealt with definitively through exorcism.

These questions also preoccupied two adversaries who engaged in a war of printed words over the case, the second focus of our enquiry. At the behest of Henri IV, Michel Marescot, a Catholic doctor in the royal house, wrote a pamphlet which tried to expose the case as a fraud, ridiculing the apparent ease with which Brossier turned her possession on and off at will. In reply, the theologian Pierre de Bérulle defended this distinctive type of possession and argued that the Church alone – as opposed to state-sponsored physicians – could judge on the presence or absence of demons. For him, the invisibility of demons was no proof of their absence, and therefore clerical expertise was needed to arbitrate on the reality of possession. Yet when we examine their debate and the works of other commentators, we find that the opposing views expressed in this case were less distant than first impressions might suggest. Each rehearsed in different ways, I will suggest, a view of religion in which education and class difference, as much as differences within theology, are the measure of religious legitimacy.

'A few certificates . . . and a few grimaces': possession and exorcism on tour

Early in 1598, Brossier's family became convinced that Marthe was possessed, and accorded her request for clerical help, seeking the aid of the curé of Romorantin. He began, with a number of other priests, to exorcise Brossier in public.[11] They appear not to have been too troubled at this stage with the tests of authenticity required by the Church: no records remain of interrogations in foreign languages, nor any checks for fraud, such as showing the 'demon' fake holy objects in the hope he would react to them as if they were authentic. We also have no record of Brossier's physical symptoms at this stage. She was endowed with demonic clairvoyance, however, and began almost straight away to perform as a public oracle, telling people whether the souls of their deceased parents were in heaven or purgatory; whether husbands would come home safe from the fields; whether people with whom they had disputes would be damned when they died; and answering, in Chevriou's words, 'a thousand other frivolous questions'.[12] According to Chevriou, however, Brossier tailored her answers to the wishes of the questioners and drew on her own knowledge of the lives of the deceased. As for doubters, Brossier hurled abuse at them or accused them of being Huguenots or apostates.[13] Her anti-Huguenot activities did not seem to have as strongly a doctrinal flavour as Obry's had, although this is possibly due to the very different nature of the records for each case.

Brossier left Romorantin, which is near the Cher River, in February 1598, to go 60 kilometres north to Cléry, on the Loire, and from there to Orléans.[14] She travelled with her father, Jacques, a burgher fallen on hard times, her sister, Silvine, and a canon from Romorantin. Another sister, Marie, was also in the party for some parts of the journey.[15] Chevriou implied that the Brossier band's motives were pecuniary.[16] The canon was the first of several exorcists to accompany Brossier on her tour, and Anne Chevriou intimated that he and Brossier were also lovers.[17] The canon subsequently died and Chevriou said that Brossier, when possessed, spoke of the welfare of his soul in paradise, saying he only spent one hour in purgatory.[18]

What would people have made of the sight of quite a large group of strangers, ordinary people and churchmen, wandering into their towns and conducting public performances of the most arresting kind? Was it typical? What could they compare it to? There were enough traditions to have made such scenes knowable, but not enough, it seems, to make them humdrum. Miracles were not necessarily part of everyday life, but were at least something to be reasonably expected to occur from time to time. Travelling preachers or mendicant friars were a Catholic tradition. And, of course, it was an itinerant indulgence-seller who had triggered Martin Luther's early and famous reflections. Gypsies offering clairvoyant services are also likely to have been known, as were troupes of entertainers – tumblers or animal acts. Indeed, critics of the performances of Brossier and her exorcists later explicitly said they were no different from such people.[19] Pilgrims, too, especially along certain routes would have been well known, and would have sought alms. Many other people had made their own pilgrimages and knew the life of the road. It is hard to know whether possessed women or travelling holy women of any kind were a common sight, but certainly the people who encountered Brossier knew what to do with her, seeing her as a Church-sanctioned seer or witch. (Unlike possessed women in later decades, however, she seems not to have been seen as a saint.) Defiantly, her sponsors took Brossier through the Huguenot heartland of the Loire Valley. While it is not clear what proportion of her demoniac performances were aimed at the Huguenots, and how much she offered the more personal services of the clairvoyant, or simply the grotesque displays of a contortionist, the likelihood of challenges to her – whether directly from Huguenots or from jittery Catholics fearing violence – was probably high. Those Brossier travelled with knew the risks, and from early on in their tour, the group began to collect written certificates testifying to the authenticity of her possession.

In the first certificate, the dean and chaplain of Notre Dame de Cléry described how they detected a sign of possession when Brossier went to the altar of the church to pray. This was the expected time: her 'demons' typically dreaded contact with anything holy. They said Brossier 'bent her knees and prostrated herself, and in the same instant, an unclean spirit took her and tormented her'.

The clerics then proceeded to 'truthfully test the matter'. They adjured Brossier's demon by invoking God, the Virgin Mary, the saints and particularly 'the blessed martyr Ignatius', and then they interrogated Brossier, and she gave 'many responses'.[20] This seems to have been enough to satisfy them. On 24 February 1598, Brossier and her group went to Orléans.[21] Anne Chevriou's account of their arrival in Orléans emphasises that Brossier established her possession in the most cursory way. According to Chevriou, Brossier and her family fooled a number of priests who 'wanted to believe, not knowing the ill will [of the family] and judging it simply on what they saw'.[22] She said that all that Brossier had had to do was to go to the theologal of the cathedral chapter of Orléans, Monsieur Burlat, a relatively senior official, and show him a 'a few grimaces . . . and a few certificates', after which he 'conjured her to make a report of what he had seen'.[23] A priest doing this kind of simple test-exorcism might not have required the permission of a bishop, but in any event the episcopal see in Orléans was vacant at this time. What the theologal (a cathedral chapter theologian) saw made him want to perform public exorcisms, too, and so, with the support of two senior Capuchins, Fathers Honoré and Raphael (and provincial guardian respectively of the Orléans house), and an Augustinian prior, Fr Rabache, Burlat applied for permission to exorcise from the dean and canons of the Cathedral of the Holy Cross, who were exercising jurisdiction while the see was vacant.[24] The priests Rabache and Raphael, we are told, had 'experience and knowledge . . . of other demoniacs in France and Italy'.[25] Permission to exorcise was granted in writing and, from 9 to 13 March, Brossier was exorcised, apparently in public.[26] Things did not go smoothly, however.

The dean and canons of Orléans changed their minds about Brossier within a matter of days. It is not clear why. Her speeches may have been inciting hostility towards Huguenots at a time when the king was beginning to make a peace. According to Chevriou there was also a rumour put about by the Brossier group that the officials had been bribed.[27] In mid-March 1598 the chapter called in a group of experts, including doctors from the University of Orléans, to test Brossier again. Two of the 'trick' tests which they conducted were subsequently described by the hostile Paris doctor, Michel Marescot. Such tests were the usual experiments which tested demons' ability in foreign languages or their capacity to distinguish holy from profane matter, a difference that was not evident to the naked eye. First, an ornately-decorated book was brought before Brossier and the mock-liturgical spell 'Nexo, xui, xum vult. Texo, xuit, indeque textum' was read to her, 'which words Martha took to be diabolical', and she fell back, according to Marescot, into 'her ordinarie friskes and gambaldes'.[28] Next, they exorcised Brossier with a fumigant prescribed in Girolamo Menghi's *Flagellum Daemonum*. Brossier had been tied to a chair, Marescot writes, then 'They did set fire to this Perfume, and offered those villainous and stinking vapours to her Nose', at which Brossier is said to have cried out: 'Pardon me, I am choaked, He is gone away.'[29] As a result of these tests, the chapters of Orléans and Cléry on 17 March 1598 revoked the initial certificate they had provided to permit the theologal and his colleagues to exorcise Brossier.[30] All clergy in the diocese were prohibited from exorcising her, on pain of suspension.[31]

Brossier stayed in Orléans until late March, then returned to Cléry, 15 or so kilometres away, where she stayed until mid-May. In that period she was exorcised almost continually, her exorcists acting in spite of the recent ban and with the permission of the dean of Cléry,[32] a clear indication of a split within Catholic ranks. According to the certificate written by an exorcist, Fr Conard, Brossier's seemingly intractable possession was due to the presence of demons of a type which is 'difficult to chase out and which requires perseverance'; here the exorcist cited the authority of books which 'treat the art and science of chasing demons out of the bodies of the possessed' – very likely including the works of Menghi.[33] In autumn 1598 Brossier and her family went to Saumur, a Huguenot stronghold in the diocese of Angers. There they met a priest who became their most vigorous supporter and Brossier's most effective exorcist, Fr Pierre Beaussier. Beaussier, who was the *curé recteur* of Saumur, spent several months travelling with the family, and his name is found on fourteen of the twenty-five certificates which support Brossier's possession. Father Beaussier, it seems, mastered the art of the possession certificate.

He obtained one certificate not from a religious official at all but from a royal *conseiller*, Hillaire Reveille, whose 'charisma of office', while not originating in the Church, clearly had sufficient cachet to appeal to the priest. Reveille may have been a League sympathiser. Using a standard introduction for a respectable person, the certificate describes how the 'venerable and discreet' Fr Beaussier had come to the official's house at Saumur on 8 November 1598 to request him to come to the Church of Saint-Pierre.[34] Reveille's presence, Beaussier told him, would render the exorcisms 'more solemn and assuage the scruples of any who doubted the possession'.[35] Reveille took two clerks with him and went to vespers. After the Mass was sung, Reveille called on Brossier to appear.[36] She was 'not at all agitated', Reveille reported, and 'with a spirit in repose and her face full of modesty' she knelt and crossed herself with holy water and began to pray. Then, no sooner than the curé opened the book of exorcisms, Brossier's face, which had been 'serene and quite lovely . . . became dull, blackened and wrinkled, her mouth gaped open and her tongue came out a good four or five fingers' breadths, and her eyes became hideous and rolled back'. After that, the official testifies, the demon, 'pushed by the virtue of the exorcism', made Brossier curve her body, put her head near her breasts and jump around, while the exorcists held the Host up to her face and put questions to her in Latin, which she answered.[37] At this point in the narrative the certificate was concluded and signed, a clear example of exorcism performed to prove a demonic presence, rather than for the demon's expulsion.

Following his own paper trail, Fr Beaussier went back repeatedly to the places where Brossier had been exorcised previously – Cléry, Angers, Orléans, Cunault – to obtain fresh certificates describing tests and exorcisms long past, and to have old certificates renewed. In their most refined form, the certificates came to testify not only to events, but even to the credibility of earlier certificates. One pair of certificates from Orléans is a particularly striking example. As we saw, the exorcisms of Brossier at Orléans and at Cléry were officially curtailed at Orléans on 17 March 1598. But in May Jacques Brossier returned to Orléans to see the theologal whose authority to exorcise had been revoked by the Holy Cross chapter at Orléans. The theologal gave Jacques Brossier a new certificate which declared that he was 'still in possession of the original mandate' which had authorised him, the two Capuchins and the Augustinian prior to exorcise Brossier, implying it was as valid as any later retraction.[38] The ban by the chapter was re-issued in Orléans on 18 and 19 September, however, possibly following an attempt by Fr Beaussier to exorcise Brossier in public, and thus the theologal's May certificate was again superseded. This prompted Jacques Brossier to go to Fr Honoré, the Capuchin Provincial of Orléans, on 23 September.[39] From him Brossier obtained a certificate which declared that Honoré bore witness to the theologal's May certificate, and that he himself had been involved with the case sufficiently to certify that Marthe Brossier 'is possessed by the evil enemy'.[40] With this new certificate in hand the family left the diocese of Orléans and began five more months of public exorcisms, said to have attracted crowds of several thousand people.[41]

As we saw in the Obry case ecclesiastical seniority carried weight in the pursuit of approval, and the support of a prelate was an especially valuable prize in making a case for or against possession. Ironically, Bishop Charles Miron of Angers came to serve both purposes equally in the Brossier case. A number of favourable certificates mention Miron as an active participant in exorcisms, and seek a little slyly to implicate him. The Capuchin, Fr Honoré, for example, attested that 'by the commandment of Monseigneur d'Angers' Honoré did a 'very brief exorcism' in front of four doctors and other observers, which involved Brossier passing tests of language skills.[42] Another Capuchin, Fr Elysée, describes the exorcism which the bishop 'commanded him' to perform and which resulted in the demon, through Brossier, obeying the exorcist's instruction to lick the floor of the bishop's chapel.[43] (Churchmen read this kind of abasement as the actions of a devil demonstrating his abdication of the diabolical vice of pride, and not the humiliation of the woman.) And one certificate implicates the bishop directly, referring to an 'exorcism done in the episcopal chapel by the bishop'.[44] Here it is clear that the exorcists relied upon the flexible meaning of the word 'exorcism' as a test, rather than an expulsion, to implicate the bishop in their accounts. Bishop Miron is also a central figure, however, in support of the case against Brossier. The Paris doctor Marescot invoked the bishop as a champion of scepticism because of some tests which he performed on Brossier, in which Brossier failed to distinguish holy water from ordinary water.[45] But it is equally clear that Marescot (perhaps unwittingly) misrepresented the bishop's activities, to make him seem less ambivalent than he actually was. There is nothing to suggest that either of these sources is a fabrication. Rather they are instructive for us, four centuries later, in showing the ways in which sources can bend the perception of events.

These stories tell us two things about possession. As well as showing the ways in which religious and social authorities determined and perpetuated the veracity of a case of possession, they highlight one of the underlying assumptions about the nature of possession: that it was an ongoing condition. A belief in the power of demons to come and go seemingly at will is the single key which gave these cases the long life they had, and allowed the cult of exorcism to develop. This was a question that divided Catholics sharply: the notion of abuse of a rite related not necessarily to essential differences between one performance and another, but had to do, for example, with the frequency and other conditions of its performance, including the question of who performed and approved it.

None of the features of exorcism in this period was new, but the sheer weight of numbers of cases, as well as their duration, made them distinctive. They also made the stories of the possessed stories of identity, not only of transient suffering. By the time Marthe Brossier reached Paris she had become a professional demoniac, threading a path between jurisdictions: her certificates played off one official opinion against another, disguising defeats and amplifying successes. The certificates did not simply bear witness to events that had taken place: they formed an indispensable part of the process of continuous proof that Brossier was worthy of credence as a successful 'career' demoniac, and showed again that a valid possession could be a semi-permanent condition. This was a central issue in the debates which followed her time in Paris.

Paris

In Paris in early 1599 resistance to the Edict of Nantes was rising as Henri IV gradually persuaded the Parlement to register the peace, the last step in formalising it. The Capuchin order, a new and zealous Franciscan order which had never known a France without war, was at the vanguard of the opposition. In December 1598 the Capuchin priest Jean Brûlart organised a procession of the Holy Sacrament through the streets of Paris which, according to the royalist diarist Pierre de l'Estoile, was 'judged by all men of acuity [to be] . . . a ceremony more of sedition than of devotion'.[46] On 6 January 1599 Brûlart preached at the church of Saint-André and said that 'all the judges [i.e. members of the Parlement] who would consent to the publication of the edict were damned'.[47] The next day the king spoke out against 'Capuchins who were carrying muskets on their habits', highlighting neatly in a single image the central contradiction of religious war, and he addressed them and other extremist Catholics, saying: 'I know everything that you do, I know everything you say. I have a little demon who tells me. Those who do not want my edict passed want war'.[48] But Henri also followed a policy of domestic diplomacy. L'Estoile describes, for example, an attempt by one of the king's aides to convince Henri that Fr Brûlart was arousing sedition. Henri, we are told, dismissed the claim.[49] And Henri also went to the Capuchin convent to visit Henri, Duc de Joyeuse, on 9 March, after the duke resumed the habit of a Capuchin, having left the order in 1592 to command League forces.[50]

Who, then, encouraged Marthe Brossier to go to Paris in such a politically and liturgically sensitive time, just prior to Easter in 1599 – a time of intense Lenten preaching and the peak period of the sacred calendar for personal devotions?[51] It is possible that the Capuchin Honoré, who is mentioned in several certificates, may have facilitated her arrival in Paris at a time when the king was at his castle at Fontainebleau.[52] It is also possible the group arrived only 'en famille', bearing their certificates. Jacques-Auguste de Thou, the chronicler and a *politique* president of the Parlement, reported that Jacques Brossier took Marthe to the abbey of Sainte-Geneviève, where he sought the help of the Church 'before anyone enquired about the life, condition, renown and disposition of the obsessed'. The Capuchin fathers, de Thou observed, were 'the first to meddle in it'.[53] Capuchin interest was not surprising. They were among the most vociferous preaching orders of this period and they were also key figures in the entrenchment of a new spiritual rigour in Paris in the 1580s, even as the power of the League, in whose ranks some of their number had died in the wars, declined. The Capuchin specialities – preaching and intense personal piety – suited the collision of inner and outer worlds so palpable in cases of possession and exorcism.[54] They were the group amid which some of the most influential mystical practices grew up in France in the early seventeenth century, influenced by the English Capuchin Benet of Canfield, who in 1599 in Paris emerged as one of Brossier's most outspoken allies.[55]

At the abbey of Sainte-Geneviève Brossier railed against the Huguenots, saying that they were all of the devil's party.[56] With the ink hardly dry on a new edict for peace it was not long before ecclesiastical officials, aware of the potential for public disturbances, scrutinised Brossier's actions more closely. News of the possession had spread throughout Paris when the bishop, Henri de Gondi, intervened.[57] The bishop immediately called in a commission of medical doctors and theologians on 30 March to examine Brossier.[58] Michel Marescot – the doctor who is our principal witness to the events of the next few days, though a hostile one – described how he tested Brossier's ability to speak in Latin, a test which he said she failed even after the bishop adjured her, or more precisely, adjured her devil, to respond.[59] Taking on the directorial role as Nicole Obry had done, Brossier said that the abbey was 'no place' for the tests and she was taken to a chapel.[60] Once in the chapel, a priest with two assistant priests 'began to exorcise', and Brossier, who had at first been on her knees praying and making the sign of the cross, 'tumbled her self backward, first upon her buttocks, then upon her backe and upon her shoulders, and then softly upon her head'.[61] Then she began to pant, rolled her eyes, poked out her tongue and spoke insolently to the bishop. Marescot noted that Brossier was able to kiss relics of the True Cross without any resistance, but that she furiously rejected a theologian's hat which was placed before her, remarking curtly 'as though the whood of a Divine, or the Miter of a Bishop had more vertue and more Divinitie in them, then the Reliques of the very Crosse.'[62] This comment is noteworthy because Marescot is not only designating here a hierarchy between objects which members of the Church were claiming to be of equal holiness, but it also seems clear that his imagined target audience is Catholic, as he was calling on their continued belief in such supernaturally charged objects. Later that day the medical doctors gave their often-cited verdict on Brossier: 'Nihil a daemone. Multa ficta. A morbo pauca.' ('Nothing from the devil. Much fraud. A little illness.')[63]

The formula whereby these doctors characterised Brossier's condition is worth contemplating. For modern readers the diagnosis of 'much fraud' might have a reassuring ring, confirming what more secular or sceptical readers would assume to be the case. But it is worth pausing before concurring with the diagnoses of doctors who, after all, allowed far more room for the diabolical element than most modern doctors would. Just as the type of natural illness they referred to in their diagnosis has changed – doctors no longer diagnose hysteria or a wandering womb – we might consider for a moment the meaning of the word 'fraud'. Did women simply decided to act possessed, if that meant knowing they were not possessed and deciding to pretend to be? (Some may have done, and we have no way of knowing. As early as the thirteenth century, the abbot Caesarius of Heisterbach had a monk in one of his dialogues say: 'I do not deny that some have pretended to be possessed for worldly gain, but in many cases there is no pretense.'[64]) It is almost impossible to know for certain how many demoniacs may have been fraudulent: the question is clouded both by the problem of perception in a Christian culture, and because most recorded confessions of fraud have tended to follow some kind of threat or coercion. A confession of fraud made after whipping, for example, is hardly reliable.

Indeed, a secularist search for the 'reality' behind the displays of the possessed rather misses the point. The reality is what the documents show was present: situations of heightened passion, confusion, coercion and suggestibility. Pressure to prove fraud arose in quite specific politico-confessional contexts, giving cases a significance beyond the immediate question of how the possessed was to be treated. Nor does an absence of fraud imply that the women were necessarily suffering from some kind of mental illness. If we instantly pathologise the behaviours of the female client, we may miss vital questions. For why would we not equally speak of the exorcists as being mentally ill?[65] They sincerely believed that the women were possessed, so their belief would be suspect for many modern readers. Moreover, exorcists often stood on the possessed, hit them and verbally abused them on the basis of their belief. We might characterise these actions as being indicative of an extreme, even pathological, state. Yet it has never to my knowledge been suggested that the problem was theirs. In such circumstances, we might equally speculate that in some cases it was possible that the possessed were terrorised. And if the possessed were frauds, they were nonetheless getting themselves into often disadvantageous and abusive situations. Better to be licking the floor of a chapel than sweeping a floor at home? A grim choice.[66]

The day after the apparent resolution against Brossier, two of the doctors, Nicolas Ellain and Louis Duret, returned to examine Brossier further.[67] Duret inserted a pin into the flesh between her index finger and thumb and noted that she gave no sign of having felt a thing.[68] Such a test was most commonly applied to alleged witches to find the devil's mark. And although it was used here to discern Brossier's 'unnatural' physical condition, showing her anaesthesia, Marescot saw the tests as analogous to witch-pricking and equally suspect. This gave him a chance both to position himself as the champion of humanitarianism, and to flatter the members of the Paris Parlement for their sophisticated views on witchcraft. He said: 'Upon such a like argument . . . we have seene poor soules condemned to be burned for Witches, and afterwards absolved and let goe by the Judges of the Court [presumably the Paris Parlement]'.[69] To further ridicule the possession Marescot underscored its selective way of manifesting. He described how, later in the same interview, the bishop ordered Brossier to show more signs of possession, to which the 'devil' replied 'Tomorrow'. Marescot noted with irony that the bishop found this 'to bee very reasonable.'[70] The next day, on 1 April, the initial group of doctors and a few new ones gathered in the church, in the presence of some members of the public. Marescot reported that an exorcist uttered the words 'Et homo factus est: verbum caro factum est: Tantum ergo sacramentum' and that Brossier 'fell as before, and used such motions, as they doe that are troubled with a Convulsion'.[71] To Marescot and the other doctors her actions seemed to be feigned. The bishop, apparently showing some sympathy for the appeal of the performances, asked the doctors to give a little more time 'for the publike benefit' and the exorcisms began again.[72]

Frustrated by the inconclusiveness of the tests the physicians began to become physically aggressive, aiming for purely physical 'disproof'. At the utterance of the words 'Et homo factus est' Brossier started to do somersaults, and then in 'foure or five skips' she went from the altar up to the door of the chapel, which, Marescot recorded sardonically, 'did astonish all the companie'.[73] At this, the exorcist Fr Seraphin called out: 'If there be any here that is incredulous, and will trouble her, the Devill will carie him away in the ayre.' Then Marescot said: 'I will take that hazard and peril upon me; let him carie me away if he can.' He then took Brossier by the neck and told her to be still. Brossier called out: 'He is gone: he hath left me', at which Seraphin approached her and said: 'Indeede this is nothing but Martha: the Devill is departed.' Marescot, triumphant, gloated: 'Then have I made him runne away.'[74]

The bishop, seeing all this taking place under his auspices and apparently growing even more bewildered, commanded: 'Let us begin againe and let us pray to God, that he would learne us the truth; let us see if the Devill will torment her again.'[75] This time, following the singing of the 'Veni creator' and the utterance of the words 'Et homo factus est', Brossier remained standing, and also did nothing when shown the holy sacrament.[76] Marescot wrote that when Brossier saw him and two of the other doctors she said: 'Meddle thou with thy Physicke.' To this Marescot responded: 'If thou do stirre, and play the foole againe, I will handle thee well enough.'[77] Then the exorcists continued to pray and Brossier went back down onto the floor. The three doctors promptly went over and held her down 'very easily'. The bishop said to Fr Seraphin, 'Good father, command her to rise.' Seraphin called out: 'Raise thy selfe upon thy feet, raise thy selfe upon thy feet'; to which Marescot responded, apparently while still holding Brossier down: 'The Devill riseth not in our presence.'[78] At this somewhat disturbing point in the proceedings, Marescot says he pleaded for the indulgence of learned members of his audience. He called out in Greek 'Nothing against nature, nothing against nature'.[79] Clearly Marescot was aware of the risk here that pious onlookers might suspect him of blasphemy were the possession shown to be real, a possibility which even he, as a believing Catholic, acknowledged in principle.[80] Then the doctor Jean Riolan furthered manoeuvred the debate so as to appease educated onlookers. He addressed Brossier in Latin to test her, but also so that only the educated would understand him, and at the same time he flattered them that only 'simple people' would seriously imagine her possessed. 'By commandment of the bishop', he said to Brossier (in Latin):

> Thou wretched woman, how long wilt thou proceede to delude us? Wilt thou never cease to deceive the simple people? Acknowledge thy fault, and crave pardon. For thy guiles are discovered: and unless though doe so, thou shalt shortly be delivered into the hands of the Judge, who by torture will wrest the trueth.[81]

Marescot reported that when Brossier was questioned whether she understood, she responded 'in good sooth, She did not', thereby showing that she was not possessed.[82] With the doctors having bullied Brossier to stop, the bishop finally retired from the chapel with 'several notable men' and ordered the doctors to give their opinion. One of the doctors, most likely Duret, declared that Brossier had the devil in her body because (in Marescot's derisive words) she had 'blared her tongue out very farre, and had indured the pricking of a pinne'.[83] Another doctor, Jean Hautin, claimed that a final verdict could not be made for three months, in view of a famous case reported by the esteemed sixteenth-century doctor Jean Fernel in which a mysterious ailment in a young man had taken that much time to show up as demonic possession.[84] But six other doctors, a majority, refuted the possession as a fraud, and according to Marescot it now seemed that 'they were now at the end of this businesse'.[85] The next day, 2 April, the Parlement and the king ordered that Brossier be taken into the custody of the *lieutenant criminel*.[86] Before the order was carried out, however, on 3 April the supporters of the possession called together another commission of doctors, this time those of their own choosing. This group was selected, according to Marescot, to exclude most of the doctors who had previously been involved, and they reported that Brossier was in fact possessed.[87] On the basis of this the bishop requested that the Parlement allow another three or four days for a definitive judgement to be reached.[88] On 5 April the Parlement denied the request and Marthe Brossier was taken to the Châtelet, where she was kept for almost two months.[89]

Brossier was imprisoned in comfort, according to Marescot, and was visited not only by doctors but by religious officials and by members of Parisian society,[90] who appear to have begun seeing the possessed as a source of salon-style entertainment. A total of fifteen different doctors on ten occasions tested Brossier, and ultimately refuted the possession.[91] As Walker and Dickerman observe, Brossier's individuality was by now completely subsumed by the question of her political significance. In a decree of 24 May expelling Marthe Brossier and her family from Paris, the Parlement cited the conclusions of these doctors and the bans made by the Cléry and Orléans chapters in 1598 as grounds for the punishment.[92]

Brossier's imprisonment, as a president of the Parlement Jacques-Auguste de Thou, narrated, caused 'murmurs . . . among the vulgar', and incensed her clerical supporters.[93] In the parish of Saint-Jean-en-Grève, before large crowds, priests fulminated against the decision of the king and Parlement.[94] They also complained to the Parlement that Huguenots were able freely to distribute their forbidden books in Paris, using this argument as leverage against the suppression of their public exorcisms.[95] Yet these men were not mere rabble-rousers. Among the group of Brossier's exorcists were figures who were to become some of the leading mystics and theologians of their day: André Duval, since 1597 the Dean of the Paris Faculty of Theology and a supporter of the defunct Holy Catholic League; Benet of Canfield, the Capuchin mystic who later wrote the influential text *The Rule of Perfection*; and Pierre de Bérulle, later the founder of the Oratorians and a cardinal, at this time a young humanist scholar and trainee priest. Duval and the Capuchin Archange Du Puis both preached 'to a population already mutinous', saying that the liberty of the Church was 'ravished by the Magistrates of the King'. It was the influence of the Huguenots, they claimed, which lay behind the Parlement's decision, because they 'cannot bear that this [miracle] was done by the efficacy of the word of God, dispensed in the true church by legitimate ministers'.[96] Duval set down the challenge to Henri, arguing 'bitterly' that public exorcisms were 'an excellent occasion presented by God to manifest his glory' and that to prevent exorcisms was to deny miracles to the eyes of the faithful.[97]

Duval and Archange were called to appear before the Parlement for giving offence to it and the king. Duval appeared and was let off with a reprimand. Archange refused to appear and would not respond to commissioners who were sent to him. Three other Capuchins – Alphonse, Brûlart and Benet – also initially refused to recognise the authority of the Parlement. Eventually all four appeared before the court. Archange was forbidden to preach for six months, and the court ordered that a defence of the papal bull, 'In coena Domini', which had been written by Brûlart and Benet to uphold ecclesiastical privilege, was to be torn up in front of them by royal officers.[98] The contents of the court's punishment was then to be read out in front of all the brothers at the convent of the Capuchins. This was done on 7 May 1599.[99] Brûlart was subsequently sent to Verona on the orders of Pope Clement VIII, following a request by Henri IV, and Benet left for England later in 1599.[100]

Even with this very public defeat, the involvement of such senior figures nonetheless shows the respectability of exorcism. As we saw, clerics across western France were prepared to put their name to Brossier's possession, and even after the official silencing of the Brossier camp, the exorcists' opponents still had to deal with the resonant fact that figures from among the Parisian Catholic elite had been against their Catholic king. Critics sought their way around the problem by various rhetorical means. In his chronicle of the case, de Thou associated belief in exorcism with 'the vulgar', whose mutinous designs he had feared during the conflict. But rather than associate the exorcists with the rabble, he affected a measure of surprise at the involvement of André Duval whom he was careful to refer to as 'an otherwise learned man.'[101] When Henri IV commissioned Michel Marescot to write a negative account of the Brossier case (published anonymously as *Discours veritable sur le faict de Marthe Brossier de Romorantin, pretendue demoniaque*, in July 1599), Marescot addressed himself to the task of inciting educated but possibly indecisive Catholic readers to share in his denigration of belief in exorcism, showing it rather as something to be shunned for its supposedly unique appeal to the ignorant. A Catholic himself, however, he made an obligatory gesture towards orthodoxy, stating: 'we doe beleeve, according to the Christian faith, that there are Devils: that they enter mens bodies: and that they torment them in sundrie sorts'.[102]

We have already seen Marescot deflate claims of Brossier's possession by deriding the use of licit means of exorcism such as fumigants, by physically grabbing Brossier to show himself as good as an exorcist in 'expelling' the demon, and by ridiculing the idea of demons coming and going in the possessed. Let us consider a little further the strategy he deployed to align education with religious superiority. First, Marescot framed his argument so as to alert the reader to the dangers of 'too great credulitie [which] is the path that leadeth headlong to falsehood, fraud, follie and superstition'[103] and he portrayed the exorcisms as a threat which drew the populace into belief in 'false miracles'.[104] To identify exorcism with superstition was a standard jibe, but any ready characterisation of its practitioners as ignorant was, however, only as tenable as polemicists were able to make it. And in this case, the supporters of Brossier had included some of the theological luminaries of the day. Notwithstanding this, Michel Marescot identified the key threat that Brossier posed as being related to the beliefs of 'weaker mindes'.[105] In order to reduce her and her exorcists to the level of popular entertainers, he said Brossier was treated 'like an Ape or a beare'.[106] He did note, however, the participation in exorcisms of members of the elite, 'Divines, Religious persons, and Phisitians', on the side of Brossier. But, like de Thou, he made as if the involvement of these people required some explanation. He said that he did not know if they believed in possession 'either through credulitie, or to follow the opinion of the people, or for some other reason'.[107] Those of 'weaker minde' were thus in a sense 'created' by reference to belief in exorcism, rather than being its natural constituency.

Importantly, however, the desire to resist the 'vulgar' was not unique to the opponents of the possession. When Pierre de Bérulle came to write his rebuttal of Marescot, just a month after the publication of Marescot's work, he too fell in step with this anti-vulgar rhetoric, to establish his own and his colleagues' elitist credentials.[108] Keen to distance the exorcists from any association with the supposed superstitions of the masses, he stated emphatically that exorcists had removed Brossier from the public view because the people are 'not fit to determine and judge truth'.[109] This move by Bérulle shows a militant Catholic defending ecclesiastical magic in spite of, rather than in the service of, the uneducated. It retrieves respectability, but in part by drawing upon anti-populist sentiment. This is significant. I suggest that, for sponsors and critics alike, to be identified with the 'vulgar' or be tainted by 'vulgar' habits in any way was to be avoided at all costs. And while we have so far emphasised the kind of questions that created divisions among Catholics in France around the use of exorcism, it remains that writers both for and against the uses of exorcism came from very similar social strata, from among the educated and, most often, the clergy. For that reason, the position of exorcism within Catholicism can also be understood in the context of a shared desire to keep religion above popular control and in the hands of the learned. Yet at the same time the reformists' caricature of the popular religion of the 'vulgar' as self-serving and material, and of the religion of the learned as altruistic and spiritual, was undermined by cases in which exorcists of high social standing stood before audiences composed of the cream of French society. For Bérulle, however, there was an even tougher assignment: to rescue his and his colleagues' credibility from the mire into which Marescot's polemic had dragged them. In this attempt he produced two pieces of writing which stand among the most elegant and sophisticated defences of possession and exorcism to be produced, and the first attempt to give each a coherent theology, founded on the central tenets of Catholicism, rather than being adjunct to them. These works pointed, too, to the 'mystical turn' in many possession cases of the seventeenth century.

Bérulle's new theology of possession and exorcism

Pierre de Bérulle was not ordained as a priest until June 1599, a few weeks after Marthe Brossier left Paris, which may explain his absence from the early part of the Brossier story.[110] However, following the publication of Marescot's *Discours veritable* in July 1599, Bérulle responded with a publication that comprised two companion works – a scholarly treatise and a 'popular' harangue – written under the pseudonym of 'Léon d'Alexis' and published without royal privilege (unsurprisingly) by an anonymous printer in Troyes.[111] The first work, the humanist theological treatise *Traicté des energumenes*, drew upon classical and scriptural authorities and on the history of the early church to argue that demonic possession was under the exclusive jurisdiction of the Church, and that therefore the king had had no right to remove Brossier from public view.[112] The second text, *Discours de la possession de Marthe Brossier: contre les Calomnies d'un Medecin de Paris*, was a rebuttal of Marescot's account of the exorcisms of Brossier and an elaboration of the jurisdictional claims of the *Traicté*.[113]

In the *Traicté*, Bérulle describes human beings as partaking of the nature of angels as well as that of animals.[114] When the devil invades the body of a person, he argues, it is out of envy of this human proximity to God, found in the angelic side of human nature, which the devil seeks to assail by disrupting the faculties of the soul through the medium of the body.[115] Having lost heaven, Bérulle writes, the devil finds a 'retreat in man, as in a little world'.[116] It is also the devil's envy

– this time of Christ – which makes him perform the act of possession in order to mimic the Incarnation of Christ. Possession can be seen as the 'shadow and idea of the singular possession which God took in our humanity in Jesus Christ: for in one it is a god, in another it is a demon, re-clothed by human nature'.[117] Importantly the same source holds good for the jurisdictional claim that Bérulle makes for the power of exorcists, which is based upon the notion of the Church as the mystical body of Christ: 'the mystery of the Incarnation, being the motif and model of this strange possession, is also the living source from which flows forever the authority to remedy it'.[118] The Church in that sense *is* Christ and so no authority outside of the Church – meaning, simply, not the state – is appropriate to confront demons. Within this framework, the position of the exorcist acquires a new significance. Christ cast out demons from the possessed in his time on earth, and the power to do this was passed on to the Church which he founded. As it was Christ who elevated humanity to partake of the divine, and the power which he had over demons was a signal aspect of his own divinity, it follows that 'the illustrious title [of exorcist] which gives us jurisdiction above demons is the appanage of our new dignity'.[119] In the *Discours*, the jurisdictional implications of this are made explicit. The Church, Bérulle argues, looks after the possessed, not by putting them in prison, but by keeping them 'in the house of God . . . carefully nourished by the hand of exorcists'.[120] It is for the Church, he argued, 'to the exclusion of all other authorities' to command demons.[121] In linking both possession and exorcism to the Incarnation of Christ, Bérulle seeks to alert his reader to the profound significance of these phenomena to the Church throughout its history, lending a gravitas to something which had been recently so severely ridiculed. In pressing into service the entire history of Christianity (but also rewriting it), Bérulle was reinforcing the point theologically, which Louis Richeome had made historically in 1597, that possession and exorcism are and always have been holy.

Bérulle was careful to note, however, that individual exorcists should not arrogate to themselves the power of exorcism outside of the Church hierarchy. He cited the 398 Council of Carthage's decree to the effect that the choice of formulae to be used by an exorcist 'was not abandoned to the liberty of particular exorcists, but reserved to public authority' (meaning that of bishops).[122] Bérulle also noted that this ordinance had been recently renewed by the 'great Archbishop of Milan', that is, St Charles Borromeo. He said this was evidence that the Church in every epoch has 'the same spirit, the same care, the same prudence' – a clear claim for the continued identity of a single Church, in the face of its historical diversity and then-current fragmentation.[123] Bérulle did not seek to refute each point of Marescot's damning account of the performances of Brossier's exorcisms. Rather, he argued from a basis which held questions of proof and individual performances to be secondary to the central purpose of possession and exorcism, which he related to the question of the display of divine authority. As the devil's 'essence is spiritual and its residence invisible', his comings and goings are not readily judged: 'a devil can be present in the demoniac without appearing to be'.[124]

Therefore exorcism can never be assumed to be final: rather than being analogous to a medical cure, it must be seen as 'an act of jurisdiction executed in relation to demons'.[125] This is a crucial point – apparently taken from Menghi – which tells us that God's plan in some sense requires the existence of devils as an index of evil, to enhance God's goodness by contrast, but that devils must nonetheless be, indeed perhaps exist to be, controlled. Emphasising again his argument of jurisdiction, Bérulle ended by drawing a suggestive analogy between the possessed and human society.[126] There are found two sides in the same man, he wrote, 'like two sorts of estates and republics', one side which has its movements founded in rules of nature and in the composition of the body, and another side which is the realm of the will and the inclination.[127] The second, spiritual side is, the reader is drawn to conclude, off-limits to secular authority.

This new emphasis on the spiritual significance of possession, as a phenomenon whose visibility was of secondary theological importance, is an early sign of the identity possession was to attain in the seventeenth century. The move also lent dignity and a new significance to the rite of exorcism and guaranteed it a place among the spiritual elite, whose preoccupations in this era increasingly involved the cultivation of the inner life. But notwithstanding his appeal to the centrality of theology Bérulle also stressed the social standing of the participants and witnesses who supported the possession of Marthe Brossier, retrieving credibility for the elite sponsors whom Marescot had scarcely spared from his derision. Bérulle referred to prelates 'experienced in the wiles of the devil' whom the bishop had chosen 'in order to be more armed by authority against this rebel'.[128] And among the witnesses to the positive tests of possession, he lists 'three prelates of note, four *conseillers* of the Parlement, some famous advocates of the court, six of the most famous physicians in Paris, three surgeons . . . some important [theological] doctors and religious people of renown and merit'.[129] In a sense, he was appealing to a respect for the social order, arguing that their belief and status were in themselves grounds for the credibility of the possession.

The Marescot–Bérulle dispute might at first glance seem to be something of a turning point in the division of church and state in France. It shows, after all, a clear example of royal authority enforcing itself over senior representatives of the Church, precipitating a vigorous response in defence of the liberties of the Church and against the rationalist arguments of the king's medical man. Yet in fact, as the seventeenth century progressed, co-operation between exorcists and a wide range of secular authorities became increasingly close. Trials which resulted in the execution of alleged witches, most of whom were priests, on the basis of demonic testimony, saw a degree of interdependence between exorcists and secular authorities. The role of the French kings is also significant, for Henri's resolve in the Brossier case does not reflect any kind of secularising shift in royal attitudes. Just as the youthful Charles IX gave subtle support to Nicole Obry while endeavouring to show a commitment to the peace, Henri, too, showed in another later case of possession, that of Adrienne Du Fresne of Amiens, greater accommodation to the aims of exorcists. There is relatively little recorded about the exorcisms of

Du Fresne, but she was said to have converted more than 500 Huguenots and induced more than 10,000 general confessions, around 1604–5. Pierre Coton, the Jesuit confessor of Henri IV, was associated with her case, as indeed was Pierre de Bérulle.[130] Coton's biography tells us that exorcisms of Du Fresne took place in the heart of the royal court and that the queen 'sometimes found herself at the exorcisms'.[131] Coton was ridiculed at court for using Du Fresne's diabolic advice to solve theological questions, but he remained nonetheless protected by his king.[132] In the reigns of Louis XIII and Louis XIV we also see direct and indirect royal involvement in possession cases.

The Brossier case might also suggest a widening gap between medical and religious perceptions of claimed possessions: what could be a clearer statement than a split between body–soul jurisdiction mirrored in a church–state dispute, than a royal doctor attacking, and a priest defending, the Church? But to envisage such a neat split would for this time be premature. We recall that it was not, after all, medical opinion which prevailed in this story, it was the main force of law: doctors themselves were deeply divided, relying on a vote to determine verdicts. Yet as the new century opened, it does seem clear that Marescot's account gave new licence to doctors to weigh into possession controversies in print, and this became a routine feature of such cases in the seventeenth century. Doctors did not, however, automatically employ naturalist explanations: several came out on the side of possession, including, at Aix-en-Provence, a royal appointee of Henri IV himself.

Nor did there emerge a clear divide between what priests and doctors argued. Doctors came almost always to take sides firstly along the lines of patronage, however subtly demarcated, and only secondarily – and not consistently – for reasons of what might be called scientific conscience. The same might be said of some priests, many of whom opposed possessions. The Catholic church was not a monolith in this period (nor is it in any) and its officials responded in diverse ways.[133] As we saw in the Brossier case, the Orléans chapter changed its mind; the Bishop of Angers was sufficiently ambivalent as to be able to serve both sides of the debate; and the Bishop of Paris also seems to have been stumped by the complexity of the situation he faced. The story of Marthe Brossier's journeys as a travelling demoniac is thus also a story of the successes and failures of her supporters and detractors to mobilise patronage in support of their views. Her story shows the intensity of conflict in the Church, but also the range of roles that churchmen saw for themselves and the Church. As the seventeenth century developed, we will see that even the theologians of Paris who were at the vanguard of the Brossier case vacillated in their enthusiasm for possession and exorcism, partly because of their desire to retain control over the interpretation of events against the claims of enthusiasts and, in some cases, apparently because of their own direct patronage concerns.

Epilogue: Marthe Brossier

In late 1599 and in early 1600, Marthe Brossier again came to public attention and again came into conflict with the king and the Paris Parlement. She had not remained in Romorantin after December 1599, but had continued her public activities in more receptive environs than Paris. She travelled this time to Avignon, with a Parisian Capuchin, her father, her sister Silvine, and the abbé de Saint Martin de Randan, Alexandre de la Rochefoucauld. The abbé appears, however, to have taken Brossier from Romorantin against her will.[134] The group was travelling with the 'aid and support' of the Jesuits and of the brother of the abbé, François, Bishop of Clermont and future Cardinal de la Rochefoucauld.[135] This time the case was projected onto an even broader canvas than that of French national politics: it began to involve the king's relations with the pope. In early 1600, the party was heading for Rome, following two unsuccessful attempts by royal authorities to curtail their activities in southern parts of France.[136] Clearly, the king saw Brossier's potential for alienating the papacy from the French monarchy if she were successfully portrayed as truly possessed, and her fate in Paris therefore depicted as a slight on the ultramontane church by a Gallican sovereign.

The king wrote to his ambassador to the pope, Sillery, and to the French cardinal d'Ossat, to prevent the group finding support in Rome. Cardinal d'Ossat spoke to Fr Jacques Sirmond, a Jesuit who was arranging lodgings for the Brossier party.[137] Here he was able to bring in a significant royal bargaining chip: the fate of the Jesuits in France, who had been banned from the extensive territory of the Parlement of Paris since 1594, because of their anti-royalist influence.[138] Ossat explained to Sirmond 'as a friend' that this new venture might harm the Jesuits' prospects of being permitted back into the regions of France under the jurisdiction of the Parlement. Ossat also spoke to the pope, and while the pope was not prepared to tell the abbé and the Brossiers to go home, he did agree to do nothing concerning their case without first consulting Cardinal d'Ossat.[139] The abbé Saint Martin went to explain his activities to Cardinal d'Ossat, saying he believed that the first *arrêt* against Brossier (of 24 May 1599) had expired, and that he had not heard about the subsequent two. While defending his motives in seeking to have Brossier delivered of her demons, he was persuaded of the wisdom of writing to the king to make his excuses.[140] De Thou reported that the abbé died a short time after 'from sadness' and that Marthe Brossier and her father 'sustained with difficulty their miserable lives with the alms given by hospitals'.[141] It is recorded, however, that Brossier was still performing as a demoniac in Milan later in 1600.[142] We know no more of her.

A reflection on women

Both Nicole Obry and Marthe Brossier attained such prominence as they did by a gradual ascent through the hierarchy of the Church, and geographically, across jurisdictional boundaries. Yet each woman was vulnerable to the highly conditional treatment such a process entailed. Even if they appeared to some to be elevated as the divinely chosen site of a cosmic battle, it remains that they were still cyphers for concerns which ignored their humanity. Denis Crouzet suggested that the possessed body of Nicole Obry might be understood as a metaphor for a divided France, whose exorcism would point to the nation's purification and unification.[143] The same might be suggested of Marthe Brossier, and each of these women may have represented more still. As members of the *menu peuple*, their bodies – non-elite, female and uncontrolled – might also be seen as an embodiment of the French public: apt to erupt into violence without warning and needing to be either choreographed or suppressed. In any event, Marthe Brossier was clearly seen by both camps as a vehicle through which contestations could be pursued. But it seems that she, too, was used as a buffer, her very lack of status permitting a more indirect conflict between male elites who thereby in a sense attenuated conflict, as well as furthering it. Her mutable status as a woman (seen as naturally duplicitous) and possessed (known to be possibly ill or fraudulent) meant that both sides perhaps acknowledged on some level the possibility that their own interpretation of her condition might be erroneous, even as they vociferously defended it. Jacques-Auguste de Thou's summation of the risks entailed in allowing Brossier to be paraded through Paris shows a degree of selectivity regarding the actual threat she posed. He said: 'Who knows if this was not . . . done to move the spirits of the people and to excite sedition in the principal city of the kingdom, from which the example will pass to others? . . . In the heat of these disputes and contestations, it is not possible to say how much the union and concord was broken and the affections of all divided'.[144] If it is not possible to say, is it not possible the risk was not as great as it was portrayed to be? Brossier was for both sides, it seems, a vehicle of domestic diplomacy, but little more.

Part II

Chapter 4

Priestcraft and witchcraft

Introductory remarks

Were Catholic priests really no different from magicians? This is in essence a political question, whose implications reverberated through the early modern era, and which had a bearing on several exorcism cases. In a provocatively titled article, 'Sacerdote ovvero strione' ('Priest or witch'), published in 1984, Mary O'Neil drew attention to the perceived interchangeability of the witch and priest in the eyes of some early modern Italian parishioners and members of the lower clergy.[1] If the magic of one did not work, there was a chance the other's might; and for inquisitors, a theologically ignorant village witch and an uneducated or under-educated member of the clergy were each potentially doing evil even if their intentions were good. Inquisitions reserved their harshest judgements for those cases in which a priest had allowed himself to be identified too closely with the laity by practising home-grown rites using church paraphernalia, for example, or by caving in to pressure to use his healing powers on a client-driven basis rather than for the purposes of worship. This ambiguity generated an undercurrent of anxiety for Catholicism, but it took on added urgency as the Church tried to counter Protestant critiques of the Catholic priest and his allegedly superstitious and blasphemous rituals. For if good Catholics could not tell the difference between witches and priests, in their practice, might not the Protestants' taunts about Catholic superstition be right? As we have seen, polemicists singled out the priestly miracle of the Catholic Mass for particular derision, disparaging it for its focus on a physical object of veneration in the Host.[2] As the Protestant Reformation evolved, the new churches fundamentally altered the status of the priest by de-mystifying, if not abolishing, the rites he performed. Most importantly, they spiritualised the priest's role by separating the idea of priest-hood from the church magic of the sacraments, the performance of which in Catholicism underscored the vital mediating power of the priesthood in the pursuit of salvation.

For its part the Catholic church responded formally to the Protestant challenge through the Council of Trent (1545–63), where the Fathers entrenched the essentials of Catholic liturgical practice rather than abandoning them. They reaffirmed the basis of the liturgy in the seven sacraments, which continued to provide the exclusive means of attaining salvation.[3] And the Church retained the notion of a priesthood that would continue to provide exclusive access to these rites and whose standing was itself made holy through the sacrament of ordination. The Catholic priesthood after Trent, however, was to be of a different order from its precursors: broad reforms were intended to purify, spiritualise and intellectualise the priestly role. This new, streamlined priesthood was to possess impeccable moral probity, greater education and an increased differentiation from the laity. Such aims reflected traditional reform anxieties about priestly immorality and theological ignorance, anxieties which had intensified in the late Middle Ages. But as with so much post-Tridentine (post-Trent) reform, its appeal fell on more fertile soil in a period of schism and uncertainty.[4] In France up to 1599 war had limited the possibilities of reform, but in the seventeenth century Catholicism became gradually more entrenched. While a strong French preference for ecclesiastical self-determination over the directives of the Roman church – the Gallican tradition – meant that the Kingdom of France itself never subscribed officially to the decrees of Trent, in 1617 many of its churchmen did, and French reform after Trent was in some ways rendered more aggressive than elsewhere because of the intensity of residual hostilities towards the Huguenots.[5] The history of demonic possession in the seventeenth century typifies this militancy. For in France, a desire to reform the priesthood and elevate the priestly office took a particularly violent turn in this period, when numerous exorcists – dozens and possibly hundreds – sought 'diabolical' testimony from the possessed to help prosecute several fellow priests for witchcraft. In what became some of the major religious scandals of the era, four of these accused priests were executed. Besides priests, two senior nuns were also charged.[6] Part II examines the question of priestcraft and witchcraft in relation to two major possession cases in convents involving alleged witch-priests: a possession at the Ursuline house in Aix-en-Provence in 1609–11 and the execution of Fr Louis Gaufridy for witchcraft, and the possession at Louviers in Normandy in the 1640s, which resulted in the execution of the priest Thomas Boullé. Let us now explore some of the dimensions of the problem of priestcraft and witchcraft, to provide a context for understanding the theological and institutional aspects of these cases.

Sacramentals and the priesthood

When exorcists pursued witchcraft accusations against priests in the seventeenth century, they were both responding to and helping shape the profile of French Catholic reform after Trent. Reform in France was characterised by a threefold sense of interior mission: a territorial mission, into the French hinterland; a mission into the institution of the Church in pursuit of reform; and a mission into the individual world of the spirit. Outbreaks of possession, and responses to them in the form of exorcism, are largely comprehensible within the framework of these aspects of the Catholic mission. As we have seen, the 'repeatability' of exorcisms on the same person or persons permitted extensive public display: numerous well-publicised exorcisms served the purposes of internal missionising in the provincial towns of France. Repeatedly, in the seventeenth century, exorcists asked the possessed to relate in public stories of seduction and betrayal by alleged witch-priests. These displays served to demonstrate to large congregations that the Church was both capable of fighting the devil through the miracle of exorcism, and sufficiently vigilant in its duty of care to the suffering possessed to challenge even its own priestly members. Thus public missionising to display the power of Catholic ritual in the provinces doubled as a means to show the emergence of a newly purified Catholic priesthood, the shocking execution of priests mirroring the expulsion of the devil from the body of the possessed. For the possessed themselves, the burgeoning of reformed religious houses in France, and an increasing pursuit of personal piety in this period, helped turn the suffering of possession into a form of holy martyrdom. (By the same token, for young women newly consecrated to God, an inability to adjust to the exigencies of religious life may have also made possession on some level an appealing and approved-of alternative to the strictures of religious life.) There was thus a triple metaphor of purification at work in these cases: ridding the country of Huguenots, the Church of its internal enemies and the possessed of her demons.

Yet exorcists in this period met a mixed reception when they used exorcism to pursue the prosecution of priests for witchcraft. Bearing in mind the historical view among Catholics that exorcists might themselves be magicians, the charge could equally be levelled at exorcists that their activities were suspect, especially when their actions threatened the reputation of the priesthood. It was after all something of a paradox for an exorcist to use rites generally regarded as those most vulnerable to priestly fraud in order to establish themselves as a more perfect type of priest. This developing role for exorcists as moral bastions of the Church, and the suspicion that their practices aroused, can be traced, in part, to the mixed status of exorcism as a sacramental.

Exorcism of the possessed was not (and still is not) one of the seven sacraments: it was a sacramental, one of the 'satellite rituals' of the Catholic church, to be performed only as the need arose.[7] It was one among many elements of liturgy and para-liturgy which aimed to mitigate the power of the devil. Others included, notably, the sacrament of baptism, with its renunciation of the devil, and other sacramentals, such as aspersion with holy water and the blessing of candles on holy days. Even crossing one's fingers is a type of exorcism, understood in the prophylactic sense, as a defence against the devil. No sacramental worked, theologians repeatedly exhorted, as a result of the action itself, the object used, the time or place of performance, or the wish of the person themselves. In this, sacramentals differed radically from the sacraments. For while the successful exorcism of a possessed person is, like the sacrament of the Mass, a priestly miracle, it differs from the Mass in significant ways. In the Mass, the words of consecration uttered by a priest have an automatic efficacy (working 'ex opere operato'), thanks to a promise made by God to the Church. By way of contrast, if the words and prayers and holy objects used in an exorcism succeed, it is the result of a decision by God pertaining to that case alone ('ex opere operantis'), in effect, a 'wholly contingent exercise'.[8] All that exorcists could do was to try to find a formula most pleasing to God, and hope that tests for the presence or absence of the devil would prove them to have been successful. This distinction had profound implications, for if no one could, theologically speaking, determine whether or not an exorcism had worked, the way was open for exorcists (in Roper's phrase) not only to 'out-miracle' each other, but even more importantly, to display miraculous power on a grander scale than that of the priest who 'merely' consecrated the bread and wine of the Eucharist.[9]

It is here, in the distinction between the sacraments and the sacramentals, that the moral implications of the difference between priests and exorcists present themselves. If the Mass of the Eucharist is performed with the correct liturgical formula the miracle of transubstantiation will occur, regardless of the moral state of the priest. This crucial doctrine was initially proclaimed by the Church to prevent heretics claiming that unworthy priests had no right to minister to the faithful. It is a principle which, in essence, endorses the institution of the Church above the morality of its individual members. A miracle such as exorcism, however, which was induced by the performance of the rite in a particular way by a particular person at a particular time permitted a differentiation between priests on the basis of their own comportment. It therefore differentiated between representatives of the Church in terms of their individual rather than their institutional power to practice the rite of exorcism. The exorcist seeks God's approval, both for the means of performance, and for his own moral worth as the mediator of a miracle in which his own moral purity might play a key part. Thus exorcists purified themselves ritually, for example, by prayer, in order to be spiritually more fit to perform the rite. In the sixteenth and seventeenth centuries, exorcists seized upon this moral aspect of their role in order to demonstrate the 'heroic virtue' characteristic of Catholic reform, and, in the most notorious cases, to allege deficiencies in other priests.[10] Thus exorcism functioned to create a hierarchy among priests, a hierarchy which had traditionally been denied in the name of the power of the Catholic church, but was now being generated by exorcists for ostensibly the same reason.

This personal holiness accruing to exorcists is why exorcisms feature so much in the stories of the lives of saints, because they display the gifts given by God to his chosen representatives. This individualised gift was something of which exorcists in the French 'century of saints' were keenly aware. One account referred to an exorcist as being known to have 'a personal gift,'[11] while other sources refer favourably to the veritable portfolios of experience that exorcists had gained. Two exorcists in the Brossier case, we recall, were said to have had 'experience and knowledge . . . of other demoniacs in France and Italy'.[12] And whereas the Mass was equally efficacious when performed by a priest for the first time in his career or the hundredth, an exorcist was able to gain experience by trying out a range of rites in order to discover which one God had blessed as the appropriate remedy, and thus to become known as a specialist. All this experimentation and gathering of experience and knowledge from individual cases was quite licit. The 1614 *Rituale*

Romanum, which aimed ostensibly to curb exorcists' excesses, nonetheless still allowed for the interrogation of demons to find out which actions by the exorcist they found most distressing, so that the exorcist might know 'at which words the devils are more upset . . . [to] give more force to them and to repeat them.'[13] But without having the guarantee of the sacrament the success of exorcisms was open to challenge, because the rite was always vulnerable to human or diabolic manipulation. It might appear to be successful, when, theologically, there was no certain way to tell if a real miracle had occurred or whether it was merely an apparent one.[14] Mistaking a fraudulent exorcism for a real one placed viewers at risk, their unwitting reverence potentially being idolatry. The fear was that crowds would be led astray by the devil, either when he faked obedience to the exorcist in order to tell lies, as the Augustinian Sanson Birette argued in his book *Refutation de l'erreur du Vulgaire, touchant les responses des diables exorcizez* ('Refutation of the error of the vulgar on the responses of exorcised devils'), or when the possession itself was fraudulent, as Michel Marescot had argued in the case of Marthe Brossier.[15]

Girolamo Menghi, the sixteenth-century Italian exorcist, had been conscious of the problems posed by exorcism, by its veritable invitation to promote personal charisma. He made explicit the need to distinguish sacraments from sacramentals, urging the exorcist not to be vain of his own prowess by imagining that his exorcisms worked automatically, and not to believe that his actions would have any direct bearing on God's decision to exorcise or not.[16] Sanson Birette, writing in 1618, echoed Menghi, and harked back to the implicitly superior rites of sacraments as the yardstick against which to measure the power of exorcism. He urged admirers of exorcism to bear in mind 'the difference that there is between the sacraments, whose effects are infallible because of the promise of Jesus Christ, and exorcisms, which, for not having such a promise, do not have infallibly certain effects'.[17] Yet, on the basis of earlier successes, exorcists in the early modern period publicised their miraculous claims, promoting 'proven' exorcisms. Jean Benedicti, a Franciscan exorcist in Lyon, introduced an exorcism in his 1611 book *La Triomphante Victoire de la vierge Marie, sur sept malins esprits* ('The triumphant victory of the Virgin Mary over seven evil spirits'), saying: 'Here follows a terrible and admirable exorcism to chase evil spirits . . . most useful for preachers, curates, religious and other ecclesiastical persons, [the effects of which] have been seen by experience, when the devil 'Frappan' ['the striker'] . . . was more tormented by this exorcism than by any other.'[18] And a collection of exorcist manuals was entitled (in Latin): 'Treasury of most terrible, powerful and efficacious exorcisms and conjurations with the most proven method, by which evil spirits, demons and all evil spells are driven from obsessed human bodies as if expelled by whips and clubs.'[19]

Not only could exorcism succeed best in the right priestly hands, using the right formulas, its difference from the sacraments was underscored by the fact that it did not even require an ordained priest in order to be successful. Exorcism was just the second of the seven priestly orders that a trainee passed through in preparation for ordination. Written permission from a bishop was generally required for an exorcist to operate, however, and membership of the priesthood could be a condition for obtaining such a licence.[20] One author, François Humier, interpreted this lesser standing of the exorcist, against that of an ordained priest, as a sign of God's contempt for the devil. He wrote: 'How admirable it is that the order of exorcist is one of the lowest orders of the Church, God so having desired to humiliate Satan, who fell as a result of his own pride. . . . [Exorcism] is properly the ministry of a cleric, and not of an ordained priest ["a sacrificer"].'[21] Indeed, successful exorcism did not technically require a cleric of any kind, which is why exorcists sought the prayers of onlookers in helping to deliver the possessed, for their prayers were good works which showed their altruism and their trust in God. In order to underscore the value of moral purity in an exorcist, Humier casually mentioned a case in which a child 'of five or six' had served as an exorcist.[22] The Jesuit Martín Del Rio, however, referred disapprovingly to laymen and clerics 'not having even the order of exorcist' performing exorcism.[23] Why then, in circumstances in which clerical authority was so publicly tested, did the Church retain such 'risky' practices? The answer seems to be that the very contingency of the sacramentals made them the perfect place to demonstrate the power of the Church and its members, the very uncertainty adding dramatic tension, as the priest struggled heroically against evil. By the end of the sixteenth century it seems that exorcism had become almost a 'super-sacrament', more persuasive to waverers and more adaptable to different environments than the performance of the sacraments, its appeal enhanced by the (at least notional) uncertainty of the outcome.

The history of exorcism can thus in some ways be understood as a demonstration of a perennial tension within the Catholic church regarding the use of personal charismatic power, as against the institutional hierarchical forces which seek to control it and thereby act as the ultimate arbiter of authenticity. Yet such a characterisation requires qualification. For although it offers a satisfactory account of some aspects of Catholic history, the case of exorcism shows institutional and charismatic authority to have been related in complex ways, belying any easy assumptions that personal charisma and institutions are inherently at odds. As a uniquely differentiated representative of the authority of the Church, the exorcist embodied both individual charisma and the force of institutional religion. He performed an act of jurisdiction on behalf of the Church, as both Menghi and Bérulle had said, but did so, paradoxically, in a highly individualised way. This created problems for the Church. What we have seen taking place in the early modern period is a development in which the practitioners and supporters of exorcism came increasingly from social positions high enough to bring exorcism into a new realm of significance, with exorcists performing increasingly extravagant exorcisms. Yet on those occasions when exorcists effectively took the law into their own hands and their displays turned to witch hunts, they also attracted suspicion and opprobrium. The exorcist inhabited a treacherous terrain. Potentially a powerful promotional spokesperson for the Church – for its miracles, and willingness to purge its own members when necessary – the exorcist's individualism and the perceived proximity of his own practices to witchcraft made him potentially destructive of precisely that institution for which he was at times the most persuasive spokesperson. The two case studies that follow describe the ways in which exorcists went about the persecution of other priests. They show that exorcists simultaneously created and confronted the limitations of their own rite – using it to promote church authority over alleged witch-priests, but exposing Catholic weakness through their own widely perceived excesses. The conflict that exorcists generated and the high public profile they were able to achieve in this period can be seen as emblematic of the convulsions of religious authority in Catholic France, in a period in which, after all, two kings, Henri III and Henri IV, were assassinated for religion's sake.

Chapter 5

The trial of Louis Gaufridy
Aix-en-Provence, 1609–11

On 30 March 1611 the Parlement of Aix-en-Provence burned Father Louis Gaufridy at the stake for the crimes of 'kidnapping, seduction, impiety, magic, witchcraft and other abominations'.[1] The story of Gaufridy's supposed witchcraft and corruption shocked France, and the case set possession and exorcism on a new, more controversial, tack. It represents an institutional turn in Catholic exorcists' practice: militancy against the Huguenot threat now turned inward, to the Church's own. Under the close control of exorcists two possessed Ursuline nuns, Madeleine Demandols de la Palud and Louise Capeau, made accusations which led to Gaufridy's death. The case awakened in would-be exorcists (and possibly also the 'would-be' possessed) a powerful new sense of the 'creative' scope of exorcism as a means to vilify publicly – or indeed eliminate – high-profile enemies.

An accusation of witchcraft against a member of the social elite was remarkable enough, but a proven case of witchcraft against a priest carried a particular imaginative force, as a challenge to religious, and to some extent social, authority. The alarming paradox of a witch trial against a priest resonated as a symbol of the urgent need for internal church purification. Other possession cases had involved witchcraft accusations, but this one revealed a new vindictive streak in Catholic reform: an internalisation, it seems, of the mood of religious warfare, a demonstration of the power of the Church, through exorcism, to punish. This shift exposed the Church as a perfect breeding ground for private grudges and long-held institutional prejudices, in which personal disputes could be given the force and legitimacy of theology and of law. But for Catholics Gaufridy's trial was an intimate attack on an internal enemy, which also deepened the fissures it exposed within the ranks of the clergy.[2]

As we have seen, exorcism is a rite open to innovation: this means in practice that if the disposition is there, the potential exists to stretch its uses almost limitlessly. If no one with sufficient authority voices anxieties about new aspects of exorcism practice, that practice can become, at least for the time being, official and authorised. In the Gaufridy case many members of the clergy expressed opposition to the use of exorcism to hunt down a priest, but none of these voices prevailed. Gaufridy was executed by the state, acting in concert with practitioners of legitimate church para-liturgical practice. I will propose here, therefore, that the case shows exorcism not to be a bizarre distraction from a new, essentially systematic and sober Tridentine reforming religious style, but an index of the depth of passions and the type of religious armoury at work in the climate of reform and renewal.

A house possessed

Like so many possession stories from the seventeenth century in particular, the Aix case can only be described with a heavy heart. It took place in a hot-house atmosphere of violence, abuse and spite. The centre of this eruption of animus was a religious house belonging to the order of the Ursulines. In 1609 the Ursulines were a new phenomenon in France. The order had been founded in Italy in 1544 by St Angela Merici, taking as its patron St Ursula, a martyr to her desire to preserve her virginity.[3] It was one of the proliferating new or reformed religious orders associated with the Catholic revival, that groundswell of reforming Catholicism which grew up in the sixteenth century as frontline religious began their own counter-reform, well before Trent. The Ursuline order (the *Congrégation de Sainte-Ursule*), once installed in France in 1597, spread rapidly: of the 320 convents which were established there by 1700, the house at Aix-en-Provence was among the first.[4] The French order developed differently from its inspiration in Italy: from the start, the French houses were stricter, following a monastic rule, though not at first fully enclosed. They appealed to the wealthy bourgeois and nobility, and their principal duties entailed the teaching of young girls in the rudiments of catechism. The house at Aix was founded under the direction of a male religious, Father Jean Romillon, himself a member of a new religious order, the Priests of the Christian Doctrine. Ursuline houses were the site of several outbreaks of convent possession, the possessions 'du jour' of seventeenth-century France, as well as being prey to witchcraft accusations.[5] The phenomenon of a convent possession was not new, however: the sceptical doctor Johan Weyer, in his 1563 work *De praestigiis daemonum*, had described a case of demonic possession among the Kentorp nuns (near Strasbourg) and writers on demonology made frequent reference to this as the model of such cases.[6] The devil's goal of deterring people seeking holiness was traditional, and he loved especially to target religious, through the medium of guilt. Put simply, the possessing demon's revulsion at holiness was most evident where religiosity was most expected, and it was common for possessing devils to strike just as the possessed began her devotions. What could be a more choice target, then, than a young woman whose whole life had been consecrated, possibly without her full consent, to such duties? (The relationship of demons to religious life took many forms, however. In one famous Italian case in 1574, a nun having problems fitting in to the convent appeared to be possessed but inquisitors suspected her own will was also at work.[7])

In mid-1609 the 20-year-old nun Madeleine Demandols de la Palud, a child of the local nobility, and Louise Capeau, the 19-year-old daughter of a converted Huguenot bourgeois, began to exhibit 'extraordinarie gestures'.[8] Other nuns were also said to be affected, though little is made of them in the story that developed. Father Jean Romillon concluded that the women were possessed, and attempted to exorcise them. He exorcised, we are told, in secret, for fear that the possession would lead to the 'defamation' of the newly established Ursulines.[9] This ambivalence is noteworthy as it indicates mixed feelings about public exorcism, and possibly even a fear that the nuns might themselves be seen as agents of the devil. For many months, Fr Romillon was unable to make the devils admit their presence. Finally, he sought the assistance of the influential Dominican Sébastien Michaelis. Michaelis was around 65 years old and the prior of the Couvent Royal at Saint-Maximum, a Dominican house in Provence. A famous reformer of female religious houses,[10] he was also an inquisitor. Significantly, he had been involved 30 years before in witch trials in Provence, and had published a treatise against witchcraft entitled *Pneumologie ou Discours des esprits* (*Pneumology or Discourse of spirits*).[11] Michaelis is the towering figure in this case: a Svengali whose experience in witch trials and Dominican eye for public display appear to have led him to see the polemical possibilities of turning exorcism into a witch-hunt. He sensed the likelihood of a successful prosecution, and later dwelt on his triumph in over 400 pages in his published account of the case, *Histoire admirable de la possession et conversion d'une penitente, Seduite par un magicien, la faisant sorciere* which saw several French editions and was also translated into English as *The Admirable historie of the possession and conversion of a penitent woman. Seduced by a magician that made her to become a witch.*[12]

Michaelis suggested that both women be brought to Sainte-Baume, a vicarage belonging to the Saint-Maximum Convent, to be exorcised by François Domptius, a Flemish Dominican from the University of Louvain. Madeleine Demandols went to Sainte-Baume first, followed by Louise Capeau, who went under sufferance, protesting that she was not possessed. This suggests Capeau was by this time seeking to reclaim some control in a situation that was getting out of hand, but exorcists employed the circular logic of demonology to claim that her protest had its origins in the devil.[13] For two weeks, from late November to early December 1610, Domptius and two Fathers of the Doctrine, Billet and Romillon, exorcised Capeau. According to Michaelis, Capeau's devil, 'Verrine', preached to growing audiences at Sainte-Baume on the sacraments of the Eucharist and of penance, on the conception of the Virgin, and on the necessity of obedience to superiors.[14] And she – rather her devil – proclaimed the possession was a way to bring glory upon the Ursulines, showing a different view to that of the hesitant Romillon.[15] Like Nicole Obry and Marthe Brossier, Capeau disputed with Huguenots and preached about the virtue of exorcism itself, defying unbelievers to contradict her. Exorcists were aware of the risk of going public and Domptius began to collect the 'sermons' of Louise Capeau systematically, in order to make the speeches available, if necessary, for scrutiny by Church authorities.[16] How much of what Domptius wrote down came from Capeau's mouth, and how much may have been interpolated by him and the other exorcists, is hard to say. The only text we have of these harangues is by Sébastien Michaelis, a trained theologian. If Michaelis did not elaborate on what Capeau said, he might at least be expected to have fine-tuned some of the theological points she made before putting them into print.

In the third week of public exorcisms, on 15 December 1610, Capeau accused her sister nun, Madeleine Demandols, of being both possessed and a witch, and she accused the priest, Louis Gaufridy, of using witchcraft to seduce Demandols into becoming a witch when she was a child (and later sexually). Demandols' consent to Gaufridy's blandishments was seen as no less real because they were given in ignorance. Saying 'yes' to Gaufridy, when he had offered her a 'charmed peach', evoked Eve's sin. This sin enslaved Demandols' will, and gave devils the power to torture her from within, when she tried to deny them. Louise Capeau, speaking as the demon 'Verrine', turned on Demandols and said, 'I am constrained to tell thee Magdalene, that thou art a Witch . . . thou wast deceived by a Priest who was thy Confessor . . . hee is of Marseille and is called Lewis: he is of the Church of Acoules.'[17] 'Verrine' also suggested the case had implications France-wide, saying, 'France is infected with this dangerous Art of Magick: all the sisters of the company of Ursula are bewitched at Marseille, at Aix, and at many other places, so that the country swarmeth with the multitude of charmes.'[18] And 'Verrine' added a chilling ultimatum: 'If Lewis will not be converted [from his witchcraft], hee well deserveth to be burned alive'.[19] Demandols herself later reiterated and expanded the claim that 'Verrine' had made, saying her devils would not depart until the alleged magician-priest was either 'converted or dead'.[20] This belief reflects the widely held view that the death of a witch could act as a kind of spontaneous dispossession. For 'demons' to claim that their successful expulsion was contingent on nothing less than the execution of a priest, however, meant that public exorcism suddenly became a high-stakes game: the reality or falsehood of a demonic presence became a matter of life and death.[21] In Michaelis's conception, exorcism was now a head-to-head battle between exorcists and a witch-priest for control of the possessed. Up until December 1610, Michaelis had been only intermittently involved in the exorcisms, but the possibility of a witchcraft prosecution appears to have led him to assert his dominance over proceedings. He brought Madeleine Demandols further into the spotlight, possibly because she seems to have been more pliant than Louise Capeau. Certainly a new element of violent physicality and sexual suggestiveness characterised Demandols' exorcisms, and her mixed status as both accused witch and possessed victim may have sharpened the drama. Capeau did not retreat, however. Her devils (acting at least theoretically under the instruction of exorcists) took direct action to save Demandols from the blemish of her witchcraft: on several occasions, she led audience members as they trod upon Demandols, in the name of reinforcing Demandols' penance.[22]

Perhaps because of scenes like this, divisions began to appear among those clergy directly involved in the case. In consultation with his deputy Fr d'Ambruc, two Capuchins and two other priests, Sébastien Michaelis decided that Romillon, Domptius and Billet should be excluded from discussion of the records of exorcisms performed to date.[23] Domptius, who had assembled records of the exorcisms, became fearful that Michaelis intended to seize his records of the exorcisms of Louise Capeau, in order to 'either teare or burne them'.[24] At one point, Domptius barricaded himself in his room and Michaelis had the door forced open in order to get to the records.[25] It is not clear why Michaelis might do this, and (perhaps curiously) we only have Michaelis's account of this unflattering incident: Jules Michelet suggested that there was a battle between the two senior priests, each backing two different protégées.[26] Failing to secure any support from the superiors of his own order, Domptius ceased to be involved in the exorcisms from this time. Clearly, the senior Dominicans were with Michaelis.

Once Gaufridy had been named, more predictable tensions began to emerge among the Catholic clergy. On 16 December 1610, a Minim friar – a member of a Franciscan order, traditional rivals of the Dominicans – confronted 'Verrine'. He used theological arguments against belief in the words of the devil, to which 'Verrine' responded by saying 'Who dares deny that Divels may speake truth? I say they may as wel denie that God is omnipotent, and that there is no authority in the Church and that all the bookes of Exorcismes are idle and of none effect'.[27] The friar implored the exorcists to desist from allowing Capeau's devil to speak so freely.[28] 'Verrine' then turned the tables and 'exorcised' the troublesome priest, implying that belief in the devil's words was an article of faith and menacing the Minim, too, with a death threat: 'I doe adjure thee by the living God to come with me, and sweare that all I have said is true. For thou deservest to bee burnt alive, if thou doest not beleeve thy God to be omnipotent.'[29] It was not only outsiders who began to bridle at the turn events had taken. Even the sub-prior of Michaelis, Fr d'Ambruc, who had initially supported him in excluding the early exorcists, now challenged the authenticity of Capeau's possession, while several Priests of the Doctrine, whose superior was the exorcist Jean Romillon, threatened to renounce their vocation.[30] Clerical friends of Gaufridy at Marseille rallied around him. On the prompting of Louise Capeau, a small group of priests and laymen had decided to summon Louis Gaufridy to come to Michaelis's priory at Sainte-Baume, but Capuchin friends apparently counselled Gaufridy to stay away. They tried to counter Capeau by enlisting the testimony of another possessed woman – their 'own' supernaturally authorised spokesperson – who declared Gaufridy to be innocent.[31] However, the nuns, especially Capeau, continued to insist that Gaufridy would have to die: when she was not saying that only his death would heal the nuns, Capeau displayed her demonic prescience, predicting his death as the outcome of the case.[32] Ominously, she said, 'you shall see the end. The silke-worme doth but now begin to weave the materials, but the tapistry that must bee made thereof, is not yet finished'.[33]

Notwithstanding the climate of menace, Gaufridy decided to go to Sainte-Baume, perhaps in a gamble aimed at putting an end to the vilification.[34] He arrived on 31 December 1610, accompanied by various supporters, and over the next ten days he faced his female accusers directly.[35] Madeleine Demandols, speaking on her own account and as the demon 'Beelzebub', accused Gaufridy of witchcraft. She enumerated the places on Gaufridy's body where the devil's mark might be found.[36] Capeau's devil 'Verrine' also accused Gaufridy, and declared again that he would be burnt at the stake.[37] Exercising his priestly rights Gaufridy attempted to exorcise the women himself, under instruction from Michaelis, but unsurprisingly, his efforts met with ridicule from the 'demons'.[38] Gaufridy's action seems a poignant statement of belief in the reality of the possession, even by the one most grievously at risk from it. Gaufridy also agreed to undergo an exorcism himself, after Capeau, expressing the prevalent belief that witches themselves were possessed, had declared that he had more need to be exorcised than the women.[39]

During this period, when Gaufridy was in Sainte-Baume, Sébastien Michaelis decided to 'proceed legally' against him. What did it mean to Michaelis to seek the prosecution in the secular courts of a brother priest for witchcraft? First we need to bear in mind that Michaelis had devoted his career to two goals: the hunting of witches and the reform of religious orders. The idea of a male witch threatening young women's religious vocation was territory he understood. According to Michaelis, Gaufridy wanted to see the Ursuline order destroyed sooner than allow Demandols to remain in it, and this had led him to use witch-craft to attack the order.[40] The figure of the lascivious priest, of course, was a stock anti-clerical theme for humorists, and priestly sexual incontinence, more recently in the confessional, one of the most common ills traditionally found by visiting ecclesiastical authorities.[41] Louis Gaufridy was not the spiritual director of the Ursulines at Aix; nonetheless, Capeau's accusations referred to his having been Demandols' confessor before she entered religion, and Demandols' later accusations situated Gaufridy's seduction (sexually and into witchcraft) at some point in her childhood. Michaelis also bore Gaufridy a traditional grudge that the regular clergy, and especially the mendicants, reserved for secular clergy (the bishops and beneficed priests). More than once in Michaelis's account of the story his position is stated as being diametrically opposed to that of Gaufridy's superior, the Bishop of Marseilles. At one point he even implied that the bishop's laxness as a superior was the reason that Gaufridy's magic worked.[42] Michaelis wanted this case to demonstrate the value of a spiritual and moral hierarchy, represented by himself and the other exorcists, whose authority was greater than that of the traditional hierarchy of the church's secular structure. Like generations of Dominicans before him, Michaelis envisaged the work of his order as bringing the authority of Rome to local communities, if necessary without (or in spite of) the involvement of local church officials, in a climate of unusually intense moral anxiety, and growing authoritarianism in the Catholic church.[43]

Michaelis's first move was to write to the papal protonotary at Avignon, Louis de Vente, who passed the letter to the king's *procureur général* at Aix.[44] It appears that the Parlement at Aix refused to act, however, until Michaelis could provide proof that the possessions were authentic.[45] From 1 January to 20 February 1611, therefore, Michaelis compiled a dossier, with the help of Fathers Gombert and Boilletot and, notably, Romillon and Billet. It describes Demandols as having all the authentic features of a possessed person, including an ability to understand

Latin and a knowledge of distant events and theology. It describes her physical disturbances, particularly in the presence of the Host, and lists twenty-four demons who, she said, were possessing her.[46] The 'devils' had also declared, in early January, that Gaufridy kept a cache of books of magic in his rooms in Marseille. De Vente, in the company of another priest and two Capuchins, went to Gaufridy's rooms and searched for the books. They found nothing suspect.[47] Michaelis recorded that 'this search displeased many at Marseille, and presently it was bruted abroad all the city, that Father Michaelis was the author of all this'.[48] This move further alienated the Bishop of Marseille, however, to whom Gaufridy was accountable as a parish priest. Once Gaufridy's innocence had apparently been established, the bishop sent four canons to extradite Gaufridy back to Marseille. Gaufridy then went briefly to Avignon 'to make declaration of his innocency', but according to Michaelis, 'he was remitted back againe' to Sainte-Baume, possibly by the papal authorities in Avignon.[49] Gaufridy remained in Sainte-Baume for several days, until this time the Bishop of Marseille used the threat of force, sending six knights to retrieve him.

The exorcists were unimpressed by such an emphatic jurisdictional claim, for they had found their own willing senior ally in the temporal authority, the Premier Président of the Parlement of Aix, Guillaume Du Vair. On 5 February 1611 Fathers Michaelis and Boilletot went from Sainte-Baume to Aix to meet Du Vair, himself an influential proponent of Catholic reform.[50] They gave Du Vair their dossier on the condition of Madeleine Demandols.[51] A fortnight later Demandols and Capeau were taken to Aix, and soon after Gaufridy was arrested and brought there too, where he was imprisoned on 20 February.[52] The Parlement then established a commission, comprised of Antoine de Thoron, Sieur de Thoart, a *conseiller* in the Parlement of Aix, and Antoine Garandeau, vicar-general of the archbishop of Aix, to investigate the charges against Gaufridy. Working in the accepted inquisitorial manner the commissioners gathered secret testimony about Gaufridy from his friends, colleagues and enemies, and from women other than the nuns, who testified that Gaufridy had seduced them.[53] The commission interrogated Demandols and Gaufridy on numerous occasions, both separately and – following an established French legal practice – in confrontation with one another. Gaufridy was also tortured. Three doctors examined Capeau and Demandols, checking, most likely, for the insensitivity of possession, and probably also to find out if they were virgins.[54]

Following a trade-off that allowed Demandols herself to be exempt from charges of witchcraft, the commission called her as a chief witness.[55] The commissioners wanted information from Demandols as an 'insider' about the locations of the devil's mark on Gaufridy's body and about the contents of the 'schedules' (demonic pacts) he had allegedly forced her to sign, in which she renounced her faith. They also required details of what Louis Gaufridy did in service of the devil at the witches' sabbat. However, Demandols was still inhabited by her demon, 'Beelzebub' (as well as other demons), and so her testimony had to be mediated at times through 'him'. This posed a major problem for educated Catholics, who knew that the gospel of St John (8:44) refers to the devil as the Father of Lies. This had been an issue raised in the sixteenth century, which now became critical when the word of the devil was expected to carry weight in a judicial forum, in a witch trial against a priest. Even when such corrosive possibilities for the Church were not involved, learned opinion nonetheless generally opposed the practice of interrogating the possessing devil.

Around the late sixteenth century, many writers – several notably in France – were equipping themselves to address the challenges that the devil's malice posed to the salvation of individual human beings, to humanity in its totality and to God's majesty. Few encouraged the interrogation of demons at all, and those who countenanced it to some degree generally discouraged too great a reliance on the devil's words. Was the aim of inducing a witchcraft accusation that would ultimately limit diabolical activity just possibly a valid case for such interrogations? The major theorists generally thought otherwise. For Jean Bodin, even though the devil might be able to tell the truth, he always did so for his own ends, 'so as to be believed when he lied'.[56] Similarly, the judge Nicolas Rémy wrote in his 1595 work *Demonolatry*: 'If anyone is so credulous as to allow himself to be influenced by them, nothing but instant destruction can result from following the Demon's ostensibly salutary precepts, maxims and examples.' Rémy here cited Acts, 16:17–18, where the devil of a possessed woman speaks and is silenced. He continued: 'For in this manner [the devil] enters the Christians' camp by means of false countersign, and then sets upon them and slays them with their own weapons.'[57] The Jesuit writer on demonology, Martín Del Rio, warned in his *Disquisitionum magicarum* of 1599–1600 that the devil should not be interrogated, either out of curiosity or even for some apparently good purpose, writing, 'just as it is forbidden by God to lend an ear to Pythons [witches], it is also forbidden to listen to demons speaking from the bodies of the possessed'.[58] One Catholic critic of exorcisms in Artois in 1616 underscored the conundrums which arose from exorcists discoursing with the devil. A Catholic exorcist there had sought to demonstrate the devil's obedience by asking a possessed woman under exorcism which religion was better, the Catholic or the Huguenot. The 'devil's' response in praise of Catholicism led an exasperated abbé of Loos-les-Lille to reflect, 'and if the bedevilled had said the contrary, [Huguenots] would have made a marvellous parade of it to the prejudice of the truth'.[59] Most significant of all was that Sébastien Michaelis himself, nearly thirty years earlier in his witch-hunting career, argued that to consult oracles was to traffic with demons, and that any help Satan gives is delusory, as he is a liar. And he emphasised that the sole job of exorcists is to cast out demons.[60]

Notwithstanding his earlier views, in his account of the Gaufridy case Michaelis marshalled arguments to support the contrary view.[61] He conceded that the devil was the Father of Lies. However, he drew attention to the phrasing of the verse in John: 'When he speaketh a lie, he speaketh of his own: for he is a liar and the father of it.' From this wording, he deduced that when the devil 'speaketh from himselfe, and of his own accord, it is most certaine, he is alwayes a liar . . . but the case is altered, when being inforced and adjured in the efficacy of the name of God, hee speaketh and answereth to exorcismes.'[62] But if the devil were the Father of Lies, how could he help but tell untruths? Michaelis cited the work of the Jesuit theologian Jean Lorini, who gave four reasons why the devil may speak the truth: 'to beguile those that are unbeleevers and faithlesse, because they may say, this is not true, for the Divell saith it'; to 'flatter and collogue with the Exorcist, that he would cease to torment him, or to cast him out'; 'when they are enforced thereunto in despite of themselves by the divine and hidden providence of God'; and 'to gaine thereby an opportunity to accuse and give attestation against unbeleeving and impenitent men'.[63] In other words, the devil might tell the truth because he was forced to, or else simply to suit himself – a versatile brief. Michaelis argued, perhaps a little oddly, that the devil 'never said it was necessary to beleeve him',[64] and implied that devils are just as likely to tell the truth as they are to be successfully expelled. He asked rhetorically, 'What ought we then to conceive of Divels, being adjured in the power of the name of God? shall they not deliver the truth, when by the vertue of the same name, they are compelled to relinquish and abandon the bodies of those, whom formerly they did possesse?'[65] This volte-face in Michaelis's views, of course, reflected the Church's historical extremes, but it can perhaps also be seen as a barometer of the times, of the heightened sense of urgency in the face of the devil's perceived threats to the purity of the reforming church. More simply, it shows that a theologian, like any good advocate, was able to muster equally orthodox opposing arguments about exorcism, depending to some extent on exigency and circumstance.

The commissioners at Aix side-stepped the theological dilemma of accepting the testimony of the Father of Lies by proposing that once Demandols' devil had testified under exorcism and then departed, she, in 'the plenitude of her understanding', as they called it, could then confirm (or refute) what the devil had said.[66] This legalistic compromise had the effect of bringing exorcism to centre-stage in the judicial process, for only exorcists could determine the presence or absence of the demon. The commissioners, occasionally joined by members of the Parlement and other officials, carried out a series of interrogations of Demandols that entailed her speaking first as a devil under exorcism, and then 'as herself', in order to confirm what the devil had said. Part of this process involved the commissioners feeling the action of the devil in Demandols' body: they felt her head when exorcists said the devil was present there and reported that it felt as if there were frogs moving there under her skin.[67] They also felt her thighs to discern the presence of the devil, as he made her perform sexual displays against her will.[68] The reward for the bewildered officials was very likely some measure of sexual gratification, in addition to the assembling of evidence against Gaufridy. This use of demonic testimony in a witch trial conveys a moving and tragic sense of the powerful and pitiful state to which the rite had descended in this period, all the while retaining its legitimacy.

Perhaps predictably, however, the identities of the devils and Demandols proved impossible to separate in practice: there was no 'still point' where the truth lay waiting to be revealed. How could there be? To assume that Demandols would tell the truth 'in the plenitude of her understanding' relied on an assumption about her capacity to be freed of the devil and to be the guarantor of truth. But as we know, from the exorcists' point of view, the need for frequent exorcisms (and hence for their services) relied on the idea of possession as a more or less permanent state, which was only attenuated, but not cured definitively, by exorcism. This nullified the idea that Demandols 'herself' could tell the truth in any definitive way. In this situation, there could be no such self. Thus, whenever Demandols began to do or say anything that did not accord with the exorcists' intentions, the exorcists were able to charge that it was the devil speaking. The exorcist became in this way the sole arbiter of the success of his own performances. This fact is especially poignant, as it highlights the doubly captive place of the possessed: both legally suspect, and captive to her role as a devil, inexorably dependent on the exorcist to arbitrate on where her own identity ended, and where that of the devil began.

On one telling occasion, the limits of Demandols' identity were clearly constrained within this circular logic, when she appeared to be defending Louis Gaufridy. The transcript relates:

> Madeleine, during the little release that she was able to have from the torments, told us sometimes, making demonstration to be in remission, that the said Louis was a good man who had made many conversions and that they [the devils] said this to cause his perdition, that he merited to be put on an altar to be adored. But in the end, she appeared to smile, at which she was interrogated who was speaking thus, answered (but smiling) that it was Madeleine. And then . . . she was exorcised and responded that it was one of the evil spirits. This having taken place, the said Madeleine returned, which we were able to know as much by her countenance as by her discourse, which tended to the recognition of herself, and the honour and glory of God. Her spirit was in repose and she was in the plenitude of her understanding, and we resumed the interrogation.[69]

The account demonstrates that when the exorcists suspected – or opted to suspect – that a demonic narrative had begun, they exorcised Demandols to make her admit the devil's presence. They exploited the flexible meaning of exorcism, which could simply be the exposure of the devil, and thus retained for themselves the prerogative of interpretation – interpretation that would in this case justify the execution of Louis Gaufridy.

There were other moments when Demandols appears to have been attempting to have some control over the outcome of the interrogations. On one occasion, when the commissioners believed they had made a satisfactory correlation between the evidence of the devil and that of Demandols and they were writing down their transcript, they recorded that 'Madeleine or rather the evil spirit . . . several times . . . suddenly lunged towards us to take our paper and that of our scribe crying . . .

all are illusions, untrue.'[70] The commissioners noted that Demandols' most violent torments occurred when she was questioned on the most important points of her testimony against Gaufridy, attributing this to the torment of the devils who feared their secrets would be revealed.[71] When she was questioned on the origin of her illness in Gaufridy's witchcraft, she was 'suddenly and so strangely moved, agitated and troubled by the evil spirits she said she was possessed by, or another cause unknown to us, that we were unable to take any categoric response . . . the words [were] far away from the common sense of regulated souls, and seemed to be rather from a person possessed by a demon'.[72]

At times during the interrogations, simple confusion seemed to prevail. In written reports, for example, the gender of the speaker – male demon or female person – changed mid-sentence, leaving in doubt who or what was thought to be speaking.[73] Further, the commissioners noted that the evil spirits made Demandols 'say the contrary of what she said in her good sense and the plenitude of her understanding for the discharge of her conscience, indeed even the contrary of what they [the demons] themselves answered, by the force and virtue of the adjurations and exorcisms conforming to the responses of this Madeleine, when she was delivered from her troubles and torments'.[74] Such complications, however, based as they were in the fact that the logic of the exorcists dominated proceedings, seem not to have affected the commissioners' decision to report against Gaufridy. Thus, in a brief and dramatic period of exorcisms, sufficient evidence was gathered to mount a successful prosecution against the priest, by the Parlement.

Demandols accused Gaufridy of seducing her sexually during visits he made to her family home in Marseille, when she was a child.[75] She said that he had given her charms – an Agnus Dei and the charmed peach – to hold her to him, and that he had sent devils into her for wanting to join the Ursulines.[76] He had, she attested, made her sign a pact in her own blood, delivering herself to the devil, and caused her to be marked with a red hot iron in several parts of her body. The pact, the baptism and the marking were all indications that Demandols had consigned her will to the devil, and they were also the means of gripping her in her possessed state. Elements of Demandols' story, of course, are not impossible, and inevitably one considers a possible case of child molestation underpinning not only the charges against Gaufridy, but also the psychological make-up of Demandols, including her experience of what was called possession. Looking for the 'really real' in this case might point to an explanation for the apparent vigour of some of Demandols' denunciations; it may even explain the apparent vagaries of her memory, as the phenomenon of repressed memory is a common feature in cases of recalled childhood abuse. Unfortunately, these are not questions that the documents permit us to answer definitively. Yet, as Walker and Dickerman have so elegantly shown in relation to another witchcraft case, a slight liberty taken with transposing witchcraft belief into a commonplace reality can yield suggestive, if somewhat contestable, results.[77]

Demandols also testified that Gaufridy had taken her to a place not far from her parents' home where she witnessed, and later joined, the witches' sabbat.

Demandols described the abominations performed at the sabbat, including devil worship, sexual orgies, the feeding of the Host to dogs and the eating of young children. And, most importantly for the aims of the prosecutors, she attested that Louis Gaufridy had performed the Mass at the sabbat. So it came about that representatives of the Parlement tested Gaufridy for witches' marks. When they found them, he asserted that he had been marked without his consent, and asked the court 'whether the Divell had power to marke a Christian without his consent'.[78] According to Jacques Fontaine, an eminent local doctor, physician to the king and holder of the first chair in medicine in the faculty founded in Avignon by Henri IV, Gaufridy's question provoked considerable debate among 'the learned' in Aix. Fontaine wrote a small treatise not long after the case, entitled *Discours des marques des sorciers*. In it, Fontaine argued that no one is marked without consenting to it, and that marks in themselves are sufficient proof of witchcraft.[79] Implicitly, then, the mark represents the will – in effect the equivalent of a signature on a diabolic pact, but legible on one's own body.[80] Michaelis, unlike Fontaine's 'learned', was less troubled by the problem, describing Gaufridy's question as 'frivolous', and holding that Gaufridy's marks were sufficient proof to convict him of witchcraft. He expressed his frustration to the commissioner Thoron: 'if this man were in Avignon he should be burnt to morrow next, for such markes doe plainely convince [convict] him, and they are never found but upon Magicians'.[81]

During Gaufridy's imprisonment the Capuchin fathers who had supported him against the early accusations of witchcraft accompanied him constantly. Yet, possibly as a result of the discovery of marks upon Gaufridy's body, which may have signalled to them his guilt and therefore the risk to his own salvation, the Capuchins began to exhort Gaufridy to yield to the accusations of the court.[82] On 11 April 1611, as he lay imprisoned, Gaufridy confessed his crimes to the Capuchins. His confession, which was later published, describes a pact he made with the devil, which gave him the power to seduce women by breathing upon them (an ironic inversion of a traditional form of exorcism, in which the breath of exorcists heals the possessed.[83]) His confession stated that he had offered his soul to the devil in return for reputation among people of high social standing and for the opportunity to 'enjoy some girls'.[84] Gaufridy told of his seduction of Demandols, and of having sought to marry her to the devil Beelzebub. The confession contains a text of the pact he said was signed by Demandols with her blood, with which she renounced her faith. He enumerated the places on her body where he had had Demandols marked, and described his trips to the sabbat and the type of activities performed there by different orders of devil-worshippers – the masks, the witches and the magicians.[85] He also described how, when children who have been baptised at the sabbat die, their bodies are eaten by devils. Concerning books of magic, which he had been accused of owning, Gaufridy said he had burnt the one he owned for fear of being caught; the ashes were still there to be found, he said. And he admitted to having consented to receive the devil's mark at the sabbat.[86]

Demandols' allegation that Gaufridy abused the sacraments (notably baptism and the Eucharist) at the sabbat was a major focus of accusations against him. But, notwithstanding his other confessions, Gaufridy would not confess to having ministered the sacraments as a witch, appearing to have been sharply conscious of the threat to the priestly office of association with witchcraft. His confession states: 'I gave myself willingly to [the devil], with all the goods which concern me privately, but for the value of the sacraments that I would administer . . . that I did not want to give, to which [the devil] agreed'.[87] A pact that Gaufridy confessed to signing also excluded the abuse of the sacraments from his submission to the devil's service:

> I, Louis Gaufridy, renounce all the goods, spiritual and temporal, which might be conferred on me by God, the Virgin Mary and all the saints of Paradise, particularly my patron saint St John the Baptist, St Peter, St Paul and Francis, and give myself body and soul to you Lucifer, here present, with all the goods that I will ever possess (except for the value of the sacraments, for regard of those that receive them).[88]

From 12 April until the morning of 15 April, Gaufridy confirmed and elaborated his confession, but he still did not admit to having abused the sacraments.[89] This displeased the Premier Président of the Parlement, Guillaume Du Vair, who saw abuse of the sacraments as a crucial charge against him.[90] Du Vair had believed that Gaufridy had accomplices, but under torture, Gaufridy said that he could not identify them, ironically (and heroically) because the devil used an ointment on him to erase his memory of their names.[91]

Louis Gaufridy decided on the afternoon of 15 April 1611 to retract his confession. The court asked him why he had confessed first to the Capuchins and later to the court. Gaufridy replied that he had confessed in order to gain the mercy of the court, fearing punishment.[92] Explicitly ignoring Gaufridy's retraction, two officers of the Parlement, Thomassin and Rabasse, delivered a condemnation of Gaufridy for 'magic, witchcraft, idolatry and abominable lubricity' on 18 April, on the basis of Gaufridy's confessions of 14 April.[93] The verdict was re-issued on 29 April, and again on 30 April, the day Gaufridy was executed. He was tortured up to and including his last day.[94] In the closing days before the case was completed, Madeleine Demandols became mute and unable to give the court any further evidence. Du Vair attributed this to the action of the devil.[95] On the day of the execution, Sébastien Michaelis was absent: he had left Aix a week earlier in order to attend a Dominican synod in Paris.

The potential for Gaufridy's execution itself to act as a sort of exorcism of the nuns had been mentioned repeatedly earlier in the proceedings, and it was said to have achieved at least some of the desired effect. The exorcists Fathers Romillon and Billet wrote in a letter to Michaelis that on the day that Gaufridy was burnt, one of the other Ursuline sisters who had been possessed was delivered of three demons, and that after some days, the demons of another two women went from them. The devils Grésil and Sonneillon also quit Louise Capeau, 'so that there remained none behind but Verrine, who said that the end of the History was not yet come'. Verrine then began to name 'complices and associats in Magick', including one blind woman called Honoria, who, according to Michaelis, was found to be marked, and thence was convicted and burned.[96]

Madeleine Demandols, who had been unable to see, hear or eat for some days, was reported to have had her faculties miraculously restored at Whitsun and was delivered of three devils. But Beelzebub still possessed her, although he was 'chained up in her body by the permission of God'.[97] Romillon and Billet also wrote that Demandols had had a vision of Gaufridy in hell and had fled to the town of Carpentras to do penance, gathering sticks among the poor women there in order to raise money for alms-giving. They recorded that Demandols 'made great reckoning of any act of humility and patience' and was 'afflicted and disfavoured by those that were neerest of her blood, by reason that shee thus debased her selfe'.[98] Thus even those closest to her appear to have accepted the legal and literal truth of the case, gained as it was through the use of the rite of exorcism in a judicial setting. A tragically ironic end to this case came more than forty years later, in 1653, when Madeleine Demandols was arraigned on a charge of witchcraft and sentenced to life imprisonment.[99] She had allegedly caused a young woman, Madeleine Hodoul, to become bewitched, necessitating exorcism. Demandols' association with witchcraft had apparently persisted in local memory: the peasant women who lived nearby reputed her to be a witch, and her accuser said she had been possessed by Demandols' demon, Beelzebub.[100]

While Gaufridy appears to have tried at every turn to control damage to the ministry, Michaelis's prize in prosecuting him was, principally, the securing of evidence that he had debased his priestly office. Michaelis's published account of the trial frames the story repeatedly in terms of the significance of Gaufridy's actions to the standing of the priesthood. His preoccupation with priestly power is evident, for example, in an embellishment he made on Gaufridy's confession, paraphrasing the pact Gaufridy made as one signed in order to 'gaine estimation and honour *above all other priests of the Country* and amongst men of worth and credit' [my italics].[101] However, Gaufridy had confessed only to a desire for worldly prominence, making no reference to his position in relation to other priests.[102] Michaelis saw the outcome of the case as part of a divine plan to protect the priesthood. He wrote: 'Observe well how God honoureth priesthood in this world, when he useth such extraordinarie and unheard of remedies for the conversion of a Priest that wandred out of his way.'[103]

The prosecution of a 'witch-priest' sharpened the paradox of a church at odds with the bases of its own sacramental rituals; exorcism was the spotlight which showed up this dilemma, intensified its significance, and proposed a way to resolve it. In 'exposing' and killing such a figure, the implicit aim was not only to purify the priesthood, but, I suggest, to exorcise from the Church the traces of its own potential contradictions, by demonstrating its ability to act with absolute power; to monopolise the interpretation of its own ambiguous rites. The exorcist's prerogative to pronounce on the presence of the devil showed a capacity for the arbitrary manipulation of Catholic sacramental forms, airing the implicit claim that if worthy priests were in charge, a correct interpretation of the visible evidence was secured. The figure of the exorcist combined the moral charismatic authority of an individual with the institutional authority of the Church to control demons: a potent blend. And even though exorcists were the butt of criticism, they also represented purification in two significant ways: in themselves, as morally superior purveyors of priestly power; and in their rite, whose aims were purificatory.

The Church, as presented and represented by Sébastien Michaelis, ritually resolved its own contradictions regarding the role of the priest as a dispenser of miracles. Where did Michaelis's drive come from? Within this one individual, church authority – or at least, its worst features and most telling doubts – was somehow distilled. Michaelis identified himself with the Church, and *as* the Church. Exorcism and execution were rites that he was able to initiate in order to ritually purify the Church, at once expunging a polluting force and deflecting attention from the risks to church unity posed by his own actions. He titled one section of his book 'Explication on the doubts' raised by the case, addressing each anxiety about the case he had encountered, or could anticipate. Ultimately, it took the death of a man to serve this purpose, which gives force to the view that the task of eliminating doubt was a sizeable one.

After Aix: Michaelis and Domptius in Lille

The publication in Aix later in 1611 of the Parlement's *arrêt* against Father Gaufridy and of his confession, and the publication in Paris of the book on witches' marks by Jacques Fontaine, brought the case to public attention throughout France. The *Mercure françois* in Paris reproduced the *arrêt* and confession almost immediately, keen to show the novelty and shock value of the case.[104] While the publication of such texts was clearly part of an effort to confirm the legitimacy of what had happened, ironically, but perhaps not unpredictably, Michaelis's exposure of a failed priest as no more than a magician confirmed precisely the suspicions that Huguenots had about all Catholic priests. Indeed, Sébastien Michaelis claims to have published his book as a defence against this kind of charge. He wrote:

> I have suppressed this History for the space of a yeere and more, and made no account to have had it published; but the zeale of the Catholicke faith hath induced me thereunto, after I had once seene a letter missive wherein [it was] advertised, that the adversaries of our faith [the Huguenots] did triumph in Rochel, when the depositions of the Magician, now in question, were put forth in print, where it is said, that the magician did celebrate Masse in the Synagogue. And thereupon they make an inference, that the Masse is a diabolicall thing.[105]

He also referred to critics who 'alleage, that it is unfitting to put it forth, to avoid thereby the scandall of many . . . when they shall understand that these things were done by a priest'.[106] Undaunted by such criticism, Michaelis and François Domptius – evidently reconciled – went to Lille in 1613 to carry out exorcisms on the possessed Brigidine nuns there. The case in Lille kept the 'character' of Louis Gaufridy alive, as the nuns described witches' sabbats – in this instance doubling as the realm of the dead – at which Gaufridy was said to have officiated. At Lille, Catholic authorities banned Michaelis's book, fearing it was being used to persecute another priest, the Canon Leduc.[107] Pope Paul V, displaying the scepticism often shown by Rome in such matters, exonerated the accused canon, and indeed offered him a richer benefice.[108] A book by the layman Jean Le Normant, *Histoire veritable et memorable de ce qui c'est passé sous l'exorcisme de trois filles possedées és païs de Flandre* ('True and memorable history of what happened in the exorcism of three possessed girls in the country of Flanders'), nonetheless praised the activities of Michaelis in Flanders, and this book and Le Normant's stories of the spectral figure of Louis Gaufridy were read with some interest. On its publication, for example, Cornelius Jansenius welcomed its confirmation of revelations made at Aix concerning the birth of the Antichrist.[109] Less satisfactorily for Michaelis and Domptius, the *Mercure françois* reported that the two exorcists had been expelled from Flanders. The Aix-en-Provence case served nonetheless as a model for later similar cases: the exorcists in major cases at Agen, Loudun, Louviers and Auxonne, as well as those involved in smaller outbreaks of possession, owe a great deal to the entrepreneurial activities of Michaelis.[110]

Theologians and exorcism

A dramatic and divisive case such as that of Aix displays some clear lines of distinction within Catholicism between what might be termed residual Leaguer militancy and 'politique sang froid'. However, shifts to be found within the writings of several individual theologians suggest that the situation in the early seventeenth century was more complex than pre-given political allegiance, or at least politics narrowly conceived, can account for. Hard and fast lines of demarcation between supporters and critics of exorcism are difficult to draw, or rather, even once the lines of argument are established, commentators very rarely stuck rigidly to one line of argument.[111] My main claim here is that it would be mistaken to assume that when theologians supported exorcism it was somehow an intellectual aberration, or that any apparent change of heart was necessarily the result of some kind of proto-enlightened inspiration, or indeed of hypocrisy. Catholic commentators assumed their positions largely on a case-by-case basis, and few if any theologians held to a single position or emphasis. Only the parameters of debate were truly continuous: the questions of reliance on externals, of leeway allowed to the devil in the speech and actions of the possessed, and of the potential effects of public exorcism on the 'vulgar', who were unable to discern what they saw. Let us consider some of the range of theological responses to the expanded uses of exorcism in this period.

It is easy to see that the large-scale exorcisms of this period, described copiously in print, would raise anxieties about the question of audience. Priests making the devil talk made other priests nervous, both about the public profile of the Church and the potential fate of souls deluded by charlatans and devils. In 1618 the Augustinian Sanson Birette wrote deploring public exorcisms as no better than the kind of divination traditionally associated with witchcraft. He describes as 'an intolerable abuse' the interrogation of possessing devils 'on the misfortunes of illnesses, of death, of accidents, of losses, of animals and of occult crimes, in order to have revelation about them'.[112] Birette's argument was founded on a paternalistic concern for those unable to tell the difference when a devil speaks 'under the honey of truth, [in order to] transmit the infection of lies'.[113] He cited a papal bull of Sixtus V, which stipulated that the devil may only be asked how many spirits are present in the possessed, the cause and subject of the possession, and the time when they entered the possessed; and he found endorsement for this in the ritual of the Norman diocese of Coutances, which he said limited the interrogation of demons to questions regarding the number of demons in the possessed, why the person was possessed, and when the possession began.[114] Yet even these strictures, which Birette implied would prevent excessive exorcist interrogations, clearly left room for eliciting information about just those 'occult crimes', such as witchcraft, whose exposure he feared would lead to belief in diabolical lies.

The Faculty of Theology at the University of Paris and its individual members made several pronouncements on cases of possession in this period: these showed equally their concern for the spiritual safety (and the potential for excessive titillation) of audiences; adherence to the traditional 'case-law' reasoning of the Church, and some corporate care for their own authority. Their various commentaries also exposed some chinks in the Faculty's collegial façade, which might also simply be read as a capacity to absorb competing views from within their own membership. When the lay promoter of exorcism Jean Le Normant submitted to members of the Faculty his *Histoire veritable et memorable de ce qui c'est passé sous l'exorcisme de trois filles possedées és païs de Flandre*, describing the possessions at the Brigidine convent at Lille, the Faculty showed some unsteadiness in its responses. All books on religious matters required official approval in order to be published: on 7 October 1622 two members of the Faculty, Soto and Le Gendre, signed an approbation, and the book was printed early in 1623.[115] On 2 May 1623, however, the General Congregation of the Faculty made the book a target for censure, after it had 'come into the hands of the Faculty . . . which had immediately . . . entrusted it to a most careful examination'.[116] The language of 'immediacy' and 'care' belies its earlier and possibly hasty approval, although the original version of the book was written in Latin and it may only have been approved in its Latin version, on the assumption that readers of that language would be of sufficient discernment to 'handle' the sensational contents.[117] The

Faculty condemned the book for four main reasons: its claims concerning the credence to be given to demons; the idea that evil spirits speaking on behalf of God should be listened to; its reports about exorcists listening to what the devil said; and its excessive descriptions of the behaviour of witches.[118] Thus two members of the Faculty saw the virtue of the book for Catholic proselytism but others – the majority – veered backed to a position of paternalism; their attitudes were shaped as much by questions regarding audience as by any fundamental theological precepts. In 1633, the Faculty declared the possession at the Ursuline house in Loudun to be authentic, but importantly, did not pass comment on the speeches of the possessed, who had accused the priest Urbain Grandier of witchcraft.[119] The Faculty's passivity in this notorious case, as Mandrou suggested, appears to have been out of deference to the *premier ministre*, Cardinal Richelieu, whose support of the possessions at Loudun was well known.

The vexed question of the devil speaking had also presented a dilemma for the Faculty when Sébastien Michaelis published his *Histoire admirable* in 1612, a book which contained extensive passages of 'demonic' speech, and described the prosecution of a witch on the basis of thinly veiled demonic testimony. The book was nonetheless given an approbation by two members of the Faculty, Froger and Dumi.[120] Yet when Sanson Birette submitted for approbation in 1617 his *Refutation*, a work that specifically rejected the practice of interrogating demons, Froger was again a signatory.[121] This shows that theologians examined books to check for orthodoxy, but that opposing positions could, nonetheless, be equally orthodox. Sanson Birette, himself fully aware of the difference between his views and Michaelis's, was still capable of being deferential. Notwithstanding that the two priests voiced opposing views on the use of demonic testimony in a witch trial, Birette was gentle when he discussed the fact that Michaelis's book had been cited in Normandy to justify the very practices that Birette opposed. Indeed he simply endorsed Michaelis's own defence of the work, which states, 'this is a History making a bare declaration of a fact, & is no foundation whereupon to build our faith, though it may serve very fitly to stirre us up to ponder upon the judgements of God'.[122] Thus, by bowing to the interpretation proposed by Michaelis (who, like Birette, was a trained theologian), Birette allowed for a distinction between interpretations of exorcism on the basis of who did the exorcising and what grounds they used to justify their practices. This distinction was also reflected in the rationale for Birette's own book: it rejected belief in demons on the basis that to do so was an 'error of the vulgar' – rather than a problem with the rite, for example – which could plunge the 'poor people' of Valognes into error.[123] Birette's piece, which might seem to be a precursor of modern humane sentiments about witch-hunting, can therefore be seen as very much a creature of its time: a document designed to reject witchcraft accusations, certainly, but because these were signs of excessive use of the sacramental of exorcism on the part of the 'vulgar', the uneducated clergy and gullible laity.

A range of sometimes irreconcilable priorities thus influenced the responses of theologians to the problems posed when demons talked: first, the inherent tensions of Catholic doctrine and traditions; second, the jurisdictional questions which affected these men's own standing as arbiters of doctrine.[124] For just as some writers saw exorcism as a symptom of all that needed reform in Catholicism, others, like Michaelis, used it as a weapon to further their own version of reform. Seen in this light, the differences between exorcists and their critics tend to diminish, and what emerges is the image of a single church torn by a desire, indeed a need, to attract the populace to public displays of exorcism, and the constant need to affirm that the aims of exorcism were spiritual and did not coincide with the supposedly superficial, short-term and material concerns of its audiences. As a final observation, we might note that this tension over audience was typified by two statements made about the Gaufridy case. One commentator critical of Louis Gaufridy associated his witchcraft with his eloquence as a preacher, something which had 'falsely deluded' the 'Marcellian [Marseilles] Vulgar', by whom he was 'exceedingly reverenced, and very much respected'.[125] Elsewhere, however, Sébastien Michaelis referred favourably to the 'great troupes' of onlookers who came to witness the exorcisms, including 'the poore of adjoyning villages'.[126] Here crowds are characterised in the same case and from the same perspective, indifferently, as a caution for their weakness, or as a source of support, apparently righteously drawn towards the truth. The most extreme forms of what moderns might see as credulity thus flourished alongside and in a fraught relationship with scepticism. And in fact, the two could co-exist in the same person: Pierre de Bérulle, who championed the cause of Marthe Brossier, later in his career rejected the practice of interrogating demons.[127] André Duval is another case in point: also a passionate supporter of Brossier's exorcisms, apparently prepared to risk his career to defend the practice, he nonetheless hedged in later responses, endorsing the Loudun possessions, but condemning outright the speeches of Elisabeth de Ranfaing.[128] But the example of Sébastien Michaelis, in particular, who became increasingly open to the possibility of dialogue with 'demons', would caution us against assuming that with age naturally came 'maturity' of judgement. Nor can we assume therefore that the reforming impulses of post-Tridentine Catholicism travelled in a straight line, that tradition was something inevitably at odds with innovation, nor that the notion of 'fringe' and 'mainstream' offers a meaningful way of seeing the kinds of fluctuations in religious passions and decision-making at work in this period.

Chapter 6

Fighting fire with fire?

Exorcism against ecstasy, Louviers, 1642–54

Historically, public and private charismatic religiosities have been contentious for Catholicism. In its public form charisma is manifest, for example, in miracles performed by saints living or dead. For individuals, methods such as prayer, contemplation and various forms of asceticism can obtain access to divine grace, which is normally only imparted through the sacraments. In each case, we are speaking of a type of religiosity that makes certain people or behaviours special within a system that, officially at least, does not require them to be special for its salvific ends to be met. Such special people theoretically pose a threat to the Church because they can be a distraction from what is supposed to be a relationship with God mediated by the sacraments, delivered, as a rule, through the everyday workings of the Church's secular hierarchy.

Judging the validity of forms of charismatic religiosity always at least implicitly requires the assessment of how much of a role, if any, the devil had in bringing to a person their apparent divinely endowed capacities. In this schema the rite of exorcism holds something of a unique place, as its job is to represent the authority of the Church itself at work, while being at the same time a form of charismatic religiosity. Through direct confrontation with the devil, exorcism can bring to light the very source of the deception which makes all forms of charismatic religiosity suspect.[1] Exorcism goes to the devil himself, but it thereby risks charges of collusion which are only able to be countered by reference to the exorcist's claim to authority over possessing demons, and his claim to greater credibility than his critics. I argued in the previous chapter that the actions of Sébastien Michaelis highlighted the central problems of priestly magic for the Church, while simultaneously harnessing the ambiguities inherent in the priest's role, and deflecting attention from the exorcist's own ambiguous status. The present chapter concerns a convent at Louviers, in Normandy, and a case of possession which spanned the 12 years to 1654. As at Aix-en-Provence, exorcists at Louviers saw it as their duty both to create and to patrol the inescapably rhetorical divide between authentic and fraudulent personal charismatic religiosity, this time by pursuing allegations that charismatic priests had corrupted young nuns by mixing witchcraft with the new affective spirituality that was typical of this period in France.

The case began with a dramatic and distasteful event, the exhumation of the body of a priest, Mathurin Picard (or Le Picard) from his burial place in the convent chapel of the Hospitaller sisters of St Louis and St Élisabeth, at Louviers. The Bishop of Évreux took this unusual step when several young nuns claimed Picard's body was causing them to be possessed. They said his witchcraft could in turn be traced back to certain spiritual practices with which the convent had been associated earlier in the century. Exorcists pursued this line of enquiry remorselessly, to establish what they saw as a history of demonically inspired control of the nuns exercised by charismatic priests, who had led the women into a state of possession in the guise of pursuing spiritual enlightenment. We shall ask, then, how practices aimed at spiritual self-development came to be associated with witchcraft, and why exorcism, itself always potentially questionable, was deployed in opposition to such practices. This second question is especially salient given that one exorcist at Loudun in the 1630s, Jean-Joseph Surin, had come to advance some forms of ritual exorcism as a means of attaining spiritual growth: neither the pursuit of spiritual enlightenment nor the rite of exorcism traced predictable paths in the seventeenth century. Rather, the possible presence of diabolical influence was something against which all religious innovation was routinely and explicitly measured in this period, and mystical spirituality, like possession and exorcism, was by turns validated and debunked in Catholic culture at this time. This seems a very obvious point to make, but it enables us to explore the changeable status of charismatic practices in this period, as they were viewed through the lens of potential diabolical interference.

This chapter will further argue that any assumption that there are two parallel tendencies of enthusiasm and sobriety in Catholicism, with sobriety characterising and sustaining a central, ultimately more authoritative view of exorcism, only takes analysis so far. When we can see that the two moods overlap historically and manifest in different ways, a different model can emerge. The tensions surrounding charismatic practices are not just those of centre versus periphery, enthusiasts versus moderates, but about what constitutes these categories in the first place, for, I will argue, they are not stable, except rhetorically. There is also no golden mean in such binary models towards which the Church naturally gravitates either over time, or even as an institution in any one moment; thus there is no maximum tolerable degree of 'fringe' behaviours. This analysis of the case at Louviers, therefore, considers the ways in which distinctions were made in the emotionally and institutionally fraught climate of Catholic reform and renewal. The story of Louviers is fundamentally about the perceived urgency of the need to separate licit from illicit charismatic practices, and about the depth of fear of the demonic nature of certain spiritual pursuits. This preoccupation, articulated through the practice of exorcism, gave free rein to other forms of dread, fear and contempt: sexual anxiety among consecrated virgins and celibate priests (again); rivalry between secular and regular clergy (again); and class division among the nuns, which led to an older, lower-class sister being tormented mercilessly for years by her younger, socially 'superior' sisters. Typically for such cases, careers and reputations were made and ruined, desires gratified, and hopes thwarted. And for one man, a secular priest named Thomas Boullé who was executed for witchcraft, the cost of the exorcists' folly was death.

The mystic turn in Paris and the campaign against illuminism

The story of Louviers had its beginning literally decades before the first outbreak of possession, indeed, even before some of the chief protagonists were born. Exorcisms at Louviers in the 1640s excavated and rewrote the history of a convent, which had begun in a climate of mystic revival in Paris after the turn of the century. To understand how exorcists at Louviers exploited the convent's history, and to trace the mixed and unpredictable status of mysticism that the story of Louviers exemplifies, we need to return to the first half of the century. While the Wars of Religion did not end finally until 1629, Henri IV's defeat of the Holy Catholic League in 1594 left many members of the Parisian social and intellectual elite with increasing opportunities to pursue the more personal side of the religion for which they had fought. They could serve the Church by diverting the energies they once used directly against the Huguenots into a range of new devotional and institutional forms. Drawing upon the innovations which had swept Italy and Spain in the sixteenth century, adepts pursued new spiritual paths; this in turn provided the infrastructure of a new Catholicism, strengthened from within, in both personal and institutional senses. It would be difficult to overestimate the impact of both the passionate inner journeys and the vigorous missions dispersed into France in this period, which came to be known as the 'century of saints'. Modern parallels at the elite level are trivial by comparison: perhaps only the modern passion for physical fitness, for example, among western elites comes close to suggesting the breadth and intensity of this movement. (Indeed, if the self-discipline of modern sports stars makes them the nearest parallel to the role model for suffering offered by saints, perhaps the parallel is not as stretched as it might at first seem.)

Much of the spiritual vigour in the early seventeenth century came not from established religious houses but from private parlours, where groups of lay men and women, together with religious, read devotional works and refined their religious devotions. One of the regular hostesses of such gatherings was Madame Barbe Acarie (in religion Marie de l'Incarnation). The wife of a League leader, Acarie modelled herself on the saintly Spanish mystic and reformer of the Discalced Carmelites, St Teresa of Avila (d. 1582). Madame Acarie cultivated a circle of elite devotees which included Pierre de Bérulle, André Duval and Benet of Canfield, who met to pray together and discuss their devotions. This kind of devotional 'cell' was to characterise much of the spirituality of this period, providing a sort of spawning pool which nurtured preaching and the development of new religious houses: Acarie was one of the founders of the Discalced Carmelites in France, for example. This movement was characterised by a strongly feminine element, and women made their influence felt at the highest levels. This pre-eminence of women, however, brought with it inevitable problems, for the women, for their supporters and, in the eyes of some, for the authority of the Church.

Traditionally, women who seek some kind of spiritual leadership role in the Church are required to submit to the authority of a priest, both in his role as a representative provider of the more accepted path to salvation, the sacraments, and also as a representative of his gender, whose presumed natural sobriety can moderate potentially deceptive female enthusiasms. Such a requirement led female religious figures and their directors to form strong bonds. Famous pairs of mystics and spiritual directors – such as Madame Acarie and André Duval, St Jeanne de Chantal and St François de Sales, Mother Alix Le Clerc (herself afflicted by demons) and St Pierre Fourier – helped, however inadvertently, to project the image of Catholic spirituality as something which was most fruitful when it was cultivated through interaction between the sexes.[2] Conspicuous male–female relationships in Catholic religious life, however, inevitably also called up anxieties about sexual contamination, particularly in a climate of heightened anxiety about diabolical activities among the priesthood and religious women. This question of sexuality, together with the broader question of women's involvement in spiritual life, became a major feature of an anti-mystic 'backlash' which took hold on several fronts in France in the 1620s. This came to be known as the campaign against 'illuminism' (false claims or delusions of spiritual enlightenment).

'Illuminist' was a pejorative term used by opponents: there was no self-avowed 'school' of illuminism among its practitioners. Nonetheless both licit and illicit spiritual practices from the period displayed some characteristic themes: the first was the idea of personal union with God, which sought the absorption of individual human will into the will of God. Like all historical attempts to gain direct access to the divinity, this aspiration posed a potential threat to the role of the Church as the primary mediator of communication with God. And beyond this 'generic' threat of mysticism, in this period, the notion that obstacles to such a union could include thoughts, reflections and images evoked the threat of crypto-Calvinism, a total rejection of external Catholic devotional practices and objects, and a degree of fatalistic spiritual complacency.[3] Union with God was to be achieved through the grace bestowed on those who practised a variety of intensive devotional techniques, such as private prayer, contemplation and, frequently, physical mortification, through whipping and other austerities. Devotional manuals proliferated, seeing new specialist vocabularies of devotion emerge, in which a focus on key words – such as 'anéantissment' (annihilation) – trained the mind towards God. One of the most influential of these was the *Règle de perfection*, ('Rule of Perfection', also known as *La Volonté de Dieu* or 'The Will of God') written by Benet of Canfield, whose activities in support of exorcism we recall from the Brossier case.

So-called illuminist practices were widespread, taking in the regions of Picardy, Artois, Cambrésis, Hainaut and Brabant, as well Paris and its environs, but the campaign to extirpate it was waged on two principal fronts. In Paris, two opposing camps in the Capuchin order were sharply divided around the new devotions. In 1623, Father Joseph Du Tremblay, Richelieu's Capuchin confessor, the famous *eminence grise*, had a translation made of the Edict of Seville, a proclamation against the Spanish illuminists, the 'alumbrados'. Du Tremblay's publication of the text implicitly paralleled the errors of proven heretics with mystical elements in his own order, but also, on the political level, it damned local enthusiasts by implying a connection with Spain, France's enemy in this period.[4] Another Capuchin spokesman for the anti-mystic camp, Fr Archange Ripaut, railed against those whom he called the spirituals 'à la mode' and 'nouveaux Adamites'.[5] This reference to Adamism referred to a dominant metaphor of spiritual renewal, the aim of 'stripping bare' the former man, taking him back to a prelapsarian state, and clothing him anew through spiritual rebirth. Such criticisms had palpable effects. The Capuchin order was purged of illuminist tendencies by the early 1630s.[6] In Picardy, the 'illuminist' priests Pierre Guérin, Claude and Antoine Buquet, and the nun Madeleine de Flers and their followers[7] were investigated by an apostolic protonotary, André Du Saussay, curé of Saint-Leu-Saint-Gilles in Paris and a friend of the Paris Capuchins.[8]

Anti-illuminist campaigns revolved in part around the suppression of suspect devotional books. A proliferation of new texts and their rapid dissemination throughout France in the early seventeenth century met with resistance, for example, from the Capuchin chapter at Chartres in 1626. They tried to stem the tide of suspect books in female religious houses by forbidding entry to people likely to introduce the books into the convents. The chapter also ordered that banned books or other 'books of controversy in the vulgar tongue' be held under lock and key and that 'little booklets', which were being circulated through France by male religious without approval, could only be read with the permission of local superiors.[9] (It is likely that one of these books was the *Règle de perfection*, by Benet of Canfield, which contained a section widely perceived to be a means for bypassing church hierarchy in pursuit of spiritual elevation.) Critics of female illuminists in Montdidier and Crécy described them as drawing together groups of women and girls to hold 'assemblies in private houses, where they conducted readings and analysed certain books, on which they found their malicious tendencies'.[10]

Finally, and most importantly for our purposes, the private and sexually mixed aspects of so-called illuminism led to inevitable charges of antinomianism, that is, a type of moral indifference, held in Catholic tradition to result from a state of indifference to the world brought on by a single-minded pursuit of spiritual goals. Critics of the emotional intensity and individualism of the new devotions, and of the influence of women in religious life, sought to undermine these practices by sexualising them: they emphasised the threat posed by the close relations of female penitents and male spiritual directors. Inevitably, critics chose to take literally the metaphor of 'stripping bare' and charged proponents with nudism. One of the 'errors' listed in the Edict of Seville's 'seventy-six errors of the sect of Illuminists' was that they gathered 'together in private homes, men and women

[to] dine and sup and at the end conjoin themselves carnally, saying there is no sin in it because they see none in it'.[11] This claim highlights anxiety about the practice of devotion by mixed groups in private, by invoking its potentially indecent consequences. Such an accusation was, of course, a traditional response to the practices of religious enthusiasts, accusations whose very consistency through the centuries suggests a probable lack of foundation. (And, for the early modern period, of course, it also evokes the spectre of a witches' sabbat.) For the French case specifically, Mauzaize has identified the state of so-called 'anéantissement' as the high-risk activity of the illuminist devotees. Once this state was reached and the soul achieved union with God, the soul could become indifferent to what surrounded it, including becoming indifferent to the actions of the body.[12] This aim called up suspicion of illicit (if oblivious) sexual contact. Thus while it would be inaccurate to say that criticism of illuminist practices would have been unlikely if women had not been involved, the actions against the illuminists show a strain of anti-feminism as well as anxiety about male–female contamination. These fears point to the crucial connection between the early part of the century and events at Louviers in the 1640s, although the campaign against illuminism had been dormant since the 1630s.

The Louviers convent: from its foundation to the outbreak of possession

Among the spiritual activists in Paris in the 1610s were two friends, Mother Françoise de La Croix and Father Pierre David (the curé of Saint-Jean-en-Grève in Paris). Their names were not identified with the illuminism scandals of the 1620s and 1630s, but they nonetheless came to be associated with the alleged illuminism at the root of the possession and witchcraft accusations at Louviers in the 1640s. In tracing their role in the early history of the convent up to the start of the possessions, we will see how each came to be implicated in witchcraft a full 15 years after either of them had been present at the convent, and indeed 15 years after Pierre David was dead. The convent of St Louis and St Élisabeth was founded at Louviers in 1616. Its principal benefactor was a widow, Catherine Le Bis (or Catherine Hannequin) who, at the suggestion of her young friend, Simone Gauguin (b. 1591; in religion Mother Françoise de La Croix), and the priest, Pierre David, wanted to found a pair of Tertiary Franciscan Hospitaller convents at Louviers, one for men and one for women.[13] All three belonged to a circle of so-called 'dévots' in Paris which gathered in the household of Charles Mangot, the royal *garde de sceaux*. Catherine Le Bis had formally adopted Simone Gauguin as her daughter in 1615.[14] Although Gauguin and Le Bis had taken the veil at Louviers in 1617, with several other postulants, no convent building existed at this time, and the nuns lived in a rented house in Louviers. It was only in 1631 that the convent was finally built. Owing to a dispute between Le Bis, Gauguin and David, and another priest, the male and female houses separated in 1622, with the women remaining Third-Order Franciscan and the men becoming

Augustinian.[15] Le Bis died in 1622 and her family reclaimed her legacy.[16] De La Croix became the Superior in Le Bis' place and she found another benefactor in Geneviève le Beau (or d'Orsay). It is recorded that de La Croix became ill and returned to Paris in 1622, where she remained indefinitely, later establishing an order of Augustinian nuns, the Hospitalières de La Charité Notre-Dame.[17] It was also in 1622 that a young woman named Madeleine Bavent, then around 20 years old, entered the Louviers convent as a postulant.[18] In 1625, as a result of plans set in motion in 1622, the convent at Louviers was effectively re-established, under its new legal provisions and at a different site, with Pierre David remaining as its spiritual director.[19]

Accounts of Pierre David's incumbency as director depict him as an enthusiastic follower of the spiritual literature popular in France in the early 1600s.[20] He is said to have instructed the nuns in reading some of the major devotional works of the period, in particular Benet's *La Volonté de Dieu*.[21] It was also said that the nuns read the *Chapelet Secret* of Mother Agnès Arnauld, the abbess of the Port-Royal convent – a work which, by the time the scandals at Louviers erupted, had been subjected to censure by the Sorbonne. In 1633 eight theologians condemned the work on the basis of what Jean Mauzaize refers to as its 'tendances dyonisiennes' and obscure language.[22] Significantly, a signatory to the censure was André Duval, who had been himself at the heart of the early mystical movement, but who by this time had become more equivocal about the value of certain devotional practices. Duval, as we recall, was also an early and vehement supporter of public exorcism, notwithstanding some later reservations. His name is significant for us in the Louviers case, too, as he was a university teacher of one of the chief exorcists, Esprit Du Bosroger.

In 1628 Pierre David died, and although a secular priest, was buried at Louviers in the robe of a Capuchin.[23] De La Croix ceased all contact with the convent around the time of David's death.[24] According to Father Antoine Laugeois (a priest who succeeded Mathurin Picard as curé of Mesnil-Jourdain), Fr Picard had himself been aware of the risks of illuminism, and had tried to curb David's influence when he became the nuns' *confesseur ordinaire*, following David's death. Laugeois said that Picard had gone to a friend, a Jesuit named Dufour, saying his 'heart was breaking' from despair over the 'damnable maxims of the Adamites' that the nuns said they learned from David.[25] According to Laugeois, Picard said that if nothing were done, he would not be answerable for the scandal that might follow when word of practices at the convent got out.[26] A short time after this, probably around 1630, the Bishop of Évreux, François Péricard, had gone to the convent and seized 'more than sixty little books that treated of the view of God' and burned them on the spot.[27] (This was the same bishop who later ordered the exhumation of Picard's body, for its supposedly corrupting effects on the nuns.) The Capuchin Esprit Du Bosroger said that he had accompanied Bishop Péricard on this mission, and that Péricard also chastened those nuns who had fallen in with David's teachings.[28] Du Bosroger later became one of the principal exorcists at Louviers, and his account of the book-burning did not of course mention the presence or influence of Picard, so we shall never know if he were there.[29] Thus we cannot know for sure whether Picard had followed David in his alleged spiritual misdirection of the nuns, or if he had tried to reverse it. Confusingly, one account states the women thought he was 'not spiritual enough for them', but when he died, aged 67, on 8 September 1642, the convent accommodated his wish that, on account of the nuns' holiness, his body be entombed in the chantry of their chapel.[30]

It appears that Picard's death came around the same time another problem arose in 1642. Sister Anne Barré, a novice in the convent, had been comporting herself 'like a girl who was starting to have visions and who was ordinarily outside of herself'.[31] In other words, she was showing signs of potential spiritual gifts, and the earliest exorcisms at the convent may well have been of the probative kind, to find out whether her behaviour meant she was under the devil's influence or not. This question mark hung over her right up until the end of the witch trial process, in 1647, and was possibly a spur to make her point suspicion away from herself, first onto the corpse of Picard, and then onto Madeleine Bavent. By February 1643 disturbances had spread through the convent.[32] Anne Barré found herself unable to take Communion, due, she said, to the presence of the body of Mathurin Picard in the chapel. Other nuns showed the same symptoms, and reported suffering 'internal and external torments', and 'visions of witches at night'.[33] The matter remained for a time within the convent's walls. A priest named Ravaut exorcised the nuns by day, and in an unusual twist, some of the senior nuns 'by the privilege of their eminent sanctity, although quite incapable of the order and function of exorcists' exorcised them by night.[34] In March the Bishop of Évreux, François Péricard, decided to act.

Bishop Péricard condemned the memory of Fr Picard for crimes of witchcraft. He ordered that his body be removed from the convent chapel, and it was thrown into a ditch known as Le Puits Crosnier, in the lands of the Archbishop of Rouen.[35] It was noted at the time of the exhumation that Picard's body, six months buried, was still 'healthy and whole'. One account of the case said that, while this would normally be taken as a sign of sanctity, the nuns' demons (who had apparently been challenged on this point) offered the novel explanation 'that the flesh of those excommunicated cannot rot in holy ground'.[36] Bishop Péricard, hoping to preserve the honour of 'priesthood [and] religion' and to avoid prejudice to the convent,[37] threatened to excommunicate anyone who revealed the exhumation.[38] On the basis of the nuns' testimony he also stripped the veil of Madeleine Bavent, and locked her up in the ecclesiastical prison of the Officialité of Évreux on a charge of witchcraft.[39] In so doing, he was using his legal authority as a bishop to proceed in a matter of ecclesiastical law, and, as far as public knowledge of the case was concerned, it might have ended there. But around 20 May 1643 some children found Picard's discarded body and thus, as Péricard reported it, 'by an accident the thing became public'. Picard's brother Estienne and his nephew Roch Picard went to the Parlement of Rouen to request that the body be again entombed in the convent. The Parlement, acting in support of the family, ordered an examination of Picard's body by doctors and surgeons, and commissioned officers of the Parlement to investigate the alleged possessions.[40] A *sergent royal* again removed the body from where it lay, this time before a reported crowd of two thousand people.[41]

Bishop Péricard sensed the Parlement's threat to his jurisdiction and his judgement, and while a *conseiller* of the Parlement of Rouen was in the process of questioning the nuns, he sought help direct from the crown. He wrote to Paris on 1 June 1643 to the chancellor, Pierre Séguier, requesting his assistance in opposing the Rouen Parlement.[42] Séguier was a friend of the newly appointed *premier ministre* Jules Mazarin, in the very early days of the regency of Anne of Austria. Three years previously he had been responsible for the suppression of the tax revolt of the *Nu-Pieds* in Normandy, which had involved reasserting royal authority over a recalcitrant *parlement* in Rouen.[43] It seems clear that an exorcism case which usurped the authority of the Parlement was a suitable means to reinforce this dominance. Péricard's letter sought the assistance of a commission made up of 'prelates or those of ecclesiastical dignity' who would report on the affair, presumably in his favour.[44] On 30 June 1643 the *conseil privé* in Paris obliged him by establishing a royal commission, which was headed by Antoine de Barillon (Sieur de Morangis, *conseiller ès conseils* of the king and royal *maître ordinaire de requestes*). By this time, Péricard's initial desire to keep the case secret had run up against his need to protect his own and the convent's reputation, by affirming the reality of Picard's posthumous influence through further, publicised exorcisms. Between the time of his request to the crown and the commission's arrival in late August 1643, at least twenty exorcisms were conducted at the convent, increasing in frequency as the commission's visit approached. At first Bishop Péricard permitted only ecclesiastical personnel to be present at the exorcisms, fearing infamy might outweigh fame, 'the affair of Loudun serving as an example on this occasion'.[45] But he was clearly torn, for he wrote elsewhere that he had read with admiration the *Triomphe de l'amour divin*, on the exorcisms of Loudun, by the senior Jesuit exorcist Jean-Joseph Surin.[46] On 24 August the commission, consisting of Morangis, Samuel Martineau (canon of Notre-Dame-de-Paris), Charles de Montchal (the archbishop of Toulouse) and Jacques Charton (penancer and canon of Notre-Dame-de-Paris), arrived at Louviers to investigate events in the convent.

The commissioners remained in Louviers until 10 September 1643. In their report, they mentioned the 'extraordinary convulsions and contortions' of the nuns and noted that the nuns had a horror of confession and Communion, but said that when they were 'in their natural [state]', they seemed 'unaffected, well-behaved, ingenuous and modest'.[47] The nuns' behaviour satisfied all the other key criteria of true possession: bodily agitation surpassing the force of nature, comprehension of commands given to their devils in Latin and Greek, and revelation of hidden knowledge, specifically the location of harmful charms around the convent.[48] Of the fifty-two nuns in the convent, eighteen were found to be either possessed or obsessed.[49] The most prominent among the possessed were Sister Marie du Saint Sacrement, the daughter of the Président de l'Élection du Pont du l'Arche, who was possessed by the demon Putifar; Sister Anne de la Nativité (Anne Barré), a novice, possessed by Leviathan;[50] Sister Marie du Sainct Esprit, possessed by Dagon, and Marie Cheron, a fifteen-year-old *pensionnaire*, possessed by the demon Grongade.[51] As a consequence of the commission's endorsement, the *lieutenant général* of Pont de l'Arche, Antoine Routier, continued investigations on behalf of the Rouen Parlement, only this time with possible prosecutions for witchcraft in mind.[52] And Bishop Péricard earned a letter of praise from Cardinal Mazarin, who doubtless saw himself as following the example of his friend, patron and predecessor, the recently deceased Cardinal Richelieu, as a patron of exorcisms.[53]

From the outset, the exorcisms of Louviers convey a sense of having been consciously appropriated for a variety of purposes: an awareness of the scale which such a case could attain, following the *succès de scandale* of Loudun, seems to pervade events. As at Aix and at Loudun, a burgeoning cult of public exorcism went hand in hand with the search for evidence of witchcraft. But whereas at Loudun the first raft of many publications emanating from the case concerned the accusations against the secular priest Urbain Grandier, at Louviers writers seized on the exorcisms to make polemical mileage on many fronts, some almost oblivious to the witch trial which was at the heart of the case. This is especially notable given that the nuns and exorcists were not preaching against any residual Huguenot threat: Louviers was strongly Catholic and witchcraft accusations, rather than preaching, dominated proceedings. Indeed, it seems indecent that, when the lives of three people (Thomas Boullé, Madeleine Bavent and Françoise de La Croix) were on the line, wit, polemic and point-scoring came first.[54] Yet this was so. It is not our aim here to examine all the polemical features of a case which generated literature second only in volume to that from Loudun; however, two major, early appropriations are noteworthy.

One paper war involved a young *médecin ordinaire* of the queen, Pierre Yvelin.[55] Yvelin had accompanied the commission to Louviers in autumn 1643, at his own request. Possibly seeing himself as a latter-day Michel Marescot, Yvelin argued that the possessions were fraudulent. The commission in its official report had glossed over his verdict, and instead reported the affirmative findings of two Rouen doctors, Pierre Maignart and Jean Lampèrière (sic), whom they had called in when Yvelin made his scepticism known.[56] This led Yvelin to embark on a campaign of ridicule of the two ageing provincial doctors, who replied in kind. The doctors exchanged a volley of pamphlets which only ended when the crown asked Bishop Péricard to rein in the two locals who were giving offence to a royal employee. Here a delicate point of patronage was again at work, for while François Péricard had successfully secured royal support to pursue the witchcraft accusations, he was nonetheless obliged to curb his local medical men, whose writings were an affront to the royal household.

While local exorcists seem to have been dominant at Louviers – unlike Loudun, where exorcists were ferried in from miles around – some helpful outsiders were also welcome. In March 1643, just as news of the exorcisms of Louviers was breaking, an itinerant exorcist, Father Thomas Le Gauffre, and his companion, a layman known as Brother Jean Blondeau, travelled to Louviers from Paris to confront the devils with the supernatural power of their late friend, another recently deceased priest, the famous Paris preacher Claude Bernard. Bernard, known as 'the poor priest', had died in 1641.[57] Le Gauffre and Blondeau spent several months at Louviers, performing exorcisms using personal devotional effects left by Bernard, such as his diurnal and his breviaries, to exorcise the nuns. According to Le Gauffre, Bernard had successfully performed an exorcism on a possessed girl at Reims by applying his diurnal to her.[58] Le Gauffre published booklets about the success of his exorcisms, which tell of the 'demons' accusing Bernard of persecuting them. Bishop Péricard also sought Claude Bernard's intercessory powers to deliver the nuns. In a letter to Le Gauffre in April 1644, Péricard wrote that he had vowed a novena (a cycle of nine days' devotions) at the altar of Bernard's burial place, in order that 'the sanctity of good Father Bernard . . . end the evil that a wicked priest had committed'.[59] Through the agency of one dead priest, in effect, the exorcists pressed back the powers of another.

The polemical uses of the case were not all, of course, so distant from the witch trial. For two exorcists in particular – the Capuchin Provincial Esprit Du Bosroger, and Pierre de Langle, the penancer of Évreux – the possessions provided an avenue for a retrospective campaign against illuminism, in which they mediated their animus against enemies real or imagined, through the vocabulary of witchcraft. From early in the case, the spectre of illuminism was present. An anonymous pamphlet which appeared as early as November 1643 (probably written by de Langle or Du Bosroger) entitled *Recit veritable de ce qui s'est fait & passé à Louviers touchant les Religieuses possédées Extraict d'une Lettre escrite de Louviers à un Evesque* refers to Fr Pierre David in relation to certain spiritual practices in the convent, which the author uses to make a direct connection between misguided mysticism and diabolical witchcraft. It depicts David's efforts to corrupt the nuns with false promises of spiritual enlightenment and claims that, having found the nuns ill-disposed to follow him, he contented himself with using an 'equally diabolic' way to infiltrate the convent: witchcraft.[60] Deploying the popular taste for paradox, the author spoke of David's 'tenebrous illumination'.[61]

Exorcists and nuns pursued the perceived link between David's illuminism and witchcraft, exposing so-called testaments which the nuns said were hidden around the convent. The contents of the testaments – which also operated as magic charms, to sustain the possession – were said to be in a script resembling Arabic, incomprehensible to the learned men present, but understood by the 'demons', who dictated their contents in French to the exorcists.[62] In one testament, Pierre David had pledged his body and soul to what he called 'our venerable assembly' (apparently meaning the witches' sabbat), and had bequeathed the spiritual conduct of the nuns to Mathurin Picard, so that Picard could continue 'these high and admirable exercises and perfections', that is, the spiritual exercises that he had founded in the convent. Picard's testament stated that he pledged to work for eternity for the glory of the god Beelzebub by continuing the 'very holy and adorable foundations of perfection' and 'high and sublime exercises' set up by David in the convent.[63] At least in the eyes of these exorcists, there was a direct link between the promotion of affective spirituality and witchcraft, a link made traceable by exorcism, and one which emerged repeatedly as the case developed. However, in the period immediately following the commission's report, the focus turned more directly to witchcraft.

The circle of accused widened, as the nuns made accusations of witchcraft under exorcism against not only Pierre David, Mathurin Picard, and Madeleine Bavent, but the founder and former superior, Mother Françoise de La Croix and the vicar of Mesnil-Jourdain, Thomas Boullé.[64] Exorcisms, which were recorded for almost every day in December 1643 and the first week of January 1644, for some reason stopped abruptly on 7 January. They resumed again briefly in March 1644 following the return of Péricard, and then intensively in May, when the commissioner Antoine Routier was beginning to formulate the case against the accused witches.[65] Exorcisms and rituals performed to intensify their theatricality took over the convent. Every day the exorcists led processions around the convent garden and cells, with other priests, friars and nuns all walking barefoot.[66] Bishop Péricard, who had spent several weeks in Paris pleading the case for the possessions to both secular and ecclesiastical audiences,[67] presided over most exorcisms, which typically began with prayers and adjurations of the 'devils' to speak. The demons usually resisted the adjurations for approximately an hour. Successfully adjured, the 'demon' then made a long and uninterrupted speech, after which it appears exorcists simply wound up proceedings. Accounts of the exorcisms usually recorded something quite perfunctory, such as 'And the demon left the girl' or even just 'the exorcism'. This may reflect the tedium for the notary of writing down Latin prayers or formulas used in expelling the demon, but it nonetheless highlights the primacy of the demons' speeches.[68] One account ends with the words 'then he said nothing but buffooneries, and we were obliged to end the exorcism'.[69] The entire schedule of convent life appears to have revolved around the exorcisms. It is hard to imagine that the non-possessed nuns would have followed a normal routine, especially when their prayers could be deployed directly to help their tormented sisters. Exorcisms took place in the morning, from around nine until lunch, then resumed either in the afternoon or at night, sometimes going on until midnight. One search for a magic charm went on until 2.30 in the morning.[70] As in other cases, the 'season' of exorcisms could be extended more or less indefinitely through the practice – by then routine – of adjuring devils to say not necessarily where a hidden magic charm could be found, but when they would reveal its location, thereby requiring a future exorcism.[71]

The nuns described hidden charms as being – often literally – the embodiment of pacts made, in most cases, between Mathurin Picard and Madeleine Bavent, which bound them both to the service of the devil. Pieces of the Host and bodily by-products of Picard and Bavent (menstrual blood, semen, hair and the aborted foetuses of several pregnancies attributed to Bavent) were, they said, mixed in with hair from the nuns whom they sought to bewitch. Many of the pacts (or schedules, as they were also known) were only implied by the fact that they contained forms of the signatures of Bavent and Picard; for example, one was a Host with the hair of several of the nuns, around which was folded a piece of paper with a circle and the letters P and B and two figures XI and IX on it, wrapped in a piece of cloth soaked in the 'blood of Our Lord', wine from the consecration at the Mass.[72] Owing to the role of Pierre David and Françoise de La Croix in the earliest history of the convent, many of the exorcisms referred to this history and the fate of the house itself. The exorcists and the possessed constructed the story of Louviers retrospectively by using exorcism as a form of historical excavation or re-invention of the convent's past. Marie du Sainct Esprit (the demon Dagon) said: 'extraordinary power from God will be necessary to save this bitch of a house';[73] and referring to the power of one particular charm, Marie du Sainct Sacrement (Putifar) said: 'it is the fundament of the house, that's why I will never give it over . . . the cement of the first stone is all bewitched'. She went on: '[T]he night after the foundation stone was cemented, all the witches came here and gave it their benedictions, and that same day they feted us at our sabbat and we wished to always have a witch here and in all the convents of this order', adding that the Antichrist would be 'born from an abbess and a bishop'.[74] These references to the foundations of the house reinforced claims that the witches had buried charms throughout its buildings. On the strength of demons' claims excavation crews dug around the clock, unearthing the foundations of the convent's refectory, its chantry, altar and garden. The holes were big enough for several people to walk down into, and exorcists carrying torches descended into them with possessed nuns in tow, there to search for the hidden charms.[75] Onlookers stood around the rim of the hole praying while the nun was pressed by exorcisms to reveal the location of the charm. Each new discovery of a charm, it was said, helped undo the witchcraft and made the devils yield a measure of liberation to the possessed.

More than once, the exorcisms were violent. The sceptical doctor Pierre Yvelin described Sister Marie Cheron as having been exorcised for eight hours to make her 'devil' do something 'he' had promised on a previous occasion and had proved unable to do. According to Yvelin – admittedly a hostile witness – Cheron came close to dying and could barely get out of her bed for three days.[76] Elsewhere, however, supporters of the exorcisms also revealed the physical violence which characterised the exorcisms. On one occasion, Bishop Péricard beat one of the nuns with a stick to make her 'devil' obey God's will. He forced Anne de la Nativité (as the devil Leviathan) to go down into a hole in the ground to search for one of the charms she had identified, and she cursed the bishop as she went. An anonymous (but sympathetic) observer wrote: 'The bishop commanded him to enter [the hole], which he did, finally, against his will and with execrable blasphemies against God, the Virgin and Saint Joseph, that I dare not repeat. And the said bishop, holding a stick in his hand, hit him with it several times, saying to him: "Work, infamous one, accomplish the will of God".'[77] In another instance, the penancer Pierre de Langle stood on the stomach of Marie du Sainct Sacrement, to make her devil obey the Virgin Mary by revealing the location of malefic charms.[78] Several of the possessed nuns also became ill and were taken away from the convent by their families. Louise de l'Ascension, possessed by Asphaxat, for example, was taken away by her parents 'to more easily recover her health' – which says much about the toxicity of the convent environment, whether it refers to her own symptoms or to her treatment by exorcists.[79]

As at Aix-en-Provence (and at Loudun up to when Urbain Grandier was executed) the ostensible purpose of the exorcisms was to both deliver the nuns and build up a legal case against the alleged witches. However, unlike the case at Aix, where Madeleine Demandols had switched back and forth between the roles of devil and victim to corroborate her diabolic testimony, the exorcisms at Louviers show another way in which exorcism was able to enter legal process. Two separate manuscript collections allow us to place side by side the nuns' exorcisms and interrogations of Madeleine Bavent. As the nuns' demons made accusations, officials took these to Madeleine Bavent and asked her to confirm them. Exorcists also brought Bavent from her prison to Louviers, to confront the other nuns directly. On several occasions she 'exorcised' them herself, in the sense of adjuring the demons, in an attempt to make them admit their accusations were false.[80] Unlike Demandols, Madeleine Bavent – parentless and from the lower classes – was not guaranteed immunity from prosecution by the Parlement of Rouen. Between June 1644 and September 1645 she was interrogated on at least twenty-three occasions.[81] Like Demandols, however, Bavent was in the ambiguous position of being treated sometimes as a witch and at other times as afflicted by devils, experiencing something like possession. There were numerous references to her being tormented by demons from within and a number of interrogations involved exorcism.[82] Bavent also displayed a classic sign of possession, forgetting what had happened to her.[83] Her 'possession' was understood as a sort of spiritual paralysis shown in her inability to complete a satisfactory confession, due to the intervention of devils sent by Mathurin Picard. The Rouen penancer and exorcist, Pierre de Langle, recorded his visit to Madeleine Bavent in her prison cell at Évreux. He described a battle between the devil Dagon (the spirit himself, not the nun he also possessed) and Bavent, in which the devil tried to prevent Bavent confessing to de Langle about her witchcraft. De Langle said that devils swarmed about her cell when he was trying to hear her confession and that they had also tried to make her kill herself in order to see her die unconfessed. Bavent resisted the devils, eventually completed a confession and renounced the devil.[84] Bavent confessed to participating in a range of diabolic activities which involved herself and a series of priests including David, Picard and Boullé. Thomas Boullé was arrested on 2 July 1644.[85] Following further exorcisms in which the nuns' demons provided testimony, Bavent implicated Mother Françoise de La Croix.[86] Thomas Boullé was interrogated and outside witnesses were questioned about his behaviour. Surgeons also searched him for a devil's mark, which they found.[87]

On 21 August 1647 the Parlement of Rouen finally made its judgement on the case. A number of the members of the court had misgivings about the case of witchcraft that had slowly evolved against Father Boullé during the exorcisms: six of the fifteen-member panel did not want to proceed with his execution without first securing the arrest of Mother Françoise de La Croix in Paris.[88] Nonetheless, the final judgement ordered that the bones of Picard be burned, along with Thomas Boullé who, finally trapped through the conceits of exorcists and the possessed, was to be burned alive.[89] The court ordered that Françoise de La Croix be arrested, and that three other nuns whom Madeleine Bavent had named as attending the witches' sabbat be questioned. This was Bavent's meagre revenge, for in giving her the central role of the witch, the young nuns also gave her the power to be the chief witness against them.[90] The court reserved judgement on Bavent herself, possibly out of pity for someone who had been locked up for four years and who would have been well known to officials. The court also ordered the dispersal of the nuns to other religious houses or to their families.[91] And it signalled the importance of the matter of spiritual direction in this case, by admonishing bishops to send *confesseurs extraordinaires* three or four times a year to the female convents in their jurisdiction.[92]

Why, if the Parlement were subject to misgivings, was Thomas Boullé nonetheless convicted? Father Antoine Laugeois, the defender of Mathurin Picard's reputation, suggests that the Parlement suffered from a failure of nerve, pressured by the persecutors of the accused priests. He said that the members of the Capuchin order from Rouen and elsewhere had staged a concerted local campaign against Boullé and against the memory of Picard, and that the vote against the priests was influenced by the Capuchins' activities.[93] While relatively little evidence suggested that Mathurin Picard had anything to do with promoting 'illuminism', even less evidence suggests the young priest Thomas Boullé – who would have been only about 18 years old when Pierre David died – had any connection with the 'sect': yet his story, almost lost in an avalanche of polemic publications about Louviers, lies at the moral heart of the case. Of all those whom the possessed nuns accused of witchcraft, he is the only one who died for it. For while the convent attracted exorcists for a wide variety of reasons, the link which some of them made with the illuminism of its earlier spiritual directors seems to be the one which motivated persistent attempts to secure a prosecution. In a case where thirty-five publications appeared over seventeen years, no one dwelt in any depth on the fate of Thomas Boullé. In this way, the case was quite different from that of Urbain Grandier at Loudun, where numerous works concerning his fate were published, before and after he died.

Another living victim of the witchcraft judgement, however, was Mother Françoise de La Croix, the order's first mother superior. The months preceding the final *arrêt* of August 1647 saw the beginnings of a legal case hatched between the Parlement of Rouen and the Archbishop of Paris, supported by the king's Conseil Privé, over the extradition of Françoise. It was probably in late 1646 that word reached the Archbishop of Paris that the Parlement of Rouen was investigating her. The Archbishop of Paris sought the aid of the king-in-council, to whom he declared that the actions of the Parlement of Rouen were 'an undertaking manifestly against his jurisdiction' and requested that it be stopped.[94] Twice in 1647 the Conseil tried unsuccessfully to obtain the documentation of the case from the Parlement of Rouen so that the *officiel* of the Archbishop, in the company of the *lieutenant criminel* of the Châtelet, could undertake enquiries into the allegations.[95] The Parlement held off til after it could publish its *arrêt*. Then in September 1647 the Conseil Privé overrode the *arrêt* by the Parlement and proceeded to take control of the investigations of Françoise.[96]

In 1648 André Du Saussay, Vicar-General of the Archbishop of Paris, interrogated Françoise on several occasions, in the presence of the *lieutenant criminel* of the Châtelet. Du Saussay provides a critical link here, as it was he who had investigated accusations of illuminism in Picardy in the 1630s. Du Saussay obliged Françoise to undergo medical tests, which is likely to have meant an invasive test of virginity, and possibly pricking for the devil's mark.[97] In late 1649 the case was made ready for judicial assessment. However, apparent reluctance on the part of the *promoteur* of the *officialité* in Paris, who refused to submit his conclusions in spite of requests by Du Saussay, combined with the disruption to state affairs in the revolutionary years of the 'Fronde', meant that from late 1649 to late 1652 nothing further of an official nature took place.[98] In 1652, however, the case was again revived by pamphleteers, who called for the judgement of Françoise to go ahead, and suggested that it had been deliberately ignored for years. A Mazarinade – a pamphlet against Cardinal Mazarin – entitled *Advis horrible et epouvantable pour detruire le Cardinal Mazarin, avec les puissans moyens de le faire hayr au Roy, & à ceux que le tiennent près de sa personne*[99] claimed that the best way to 'make the king hate Mazarin' would be to have the case of Françoise judged by the Paris Parlement. It stated that the case had been ready to be judged five years previously, and that the cardinal had deliberately sought to keep the queen regent ignorant of it.[100] It called for Bavent to be confronted, as in that way 'one would learn prodigious and abominable things',[101] and it suggested that Barillon (Morangis), the royal commissioner involved with the case in 1643, had hidden from the queen information about the trial given to him by Bishop Péricard in 1646, despite her repeated requests to see the transcripts.[102] In a set of complex power-plays whose basis is difficult to unpick, it seems that critics of Mazarin were trying to drive a wedge between him and Queen Anne of Austria, by using the Louviers case to promote the view that Mazarin did not have respect for his queen.

Another pamphlet took a different tack from the Mazarinade.[103] It called upon the *lieutenant criminel* to conclude the case, but defended Françoise, on the grounds of her holiness.[104] Ironically, this takes us back to the illuminist slur against her, but here she is championed because of the supposedly divine favours she has received. The pamphlet referred to the 'natural and supernatural actions, such as ecstasies and levitations practised by the Mother since her childhood' and it stated that the Archbishop of Paris had often seen her in ecstasy.[105] In December 1652 Du Saussay again questioned her and she gave a profession of faith in front of several officials and theologians, as well as the sisters at her convent.[106] In 1653 the ecclesiastical investigations ended, and in 1654 Chancellor Séguier declared her innocent of all charges.[107] Mother Françoise was never reinstated as superior of her convent, however, and died in 1657.

Histoire de Magdelaine Bavent

As we have seen, the case at Louviers occasioned a flurry of publications, as peripheral figures sought for themselves a place among the inner circle. Madeleine Bavent was a central figure, but the witchcraft accusations consigned her to relative silence. Yet a local priest, the sub-penancer of Rouen, an Oratorian named Desmarets, saw in Bavent's continuing incarceration after 1647 an opportunity to defend her name and to make his own. He published, as a companion piece to the Mazarinade we considered above, a work entitled *Histoire de Magdelaine Bavent*. The book comprised an extract from the interrogations of Bavent by the *lieutenant criminel* of Pont de l'Arche, Antoine Routier, and a long autobiographical piece, said by Desmarets to have been dictated to him by Bavent at her request, at Rouen in 1647, some time after the execution of Boullé, and when her own fate remained undecided.[108] Critically, Desmarets' ghost-written account of Bavent's life was framed as her general confession, and aimed to demonstrate two things: first, that Bavent's confessions to the Parlement had been obtained under duress, due to the pressure of continuous new accusations put forward by the 'demons' (principally Anne Barré's demon Leviathan); and second, that this new confession was in effect the first time she had been able to confess herself fully since the beginning of the story, due to a succession of corrupt spiritual directors and hostile female superiors at the convent. In other words, Desmarets was shifting any blame from Bavent onto the succession of priests who directed the nuns, in order to highlight how vulnerable penitents are when they have no choice as to spiritual director. In effect, he represented himself as the ideal director, revealing the truth of the case, after the fact.

We recall that Bavent was virtually the only living person who had been in the convent from its early years until the possessions began. She was therefore by now around 50 years old. In an attempt to shake off the charge that her activities were a fundamental part of the witchcraft at the convent, Bavent said that the convent was already infested with evil before she entered. She cited the case of a woman named Charlotte Pigeon who had tried to enter in 1619, but had left owing to difficulties experienced while performing the sacraments of penance and confession.[109] Bavent traced this evil to the illuminism of Pierre David, providing a distasteful narrative of David's abuses in the convent. During his incumbency, Bavent said, the book *La Volonté de Dieu* by Benet of Canfield was 'virtually the only rule' in the house, and through it, sexual coercion had been given a powerful rationale.[110] She said that David had taught the nuns that 'it was necessary to effect the death of sin by sinning, to return to innocence and resemble our first parents [Adam and Eve] who were without shame of their nudity before their first sin'.[111] Invoking images reminiscent of the witches' sabbat, Bavent said that David had made the nuns dance naked around the convent chapel and garden, and, in a rare mention of lesbianism in this period, she alleged he had directed them to have sexual relations with one another. Bavent related that David would not let anyone speak of these events to him in the confessional, saying that there was no offence in them. The mistress of novices, she said, had given her the same response when Bavent had asked for a new confessor.[112] When David was dying, Bavent recalled, he gave Picard a piece of paper with mysterious writing on it and entrusted him to conduct the nuns in the manner he had instigated. Bavent was then to take the paper to the convent. Bavent subsequently saw the paper at the sabbat many times, she said, where its contents ('blasphemies and horrible imprecations') were read at the diabolic Mass, at which, she said, it served as a canon in processions and at acts of profession.[113] Its symbolic status is clear in this narrative, signifying an unbroken link in the chain between the convent's directors.

When Bavent had tried to confess to Picard, she said, he had seduced her instead, leading her then into witchcraft. Here the issue of her free will was paramount. There are several instances in her story where she described having given her unwitting consent to things Picard had said to her, thereby consenting to witchcraft.[114] For example, when Picard had taken her to look over some new buildings on the convent site, he had said to her 'My dear, I am having this church built; after my death you will see marvels. Do you not consent to it?', to which Bavent said, she had responded 'yes'.[115] Bavent lamented that she had made what she now saw as her first consent to witchcraft without any ill intention, and said she had done so 'through ignorance and not through malice'.[116] Much of the remainder of her account describes attempts to have herself confessed, attempts which were thwarted, she said, through the witchcraft of Picard and the hostility of the superiors in the convent, whom she also implicated in Picard's witchcraft.[117] It was, she said, 'a great pity to not give any liberty to souls in the choice of confessor, and to make them stick with one alone, who might cause their perdition'.[118] Bavent was not called to trial again after 1647, but she remained imprisoned, later being moved the *hôpital général* in Rouen, where she died in 1653.[119]

The exorcist's story: *La Pieté affligée*

Desmarets' book of Bavent's life was rapidly followed by a lengthy rejoinder by the Capuchin exorcist and provincial, Esprit Du Bosroger, *La Pieté affligée, ou discours historique & Theologique de la Possession des Religieuses dittes de Saincte Elizabeth de Louviers,* ('Piety Afflicted, or true historical and theological discourse of the possession of the nuns of Saint Elizabeth of Louviers'). Bosroger wrote in defence of the nuns at Louviers, contesting Bavent's claim that some of them had been implicated in the illuminism and the witchcraft at the convent.[120] The concerns of Bosroger perpetuated the themes of French ecclesiastics in the 1620s and 1630s who sought to extirpate illuminism from northern France and from religious houses in Paris. It is perhaps no coincidence that Du Bosroger had been a student of André Duval, whose own career had seen him defend public exorcism, who was a leading light in the circle of Madame Acarie, and a defender of the alleged illuminist Madeleine de Flers, but who nonetheless opposed the Mother Agnès Arnauld's 'illuminist' *Chapelet Secret*. Du Bosroger's book was a late salvo in this campaign, apparently written primarily to protect the reputation of the Capuchin nuns under his care at Rouen, one of whom had formerly been at the convent in Louviers.[121]

In a chapter entitled 'Of the error and the false spirituality that devils and magic have tried to introduce subtly into this house',[122] Du Bosroger described the convent as having fallen, under Pierre David's direction, into the 'error of a deceptive spirituality' which 'under the guise of suppressing the passions made them all the more violent'.[123] Du Bosroger's awareness of paradox here makes an ironic counterpoint to what might be said equally of exorcism itself in this period, which in the guise of expelling demons appeared to give them unobstructed access to the public eye. Du Bosroger had known Pierre David personally and *La Pieté affligée* provided an arresting portrait of David as he remembered him at least twenty-four years after the fact, and after Du Bosroger had successfully kept the Capuchin order's anti-illuminist sentiments alive, while helping to bring about the death of a man for witchcraft. Du Bosroger wrote to emphasise the need to distinguish the appearance of piety from real piety – the need to play down externality – and his account highlights the way that, in this period, the indices of spiritual power were registered within what Certeau termed 'a vocabulary of the body'.[124]

Pierre David, according to Du Bosroger, 'composed his gestures, his walk, his words, his face, his actions, so that with these disguises he would be seen as a good man'. Du Bosroger went on:

> His step grave and moderate, his eyes lowered, his beard long and neglected, the pallor of his face, which he hid, concealed by design, the sweetness of his discourse, his amiability with those to whom he spoke, the ardour of his zeal, the purpose in his actions, the elevation of his spirit showing on his forehead, the serious delivery of his ideas, his very studied reserve, some fiery words which conveyed a feeling for God and Paradise, some fervent sighs, his face lost in contemplation, his long Masses during which he appeared quite ecstatic, his actions of grace marked with sobs and suddenly arrested by a peaceful silence – in a word all his exercises and all his postures promised only great things. He had the way of a great servant of God, a great spiritual, a great director. He was great, I admit, but a great Pharisee and great hypocrite, a great and furious wolf. Oh cruelty, enclosed in this poor, innocent sheepfold that he would have inevitably ruined if God, who is the protection of virgins and the conserver of their virtues, had not dispelled the malice of this great seducer.[125]

Du Bosroger's principal objection to the spirituality of David was that it sought perfection and union with the divinity at the cost of abandoning penitential self-examination. He said that David taught the nuns that self-abnegation, taught by

Jesus, 'should extend to all actions and especially to one's own judgement and reason, and to that human prudence which wants in all occasions to discern too much'. When the nuns questioned his instructions, he had assured them that 'these discernments and repugnances that were felt in relation to the opinions of the director came from flesh and blood, and that one had to overcome and destroy them, since this annihilation represented the triumph of the holy soul'.[126] Du Bosroger wrote that David only used words chosen to give pleasure, speaking of 'contemplation, inaction, light, ecstasy, union, transformation, adhesion, suspension, death, annihilation, sublimity, the hidden and unknown life of the spirit, of rapture, and of the glorious passage to divinity'. Du Bosroger's reaction to this type of spirituality was contemptuous; he concluded: 'what baseness!'[127]

Where physical discipline was concerned, Du Bosroger, on the one hand, rejected an absence of physical self-discipline and, on the other, regarded its excesses as vanity.[128] Rejecting the path of 'easy' spirituality, he spoke of people who claim ecstasies and revelations but who have 'never borne the mortification of Jesus Christ in their flesh nor in their souls'.[129] Elsewhere, however, he rued the fact that some of the nuns were caught in the spirit of error disguised as austerity and had 'tyrannised their bodies with cruel mortifications'.[130] And here Du Bosroger made the critical link between David's spiritual practices and demonism, concluding: 'who cannot see that his way of acting was from magic, from the sabbats and like the alphabet of the dark science of hell'.[131] Du Bosroger spoke of the 'dirty desires' of David, who had argued that 'this spirituality' had to be achieved by sensuality and through actions that David 'did not dare openly explain'.[132] Instead of fleeing from the desires of the flesh, David had taught that sin 'was not in the body, nor in corporeal actions, but in the discernment of human prudence and . . . whoever discerned it was cursed and damned' and that therefore 'the modesty of the girls was an error'.[133] And Du Bosroger said that David made the nuns keep his teachings secret, for fear of scandalising the ignorant.[134]

Du Bosroger, invoking the catch-cry of the new devotions of 'stripping bare the former man to clothe him anew', said that David had protested to the nuns that 'nudity is the appanage of true innocence', and that provided that no sin was seen or discerned, there was none, because 'the spirit united with God does not sin'. Du Bosroger drove home the claim of diabolic influence, asking: 'Oh impiety! Oh brutality! Is this a Gnostic, a satyr or a devil who put forward these hateful words?'[135] When some of the nuns took exception to David, wrote Du Bosroger, he pacified them by talking about the 'illuminative life'. Du Bosroger added that their peace was no doubt 'caused by demons'.[136] By sexualising and demonising David's teaching, Du Bosroger asserted retrospectively a paternalistic concern to prevent women religious from being exposed to the new literature of devotion in circulation in France in this period. In Du Bosroger's schema, the chastity of the nuns was threatened by the act of reading.[137]

Ecstasy, books and reading

Anti-illuminists such as Du Bosroger depicted alleged illuminists as having permitted the breakdown of distinctions between spiritual and physical, a collapse of the distance between the real and the metaphorical in physical metaphors of spiritual achievement, and a collapse of any distinction between actions of grace and actions of human will. In a chapter of *La Pieté affligée*, 'Of false spirituals and of the means to discern between true and false spirituality',[138] Du Bosroger drew on church authorities to examine the critical question of how far human will should be directed in the pursuit of its own abandonment. Du Bosroger emphasised the importance of not allowing the sin of pride to lead people to mistake the effects of human actions for divine ones. True ecstasies, he says, are priceless but false ecstasies are to be feared.[139] 'As soon as a man or a woman finds a way to produce ecstasies, it must be concluded that these ravishments are but vain elevations born of pride and magic'.[140] He cited Martín Del Rio as saying that there is no greater index of magic than voluntary ecstasies which 'can only be born from a sacrilegious pact contracted with the demon'.[141] To this he added a reflection on the collapse of male authority over female, where authority was either abused by priests for sexual ends or priestly authority was claimed illegitimately by women. The brokerage of the divine by 'illuminist' directors who advocated passivity was implicitly an abdication of their priestly authority, or rather an assertion of it in a new way which, by encouraging excessively individualised spiritual pursuits, could be seen as 'privatising' their priestly authority as representatives of the institutional Church. In this way, of course, the alleged practices of illuminist priests resembled precisely the activities of exorcists.

Du Bosroger pursued his anti-illuminist theme by alerting readers to the particular dangers of female 'false spirituals' occupying quasi-sacerdotal roles. He described the case of a nun in Flanders 'not long ago' who posed as possessed and took on the role of a priest, even to the extent of conducting – or (technically) making as if to conduct – the Mass.[142] Du Bosroger said the nun pretended that her voice was the voice of Christ, a fascinating accretion on the cross-gender aspect of possession: '[N]ow the devil pushing a frightful voice and then offering words of sweetness, with her voice deliberately deceitful, that she said was that of Our Lord . . . had the insolence to pronounce words over Hosts by an impious sacrilege [and] she offered to the vulgar ignorant the Hosts to be adored and received at the time of communion'.[143] And here emerges the other theme of the anti-illuminists: the risk of women aspiring to have access to spiritual and theological power through their reading.[144]

As we have seen, the witchcraft at Louviers identified the effects of reading controversial spiritual books with the effects of diabolical power. The 'little books' which exorcists portrayed as being at the root of the outbreak of illuminist practices in Louviers in the 1620s and 1630s, were understood to have had a direct effect upon the bodies of their readers, bypassing any cognitive screening, and making the nuns susceptible to the corrupting influence of the priests who had given them the books.[145] Bosroger said the books had disrupted the inner lives of the nuns, in a way which they mistook for promptings of the spirit. The status of the words in these books was not related to their literal interpretation, then, but to the inspirational power of the techniques of devotion they proposed, and also to their own intrinsic power to move. The exorcists at Louviers thus employed exorcism as a means to intercede in this process, and block the influence that was drawn down through the act of reading. In *La Pieté affligée*, Du Bosroger referred to several 'books with striking titles' given to the nuns by Pierre David: *La perle évangelique* ('The evangelic pearl'), *Thrésor caché dans le champ* ('The treasure hidden in the field'), *La théologie germanique*, 'the most unintelligible' he complained, being seen as 'the most useful and the most divine'.[146] He suggested that David wanted to 'revive the sect of the Valentinians' (a spiritually elitist Gnostic sect) and to make people out to be idiots if they misunderstood his doctrines.[147] In effect, Du Bosroger sought in his writing and in his exorcisms to limit the possible uses of books, thereby establishing his presence as a gate-keeper within the spiritual director–devotee relationship and as a mediator in the use of books for the purposes of spiritual advancement. Reading was seen as contentious, not just because it could give ideas to women, but because of what might occur in the act of reading itself. Exorcism in the case at Louviers attempted to control these effects by insinuating a position of authority to stand between book and reader. Books can be seen as a medium for inspiration, introspection and spiritual enhancement. The world of the text is an inner world, in some ways not unlike the witches' sabbat, in which anything can happen and no one need know. The exorcist made it his business to know.

The possessions at Louviers allow us to examine issues of personal inspiration and church authority in seventeenth-century France. First, let us consider the changing role of exorcism in relation to two figures who early in the century saw the rite as a means to reinforce Catholic authority. The first is the Capuchin Benet of Canfield, who in 1599 was himself prepared to face deportation for defending the rite of exorcism. Yet he wrote a work, *Règle de perfection*, whose alleged diabolical effects at Louviers only the rite of exorcism could expunge. In this case, the illuminist purges in the Capuchin order appear implicitly to have 'demoted' Benet, and it could be argued that both his promotion of exorcism in the case of Marthe Brossier and his writing represent a style of religiosity characteristic of its time, each apt to be seen in different times and contexts as suspect. Capuchin exorcists at Louviers used the rite of exorcism, which Benet had promoted to his cost in 1599, in order to purge his influence on other aspects of spiritual life. And André Duval, the close ally of Benet, and himself a founding figure of the mystic movement, articulated increasingly differentiated views about exorcism and about charismatic religiosity as the century went on. As we have seen, the Paris Faculty of Theology, where Duval was a leading figure, gave little sense of a consistent line, still less of a trajectory of increasing conservatism. Thus at Louviers one of Duval's students, Esprit Du Bosroger, used exorcism to extirpate what might be seen as precisely the kind of mysticism which Duval had once endorsed, in his support of the Picardy illuminist Madeleine de Flers. It is difficult to gauge in what precise ways Bosroger modelled himself on Duval, but what is clear is that he gained from his teacher the view that these liminal zones of Catholic practice are where the crucial battles of the Church are fought.

The Louviers case also suggests that the more ostensibly 'Dionysian' forces of charismatic religiosity were not necessarily always opposed to more sober, hierarchical tendencies. Although the rules governing exorcism required exorcists to seek permission from a bishop before acting, this does not mean exorcists necessarily represented a 'rogue' element in relation to more powerful figures in the secular hierarchy. At Louviers, the co-operation, apparently over several years, between Esprit Du Bosroger and François Péricard is a good example of a vigorous regular working hand in hand with a senior reforming member of the secular hierarchy to promote exorcism, while also defending the right of episcopal authority against a local Parlement. What I am hoping to posit, therefore, is that charismatic methods and the institutional goals of the Church in this case were not inherently incompatible. At Louviers, the power exorcists wielded – arbitrary and flamboyant – was not the same as the steadying and sober power they stood for, in their fight against illuminism.

Nor can we detect anywhere in this case a jurisdictional body which represented by definition, or consistently, a 'moderating' force. The crown, as a prime example, first lent its support to a witch trial, in support of Péricard and against the Parlement. But once the Parlement expressed the wish to question Françoise de La Croix, the Crown reclaimed its prerogative and took the case away from Rouen, to be handled by a local church official and later the chancellor, apparently because the Archbishop of Paris supported Mother Françoise. And while it was Françoise's reputation for attachment to charismatic religious practices which her Norman antagonists sourced to witchcraft, a pamphlet written in her defence identified these very practices as her strength. André Du Saussay prosecuted illuminism in the 1630s, but in this case his brief appears to have been to exonerate someone accused of it, because of the jurisdictional tussle between Rouen and Paris which returned the case to him. The actions of exorcists were vindicated up to a point – they succeeded in having Françoise investigated – but a centralising authority worked against their aims, and in favour of her as an acknowledged ecstatic. And the whole edifice was poised precipitously on the initial testimony of a woman such as Anne Barré, whose identity appears to have shifted from being spiritually endowed, to be being a demon, to being possessed but innocent, to being in the end, formally suspected of witchcraft. In short, she embodied, in a sense literally, the mutability of sources of authority at work in this case. Through this somewhat bewildering morass of claims and counter claims, what emerges is not so much a minefield of contingency, though doubtless this was what it was, but a variety of constellations of authority in a culture where the values of charismatic religiosity were pre-eminent, at the same time as being subject to circumspection.

Let us consider for a moment, then, the inner worlds in which these actors found their language and their power. Illuminism and exorcism, it might be said, competed for the same ground, as means whereby the inner worlds of desire, of reading, of the witches' sabbat, of the will of the possessed – the same spiritual 'territory' – became accessible. These were the worlds in which the possibility for a new spiritual hierarchy gained ground. So rather than there being a tension at the heart of Catholicism between charismatic and institutional forces, a more useful model, for this case at least, is one in which competing sources of authority are each vulnerable to accusations of association with the devil, but also equally entitled to refer to the devil as a threat. The fact therefore that exorcism was used as part of an anti-mystic backlash and was also resisted for its own 'freelance' style suggests there was no uniform march in the mid-seventeenth century to an inevitable triumph of the 'dry' view. Rather, exorcism stood at the crossroads of mysticism, witchcraft and reform, because of its ambiguous relation to authority. A model which posits sobriety versus enthusiasm as a central pre-occupation of the Church can miss the nuances of a deep ambivalence at work in a case such as this. Charismatic religiosity helped shaped new constellations of hierarchy, and gave strength to institutional hierarchy as well as to individuals.

If we assume a strict distinction between individual charisma and centralised institutional cohesion or strength, we miss the point that each one can serve the other. To assume that exorcists were aberrant representatives of Catholicism would be to misconceive the ways in which Catholic authority worked in seventeenth-century France. That does not mean that such a distinction cannot be present, but to assume it can lead to inaccurate understandings about the nature of exorcism, a rite which bears a very complex relationship to centralised religion. Thus I am suggesting that exorcism did not bear an automatic affinity with any particular model of Catholic reform, nor with only one form of Catholic revival. Rather, this case suggests reform and revival in the seventeenth century were intertwined in unexpected ways. In a sense, the association of Catholic reform with the programmatic reforms of the Council of Trent disguises the haphazard nature of much reforming activity. For distinctions and difference within Catholic reform were mediated in part through relations with the diabolic realm, and this realm was as much feared as it was available as a weapon against opposing models of apostolic and devotional life.

Part III

Chapter 7

Ecstasy, possession, witchcraft

The will to hierarchy

William Monter once described the seventeenth century in western Europe as the 'golden age of the demoniac',[1] but the same period in France is also referred to as the 'century of saints'; and overlapping in time with the rise in cases of demonic possession and the Catholic spiritual renewal was the witch hunt. Traditional historiographies of demonic possession, ecstatic spirituality and witchcraft have tended to treat these categories as separate, but recent work has identified significant areas of overlap between them. In this period, many individual women – and we are speaking almost exclusively of women – found themselves in more than one of these categories at different times in their lives, or even at the same time, depending on the views of outsiders. Some early modern ecstatics were seen as witches, or were made the object of probative exorcism; while possession was arguably a subcategory of ecstatic spirituality.[2] Witches for their part were seen as those who caused possession, but at times as themselves possessed, all depending on the case. The performances of the possessed as demons under exorcism were the functional equivalent of the raptures of ecstatics, and indeed they were characterised by similar symptoms, such as 'falling as if dead', and a return to consciousness, after which they were able, for example, to bring news from purgatory.[3]

Concentrating predominantly on French possession cases, we will outline here what might be called a sliding scale of rapture. At one end was the ecstatic spiritual who had surrendered her will to that of God and was rewarded with ecstasies and insight, and a possible reputation for sanctity. At the other end was the witch, whose renunciation of her will, and her baptism, in exchange for extraordinary powers (or at least a belief that she possessed such powers) aligned her totally with the devil. In between was the possessed, whose state, unlike ecstasy, always involved the devil, but which, unlike witchcraft, could be turned to good ends. I want to suggest that what took place in the murky realm where the role of the devil was constantly at issue and difficult to determine, can give us further insight into Catholic reform, and the possibilities for, and limitations on, female identity within it. I shall begin by describing a shift which occurred in this period from a traditional understanding of possession as a punishment for one's own or another's sin, to possession being increasingly represented as the consequence of witchcraft, with the possessed as victim. This victim status, in turn, emphasised suffering as the foundation of holiness, and for this reason, possession became in many cases a feature of devotional life. At the same time, however, critics feared diabolic manipulation in cases of positive possession, as they did in cases of ecstatic spirituality.

Theological and medical explanations of possession in the sixteenth century, and even in the seventeenth century, tended to emphasise the responsibility of the possessed in bringing about their own misfortune. Yet these explanations were often out of step with the actuality of events.[4] From the mid-sixteenth century on, positive possessions became the dominant mode in public life, and something of a gap developed between theory and reality. The traditional and one might say non-empirical view was expressed by Pierre Crespet, a Celestine, when he wrote in 1590 that the 'devil never possessed anyone he does not find to be in mortal sin'.[5] In 1618, the Augustinian Sanson Birette noted that devils have an 'extensive jurisdiction over men infected by sin' and he enumerated the sins for which possession could be a punishment.[6] These were pride, hate, envy, lust (notably between married people), attacks on good and holy people, apostasy, blasphemy and the mocking of sacred things.[7] In a similar vein the physician Barthélemy Pardoux, writing in 1639, gave the following reasons for possession: infidelity, vexatious arguments, abuse of sacred things, the persecution of good people, contempt of religion, mistreatment of parents and 'horrible curses'. Pardoux also noted that 'the impiety of magicians' and 'ecclesiastical censures' could open the door to possession by the devil.[8] ('Ecclesiastical censures' seems to refer to the view that the Church itself could effect some sort of possession as a punishment, in light of Paul's punishment of incest in Corinthians 1:5. However, this does not appear to have been the attribution in any recorded cases of possession.[9])

There was some awareness of blameless possession, however. Birette cautioned that 'it is not necessary to have a bad opinion of all those agitated by evil spirits, seeing that they might be in the grace of God and may die in it', and he devoted considerable space to stories of parents making their children possessed by cursing them.[10] Pardoux similarly noted that God permits 'persons of good and holy life and of irreproachable appearance [to] fall into this discomfort' in order to avenge the sins of parents on their children, or for some other 'incomprehensible effect of His providence'.[11] Possession caused by the sins or curses of parents pointed to external causes, to something like witchcraft. In a possession case from 1586, Jeanne Féry, a Soeurs Noires nun at Mons-en-Hainaut in the Spanish Low Countries, became possessed partly as a result of her father having cursed her when she was 2 years old. Through Jeanne's mouth, her devil 'Cornau' reported that once when her mother had gone with Jeanne in her arms to a tavern to retrieve her husband, the child's father said the girl could go to the devil. After this, the devil had gained power over Jeanne, and when she was four years old, the devil asked her if she would take him as a father, to which she agreed. Her infantile act of apparently free will led to the devil looking after Jeanne and replacing the father who had consigned her to him.[12]

In the late sixteenth and seventeenth centuries, however, outright witchcraft came to be the most common cause of possession leading to exorcism. Some contemporary commentators noted the shift. Father Gerard Grudius wrote simply: 'It is a great pity to see today that witches have such power, which is a bad sign.'[13] And an exorcist involved in the exorcisms of the Ursulines at Loudun wrote in 1634: 'In these unfortunate times we see that most possessions occur through evil witchcraft, God permitting that demons afflict the bodies of the most innocent through the intervention of witches and magicians.'[14] Henri Boguet argued for the exemplary value of the suffering of the innocent possessed, when he wrote:

> Sometimes . . . God allows Innocents to be possessed and afflicted, not for any sin, but that His justice and His works may thereby shine the more gloriously. . . . Loyse Maillat, at eight years old, was possessed of five devils; but what ensued from this? It led to the discovery of countless witches who have been punished as the gravity of their crimes deserved.[15]

Concern for the welfare of the possessed reflected a new premium attached to innocence and suffering. In the several dramatic possessions in seventeenth-century France, for example, in which possessed women successfully accused prominent men of witchcraft, exorcists defended their own witch-hunting by referring constantly to the suffering of the 'poor girls'. For possessed women themselves the traditions of martyrdom, which emphasised internal struggles with devils, increasingly informed understandings of possession.[16] Possessing devils thwarted their attempts to participate in religious life by preventing the possessed saying the words of confession, or making them reject the Host. Typically when priests offered the Host to the possessed, their 'devils' bellowed curses such as 'I'm burning! I'm burning', showing their torture in the presence of God.

The possibility that possession could be seen as holy, however, also made it more likely to attract suspicion, a risk shared with more traditional forms of ecstatic spirituality. Both ecstatic spirituals and the possessed existed in an ambivalent sphere in which claims of direct, divine intervention in the body were open to charges of being willed, merely physical manifestations, or false claims to divine illumination (illuminism). True ecstasies or holy possession were by definition not something which could be willed. Rather, they signalled a victory over the human will by the will of God, in the gracious endowment of 'favours', which could include ecstatic experiences (in St Teresa's word, 'lights'), or the granting of insight into the true nature of apparently holy phenomena. Critics saw attempts to force these favours as a culpable, and possibly diabolical intervention in devotional life, and numerous accounts show women as vulnerable to accusations of having feigned sanctity or cultivated its outward signs, in order to advance their worldly standing.[17] Such cases show a preoccupation with the power of the will. One could achieve the appearance of divine favour by assigning one's will to the devil through a written pact, for example, or as a result of seduction by a devil or male witch, or through the donation to the devil of something personal like a hair. Martín Del Rio regarded voluntary ecstasy as a sure sign of witchcraft, and he cited a case of a girl in Saragossa whose fraud was discovered in 1585, her 'frequent raptures' made possible by a pact she had made with the devil while minding her sheep.[18] Both Del Rio and Jean Bodin cited the well-known case of Magdalena de la Cruz of Cordova, an abbess in the mid-sixteenth century, who was regarded by some as a saint. Some of her nuns suspected her of being a witch and in the end she confessed that she had given herself to the devil in the form of a Moor when she was 12, and had had sexual relations with him over the next 30 years.[19]

Another noteworthy case from France in the 1590s is recorded in the biography of Madame Barbe Acarie, the great Discalced Carmelite, and in the biography of the cardinal and promoter of positive possession, Pierre de Bérulle.[20] Each work describes the career of a young woman named Nicole Tavernier of Reims. Tavernier was intensely pious: she had revealed people's sins, discoursed on passages from the Bible, foretold the future, had experienced ecstasies, revelations and visions, and people asked her to pray for them. Once she had even appeared to come back from the dead. During the Wars of Religion, militant Catholics undertook a general procession through Paris under her advice.[21] She had been examined by the leading theologians of the time and had satisfied their doubts.[22] Yet Madame Acarie was suspicious of her. In one instance, Tavernier had disappeared for an hour while on the way to Mass with Acarie, claiming on her return that she had gone from Paris to Tours to discuss religious affairs with a 'powerful person in the kingdom'.[23] Reflecting on this claim, Acarie recalled the debate on the possibility of witches' transports, saying: 'Isn't it so that those over whom the devil has power say customarily that they have been in distant places, even though they have only been there in their imaginations?' Besides, added Acarie, if Tavernier really had gone to Tours, the devil could have taken her there.[24]

Acarie's biographer, the theologian André Duval – someone accustomed to reflecting on the powers of the devil, as we have seen – reported that one day Acarie and Tavernier and several priests were in a room together when a trail of gunpowder appeared on the floor before them, blowing up and leaving a foul odour. This they took to signify outwardly the departure of the devil from Tavernier's body in a sort of spontaneous exorcism, with the result that Tavernier was no longer able to speak in 'fine discourses and high conceptions'.[25] In the words of Germain Habert, Pierre de Bérulle's early biographer, the devil 'left this girl, who appeared a miracle of knowledge and piety, coarse, ignorant, stupid, and hardly different from an idol, that the spirit, which had provided it with false oracles, has quit'.[26] Habert's simile suggests how much was seen to be at stake in such a case: the image of Tavernier becoming like an idol promoted the idea that a powerful female autodidact was as menacing as a false god. It may be noted, however, that as the primary intention of these accounts was to publicise the spiritual acuity of Acarie and Bérulle, this anecdote had none of the militancy of more moralistic tales, such as Del Rio's. Duval told the story in order to praise the capacity of Acarie to detect deceit behind the outward appearance of spirituality, and Habert also takes a relatively sympathetic view, concluding that Tavernier had been taken in by the demon.[27]

The exorcisms of the nun Jeanne Féry – whose drunken father had cursed her as an infant – produced at one point a strikingly similar result to that of the 'exorcism' of Tavernier. As her consent to the devil at 4 years old shows, Féry was depicted as having been possessed partly as a consequence of her own volition. When she was being exorcised as a nun in her twenties, her devil pleaded with her that he not be abandoned. He even spilled candy ('little round sweets called Anis d'Alexandre') about the room to tempt her, then threatened that if she let the exorcisms deliver her, she would lose her intellectual powers. This was a very subtle entreaty to her nature, the narrator claims, as Féry had all her life been endowed with a sharp mind.[28] The implication is clear, that Féry's intellectual pride was demonically inspired. Her exorcist, abbé Mainsent, resolved that he would sooner see her mind reduced to that of a child than see her possessed.[29] Having reassured Féry that he would be like a father to her, as the devil had been, he continued the exorcisms.[30] During one unconventional and aggressive 'exorcism', exorcists held her head under water for as long as she could stand it. Then Féry, emerging from the water to breathe, miraculously produced from her mouth a letter, which declared that, thanks to the intercession of Mary Magdalene, she was free from the possession of devils and might now be 'instructed and indoctrinated surely in the praise of God, of which she is ignorant'.[31] The story goes on: 'After the rendition of the said letter . . . the nun remained with the understanding of a mere child of four, ignorant and idiotic.'[32] Thus an opening was made for officially approved learning, and the episode concludes: 'So little by little the rudiments of Christian piety were taught to her, even though she had to go back to her ABC to learn to read.'[33]

These stories are especially poignant in relation to the educational standing of women in the context of Catholic reform. They clearly suggest a disjunction between the level of religious knowledge that was accessible and often encouraged for young women, and what was seen as fitting. What was emerging in the late sixteenth century, was, in effect, a tension between a growing responsiveness in the Catholic church to the desire of young women to participate in public religious life, and a parallel anxiety about the legitimacy of female authority. In this scenario, broader fears about the value of female charismatic spirituality and demonic possession were fed by concern about the powers of the devil in the world. This made it critical to discern divine from diabolical inspiration.

The so-called 'discernment of spirits' required either the sufferer to interrogate her own experience, or an outsider to scrutinise it, in order to provide an official hierarchical intervention.[34] St Ignatius described the minute attention which was required to discover the source of apparently divine prompting. He described the process whereby the whole experience of an emotion, from its source in thought to its expression in feeling, helped one 'little by little . . . to know the difference in the spirits that were at work, one of the devil and the other of God'.[35] Jeanne Féry said that Mary Magdalene had visited her and explained how to discern the actions of good and evil spirits: 'Good spirits when they arrive bring fear to the person, but when they leave, leave them full of joy and consolation. In contrast, evil spirits cause when they arrive some apparent recreation, and when they leave, leave the person confused, perplexed, bewildered and ill at ease.'[36] Willingness to submit oneself to scrutiny in case of doubt was also seen as a mark of holiness: St Teresa of Avila had stressed that a devotee who believed she was the recipient of some kind of personal divine communication should submit herself to a confessor[37] and Madame Acarie, following the founder of her order, had her own ecstasies scrutinised by two churchmen.[38] To correctly 'discern spirits' in others was itself also regarded as a divine gift. André Duval praised Madame Acarie's capacity to discern 'whether it was the spirit of God or the evil spirit that attended a soul',[39] saying that, in the Tavernier case, she saw 'more clearly than the most famous doctors and those most advanced in the interior life'.[40] The act of discernment thus generated a hierarchy among candidates for spiritual credibility. Significantly, however, as Duval's deferential tone suggested, this establishment of a spiritual hierarchy occurred sometimes in the absence or even instead of official church hierarchy. Indeed what we see in the Tavernier case are the workings of a parallel and sometimes competing spiritual hierarchy: here, one member of this hierarchy, Madame Acarie, was denying another, in Tavernier, status and authority.

Patronage from within the traditional institutional hierarchy also continued to figure in these cases, however. In one notable story, Claude Pithoys, a Minim priest, approached the Bishop of Toul in 1620 after the possessed Lorraine widow Elisabeth de Ranfaing had accused a Minim provincial of witchcraft. Pithoys told the bishop he thought Ranfaing's possession may be the result of 'a diabolical illusion caused by means of some demon present, but not possessing', implying heavily it was her own witchcraft.[41] Unfortunately for Pithoys the bishop was Ranfaing's chief sponsor, and after hearing Pithoys out, he demanded what Pithoys knew of possession, and finally ordered him out of his sight, saying: 'Get out! Go! Get away!'[42] And while this alienating experience may have influenced Pithoys' subsequent conversion to Protestantism,[43] papal officials later turned the tables on Ranfaing herself. Bypassing her local patronage networks, they worked to dismantle her personal cult after members of the Jesuit hierarchy accused her of having a possibly diabolical hold over some of the order's younger members.

Even when positive possession was legitimated, the role of the holy possessed usually aroused a degree of suspicion, and the status of possessed women – even those of high social standing or who were supported through many strands of church hierarchy – was rarely free of the taint of the primary association of possession with the devil and with the body. Robert Mandrou's characterisation of people such as Mother Jeanne des Anges (the possessed superior of the Ursulines of Loudun) as 'second-order mystics' is itself a reflection of the notion, which was pervasive in the seventeenth century, that possession, even when interpreted favourably in some quarters, was a suspect source of spiritual worth.[44] The fate of the 19-year-old Ursuline nun Madeleine Demandols, whose admissions under exorcism facilitated the execution of Louis Gaufridy for witchcraft, attests to this ambivalence. As we have seen, she became a social outcast after the execution of Gaufridy and, at the age of 64, was herself prosecuted for witchcraft for having caused a young woman to become possessed.[45] And two of the most successful possessed women from this period, Mother Jeanne des Anges and Elisabeth de Ranfaing, each of whom became a religious leader of some note, only achieved their status after distancing themselves from the initial demonic possession which had provided its foundation.

Finally, the legitimacy of demonic possession was largely dependent upon the possessed being seen to be totally in the sway of demons, and upon their (or their demons') active submission to higher authorities. In the case of Elisabeth de Ranfaing, the Paris Faculty of Theology made this clear. The Faculty did not condemn Ranfaing's many demonic speeches outright, but tried to nuance its response by judging her performances to be suspect because they went on for too long, 'without syncope or interruption'.[46] In other words, for her displays to be legitimate, Ranfaing should have either fallen into a faint (showing an unambiguous sign of the devil's physical domination of her body), or have been interrupted in some other way, possibly by the exorcist. The Faculty appears to have seen an uninterrupted performance as inherently suspect, occurring as a result of the unmediated desires of either Ranfaing herself, or the devil. Anything which allowed for the interpolation of the exorcist's authority, and showed control over the woman or the devil, it appears, would have made the performances authentic, in the opinion of the Faculty.

Similarly, the many instances of physical interaction of the possessed with audience members at public exorcisms might be interpreted as a way in which the possessed 'purchased' both their credibility as truly possessed, and belief in what they said. As we have seen, Nicole Obry was said to have felt like wood, and at Aix, commissioners of the Parlement were invited to feel the action of the devil in Madeleine Demandols' body.[47] At Loudun a member of the Parlement of Rennes, Sieur Queriolet, was told by the exorcists to put his hands on one of the possessed nuns, which the 'demon' resisted, saying 'no, I don't want him to touch me. His hands are smelly. Oh you're crazy – it pains me to see you'.[48] And a visitor to Loudun related that audience members were also permitted to touch the protruding tongues of the possessed, to discern their unnatural hardness.[49]

Indeed, exorcists appear to have offered direct contact with the bodies of the possessed as enticement to audience members to gain their support. I do not suggest that exorcists necessarily consciously 'used' the bodies of the possessed. That would imply that exorcists perceived a distinction between the sexuality or physicality of the possessed, and the religious significance of their physical state, and there is no evidence for such a claim. However, their imperviousness to what modern eyes can see as abuse, does not alter the reality of the imbalance in the power relations between exorcists and the possessed, an imbalance that was at times characterised by physical and psychic violence. In fact, possession showed few signs of anything like true ecstasy. Notably lacking from cases of possession was the kind of celebration of divine gifts found in the work of St Teresa, for example, or the 'joy and consolation' promised by Mary Magdelene to Jeanne Féry. This was a joyless and morbid religiosity, which permitted cruelty in exorcists and, at times, the possessed. The ability of the possessed in some cases to generate witchcraft accusations and to gain support for their spiritual quests could make them powerful, even dangerous, women. Thus, while it is important to understand the limitations that possession could place on female power, it remains that the power and authority the possessed could claim was sometimes significant. Even so, authority came at a cost, giving credence to what 'demons' said depended on an oscillation between the possessed being seen as a suffering female body, and being listened to for the content of her speech. Father Tranquille, an exorcist at Loudun, made clear that he saw the physical violence of demons in the bodies of the possessed as an index of the credibility of what the women said. He argued that if the demons were tortured, exorcists must be hitting their mark. 'We can see well', he wrote, that when the demons 'can only speak with great constraint and violence, the interrogation is exact and pressing . . . especially when the authority and intention of the Church is interposed'.[50] Credibility, in other words, was measured in physical suffering.

Yet a woman might find a potent form of devotional expression in demonic possession, even if she did so unconsciously, or indeed, on condition that she was seen to do so unconsciously. For claims to spiritual authority or access to divine mysteries through possession were subject to the same scepticism as ecstatic spirituality, as, by promoting direct contact with God, each claim to spiritual authority implicitly challenged the position of the institutional hierarchy in the Church. At the same time, it was this kind of spiritual fervour that kept alive the devotional core of the Church as a whole. The case studies that follow demonstrate the kind of power to which the possessed could lay claim, by showing the potency of possession as an aspect of proselytism. They also reveal the vulnerability of the possessed to challenges that could arise partly as a consequence of the particular characteristics of possession, discussed in this chapter, and partly as the result of specific political and institutional conditions. Possessed women performed within a treacherous terrain in Catholic devotional culture, which they, with their exorcists, constantly manipulated and expanded. Buttressed by an understanding of possession as analogous to spiritual ecstasy, they were nonetheless subject to intense scrutiny because of their inescapably demonic associations. When accusations of witchcraft were involved, the stakes were very high. Working in a volatile religious atmosphere, subject to jurisdictional tensions within and between secular and religious hierarchies, possessed women were exposed to the full implications of the proximity of diabolic power which their possessions entailed. For every successful religious career launched by a woman's public displays of possession or ecstasy, another ended in obscurity or ignominy.

It is saying nothing new to claim that women seeking a holy life in western Catholicism have often needed to do so by means of affective spirituality, due to their relative lack of authority within the male hierarchy. We have considered here the distinctive role that demonological speculation and the backdrop of witch-hunting had in shaping how these women saw themselves and how others saw them, in order to suggest that the volatility of notions such as ecstasy, possession and witchcraft made it difficult for the women in such cases to retain any kind of secure identity. These events took place in a period of Catholic history in France when notions of hierarchy were being both severely tested, and expanded, by charismatic spirituality and positive possession. What the performances of the possessed and the tests they underwent reveal is not only instability in meanings and sources of authority, but the persistence of a distinctive process whereby authority was constituted in the Church. The emphasis on the need for discernment between divine, demonic and human activities is evidence of what could be called the force of a *will* to hierarchy, an impulse which served not only pre-existing institutional hierarchies, such as the secular hierarchy, but also those people and groups who stood to gain esteem by staking a claim for what might be called a spiritual hierarchy. Even, or especially, these spiritual parvenus needed to reinforce some kind of scale of authenticity, to vouch for their own place in the institution of the Church. That the entrenchment of notions of hierarchy came about partly through the agency of apparently centrifugal forces is, like possessing devils preaching for the Church, one of the productive paradoxes of Catholic reform.

Chapter 8

'God's witches'[1]

Two possessed women

Lucetta Scaraffia and Gabriella Zarri, in their introduction to the collection *Women and Faith*, consider the place of activist women in the history of Catholicism. They provide a model for understanding women's place in the Church within a cyclical theory of innovation and change. They say:

> So far, research on religious movements and on successive models of sanctity in which it is easy to find analogous characteristics has enabled us to prove that indeed institutions and models challenged in times of fresh openings and social crises do, once the revolutionary crisis and subsequent reaction are over, reconstitute and impose themselves as elements of a new order. . . . In religious movements, in fact, it was mostly women who offered the principal discourse on reform: whether in an operative sense – as with Catherine of Siena or Teresa of Avila, to mention two of the most noted examples – or in a mystical or prophetic form, as with Bridget of Sweden. In periods in which the ecclesiastical and hierarchical fabric is being put together again, such women develop models of role reversal and opposition. . . . Thus, while in the first case women exert themselves in the same direction as history in general – indeed often accelerating it and giving it direction – and are thus accepted and glorified by the ecclesiastical hierarchy, in the second they are swimming against the current and are thus marginalized and repressed. [2]

While Scaraffia and Zarri situate these trends within a model of historical flux, of action and reaction, the stories of two possessed women in the seventeenth century show the historical tides they identify as being able to move in contrary directions at once. The lives of Marie des Vallées at Coutances, in Normandy (1590–1656) and Mother Jeanne des Anges at Loudun (1605–65), are benchmark possession cases: they show demonic possession to have been simultaneously the means for gaining spiritual authority and a source of profound vulnerability. Their stories indicate the level to which demonological thinking and its accompanying moral panic penetrated the spiritual life of the seventeenth century.

The stories of Vallées and Jeanne have much in common. In each case, the spells of an alleged male witch summoned unwanted and agonising sexual desires: demonic possession became a sign of tortured resistance to sexual temptations. But the imputation of witchcraft as an outside cause of this temptation also provided a springboard for a form of meritorious suffering, endured because of the sufferer's desire to be virtuous.[3] The experience of demonic possession thus formed the basis of the spiritual life of each woman, and led each ultimately to attain a degree of spiritual authority. Vallées became regarded as a local holy woman and Jeanne toured France to display the God-given signs of her successful deliverance. Each took on to some degree the role of spiritual consultant, offering her own views on spiritual matters and evaluating the spiritual aspirations of others. These stories show how far the careers of possessed women were able to go, if the right patrons were found and circumstances were propitious. Their lives are in many ways typical of would-be saints from any era, yet the discourse of demonology provided these women with a unique language through which to attain their spiritual goals. The proximity of demons, who inhabited their very bodies, heightened the intensity of the traditional discourses of martyrdom and temptation. Each experienced (and in some ways practised) intense psychic and physical violence, which dramatically displayed conflict with the devil and amplified through their bodies a religiosity of struggle, punishment and proof. The theme of punishment especially resonates throughout: this includes the punishment of others, when witchcraft accusations called for vengeance against the ungodly; and of the self, through rigorous self-accusation and physical self-mortification.

Public attention to the suffering of the possessed and the drama of witch trials caught the eye of potential patrons, and these women found support among several influential male religious figures of the day: figures as significant as Pierre Coton, Pierre de Bérulle, Jean Eudes and Jean-Baptiste St Jure. Each woman in different ways also achieved a degree of almost priestly authority, promoting a powerful spiritual elitism, which in turn – and perhaps inevitably, given her sex – aroused envy and suspicion. The spectre of demonic possession came back, as it were, to haunt them until late in life, as each proved unable to rid herself entirely of the taint of possession, and the suspicions it prompted among sceptics of a compact with the devil. The cases of Marie des Valiées and Jeanne des Anges show that a personal history of possession always left an opening for hostile forces to exploit: each woman's position in relation to the institutional hierarchies of the Church was characterised by fluctuations in her credibility. The discourse of demonic possession that had aided each to achieve a reputation for sanctity also, to an extent, disallowed them a place in the forefront of the century of saints. Seeing how the possibilities of sainthood for the possessed worked at personal, interpersonal and public levels in these cases can provide us with insight into the workings of charismatic spirituality in this period; show its interpenetration with institutional and hierarchical religion through patronage; and most importantly, convey an understanding of the vital dimension brought to these stories by the discourses of demonology and demonic possession. I argue that it is this demonological dimension of Catholic theology which makes it possible for a historical pendulum which swings for and against female (or indeed, any) charismatic figures to do its work in the same lifetime and in the same historical moment.

The emergence in France of the saintly possessed can be seen as part of a continued but controversial fascination with, and devotion to, so-called 'living saints' in Catholic Europe, which dated from at least the fifteenth century.[4] Most of these 'saints' – some of whom were officially beatified or canonised – were women. The Spanish *beatas* and and other more elite women, notably St Teresa herself, and the *sante vive* of Italy are testimony to the efflorescence of local cult veneration from as early as the 1400s.[5] In the tradition of sanctity, many of these women experienced a path to holiness via temptation by demons. For many this took the form of something often called 'obsession' – the torment of demons through outward suggestion and temptation, in the manner of Job (and indeed of Christ himself). In the cases we will consider here, the devil attacked through outright possession – a seeming capture of the whole person, body and soul, using the deceptive and vulnerable outward shell of the body – a phenomenon which could entail the same moral torments of obsession.[6]

Our principal sources for the lives of Marie des Vallées and Jeanne des Anges are hagiographical. Vallées told the story of her life to two male admirers: the layman Gaston de Renty and the Oratorian (and later Saint) Jean Eudes. In 1644 Jeanne wrote a story of her own life in what might be called an auto-hagiographic mode, ostensibly on the instruction of her spiritual director.[7] Other writers, most notably Jean-Joseph Surin, also promoted their belief in Jeanne's sanctity and conserved stories of her suffering at the hands of demons and of her spiritual insight. Not only did the admirers of these women record their lives in hagiographic mode, the women lived their lives according to the inspiration of the lives of other saints. It is unlikely that historians trained in the past thirty years would argue that hagiography is a distorting mirror that limits our access to the 'reality' of events, making its value as an historical source only ever partial. Hagiography is a usefully opaque medium for seeing the ways in which these lives as written were shaped by the authors' priorities. I would further argue that it was also a code by which the women lived, by which they understood the world around and within them. For both of those reasons, there is potentially no 'deeper' explanation of the truth of their lives than the one which this literary form provides.

Holy stories of struggle which sought to compare the subject to the saints of the past, and commend them to posterity, were for the devout of this period among the most potent 'narratives of self' available. Marie des Vallées and Jeanne des Anges were each familiar with the lives of the saints: the biographies of each make specific reference to admired holy women, including the saints Angela of Foligno, Magdalena de' Pazzi, Catherine of Siena, and especially Teresa of Avila. (The *Life* of St Teresa, who was canonised in 1622, saw more than thirty French editions before 1700.) A hagiography is above all intended to be a story about proof, and so nothing is left to chance: all actions are guided from the start of the life by a divine hand. The life is the story of a confrontation between the spiritual world and the material world. Birth and death are barely relevant: proof of one's essence, for good or ill, is all that matters. Even though this determinism might seem to go against the essential optimism of Catholicism – expressed in the notion that good works can be of benefit – the discourse of hagiography provided these women with the possibility of achieving the status of a living saint, and even, they might have imagined, canonisation after death. Hagiography offers considerable moral flexibility in life as lived: there is no moment when it is too late to be saved, no assertion of sinfulness too abject – the cavalry can arrive at any moment, as it were – and in that sense hagiography also reinforces for its readers a theology of redemption, as well as offering comfort. The future in a sense guides the past, drawing it ever closer to its 'natural' conclusion.

Hagiography underscores the theme that the real world is the world of the spirit, but that the body, as a temporary home for the soul, can nonetheless jeopardise eternal salvation through its desire for worldly gratification. Forbearance in the face of suffering shows the desire to destroy love of the flesh, and heightens receptiveness and readiness for divine grace. These are clichés of Catholic asceticism, but they need to be made explicit here, because of the many ways in which they recur as themes in these cases. From the rigorous self-interrogation and physical torment to which these women submitted themselves, to the accusations against men who supposedly led them into the sin of sexual desire, fear and suspicion about the world of the flesh and of appearances were the dominating themes. But more than that, these fears were the mobilising forces which, for the women involved, were creative spurs whereby they disciplined themselves, honed their personalities, generated charisma, and ultimately, established power and influence over others.

Hagiography is form of triumphalism, a narrative mode whereby everything that happens does so in order to show the hand of God at work, and which can thereby glorify even the sinning subject of the story. Demons have an express function in triumphalism: obstacles placed by demons are turned to advantage. Demons both incite and exploit human weakness, but this weakness is helpful, if it makes a story of triumph possible. The devil amplifies and displays this human weakness, showing up the depth of moral abjection, and thereby providing a means for divine triumph to be magnified. This function of demonic power has been argued more generally for this period, encapsulated in the famous mot: 'no devils, no God'.[8] On an individual, human level, though, while the devil is in himself the source only of pure abjection, the projection of this diabolical threat into a triumphal narrative offers the sinner at the end a hope of redemption.

Marie des Vallées[9]

Marie des Vallées, the so-called Saint of Coutances, was born into a peasant family in 1590, in Saint-Sauveur-Lendelin in the diocese of Coutances in Lower Normandy. She was possessed for 46 of her 66 years, during which time she evolved a devotional style constructed largely around her conflicts with demons. She became well known in Normandy as a local mystic, somewhat like a medieval anchorite, eventually to be consulted by members of the reforming religious elite.

Lay supporters of the Catholic spiritual revival, such as Gaston de Renty and Jean de Bernières, came to be her close friends. She is remembered in particular as a friend and inspiration of St Jean Eudes, the founder of the Congregation of Jesus and Mary (the Eudists). These were significant connections given that Vallées (unlike Jeanne des Anges) never actively aspired to life in a religious order and worked as a housekeeper for two priests for most of her adult life. In her conversations with Jean Eudes, she mentioned wistfully having as a child seen some preaching friars, and admired them, and of having decided she wanted to be married to God.[17] Otherwise, there are no signs she contemplated a life in religion. This is unusual, given that other lay possessed such as Marthe Brossier and Elisabeth de Ranfaing (who later became a nun) had failed in attempts to join religious orders before they were diagnosed as possessed and appear to have understood possession as a means of entering religion via the back door.

Marie des Vallées' father Julien des Vallées died when she was 12 and not long after her mother Jacqueline Germain, married a butcher, 'whose humour and manners resembled those of the animals he worked with',[10] and who beat Marie with a stick.[11] As a consequence, Marie left home and moved through a number of unsatisfactory living arrangements over the next two years. She was living with a female 'tuteur' when she began to experience the symptoms of possession by demons, in May 1609.[12] She described the event to Jean Eudes in these terms, some thirty-five years after it occurred. She said a young suitor, who had proposed marriage to her and whom she had rejected, had sought the help of a witch to win her affections. On the feast of Saint Marcouf, the young man pushed against her in a procession near a parish church, and Vallées said, 'she felt within her straight away an extraordinary movement for this young man . . . the great infernal fire of concupiscence'.[13] For Marie des Vallées, this was the foundational moment of her spiritual life. On returning home, she immediately fell down 'her mouth agape, giving out terrible cries'.[14] Subsequently she found it difficult to pray or go to church.[15] The identity of the young man who she said bewitched her is never given, and Vallées reported that he later left the district permanently. She nonetheless told Eudes that the witch known as 'La Grivelle', from whom the man had obtained his spell, was later burned in Coutances, in a case unrelated to that of Vallées.[16]

The theme of conflicted sexual desire is a consistent one through several major cases of possession, and Vallées' story here is remarkably similar to that of the young widow Ranfaing, who became possessed in 1618 during a social gathering, after a small pilgrimage near Nancy. In this story, the suitor was himself the witch – a local doctor, Charles Poirot – who, Ranfaing alleged, forced a charm into her body by tempting her to eat a piece of salted pork. After a long period of public exorcisms, which led to a witchcraft trial, Poirot was burned in 1622 for having caused Ranfaing's possession. It seems no coincidence that each of these two women's encounters with temptation occurred on a day of religious devotion. Both Ranfaing and Vallées portrayed themselves as metaphorically crucified on their own mixed feelings, experiencing a desire to be in the world, which was symbolised by the passions of the flesh, and the equal but incompatible desire to participate in the religious renewal of their times, the tension manifesting as possession.[18] Thus in cases of possession involving unwanted sexual attentions, the fear of witchcraft on the one hand and a focus on suffering in devotional life on the other underpinned the notion of possession as martyrdom.[19] One of the critics of Marie des Vallées, writing after her death when her cult was under scrutiny, gave an alternative explanation for her possession, however. He said that he had been told that Vallées became possessed not as a result of a spell over which she had no control, but as a consequence of 'a lascivious and sacrilegious dance' she had shared with a young man in a parish cemetery, on a feast day.[20] And indeed Marie des Vallées herself was clearly aware of the possibility of her guilt being seen as the cause of her possession. She rehearsed the range of explanations of possession, as part of her own intense self-scrutiny, reflecting: 'I am quite certain that I never gave myself to the evil spirit, and that my parents did not do so, for I never gave them cause. And so it is doubtless God himself who wished it . . . for my salvation. And I would not change places with the greatest queen in the world.'[21] Thus although Vallées embraced her state of possession, in order to serve God through suffering, she nonetheless demonstrated that her condition was unsolicited. This made a critical distinction, because it highlighted her passivity and served to deflect possible accusations that she had treated with the devil.

Over the next three years, Vallées 'believed she did not sleep for one hour' and sought help from medical doctors, to no avail.[22] In 1612, her relatives took her to the bishop of Coutances, Bishop Briroy, to seek his assistance. He had her exorcised, initially simply in order to ascertain that she was in fact possessed. This included standard tests in Greek and Hebrew, which she passed, although she had not yet learned to read even in French.[23] The bishop also made enquiries about her background, to ensure her own life was irreproachable, and that her possession could not be attributed to her own or her parents' sin, 'the punishment for which God permitted or commanded this affliction'.[24] His attempts over the following three years to make her devils depart, however, were fruitless. Vallées then travelled to Rouen in 1614, where the archbishop, Mgr de Joyeuse, and several 'great doctors', exorcised her, but still her devils clung on.[25] At one point, her devils declared that they would depart at an appointed time but then they failed to do so. The bewildered clerics asked why her devils were still there, when they had promised to leave. The response of her 'demons' propelled Vallées into treacherous territory: they said that the witchcraft of a local gentleman was preventing them from leaving her body. The nobleman – a different man from the young man in the first story, but whose name is similarly omitted from accounts of the case – in turn denounced Vallées to the Parlement of Rouen as a witch, and the Parlement duly had her arrested.[26] Such a turn of events was not entirely unpredictable, as a claim of possession and an accusation of witchcraft in this period were often only separated by a chance act of patronage. In the case of Madeleine Demandols, for example, it was only the support of the exorcist Sébastien Michaelis that had stood between her and a prosecution of witchcraft.[27]

Marie des Vallées' experience as a witchcraft suspect makes disturbing, if familiar, reading. For six months in 1614 she was a prisoner of the Parlement of Rouen.[28] First, a court-appointed surgeon was called in to strip and shave her to look for the devil's mark, and to 'matron' her, that is, assess if she were a virgin.[29] Then a group of six or seven members of the court stood by while she was pricked all over by doctors and surgeons, after being shaved a second time.[30] Her virginity, Eudes tells us, ensured her release, 'virginity being in no way compatible with witchcraft'.[31] These events feature as key elements in the narrative of her martyrdom, a martyrdom that Vallées later believed her devils had planned for her all along, when they made their initial witchcraft accusation.[32]

Vallées continued to be possessed, but accounts of her life begin here to represent her suffering increasingly in terms of a personal campaign against witchcraft. The compassion she had for the witches who, she believed, wanted to destroy her was so great, we are told, that she volunteered to God to undergo all the punishment that they deserved for their crimes.[33] She also wanted to suffer by taking upon herself all the spells that witches set for other people, absorbing their evil to protect others, as a kind of lightning rod.[34] In particular, she wanted to suffer for the young girls of the parish affected by witchcraft.[35] Witchcraft, with its frequently sexual overtones was, for Vallées, the ultimate expression of all human sin, and she dedicated herself to its destruction. Later, she even descended into what she referred to as 'hell' for two years (1617–19), in order to suffer the tortures merited by all the witchcraft in the world.[36] The psychological suffering she describes in hell was acute: she speaks of unbearable torture at the hands of demons, who gathered around her and accused her of sins she had not committed, but for which they said she would be punished anyway.[37] In worldly terms, however, her suffering appears to have been constituted by traditional ascetic behaviour, such as fasting, wearing a horsehair ceinture and a pigskin shirt with bristles.[38] (Indeed, a hostile writer jeeringly queried how she could have been in hell, when she was seen eating, conversing and going to church at Coutances, as before.[39]) Her suffering for witches in order to destroy their sin had the desired effect, however, in its own martyrological terms: the witches of the world repeatedly mobilised against her.

Two notable stories illustrate the efforts of witches to bring about her downfall. According to Eudes' account of her life, the witches of Paris plotted against Vallées to make her commit some kind of crime. He tells us that a certain merchant from Coutances was returning from Paris and was approached by a group of well-dressed horsemen. They told the merchant they had heard of Vallées and of her suffering and asked him to take some relics of Saint Geneviève to her in a little box they gave him. When friends exposed Vallées to the relics, she was pitched into a paroxysm of blasphemy, 'exciting her to murder and massacre, pushing her to strangle, choke, dismember and devour everyone'.[40] This dramatic display of discernment of evil on the part of Vallées showed the relics to have been diabolical fakes, sent by witches to incite her to perform a criminal act. Another story she related to Eudes tells of a young female witch discovered going from town to town throughout Normandy, passing herself off as none other than Marie des Vallées, trying to ruin the real Marie's reputation for purity by taking her clothes off and 'doing wicked things'.[41] The woman said she had done this because the devil tempted her to, and she even showed an insensible mark on her forehead 'to a man of probity', to show she was in league with the devil.[42] Eudes gained 'insider' corroboration of such activities from a former male witch whom he had converted, who told Eudes that the girl was likely to have been put up to her high jinks by the 'infernal troop' of witches.[43] But perhaps the greatest torture Vallées endured was to be excluded from devotional life through the actions of demons.

Repugnance at holy objects and religious ceremonies was a common experience for the possessed. In many cases, most notably the prototypical miracle of Nicole Obry at Laon in 1566, proximity to the Host was sufficient to drive possessing devils into a frenzy of resistance.[44] In the case of Marie des Vallées, a paralysing inability to take Communion and to make a confession arose as a result of a distinctive and controversial spiritual bargain she reported striking with God in 1615. Vallées undertook to 'exchange her will' with that of God, which meant, among other things, that even though she wanted to take Communion she wanted even more to suffer through being deprived of it, according to God's will, for the sins she might commit. The suffering she endured when demons kept her from confession and Communion, in particular, thus became the source of her greatest claim to sanctity. By this time she had read widely in the lives of saints and took inspiration from them. The idea to exchange her will came from reading a contemporary devotional text, the *Occupation intérieure* of Fr Pierre Coton, the great Jesuit confessor to Henri IV and Louis XIII.[45] She told Jean Eudes of the reasoning she used to reach her decision to renounce her will: '[T]he Divine will', she said, 'is God. Holy Communion is also God, but when I take Communion every day, I can still sin after that, and if my own will is annihilated and that of God is given me in its place, I will offend no more, for it is only my will which can sin. That is why I renounce with all my heart my own will and give myself to the adorable will of my God in order that he possess me perfectly, that I never offend'.[46] She begged God to punish her for her sins, rather than have her commit them.[47]

Devils assisted in this divinely approved plan by making Vallées physically unable to take Communion. Typically, the demons prevented her approaching the sacrament by 'twisting her head aside, making her fall to the ground', or 'through agitation of her body in some other way',[48] and they prevented her from leaving her bed on Sundays and feast days.[49] When exorcists asked the devils why, when they were adjured by the power of the Church to allow Vallées to take Communion they would not let her, they answered that they could not because 'it was an order from God not to'. When quizzed as to a reason for this, they replied that 'they were not privy to God's designs'.[50] Like so many *dévotes* in this period, Vallées rejoiced in her suffering and challenged the demons to attack her: 'Is that the best you can do?' she said, 'you're pretty weak. Here I am, do your worst. Do not wait for God to tell you to strike me, it is enough that He permits you.'[51] However, unlike Jeanne des Anges and Elisabeth de Ranfaing, who succeeded as more mainstream spiritual leaders after seeming to have overcome their possession, Vallées never moved to distance herself from her state.[52] Rather, her direct communications with God inspired her to absorb her possessed state into a more or less routinised alternative form of devotional life. Exorcists largely set aside their fruitless 'anathemas and excommunications'[53] and allowed her to get on with being possessed, as an expression of her private devotion and suffering.[54] She did not take Communion or confess for more than 30 years, and she remained possessed from 1609 up until 1655, the year before she died.

Vallées' devotional life and public life were shaped by the rejection of worldliness and sensuality in any form, and tinged with violence, both physical and psychological. It is hard to gauge exactly how her public reputation evolved. She tells us that children laughed at her once as she performed devotional acts, and at least her early demonic convulsions also seem to have taken place in the more or less public place of chapels. Yet much else of what we know of her is mediated through the retrospective accounts of her own earlier life provided to Jean Eudes and Gaston de Renty, and these speak more of her own cherished attitudes to potential immorality in herself, and the perceived immorality of others, than they do of public events.

Her objects of opprobrium were church and lay figures alike, and, of course, her own potentially sinning self. Punitive and self-punitive impulses are everywhere in these accounts. They lie along a spectrum from 'routine' devotional self-abasement, such as making five processions around a church on her bare knees, with relics around her neck and carrying an image of the Virgin,[55] to the expression of chilling sentiments of vengeance. She said that when she encountered a young woman who dressed with her neck exposed (in the new fashion of the times) she had wanted to say something to her. On this occasion, God stopped her, saying 'vanity will soon end and her pain will be eternal'. Vallées reported that the woman died not long after.[56] In another instance, she reported that God provided corroboration for her negative opinion of a churchman who sold benefices: God told her the man was already damned.[57] God also told her that demons would cause to be possessed all those who did not wish to convert.[58] And when one of the priests for whom she worked entertained a fellow priest and gave him wine, Vallées waited for the visitor to leave the house, then smashed his glass and the wine jug and fed to pigs the bread he had left uneaten.[59] At one point she also attempted suicide, yet God saved her. Her arm had stiffened and the knife dropped. She was able to say to herself: 'I am not yet lost: God has stopped me from killing myself.'[60] (In this Vallées was probably recalling the experience of St Magdalena de' Pazzi, who had said this happened to her when she attempted suicide.) These diverse sentiments of torment and rage, packaged in her accounts as parts of a campaign against sin, suggest the stepfather's beatings which she claimed occurred may have been both real and profoundly affecting. It is equally important to recall, though, that important as family influence is, religion not only offered a means of expression and resolution for such embedded emotions, and that the values abroad in Catholicism in this period, in particular, also went far to inculcate such violent emotions.[61] The intensely moralistic cases of demonic possession we have seen on the cultural map are but one example of this trend.

How then was the housekeeper Marie des Vallées able to make friends with some of the major luminaries of the Catholic revival? It seems clear that there was in this period something of an informal network of French holy men who tracked the careers of would-be female saints and the positive possessed throughout France and French-speaking territories in Europe. Indeed there was a notable overlap in these cases among patrons of the possessed: the connections abound. Pierre de Bérulle, known already for his support of Marthe Brossier, was also involved with Elisabeth de Ranfaing. Pierre Coton was involved with Adrienne Du Fresne in Paris, corresponded with Elisabeth de Ranfaing, and supported Vallées, who took inspiration from his writings. Vallées was influenced by the work of Benet of Canfield, and she knew François Domptius, the confrere of Sébastien Michaelis. Jean-Baptiste Saint-Jure, the spiritual director of Jeanne des Anges, directed Gaston de Renty, who wrote Vallées' first biography. It has also been suggested that the convent, Notre-Dame de la Charité du Refuge, set up by Jean Eudes was modelled on that of Elisabeth de Ranfaing.[62] Renty wrote to Marie des Vallées telling her about Ranfaing; Vallées knew Mgr Harlay Sancy, Bishop of St-Mâlo, who had been one of Ranfaing's exorcists.[63] Specifically, Normandy was the region where Jean Eudes was at his most active, founding a religious order, and missionising against immorality in the countryside. It is likely that as he passed through Coutances, local priests told him of Vallées' extraordinary conduct. The same appears to have happened in relation to the local nobles Gaston de Renty and Jean de Bernières. It seems most likely that kindly disposed priests sensed that here was a possible way to bring people closer to God, and reported Vallées' experiences and performances to those who they thought might regard them with sympathy.

Let us imagine a degree of desperation in all this, a desperation to be closer to things divine – it's a sentiment present in many of these cases.[64] We saw in Chapter three that Pierre Coton was quite prepared to undergo humiliation when he referred theological problems to the devils of Adrienne Du Fresne. And as we saw in the cases of Obry and Brossier, as well as that of the ecstatic Nicole Tavernier, in a religious tradition which celebrated humility and was responsive to paradox, socially and intellectually elite men felt a perhaps wilful, even perverse, assurance that holiness was to be found more readily in, what was for them, the most unexpected of places, among the lowliest and most 'misunderstood' of females. There is a tendency to celebrate this sense of spiritual desperation – as Vallées herself said (in comparing herself to, and distinguishing herself from, St Teresa), 'I walk "à la desperade"' where Teresa was more moderate.[65] Vallées' friends were even prepared to entertain the prospect that she was an incarnation of divinity. They recorded her experiences at a church of the Capuchins and again of the Dominicans, when she saw, unusually I think, a vision of herself in the Host. She understood that this meant she was 'quite deified and transformed into Our Lord' and said that God had promised her several times that He would 'leave no more of her than in a consecrated host'.[66] And while there was one occasion when Vallées criticised Jean de Bernières for being too passive in his prayers – thereby perhaps assuming too much of his own capacity for goodness and ignoring the ways the Church provided to save him – Vallées' own apparent choice to bypass consistently, or indeed replace, the Church's channels of grace perhaps inevitably smacked of spiritual elitism.[67]

The degree to which Vallées revelled in this imposed distance from the sacraments and the ministrations of the clergy became, because of its seemingly 'pre-quietist' tendencies, her greatest source of vulnerability. In 1651, following a shift in her local patronage networks, and possibly as a result of her recent close friendships with Jean Eudes and Gaston de Renty, Vallées had to face a tribunal of local clergy.[68] Under the instruction of the grand-vicar of Coutances, Fr Bazire, two priests, Bertout (canon of the Church of Coutances) and Ameline, declared their fear that 'she was fooled' (implicitly, by the devil). They also, significantly, referred to her exchange of will as a 'pact', and expressed concern about her apparent belief that she was 'impeccable'.[69] Vallées was ordered to fall in line with the requirements of the Church. She agreed to do so, although (subversively) only following a communication from God, who, she said, told her, 'Just as you gave yourself to me, I now give you to the Church to dispose of you as it pleases.'[70]

The importance of demons in Vallées' spiritual profile was always controversial, however, attracting ridicule and suspicion during her lifetime and long after her death, when it was invoked to undermine her reputation as a saint, and to deride Eudes' faith in her. After Vallées' death in 1656, Fr Bazire reiterated his attack on her spiritual conduct for its 'perilous consequences regarding religion and against the order of the Catholic church', in order to prevent others following her example.[71] And he queried whether she was free of demons, implying that possession was a diminished rather than an elevated spiritual state.[72] One of his chief aims this time was to stifle a thaumaturgic cult which had developed around her. Stories of miracles performed in her lifetime and after her death – she was said to have obtained for Jean Eudes a new lung, for example[73] – and the use she had made of expressions such as 'deification'[74] to describe her own condition, along with her calls for a so-called 'general conversion' to take place before the end of the world, only added to the suspicion that had developed around her: that she had come to be seen in some circles as a 'female messiah'.[75] Later, when Vallées had been dead for nearly twenty years, Jansenist sympathisers opposed to Jean Eudes (who had strong links with the Jesuits) used his association with Marie des Vallées to undermine the reformer's credibility. In 1674, Charles Dufour, the Abbé d'Aulnay, wrote in an anonymous tract that Fr Eudes should blush for getting involved in 'this infamous demonomania', for declaring himself a defender of a demoniac who was 'deceived by the devil'.[76] In Vallées' defence, Jean Eudes praised her suffering at the hands of demons, saying 'it was no crime' for her to have been possessed.[77] And he wrote that it was 'a calumny quite false and dark, to say that this good woman was a witch, and that she was condemned as such by the Parlement.'[78] Investigations in 1869 which led to Eudes' canonisation in 1925 entailed a consideration of his relations with Vallées, which clearly found in their favour.[79] Since then, Vallées has increasingly come to be counted among the significant mystics of her era.[80]

Jeanne des Anges

The demonic possession of Mother Jeanne des Anges, superior of the Ursuline convent in Loudun in the 1630s, and the trial of the parish priest, Father Urbain Grandier, executed for witchcraft following accusations made by Jeanne and other nuns under exorcism, is perhaps the best-known story of possession in western history. The 'devils of Loudun' has been the case of possession beside which all others are viewed, and it has been celebrated – or lamented – in fiction and in the performing arts.[81] Its seventeenth-century documentation, in manuscript and print, is vast.[82] While historical interest in the case has traditionally focussed upon the trial of Urbain Grandier – another chilling case of punishment of sexuality – a major 1970 documentary study by the pre-eminent historian of French seventeenth-century mysticism and cultural theorist Michel de Certeau brought to the case a fresh interpretation. Certeau focused upon the significance of the case in the context of seventeenth-century spirituality, drawing attention to the fact that a cult of exorcism which grew up around the Ursuline convent of Loudun, and which was promoted widely in pamphlets and conversion stories, came only after the death of Urbain Grandier.[83] In this context, a considerable personal cult around Jeanne des Anges and her struggles to overcome demonic forces saw her become, in Certeau's words, 'the new Teresa of Avila after having been the new Madeleine de Demandolx (sic), the "mystic" after having been the "possessed"'.[84]

Unlike Marie des Vallées, Jeanne des Anges began her career in religion from a position of authority in a powerful religious order, and for all but three years she remained as superior of the Ursulines at Loudun, from 1627 until her death at the age of 60 in 1665.[85] Yet her story reveals some similar responses of doubters to a case of positive possession as we saw in the case of Vallées. Even after supporters had failed in their attempt to save the life of Urbain Grandier by alleging the rash of possessions at the convent was fraudulent, scepticism lingered about the cult that developed around Jeanne des Anges. As late as 1662, three years prior to her death, Jeanne's spiritual authority encountered scepticism. As the Jesuit Jean-Joseph Surin, her lifelong friend, and sometime exorcist and spiritual director, wrote: 'She was accused and subject to calumny as if she were a witch, a magician . . . and it is the idea that was held of her for a long time.'[86]

Jeanne des Anges' spiritual authority derived from both her suffering at the hands of demons and from several miraculous exorcisms, which, over a period of several years, gradually led to her being declared free of her demons. Jeanne did not retire quietly to the life of a convent superior after she ceased to be possessed. Her claim to divine favour was reinforced by her reported interaction with a guardian angel, a spectral figure who Jeanne said gave her interior responses to requests for guidance on matters of faith. As someone regarded as an 'insider' on spiritual matters, she nonetheless found herself on several occasions opposing the claims of male spiritual directors who wanted her endorsement of their own spiritual protégés. The hostility she aroused in these directors, as well as in other local churchmen, reflects the tension between an authority based on direct divine communications, and the workings of the more traditional male hierarchy within the Church.

Jeanne des Anges was born Jeanne de Belcier in 1605, the child of a noble Gascogne family. Her father was Louis de Belcier, Baron de Cozes, and her mother was Charlotte de Goumard, of the family des Chilles. At the age of 16 Jeanne entered the Ursuline convent in Poitiers, where she remained until 1627, transferring in July of that year to the new Ursuline house at Loudun. Shortly afterwards, and possibly because of her social position, she became the superior at Loudun while only 22 years old.[87] Father Urbain Grandier – the parish priest at Saint Pierre-du-Marché in Loudun and a prebendal canon of Saint-Croix de Loudun – was a prominent figure in the town, with powerful friends. He was also prone to involvement in scandal and litigation, and had written a treatise against the celibacy of priests.[88] Jeanne tells the story of her inner battles concerning her sexual fascination with Grandier: 'When I did not see him, I burned with love for him and when he presented himself to me . . . I lacked the faith to combat the impure thoughts and movements that I felt. . . . Never had the demons created such disorder in me.'[89] Articulated within the framework of demonic possession, the desire to avenge desire – whether conscious or unconscious one cannot say – became a sharpened instrument in the pursuit of sanctity.

In September 1632, the convent was disturbed by movements at night. Nuns saw the shadowy figures of men moving through the house, among them the spectre of the convent's former spiritual director, Fr Moussaut, who had recently died, and that of Urbain Grandier.[90] The troubled nuns reported under exorcism that Grandier had caused their possession.[91] In total, twenty-seven nuns were classified as either possessed, obsessed or bewitched.[92] Chief among the eight possessed nuns was Jeanne des Anges, who was possessed by seven demons. Within weeks of the nuns' first signs of disquiet, priests began exorcisms at Loudun. Public exorcisms rapidly became something of a citywide circus, taking place not only in the convent, but in local chapels, and even in private homes, up until 1637.[93] Canon Jean Mignon, an enemy of Grandier, and Pierre Barré, the curé of Chinon, initially carried out the exorcisms. Later, regular priests came to dominate proceedings: in particular Capuchins, most notably Fr Tranquille (superior of the Capuchins at La Rochelle) and, subsequently, the Jesuits.[94] 'Spiritual tourists' from within France and beyond, such as Thomas Killigrew, with whose letter this book began, passed constantly through the town. As the prioress of the Ursulines at Loudun, it fell naturally to Jeanne to be the focus of the exorcisms, and as time went by Jeanne took over as her own the high profile that it took all the priests and nuns (and several other women) at Loudun to generate.

Fatally, the case of witchcraft against Grandier was also shaped by a 'real-political' dimension. A royal official, Baron Jean Martin de Laubardement, was present in Loudun overseeing the destruction of the town's castle, under royal authority. The Governor of Loudun, Jean d'Armagnac, resisted this intervention, and one of his supporters was Urbain Grandier.[95] In November 1633 Laubardemont sought from Cardinal Richelieu a special commission to investigate the charges against Grandier, who was imprisoned almost immediately, on 6 December 1633.[96] Laubardemont appears to have pursued the case in part to humble the governor through Grandier, and in so doing, to assert his own political position in the region. As Laubardemont built up a dossier against Grandier, exorcisms continued to take place in several churches around Loudun, where before large crowds the nuns made accusations against Grandier and revealed charms and demonic pacts said to have been made by him.[97] According to Jeanne, all the nuns in the convent had been affected by the witchcraft which Grandier had used to lead them into debauchery. In Jeanne's case, Grandier's alleged witchcraft led her to be assailed constantly by impure thoughts of him, which she struggled to suppress.[98] Despite vigorous efforts on the part of Grandier's friends and family to save him, he was burned for crimes of witchcraft on 18 August 1634.[99] His treatise on the celibacy of priests was burned with him.[100]

How is it possible for us to calculate the impact the death of Grandier may have had on contemporaries' views of Jeanne des Anges, and on her own opinion of herself? It is not unlikely that it contributed to fear of her, yet it may also have generated a morbid attraction. After all, this was real power. Her leading role in the exorcisms was sustained as long as male religious figures expressed an interest in her, and there was never a lack of such admirers. As to her own views, it was reported that after Jeanne testified against Urbain Grandier she began to act strangely, standing in the rain for hours with a rope about her neck and a taper in her hands, and was only prevented from hanging herself by her sister nuns (apparently the first of two suicide attempts). It was also recorded that Jeanne told one of the chief orchestrators of the case against Grandier, Baron de Laubardemont, that she believed she had offended by testifying.[101] Perhaps we can infer here a certain urgency for Jeanne in establishing for herself a reputation as someone holy, and therefore implicitly benign. The opportunity to achieve this presented itself when she met the Jesuit Jean-Joseph Surin.

Father Surin arrived in the town in December 1634 with an older priest, Fr Bachelerie, following the express order of Cardinal Richelieu that Jesuit exorcists be sent to Loudun to take the place of the Capuchins.[102] The two were later joined by five more Jesuits and two Carmelites.[103] The arrival of Surin saw the beginning of a long and intense spiritual partnership between him and Jeanne des Anges. Both were around thirty years old and their friendship became life-long: they died in the same year, 1665. Surin set himself the task of re-making his relationship to Jeanne from that of exorcist to spiritual director.[104] He began to prescribe prayer regimes and mortifications to assist her in finding her 'liberty' – that is, a kind of spiritual equilibrium that would ultimately lead her away from the vexations of possession.[105] What Surin did, in effect, was to use exorcism as one of many means for providing spiritual comfort to Jeanne,[106] who later wrote that the nuns in the convent saw a more introspective mood affecting her and gave her the nickname 'le diable dévot'.[107] Since early 1635, Father Surin had also been conspicuous among the exorcists for the fact that he had 'caught' the possession, and was at times perturbed by the very demons over which he was supposed to have command. During one exorcism, Surin himself had to be attended to by other exorcists who applied the Host to his mouth. In another encounter the demon possessing Jeanne des Anges 'jumped' from her body into that of Surin, recalling the demons of the demoniac of Gadarene, which Christ caused to jump from the man's body into the herd of swine.[108]

Jeanne's relationship with Surin saw the two of them turn exorcism inwards, away from public display, and importantly, away from what Jeanne referred to as 'the violence ordinarily practised in exorcisms'.[109] Jeanne described one of Surin's exorcisms in detail: 'To acquire liberty, the Father applied himself strongly to exorcising me, not as they did ordinarily, nor with all the violence they usually employ, but holding me on a bench, with the Holy sacrament in my hand, he paraphrased some psalms of David on the spiritual life, and reproached the demons for the perdition of sin and for having quit God.'[110] Surin's use of a type of exorcism to soothe Jeanne's spirit, in the context of an overall programme of spiritual exercises, was nonetheless seen to detract from the aim of expelling the demons, which was what his superiors appear to have desired.[111] Like Marie des Vallées, Jeanne was in a sense learning to live with her demons, to recognise them as an aspect of her own personality, and thereby give her spiritual pursuits meaning. Surin led her to an understanding that her own reluctance to yield to the ordinary requirements of convent life was diabolical. Indeed, it could be said that her life in religion was in the end entirely defined by the inability to come to terms with its strictures. Surin referred to Jeanne's 'extraordinary distraction of her wits, with a perpetuall inclination to eat and sleepe',[112] and she admits to having indulged at one point in a 'quantity of drinking songs'.[113] Surin did not wholly indulge this theologising of the mundane: he also made her turn to and wash the convent dishes. It was from such things that her 'triumph' emerged, and the reward of introspection was never far from view.

Yet Jeanne's exorcisms did come to an end. Between 1635 and 1638, she underwent a series of exorcisms which resulted in the dramatic expulsion of several of her devils, and which in the end left her altogether free of her possession. The first of these expulsions came at a critical time in late 1635, when the tenure of Surin as an exorcist at Loudun seemed threatened by interventions from his superiors. The Jesuit hierarchy had expressed disquiet about the involvement of Jesuits in the exorcisms at Loudun from the outset,[114] and this had deepened when it became apparent that Surin had taken to the role of exorcist with relish and was following unconventional methods in his practice.[115] In early November 1635, Surin was given eight more days to exorcise before he would be called away. Jeanne recorded that she was disturbed by the thought of Surin leaving – attributing the plan, unsurprisingly, to the work of demons – and wrote that she was also concerned for Surin's honour.[116] In her prayers, she undertook to increase her devotional activities in order to humiliate the 'demon' who was plotting to undermine her well-being.[117] She wrote that the devil tried to weaken her, to make it impossible for her to undergo exorcism, but she persuaded Surin that she was well enough to be exorcised and on 5 November the demon Leviathan was chased from her body, leaving her forehead marked with a big, bloody cross, which stayed on her for three weeks afterwards.[118] 'This departure', she recorded, 'made people think, because it was the first exorcism done after Father Surin was recalled by the provincial'.[119] Surin was permitted to remain.[120] Another four such dramatic expulsions took place, leaving the names of Mary, Joseph, Jesus and François de Sales inscribed upon Jeanne's hand.[121]

Jeanne's reputation as the beneficiary of miracles was further enhanced in 1637 by the first of two miraculous cures effected on her by St Joseph.[122] Jeanne was suffering from an illness said to have been induced by the excessive demands placed on her body during an exorcism by a Fr Ressès. From her sick bed, she saw the figure of an angel 'of rare beauty', resembling a young man of around 18 years of age, with long blonde hair.[123] This was an early visitation by her guardian angel, who came to play an increasingly important role in her spiritual life from this time. She also saw the figure of St Joseph. The saint applied to her right side an unction and she felt herself to be 'entirely cured'.[124] Two days later, she and her sub-prioress examined the nightdress that Jeanne had been wearing at the time of the visitation. They found it to possess an 'admirable odour', and to have retained five drops of the miraculous unction.[125]

The names on her hand, and the nightdress, immediately became the focus of veneration and a source of further miracles, although the capacity for a cult to develop around her was enhanced by the fame of Loudun and underscored by her own leadership position. People came to Loudun to touch and to kiss the bright red letters, and to touch Jeanne's hand with pieces of cotton and paper.[126] Baron de Laubardemont, who had continued to sponsor the exorcisms, sought the intercession of St Joseph through the miraculous nightdress when his wife was experiencing a difficult pregnancy.[127] The Jesuit superior-general in Rome expressed misgivings about the involvement of members of his order in this cult, and he tried to make the Jesuit rector in Loudun ensure that the case was not perpetuated 'eternally', when apostolic workers were needed in other fields.[128]

Following the departure of her last demon, Behemoth, in October 1637, Jeanne undertook to fulfil a vow of pilgrimage to the tomb of François de Sales at Annecy. Accompanied by two nuns and a confessor, Fr de Morans, she travelled for five months in 1638, her tour taking in most of the major cities in France including Orléans, Lyon, Grenoble, Blois, Paris, and Annecy.[129] Crowds flocked to see Jeanne and to see her hands, and she became, in effect, a mobile pilgrimage site and miracle-worker. At Annecy a possessed girl was cured using the nightdress.[130] In Paris, Jeanne was displayed to the public from four in the afternoon until ten at night (when she could be seen under lights), her hand protruding through a window into a courtyard for spectators to see.[131] Her party also met theologians, prelates, and dignitaries, including Richelieu, Anne of Austria, Henri II de

Bourbon (the prince of Condé) and the king, Louis XIII.[132] She told the queen stories of the possession at Loudun, and the queen touched some chaplets with the miraculous unction, even asking Jeanne if she could keep a snippet of the nightdress for herself – a request that Jeanne politely refused.[133] Jeanne remarked that many people offered alms, but she had only accepted a small gift from Richelieu, and a letter of recommendation from the king for the rest of their journey.[134] There were doubters, however. Huguenots questioned the possession, and one man tried to inscribe letters on his own arm to prove that Jeanne's were fake, which Jeanne said caused inflammations on his skin.[135] Even the second Cardinal Richelieu, Alphonse, brother of the *premier ministre*, wanted to cut the names off Jeanne's hand using scissors or a razor. She told him that he was causing her pain, and cautioned him that his brother had not asked her to undergo these tests.[136] Overall the trip was a success, however, and Jeanne's cult continued to flourish following her return to Loudun.

Father Surin ceased to be Jeanne's spiritual director in 1639, only resuming the post again from 1657 until 1665.[137] He wrote to Jeanne frequently, though, offering spiritual guidance, as he did to many correspondents throughout his career.[138] From 1643 until 1657 Jeanne was directed by another Jesuit, Jean-Baptiste Saint-Jure, with whom she also maintained a correspondence.[139] It was under the direction of Saint-Jure, but on her own initiative, that she wrote her autobiography in 1644.[140] The autobiography was modelled upon the *Life* of St Teresa.[141] In it, Jeanne described her life in terms of a spiritual quest, marked by an almost infinite degree of scrupulosity concerning her motives and the ways in which she allowed demons to have scope to act, as a consequence of her own defective will. Like Marie des Vallées, Jeanne reports surviving a failed suicide attempt, stopped only by the divine hand. Her story moves through descriptions of early, hypocritical attempts to appear holy, to her possession, and then, changing tone to fit its triumphalist trajectory, describes the success of her tour around France.[142]

The discernment of spirits

After the cult of public exorcisms on the nuns at Loudun diminished in the late 1630s, Jeanne's personal cult came to focus increasingly upon a relationship with her guardian angel. The angel would periodically renew the letters on her hands, and Jeanne received from him revelations and counsel.[143] In this period, claims of spiritual insight gained through prayer and intuition and in consultation with her angel, gradually came to supplant the physical indices of her spiritual state. Jeanne was sought out for advice on spiritual matters on numerous occasions, and she would often refer questions to her angel, in a gesture which demonstrated her own humility and deference to higher authority. A constant requirement to affirm that the giving of spiritual advice was undertaken with humility was something also sought in male religious, of course, but it was a much more contentious question for women, and especially for the 'recovering' possessed. This attachment to a guardian angel, was, as Certeau noted, relatively common in the post-Tridentine era.[144] St Teresa, as a notable example, had been influenced throughout her life by an angel. The place of the guardian angel in Jeanne's life was something like that of a spiritual director – a divinely dispatched interlocutor who mediated Jeanne's claims to special insight. For example, when Jeanne believed she was communicating with the soul of a deceased sister from the convent, in purgatory, she asked her angel to confirm that the nun's apparition was real.[145] Jeanne would also relay the responses of the angel to her human spiritual director for confirmation.[146] She was aware of the risks that could accompany claims of divine communications and, in 1643, she expressed the fear that the visits of the angel 'may not be from . . . God', finding reassurance after presenting the matter to the Jesuit Fr Barthélemy Jacquinot for examination.[147] On another occasion, Jeanne asked the angel for advice about himself: she asked what to do if the counsel the angel gave her contradicted that of her own spiritual director, to which the angel replied appropriately that it was possible to be fooled by an angelic form, but not by being obedient.[148]

After the possession, communication with the angel sustained the very high public profile enjoyed by Jeanne in her position as a spiritual authority. The maxims of the angel were even published by an anonymous Jesuit in 1656, at Valenciennes, under the title La Gloire de S. Ursule.[149] While Fr Saint-Jure seems to have encouraged Jeanne in her relationship with the angel, Certeau suggests that Surin was less enthusiastic. Surin urged Jeanne not to 'run a sort of advice shop' ('tenir comme une boutique'), where the angel responds to enquiries about marriages, law suits and the like, just as demons did during exorcism.[150] This response, even coming from a friend, again reflects some of the ambivalence of members of the Jesuit order to female mystics. And a letter from Jeanne to Fr Saint-Jure, written in 1650, expresses regret that the Jesuits of Loudun, under orders from their vice-provincial, Fr Le Gualez, rarely came to the convent and never alone because of the belief among those in authority that she was 'fooled' (by the devil) in the many extraordinary things that had happened to her.[151]

Like Madame Acarie before her, Jeanne was believed capable of discerning the effects of God from those of the devil, and she was often asked to give her opinion in cases of claimed possession or ecstasy. A manuscript account of her life, assembled by friends and drawing on her own writings, gives further insight into the processes whereby claims to divine inspiration were investigated and negotiated in this period.[152] Perhaps surprisingly, these cases show Jeanne playing the role of 'spoiler', carefully shoring up the bounty of divine inspiration by helping to keep successful claims to a minimum.[153] Cynicism cannot be assumed, however: the need to interrogate and limit claims of access to the divine was simply part of what sustained its value. And while Jeanne had been on the other side of the fence when she was possessed, undergoing tests to affirm the legitimacy of her possession, its success had also elevated her in the spiritual hierarchy. In several cases, the spiritual authority she claimed, and which was attributed to her, brought her into conflict with male religious figures, whose authority was vouched for more strictly within the traditional institutional hierarchy. The narrators of Jeanne's story emphasised the value and power of her intuition and divine communications over the perceptions of male custodians of authority. What is of especial interest for us here, though, is what these stories reveal about the function of the sacramental side of Catholicism in relation to a woman in authority. For as I have suggested, the sacramental nature of Catholicism relied upon the constant generation of hierarchies, as each claim to divine favour is assessed. Jeanne and her supporters positioned Jeanne herself at the top of such a scale for judging such claims, and then called upon her to evaluate claims of others seeking to ascend it. But because she had been so close to the devil when possessed, when she expressed views unpalatable to the promoters of these new claims, she herself became suspect. The cases we find described in the manuscript collection on Jeanne's life convey a sense of the highly charged and competitive devotional climate that characterised France in the mid-seventeenth century.

In 1653 Jeanne received a letter from her friend and regular correspondent, Mother Du Houx of the Visitation order in Rennes.[154] Du Houx wrote concerning a young nun, an extern, from a convent in Pontivy, who was said to be displaying 'extraordinary dispositions' which suggested she was divinely inspired.[155] The young woman was illiterate, but she had asked someone to write on her behalf to Du Houx.[156] When she saw the woman's letters, Du Houx immediately suspected she was not receiving appropriate spiritual direction, and so wrote to Jeanne. One of the young woman's spiritual directors was Vincent de Meur, a significant figure in the spiritual revival of the time.[157] It was recorded that Du Houx did not let Jeanne know her own feelings on the matter, and only mentioned the extraordinary things she had been told about the young woman. In this way the narrative underlined the role of divine intuition in Jeanne's response.[158]

Jeanne wrote to Du Houx: 'Good Lord! Is there not some mixture of the spirit of darkness with the spirit of light here, and a mixture of strong imagination with true visions.'[159] And she went on to say she that she had severe doubts on the matter, which came through her prayers and communion, doubts which she could not shake off.[160] Du Houx next sent Jeanne details of interrogations of the woman by her directors, and some letters containing a range of opinions from other priests. She also enclosed a cloth tinged with blood from a wound that the young woman had, as well as some little papers marked with white wax, which the woman claimed had been brought to her from heaven.[161] Jeanne again expressed fears about the authenticity of the claims, fears which 'deepened the more she tried to make them go away'. And she hinted that Du Houx and the woman's director were 'a little too ready' to believe in the woman's claims.[162] She would not make a final declaration, however, and tried to defer to the authority of the director, saying the tests he had made 'appeared sufficient' to have found the truth.[163] In a subsequent letter, she wrote that she saw 'many very doubtful and strange things' in the young woman's letters.[164]

In the end, the narrator tells us, Jeanne 'received . . . true lights'.[165] Revelations came to her on a series of occasions through the period of a novena (a nine-day prayer cycle). On the second day of the novena, as Jeanne was leaving the altar, holding the blood-stained cloth and the marked papers, a voice said inwardly to her 'Take away the work of my enemy from this place, for I want her to belong to me.'[166] And on the fifth day of the novena, a voice said to her: 'The spirit of darkness acts in this soul [but] without great sin'. The voice then urged the need for charity to save the woman from the devil.[167] On the last day of the novena Jeanne consulted her angel, who told her to tell the priest that it was all an illusion, but that the young woman was simple and that she was in the care of God and the Virgin. And hinting that interest in the young woman might diminish if she turned out to be merely deluded, Jeanne's angel urged the director not to abandon her, but to work to save her.[168]

Evidently frustrated by Jeanne's responses, the spiritual director wrote to Jeanne again, this time mentioning another similar case and asking her to ask her angel if that, too, were illusion.[169] Notwithstanding the growing pressure on her to give a positive response, she replied that there were demonic operations in both cases. The account goes on: 'None of the directors of this poor soul (who were of different orders and all very capable persons) gave credence to what the Mother said of her state, thinking the woman to be truly led by the good spirit and really maltreated by Satan, the visible marks of which appeared on her body.'[170] The directors of the young woman let her know ('perhaps unintentionally') that Jeanne was opposed to her claims, leading the woman to become very annoyed and to attempt to gain advantage over Jeanne, by saying that Jeanne was the one who was deceived. The directors also wrote to Fr Saint-Jure, to complain about Jeanne. Over the next two or three years Jeanne was vindicated, however, the devil making his influence more and more obvious, as the woman began to lead a 'very unruly' life. In the end, the woman died, but only after having been 'entirely disabused' of her belief, seven or eight months before her death. Underlining the need in cases like this for spiritual insight such as Jeanne's, the account concludes by suggesting that the devil may have been using his artifices in this case to discredit the woman's directors.[171]

Other cases described in this hagiographical text show Jeanne's insight to have been similarly vindicated. She was sent two holy images that were said to have come from heaven as blessings to a young male novice, who was reputed to have had divine revelations.[172] When Jeanne held the images up with other items for her angel to bless, the angel pointed to the images and said angrily: 'The abuses which are committed are strange', and blessed everything but the two images.[173] This led Jeanne to believe that the young man was under an illusion, and this was later borne out when he left his order. Again a lack of 'light' on the part of his directors had led them, Jeanne believed, to put too much faith in his claims.[174] And in the case of a girl in Rennes who was said to be possessed, Jeanne again prayed for 'true lights'. As a result, the thought came to her that the girl was not possessed, but that the devil had the power of obsession over her, due to her own frailty and ignorance, 'rather than from malice', and that she was in 'more need of charity to assist her soul . . . than of exorcisms'. Jeanne added that the girl needed to be applied to manual work and hinted that she had poor spiritual direction.[175] Again Jeanne was proven correct in her intuitions when the girl confessed to a jailer, only, however, after having been threatened with a beating and imprisoned by the Archbishop of Rennes. In this case, too, the vulnerability of male spiritual directors was underlined, as was the capacity of a woman to manipulate the visible signs of divine intervention; the writer records that the girl had initially 'fooled the abbé de Montfort, though he was a learned, knowledgeable and experienced man, who exercised much charity towards this poor creature'.[176] One can only picture the reaction of the abbé upon hearing such a diagnosis.

It seems difficult to imagine that there was not a lingering awareness among Jeanne's critics that she had, effectively, sent a man to his death – a likely source of some circumspection. This may be a reason why her possession, and the spiritual authority that came circuitously but certainly as a result of it, were viewed with ambivalence. Even as late as 1661, Jeanne was herself suspected of being susceptible to the devil, and it was charged that the visions of her angel and the holy names on her hands were diabolic illusions.[177] A commission was established in Poitiers to examine her life, habits and 'the extraordinary things that happened within her'.[178] The commission came to nothing, however, as one of its members, a priest, died suddenly, and unconfessed.[179] Jeanne offered to suffer for his soul in purgatory and it is recorded that she suffered terrible pain for a long time, an observation which implicitly shows it was he who was the sinner of the two.[180] With a discomfiting hint of satisfaction, reminiscent of her response when the exorcisms of Surin had proved indispensable, Jeanne noted that the death of the priest 'had given people pause to reflect', and thus re-stated her own claim to divine partisanship.[181]

Conclusions

Charismatic spirituality relies upon manifestations of divine presence in the physical world, and upon the idea that individuals can be chosen to be the repository of divine inspiration. And while institutional hierarchies are by their nature sceptical, it remains that the relationship between these two aspects of Catholicism – between the idea of a spiritual hierarchy and of an institutional hierarchy, in effect – is a symbiotic one: without hierarchical support, charismatic figures remain in obscurity, but without the sustaining signs of arbitrary supernatural power, the Church itself loses spiritual vigour. In seventeenth-century France, the balance was in favour of charismatic religiosity: if ecstatic spirituality had not been widely favoured, it is doubtful that demonic possession would have surfaced as a form of spirituality. As it was, the traditional presence of the devil in the lives of saints and the possibility of the devil being at work behind attempts to lead a Christian life was a fertile tradition within which demonic possession was able to develop. Battles with the devil were a 'routine' part of saintly existence: what possession did was to both heighten the suffering of would-be saints and, as we have seen, remove to a degree the possibility of blame for one's own possession. However, it remains that the devotee must always interrogate her own motives, and to this extent possession retained, even for the victim-possessed, a degree of self-blame, or at least self-doubt. Thus in the lives of the two women we have considered here, their demonic possession was part of their self-inscription as sinners. Charismatic spirituality, for all its connotations of individualism and anti-institutional, even antinomian, tendencies can nonetheless belie a powerful authoritarianism. Indeed, success for saints in this period invariably entailed a capacity to project a punitive attitude to the self onto a larger social canvas, at least in part with the purpose of retaining institutional approval, and partaking of hierarchy. Catholic revival in France in this sense was at once supple and authoritarian. In this type of female charismatic spirituality, the discourse of demonic power facilitates the development of both action and reaction at the same historical moment.

What is traditionally defined as marginal is not always to be found *at* the margins. The body of church hierarchy was penetrated to some extent by a sense of positive excitement and exhilaration at the potential of new paths to salvation and spiritual growth, as well as a need for struggle with the devil and triumph over the world of the flesh. They were part of the same schema. And here I want to explore the argument of Certeau in his important essay, 'Discourse disturbed: the sorcerer's speech'. Certeau argues that the speech of the possessed can be seen as subsisting always outside other (male) discourses, namely medical and theological discourses, which nonetheless induced, defined and sought to contain it.[182] He wrote: 'the treatise of demonology (or the exorcist's interrogations) assigns in advance to the possessed woman the condition and the place of her speech . . . her locus is not that of the discourse of knowledge being held about her'.[183] Certeau noted, for example, that Jeanne des Anges could not have written an account of her possession when she was actually possessed. The speech of the possessed, when the woman takes on the identity of a demon, is typified by a severance between the speaking position 'I' and its human subject. Only afterwards can the possessed speak: 'These are discourses written later, when she objectifies herself by saying, "I used to be, I used to do".'[184] Certeau saw an analogy between the speech of the possessed and that of the mad person within psychiatry, or the utterance of the indigenous person within accounts of the colonising of the New World.

The possessed woman is undoubtedly situated as 'other' in relation to some aspects of demonological discourse: she is a devil for one thing; nonetheless, the possessed, as accuser, also speaks on behalf of the Church, and for a judicial authority which also adjudicates her fate. For this reason, I would suggest, the possessed woman cannot be seen as precisely analogous either to the indigenous person in the New World or to the psychiatric patient. Even if the woman had little or no social value outside of the system the possession gave her, she was poised to be able to secure personal power and an identity through a system which kept an option on exclusion. It was the capacity of some possessed women not only to endorse the power of exorcists, but also to amplify it, and even partake of it, that made their position singular.

Possessed women in this era were familiar with accounts of the lives of female saints and with the possibilities of divine intervention, and their actions were, as I have tried to suggest, interpretable within and largely shaped by martyrological and hagiographical understandings of possession. For that reason, and without diminishing the decisive role of medical and theological discourses of possession, it might be suggested that the discourse of hagiography was an equally powerful one in these cases, giving the possessed an opportunity to make their words their own, to speak in their own interests, as they understood them, within an approved system of meaning. As themselves potential objects of veneration, these women are the insiders. Hagiography, it may be suggested, was a potent narrative device that was a living code for the interpretation of the possibilities, actions and responses of the possessed, and a source of 'real power'. It placed its subject at the centre, or at least as close to the centre as was possible in a tradition where the self has to be set aside.

Beyond this, for both the males and females concerned, there were also strategic reasons for consistently affirming that the speech of the women was still ultimately in the hands of the exorcist, even when all the evidence suggested the contrary. Exorcists were keenly aware of the risks if the devils of the possessed appeared to 'command the exorcist', as Sébastien Michaelis wrote.[185] Thus, representing the speech of possessed women, however much it was their own, always had to be framed within their relationship to their male interlocutors, in order to safeguard the notion of successful exorcism as an act of obedience. Exorcists theoretically controlled the release of utterances by the 'demons', but at the same time, exorcisms occasioned almost unprecedented belief in the supposed utterances of the devil. The exorcism of the possessed thus both bore witness to the authoritarianism of French reform, as well as typifying its permissiveness, in relation to women as well as demons.

Demonic power and witchcraft were concepts fundamental to the spiritual quest of Marie des Vallées and Jeanne des Anges. These volatile discourses provided means at once potent and fragile of climbing the spiritual ladder of Catholic renewal in France, providing as they did a wide range of agonistic metaphors that were well suited to spiritual warfare: torture and persecution by witches and demons, divine consignment to suffering in an internal hell, paralysing self-doubt. What makes this kind of demonology such a powerful discourse? As contemporaries were deeply aware – and as Stuart Clark has underlined – there is no Christian moral universe without the notion of demonic power, but there is also the possibility that there will be no meaning at all, if that power is present in excess.[186] Demonic power is necessarily both central and peripheral to Christian discourse: it defines the moral universe, but the purpose of the very same discourse is to expel it. The devil's absence from mainstream discourse is only ever provisional. And so, in a way, mixed responses to people such as Marie des Vallées and Jeanne des Anges, who used the discourse of demonic power to great effect, are an expression of the ambivalence about the place of the devil at the heart of Christian discourse. It is a fundamental tension that is difficult to expunge. And in a century marked by apocalyptic anxieties and fears about the power of the devil in the world, the vexed situation of demonic power at both the centre and the periphery of Christian discourse became insupportable to some, but equally, invigorating to others. Adepts mobilised the discourse of demonic power in a way which challenged actively the nature of the hierarchy and possibly the very identity of the Catholic church. Precisely what constituted legitimate church hierarchy in France was highly dispersed and highly contested in this time of consolidation after the Wars of Religion: the spiritual hierarchy and the institutional hierarchy were not necessarily easy to differentiate, particularly as the new religious orders established their own institutional bases, and claims of mystical experiences found receptive listeners in high places. Charismatic figures, and especially the saintly possessed, posed this problem forcefully, by challenging those who held more traditional views to prove that they represented the true church.

Conclusion

This book began with an excerpt from a letter by Thomas Killigrew describing the violent exorcisms at Loudun in 1635. The use of this letter as evidence in an Australian courtroom in the late twentieth century demonstrates the fallacy of assuming that belief in the reality of possession and the efficacy of exorcism have been 'superseded' by more 'rational' beliefs, and of assuming that belief in possession and exorcism is confined to the realm of the uneducated and to the fringes of western Christianity. By considering the history of possession in early modern France, this book has established a number of arguments as to why these assumptions did not apply even to that historical period, in a society where the view that possession and exorcism were the domain of fools already had some currency. On the basis of our understanding of seventeenth-century possession, it is my claim that the presentation of Killigrew's letter as evidence in an exorcism-manslaughter trial in a modern secular court is not to be marvelled at, and the examples we have examined make it possible to say why. More broadly, I am arguing that if analysing the past can help us to see or to consider things about the present which might otherwise have passed without comment, or be assumed to be already fully understood, then the value of opening up a historical moment is demonstrated.

Possession and exorcism were in one sense marginal in the early modern era: they appealed to sensibilities which might seem to be at odds with a religion whose central tenets are altruism and denial of the flesh rather than its apparent celebration. And they seem never to have ceased to shock. They were nonetheless central in that they reflected preoccupations which cannot be eradicated from Catholicism without undermining some of its central doctrines, and abandoning biblical and historical examples. Thus I have argued that exorcism in early modern France was a licit rite enthusiastically deployed by elite religious figures, that exorcism and possession became respectable, and that their history in this period does not therefore trace a growing maturity of learned or popular attitudes in the face of bizarre and atavistic abuses. Rather we learn that educated people, exposed to scepticism, nevertheless endorsed exorcism: Sébastien Michaelis, grew 'into' rather than 'out of' belief in the practice. To be sure, some commentators saw the lengths to which these cases were going, and took a more sceptical stance. But this was more a question of a change of emphasis than a change in basic beliefs. The only Catholic sceptic regarding exorcism who is known to have renounced the Church was a Minim friar, Claude Pithoys, who wrote against the possession of Elisabeth de Ranfaing.

As we have seen, the status of exorcism was related to questions of social stratification. The spiritualising tendencies of the era made elites sympathetic to a view of possession that emphasised the suffering caused by the devil in those who wanted to participate in religious life, while exorcists sought patronage in the form of letters of support from officials and approval by theologians. They also sought audience participation and wrote promotional literature. Notwithstanding this support from elites, opponents of exorcism attempted to associate the rite rhetorically with 'the vulgar'. Supporters, too, sought to distance their motivations, rhetorically and in fact, from the 'vulgar' audience, while relying upon that same audience to attract attention to the rite.

While exorcism aroused suspicion and controversy, very few debates about possession were purely theological. Theologians expressed a wide variety of views, which were often affected by the precise political and strategic circumstances in which they arose. But seeing the political benefits of a case of possession is not identical to disbelieving the reality of it: we cannot assume that just because a powerful political figure such as Cardinal Richelieu saw the political advantages for the crown of the possession at Loudun, he did not believe that the possessions might be real. Catholic tradition allowed for both enthusiasm and scepticism, and the argument of this book has been that a tradition of this kind, whose sources of authority date back so far and are so readily placed at odds with each other, does not yield to simple models of progress. In that sense, we must acknowledge that tradition, so powerful rhetorically, is a contentious rather than a reliable source of authority.

The book has also invited discussion about images of Catholic reform in the early modern period. One might assume that reform would inevitably imply a move away from a focus on the physical aspects of the religion towards more consciously intellectual and metaphysical versions of holiness. However, the examples we have seen point to the need for greater differentiation in our understanding of the meaning of Catholic reform in the early modern era. The complex role played by demonology in reform and in revival suggests that there is no uncomplicated or consistent meaning of the word 'reform' in this era. There is no sense that sober reform, on the one hand, and charismatic revival, on the other, for example, were two parallel streams with essentially one goal; rather, these two streams overlapped and at times conflicted around possession cases. Thus exorcism worked both as a centrifugal force and as a centralising one: it supported claims of authority within the Church and the authority *of* the Church, but it was nevertheless able to undermine Church authority and institutional cohesion.

In designating something like a 'will to hierarchy' or a hierarchical imperative in relation to the phenomena of possession and exorcism, the book has sought to find a framework for institutional responses to the sacramental aspects of a religion that was suspicious of their value. This, in essence, has been my argument about the tensions within Catholicism as a sacramental religion. Belief in the reality of the devil and his powers is fundamental to Christianity, as is belief in the power of exorcism. A sense of the urgency of the need for a struggle with the devil, and triumph over the world of the flesh, affected both those who embraced and those who were sceptical of exorcism as a practice. Tension over the place of the devil in Christianity points to tensions between the theological notion of Christ's message – to reject the devil – against the historicity of the 'Christian story', which includes accounts of Christ's and the saints' dealings with demons.[1]

By the end of the seventeenth century, public exorcism had 'retired' to inhabit territories more strictly identified as 'scandalous', and to take place in relatively localised outbreaks. This shift of possession away from the forefront of religious practice and debate has not been explored in detail, but the change in the profile and agendas of possession cases can be associated with the end of religious wars, the decline in witch hunting, and a retreat from a mystic and affective spirituality which exploited the potential of demonological discourse. (Nonetheless, the cults of Marie des Vallées and Elisabeth de Ranfaing in Lorraine arguably did not decline out of sight. Both are enjoying a resurgence today, as is exorcism as a rite.) This decline also arguably came about simply as the result of the deaths of the chief sponsors from this era, whose values and enthusiasms infused these practices. There is an argument to be made that this spate of cases was the indulgence of a relatively small number of people in France – that no more than a handful of names can be identified as the prime movers of militant exorcism practice. It remains nonetheless that these promoters drew dozens and probably hundreds of other religious figures into their activities, not to mention thousands of laity who participated as onlookers.

There was, then, no thread of scepticism about possession and exorcism which grew and led irresistibly to a modern state of heightened scepticism in the Church. On the contrary, as we have seen, the most extreme examples of what moderns might see as credulity in cases of possession flourished alongside and in dialectical relationship to a large measure of scepticism – the weight of each depended to some extent on the other. Modern secularist scepticism can mask the fact that scepticism within Christianity was and still is part of a scheme that *sustains* belief in the reality of demons and possession, and the efficacy of exorcism. This observation sits oddly with modern assumptions that belief in demons and possession is something that was purged in the wake of the rise of a more 'rational' religion. Because our own age is steeped in this self-image of rationalism and secularism – in spite of clear countervailing evidence – it seems necessary to state firmly that it was never a foregone conclusion in the early modern era in France that the voices of opposition to exorcism practices would prevail. Indeed, there is very little evidence to show that they did. To imagine that the process of marginalisation was somehow inevitable would be to presume something about the twentieth and twenty-first centuries which cannot be proven, and something about the history of Catholicism which also cannot be proven. The equivocation we saw among theologians in the early seventeenth century points to a set of sometimes competing, sometimes compatible parallel traditions, rather than to a linear progression towards a final, modern rational view. What seems to have happened is that the significance of possession and exorcism declined in France at the elite level. That is all that can be said with certainty. The model I have developed does not imply that Christian tradition makes anything possible at any time, but it does support a view of Christian history as something whose meaning for believers is above all moral, and only adventitiously sequential.

The debates about possession and exorcism in early modern France were part of debates between churches, as well as within them. Since the schism of the sixteenth century, western Christianity has been in a state of free fall and fission: as each element of theology or practice has become marginalised in the actions of one section of an institution, the possibility of creating a new church or a new branch of that church has arisen. In recent years, non-mainstream Christian groups have increasingly used exorcism as part of their way of Christian conduct and ritual. Possession and the rite of exorcism also appear to be on the rise in the mainstream Christian churches, or in sectors of them, partly as a response to the fact that revivalist churches are rapidly increasing their reach and congregations. The Catholic and other 'mainstream' churches are also responding to calls for greater responsiveness at pastoral level, possibly to retain those believers in search of more spectacular and more affective modes of religiosity. Secular leaders are less likely now to seek a 'photo opportunity' alongside an exorcist in the way that some secular figures of authority sought to associate themselves publicly with leading practitioners in the early modern era. However, it remains that such a vision is perhaps not as far away as one might imagine.

For early modern Catholicism, the reality of possession and exorcism was endorsed along primarily social lines, with the support of the elite. A similar case can be made for the way in which exorcism was defended in the trial following the death of Joan Vollmer in 1993. Killigrew's description of events at Loudun was used because the defence sought to argue, in essence, that Joan Vollmer was not 'herself'; that her struggle to be freed of her four lay exorcist captors was a violent manifestation of demonic possession – not human action – that could legitimately be met with force. In this case, the force proved to be lethal. The fact that the exorcisms of Loudun were both violent and licit was the reason they were invoked: as part of a claim that physical aggression could be a legitimate element of church ritual. Significantly, in the Vollmer case, a Catholic vicar-general appeared for the prosecution and repudiated the ultimately fatal form of exorcism performed on Joan Vollmer. But the defence were able nonetheless to recruit the services of a rural Catholic priest whose testimony was used to defend (up to a point) the actions of the assailants. This example indicates an ongoing openness and tension in the Catholic church regarding the practice of exorcism. The secular court also allowed for the possibility of possession being real, because, it seems, the prosecution and the judge did not wish to risk a mistrial, or that the jury be alienated. This was exploited by a defence barrister who put the case that if it were possible to be possessed, then his client's conduct could be legitimate. Paradoxically, the preparedness of a modern, pluralist court to leave open the possibility of demonic possession allowed the defence to affirm the legitimacy of the 'exorcists" actions. Fringe was suddenly mainstream.

Meanwhile, the Catholic church in Italy has been subject to debate over exorcism: in response to an ongoing cult in Milan associated with exorcisms performed by a bishop, the Church issued its first guidelines on exorcism since the *Rituale Romanum* of 1614. The principal aim was to deter priests from too readily ascribing a diagnosis of possession to those who sought their aid. A year later, newspapers proclaimed that the pope had performed an exorcism. Subsequent Vatican reports denied that this was so.[2] These developments seem to suggest that the Church is still struggling with the implications of its own doctrinal precedents.

The argument of this book has been that because the line between mainstream and fringe cannot be assumed for any historical era, such a division cannot be said to exist other than as a rhetorical construct. For the early modern period, I have sketched the system of authority whereby the uses of exorcism expanded, and the fringe became mainstream. I also argue that the mainstream is implicated in beliefs about possession and exorcism. That is not to say that all Christians are implicated as individuals in all the behaviours others have undertaken in the name of Christianity, nor that abuse has not been actively resisted. Nor has the book sought to promote a thinly veiled secularist position. It has nothing to say about the promises of the life of the spirit, nor about the worth of Christ's message, nor even about the benefits of collective belief. But if the question is, 'how could this happen', relating both to the early modern period and to the Vollmer case, I have offered some guides to an answer.

It is arguable that Christianity has sought to distance itself from the fact of the devil in its history and it is even possibly the case that it has survived at the elite level for having been, in a sense, delivered of its demons. The past three hundred years have seen the growing ascendancy of intellectualist religion, of a distancing from the physical world, and hence – to some extent – from the less educated classes. But there is no reason to see this as a one-way process. Before assuming that the 'rise of science' is something intrinsically antipathetic to certain types of religious attitudes – intense belief in the devil, for example, or biblical fundamentalism – it is worth bearing in mind that science can now be used in a relativist, even post-modern way in order to support just such religious beliefs. So-called 'scientific creationists' invoke a form of radical doubt in order to question the scientific bases of evolutionary theory. In the same legal trial which used the Loudun exorcism as a precedent, an Assembly of God bible college lecturer with a Cambridge Ph.D. in aeronautical engineering defended belief in the reality of demonic possession and exorcism by arguing at some length that we now live in a 'post-scientific age' where 'religious reasons' can compete on equal terms with scientific ones.

I found it remarkable that the Killigrew letter was unearthed in 1993 like a magic charm to defend violent exorcism, and the fact of its use to validate extreme exorcist practice has enabled me to re-think the cases which were the subject of my initial study. It is my hope that by now the reader understands why possession and exorcism can be part of an intellectually sophisticated society, and crucially, can accept that educated people exposed to sceptical views can still hold to belief in the reality of demonic exorcism.

Notes

Introduction

1 Killigrew lived from 1612 to 1683. Alfred Harbage, *Thomas Killigrew, Cavalier Dramatist* (New York: Benjamin Blom, 1930). On the modern case, see Sarah Ferber and Adrian Howe, 'The man who mistook his wife for a devil: exorcism, expertise and secularisation in a late twentieth-century Australian criminal court', in Hans de Waardt, Jürgen Michael Schmidt and Dieter Bauer (eds), in co-operation with Sönke Lorenz and H.C. Erik Midelfort, *Dämonische Besessenheit. Zur Interpretation eines kulturhistorischen Phänomens/Demonic Possession. Interpretations of a Historico-Cultural Phenomenon* (Hexenforschung 9) (Bielefeld: Verlag für Regionalgeschichte, 2003), 299–312. Spiritual tourism of this kind was not uncommon: Michel de Montaigne saw a (similarly violent) exorcism on his visit to Rome. See his *Journal de voyage en Italie par la Suisse et l'Allemagne en 1580 et 1581*, Charles Dédéyan (ed.) (Paris: Société des Belles Lettres, 1946), pp. 219–21.

2 J. Lough and D.E.L. Crane, 'Thomas Killigrew and the possessed nuns of Loudun: the text of a letter of 1635', *Durham University Journal*, vol. 78, no. 2, (1986), 259–68, at pp. 262–4. Throughout, for English and French, I have modernised spelling when the letter 'v' has been used instead of 'u', or vice versa, or the letter 'j' instead of 'i', or vice versa. Accents have not been altered from the original.

3 D.P. Walker, *Unclean Spirits: possession and exorcism in France and England in the late sixteenth and early seventeenth centuries*, (London: Scolar Press, 1981), p. 4. Walker's innovative survey provided an elegant and suggestive guide for future research. The numerous other scholarly and intellectual debts incurred in researching and writing on this topic will be clear to specialists. Two foundational works on French possession deserve special mention: Robert Mandrou, *Magistrats et sorciers en France au XVIIe siècle: une analyse de psychologie historique* (1968) (Paris: Seuil, 1980), is the early and defining work on this subject which argued that possession scandals had a powerful influence on French elites' attitudes to witch-hunting; Michel de Certeau, *The Possession at Loudun* (1970) (trans. Michael B. Smith, with a foreword by Stephen Greenblatt; Chicago, Ill. and London: University of Chicago Press, 2000), is a magisterial meditation on a collection of texts from one case. Other essential contributions to the understanding of possession, exorcism and Catholic sacramentals are cited here in order of publication: Peter Brown, *Relics and Social Status in the Age of Gregory of Tours* (Reading: University of Reading, 1977); David Mark Jones, 'Exorcism before the Reformation: the problems of saying one thing and meaning another' (MA thesis, University of Virginia, 1978); Marc Venard, 'Le démon controversiste', in Michel Peronnet (ed.), *La controverse religieuse (XVIe–XIXe siècles)*, 2 vols, (Montpellier: Université Paul Valéry, 1980), vol. 2, 45–60; H.C. Erik Midelfort, 'Madness and the problems of psychological history in the sixteenth

century', *Sixteenth Century Journal*, vol. 12, no. 1 (1981), 5–12; Mary R. O'Neil, 'Discerning superstition: popular errors and orthodox response in late sixteenth-century Italy', Ph.D. dissertation, Stanford University, 1982; D.P. Walker, *Unclean Spirits*; Henri Weber, 'L'exorcisme à la fin du XVIe siècle, instrument de la contre-reforme et spectacle baroque', *Nouvelle revue du XVI siècle*, no. 1, (1983), 79–101; Robert W. Scribner, 'Ritual and popular religion in Catholic Germany at the time of the Reformation', *Journal of Ecclesiastical History*, vol. 35, no. 1, January (1984), 47–77 (republished in his *Popular Culture and Popular Movements in Reformation Germany*, London: Hambledon Press, 1987, 17–47); Bodo Nischan, 'The exorcism controversy and baptism in the late reformation', *Sixteenth Century Journal*, vol. 18, no. 1 (1987), 31–51; Giovanni Levi, *Inheriting Power: the story of an exorcist*, trans. Lydia G. Cochrane (Chicago, Ill.: University of Chicago Press, 1988); H.C. Erik Midelfort, 'The devil and the German people: reflections on the popularity of demon possession in sixteenth-century Germany' (1989), in *Articles on Witchcraft, Magic and Demonology*, vol. 9, 'Possession and exorcism', edited and with an introduction by Brian P. Levack (New York and London: Garland, 1992), 113–33; Lyndal Roper, 'Exorcism and the theology of the body' (1991), in *Oedipus and the Devil: witchcraft, sexuality and religion in early modern Europe* (London: Routledge, 1994), 171–98; Michael MacDonald (ed.), *Witchcraft and Hysteria in Elizabethan London: Edward Jorden and the Mary Glover case*, with an introduction by Michael MacDonald (London and New York: Tavistock/Routledge, 1991); Alison Weber, 'Between ecstasy and exorcism: religious negotiation in sixteenth-century Spain', *Journal of Medieval and Renaissance Studies*, (1993), vol. 23, no. 2, 221–34. Irena Backus, *Le Miracle de Laon: le déraisonnable, le raisonnable, l'apocalyptique et le politique dans les récits du miracle de Laon (1566–1578)* (Paris: Vrin, 1994); Robin Briggs, *Witches and Neighbours: the social and cultural context of European witchcraft* (London: Fontana Press, 1996); Anita M. Walker and Edmund H. Dickerman, 'Magdeleine Des Aymards: demonism or child abuse in early modern France?', *Psychohistory Review*, vol. 24, no. 3 (1996), 239–64; Stuart Clark, *Thinking with Demons: the idea of witchcraft in early modern Europe* (Oxford: Oxford University Press, 1997); Denis Crouzet, 'A woman and the Devil: possession and exorcism in sixteenth-century France', trans. Michael Wolfe, in Michael Wolfe (ed.), *Changing Identities in Early Modern France*, with a foreword by Natalie Zemon Davis (Durham, N.C.: Duke University Press, 1997), 191–215; Barbara Newman, 'Possessed by the spirit: devout women, demoniacs, and the apostolic life in the thirteenth century', *Speculum*, no. 73, 1998, 733–70; Jonathan L. Pearl, *The Crime of Crimes: demonology and politics in France, 1560–1620* (Waterloo, Ontario: Wilfred Laurier University Press, 1999); James Sharpe, *The Bewitching of Anne Gunter: a horrible and true story of football, witchcraft, murder, and the King of England*, (London: Profile Books, 1999) and Walter Stephens, *Demon Lovers: witchcraft, sex and crisis of belief* (Chicago, Ill. and London: University of Chicago Press, 2002). The pre-eminent work for witch trials in France is Alfred Soman, *Sorcellerie et justice criminelle: le Parlement de Paris (16e–18e siècles)*, (Hampshire and Brookfield: Varorium, 1992). For Francophone territories see E. William Monter, *Witchcraft in France and Switzerland: the borderlands during the Reformation*, (Ithaca, N.Y.: Cornell University Press, 1977) and Briggs, *Witches and Neigbours*. The present work relies on printed and manuscript accounts. The existence of major studies on each of several French cases make an exhaustive study unnecessary, and the range and depth of sources make it almost impossible. I have canvassed what I believe is a sufficient sample to make the book's claims sustainable.

4 Ferber and Howe, 'The man who mistook his wife for a devil'.

5 Natalie Zemon Davis, 'The rites of violence', in *Society and Culture in Early Modern France: eight essays* (Stanford, Calif.: Stanford University Press, 1975), 152–87, at p. 186.

6 Davis, 'The rites of violence'; Crouzet, 'A woman and the Devil'; Barbara B. Diefendorf, *Beneath the Cross: Catholics and Huguenots in sixteenth-century Paris* (Oxford and New York: Oxford University Press, 1991).

7 The notion of the devil as one evil spirit derives from the Old Testament idea of Satan, God's single, most powerful, adversary. References to 'the devil' (definite article, sometimes capitalised) are usually taken to mean this singular figure, and his lackeys referred to either as devils or demons. In the texts we shall be considering the words 'devil' and 'demon' were frequently used interchangeably. The names for individual demons could derive from those of pre-Christian demons, monsters and gods, such as Beelzebub, Asmodeus, Astaroth, Behemoth, Baalberith, and Leviathan. Karel van der Toorn, Bob Becking, Pieter W. van der Horst (eds), *Dictionary of Deities and Demons in the Bible* (Leiden: E.J. Brill, 1995), columns 293–6; 197–200; 189; 315–22; 266–72; 956–64 (for each of the preceding respectively). Other names could simply resemble French pet-names, and 'names' also emerged from the mouths of the possessed as total gibberish. The devils of Denise de la Caille in Beauvais in 1623 declared their names to include Brissilolo, Milola, Sililolo, Cyria, Silala, Brisola and 'eighteen other less singular names', leading the notary taking them down 'to want to tear his papers with his teeth'. *Histoire veritable arrivee de nostre temps en la ville de Beauvais touchant les conjurations et exorcismes faicts à Denise de la Caille, possedée du Diable* (Paris: Pierre Billaine, 1623), p. 4.

8 See Roper, 'Exorcism and the theology of the body' in *Oedipus and the Devil*.

9 Matthew 10:1 and 8; Mark 6:7; 16:17; Luke 9:1; 10:17.

10 The exact number of major possession cases in France is difficult to state, as criteria for significance vary. Between 1550 and 1690 many more or less well-publicised cases arose: at Laon (1566); Soissons (1578); Berry (1582–3); Annonay (1581); Rouergue (1597); Louviers (1591); Paris (1599); Aix-en-Provence (1609–11); Agen (1619); Beauvais (1623); Loudun (1630s); Chinon (1634–40); Louviers (1642–7); Coutances (1613–56); Auxonne (1662) and Toulouse (1682). There were also countless minor possessions, some referred to only in passing, as well as related cases in the French-speaking Low Countries and the Duchy of Lorraine. In all, hundreds of manuscripts documented these cases and over a hundred printed works were produced. See index and later chapters for further references, and Mandrou, *Magistrats et sorciers*, for the best single survey, which has been nonetheless added to by later research.

11 The centrality of eschatology in contemporary understandings of possession and exorcism is underscored in Backus, *Le Miracle de Laon*, Clark, *Thinking with Demons*, Part III and Crouzet, 'A woman and the Devil'. It is very likely that outbreaks of possession and some instances of witchcraft could be identified with sources of personal and social stress. Michel de Certeau alerted his readers to the presence of plague in Loudun in the 1630s, for example, seeing it as both a metaphor of possession and a contemporaneous instance of social dislocation. Lyndal Roper identified the witchcraft of Regine Bartholome in the context of fraught personal relations ('Oedipus and the Devil', in *Oedipus and the Devil*, 226–48), a commentary glossed in turn by Walker and Dickerman ('Magdeleine des Aymards' pp. 258–60). Their article located the source of a witchcraft self-accusation in the context of perceived sexual abuse, a factor they also identified in relation to the possession of Françoise Fontaine, who had been raped by soldiers in the Wars of Religion (Anita M. Walker and Edmund H. Dickerman, 'The haunted girl: possession, witchcraft and healing in sixteenth-century Louviers', *Proceedings of the Annual Meeting of the Western Society for French History*, vol. 23 (1996), 207–18). The hagiographical writings on Marie des Vallées and the possessed Lorraine widow Elisabeth de Ranfaing also seem to point to a background of family violence, yet such an observation is nonetheless clouded by the typically agonistic contours (and hence limitations) of the genre of hagiography. Grief also seems a factor: the stories of Nicole Obry, the nuns of Loudun and the nuns

of Louviers (see Chapters 2, 6 and 8) relate directly to the death of significant figures, a grandfather and two recently deceased spiritual directors, respectively. And the constricted lifestyle of convents as a more or less ongoing source of stress also either triggered belief in real possession or created sufficient personal and interpersonal pressures to make fraud or intense self-persuasion more likely. However, isolating such instances and contexts does not imply that any similar events in a Catholic culture will necessarily result in an outbreak of possession, nor does the absence of such events imply the impossibility of an outbreak of possession. Possession, put simply, is no more reducible to mono-causal explanations than any other kind of event. Yet one seems led, instinctively, to accept possession as likely to be related to dramatic or tragic life circumstances, while acknowledging that the discourse of possession itself, with its own distinctive and multifaceted history, bears with it a violence and potential for disruption that can feed into, as well as draw nourishment from, psychic dislocation.

12 Denis Crouzet, *Les guerriers de Dieu: la violence au temps des troubles de religion*, 2 vols (Seyssel: Champ Vallon, 1990), vol. 1, p. 45.

13 Mack P. Holt, *The French Wars of Religion, 1562–1629* (Cambridge, New York, Melbourne: Cambridge University Press, 1995), pp. 18–21; Robin Briggs, *Early Modern France, 1560–1715* (Oxford: Oxford University Press, 1977). The French Catholic term for Calvinism was the 'supposedly reformed religion' ('religion prétendue reformée', or RPR).

14 Barbara B. Diefendorf, *Beneath the Cross*, pp. 38–48.

15 See Richard H. Popkin, *The History of Scepticism from Erasmus to Descartes*, rev. edn (New York: Harper and Row, 1968). On Obry and Brossier, see also Carleton Cunningham, 'The Devil and religious controversies of sixteenth-century France', in *Essays in History* (published under the auspices of The Corcoran Department of History, University of Virginia, Charlottesville), vol. 35 (1993), 33–47.

16 Jean Bodin, *De la demonomanie des sorciers*, rev. edn (Paris: Jacques du Puys, 1587); Nicholas Rémy, *Demonolatry* (1595), trans. E. Allen Ashwin, edited and with an introduction by Montague Summers (Secaucus, N.J.: University Books), 1974; Henri Boguet, *An Examen of Witches* [*Discours execrable des sorciers*, 1602 edition], trans. E. Allen Ashwin, ed. Montague Summers (John Rodker: London, 1929); Pierre de Lancre, *Tableau de l'inconstance des mauvais anges et démons où il est amplement traité des sorciers et de la sorcellerie* (1612), critical introduction and notes by Nicole Jacques-Chaquin, Collection Palimpseste (Paris: Aubier, 1982). Cf. the work of the influential Belgian Jesuit Martín Del Rio, *Disquisitionum magicarum libri sex* (Louvain: Gérard Rivière, 1599–1600).

17 Gabriella Zarri, *Le sante vive: cultura e religiosità femminile nella prima età moderna* (Turin: Rosenberg and Sellier, 1990).

18 John Cruickshank, 'The Acarie circle', in *Seventeenth-Century French Studies*, vol. 16, (1994), 48–58; William M. Thompson (ed.), *Bérulle and the French School: selected writings* (New York and Mahwah, N.J.: Paulist Press, 1989).

19 Jacques Le Brun, 'Mutations de la notion de martyre au XVIIe siècle d'après les biographies spirituelles feminines', in Jacques Marx (ed.), *Sainteté et martyre dans les religions du livre* (Brussels: Institut d'Études des Religions et de la Laïcité, 1989), 77–96. My thanks are due to Albrecht Burkardt for kindly providing this reference.

20 R. Po-chia Hsia, *The World of Catholic Renewal, 1540–1770* (Cambridge and New York: Cambridge University Press, 1998), Chapter 9, 'Holy women, beatas, demoniacs'.

21 The term is Alison Weber's.

22 Beyond this paradox of material manifestations of spiritual forces, François Le Brun draws attention to a range of other characteristic contradictions within Catholicism. Speaking of the contradiction between personal religion and communal religion, he states: 'This contradiction lies at the heart of Christianity, along with that between

contemplation and action and between the Church as institution and the Church as mystical body'. 'The two reformations: communal devotion and personal piety', in *A History of Private Life*, Vol. III, *Passions of the Renaissance*, trans. Arthur Goldhammer, ed. Roger Chartier, (Cambridge, Mass.: Harvard University Press, [1989]), p. 69.

23 Ann W. Ramsey, *Liturgy, Politics, and Salvation: the Catholic League in Paris and the nature of Catholic reform, 1540–1630* (Rochester, N.Y.: University of Rochester Press, 1999), p. 4.

24 'Of the nature of, relating to, or expressed by, an outward sign or symbol', *Shorter Oxford English Dictionary*. This definition could nonetheless also apply to language, as a student, Liz White, pointed out to me.

25 Alison Weber, 'Demonizing ecstasy: Alonso de la Fuente and the Alumbrados of Extremadura', in Robert Boenig (ed.) *The Mystical Gesture: essays on medieval and early modern spiritual culture in honor of Mary C. Giles*, (Brookfield, Vermont: Ashgate Press, 2000), pp. 143, 158. A clear analysis of the system of Catholic sacramentals is found in Scribner, 'Ritual and popular religion'; Lyndal Roper situates possession and exorcism within a broader analysis of Protestant and Catholic attitudes to the body and the material world. 'Exorcism and the theology of the body', *Oedipus and the Devil*.

26 Jean de Viguerie, *Notre Dame des Ardilliers à Saumur: le pèlerinage de Loire* (Paris: O.E.I.L, 1986), p. 17. Except where noted, all translations are mine.

27 Clark, *Thinking with Demons*, pp. 474–9.

28 Two classic late-medieval texts on the so-called 'discernment of spirits' by the reformist theologian Jean Gerson may be found in *The Concept of* Discretio Spirituum *in John Gerson's* 'De Probatione Spirituum' *and* 'De Distinctione Verarum Visionum A Falsis', trans. and ed. Paschal Boland (Washington: Catholic University of America Press, 1959). See also M. Viller *et al.* 'Discernement des esprits' in *Dictionnaire de spiritualité, ascétique et mystique: doctrine et histoire* (Paris: Beauchesne, 1937–95, vol. 3, cols 1222–91); Jean-Michel Sallmann, 'Théorie et pratiques du discernement des esprits', in *Visions indiennes, visions baroques: les métissages de l'inconscient* (Paris: PUF, 1992), 91–116; Christian Renoux, 'Discerner la sainteté des mystiques: quelques exemples italiens de l'âge baroque', *Rives nord-méditerranéennes*, 2e série, no. 3 (1999), 19–28; Alison Weber, 'Spiritual administration: gender and discernment in the Carmelite reform', *Sixteenth Century Journal*, vol. 31, no. 1, (2000), 123–46.

29 For a discussion of the ways in which social hierarchy and the hierarchy of holy objects interacted in the time of Gregory of Tours, see Peter Brown, *Relics and Social Status*.

30 Roy Porter, 'Witchcraft and magic in Enlightenment, romantic and liberal thought', in Marijke Gijswijt-Hofstra, Brian P. Levack and Roy Porter, *The Athlone History of Witchcraft and Magic in Europe: The eighteenth and nineteenth centuries*, v. 5, general editors, Bengt Ankarloo and Stuart Clark, (London: Athlone Press, 1999), 191–282, p. 213. Denis Crouzet, 'A woman and the Devil', p. 191. Fernando Cervantes argues that early modern demonology shows a shift in the very identity of the Christian God, to a more punitive version. 'The devils of Querétaro: scepticism and credulity in late seventeenth-century Mexico', *Past and Present*, no. 130 (1991), 51–69.

1 Scepticism and Catholic reform

1 [Ciruelo, Pedro], *Pedro Ciruelo's A Treatise Reproving all Superstitions and Forms of Witchcraft: Very Necessary and Useful for all Good Christians Zealous for Their Salvation* (c. 1530), trans. Eugene A. Maio and D'Orsay W. Pearson, annotated and with an introduction by D'Orsay W. Pearson (Cranbury, N.J. and London: Associated University Presses, 1977), p. 266. (Cited hereafter as Ciruelo, *Treatise Reproving all Superstitions*.) Mary R. O'Neil discusses the problems of exorcism in 'Discerning superstition: popular errors and orthodox response in late sixteenth-century Italy', Ph.D. dissertation, Stanford University, 1982, especially Chapters 6 and 7.

2   Stuart Clark, *Thinking with Demons: the idea of witchcraft in early modern Europe* (Oxford: Oxford University Press, 1997), p. 390.

3   Richard H. Popkin, *The History of Scepticism from Erasmus to Descartes*, rev. edn (New York: Harper and Row, 1968), p. xiv.

4   See, for example, Ciruelo, *Treatise Reproving all Superstitions*, p. 267, and David H. Darst, 'Witchcraft in Spain: the testimony of Martin De Castañega's treatise on superstition and witchcraft (1520)', *Proceedings of the American Philosophical Society*, vol. 123, no. 5, (1979) 298–322 (cited hereafter as Castañega, 'Treatise on superstition'), at p. 317.

5   Mary R. O'Neil describes the problems generated among the clergy by different levels of theological education in '"Sacerdote ovvero strione": ecclesiastical and superstitious remedies in sixteenth-century Italy', in Steven L. Kaplan (ed.), *Understanding Popular Culture* (Berlin: Mouton, 1984), 53–83.

6   Ciruelo, *Treatise Reproving all Superstitions*, p. 266.

7   Castañega, 'Treatise on superstition', p. 311.

8   Heinrich Krämer (Institoris) and James Sprenger, *Malleus Maleficarum*, trans. with introductions, bibliography and notes by Revd Montague Summers (New York: Dover, 1971), part II, qn 2, ch. 6, p. 181.

9   Krämer and Sprenger, *Malleus Maleficarum*, p. 181.

10 [Bérulle, Pierre de], 'Léon d'Alexis', *Traicté des energumenes, suivy d'un discours sur la possession de Marthe Brossier: contre les calomnies d'un medecin de Paris*, Troyes, no printer, 1599, second section, *Discours*, pp. 19–20. The council was that of 398, <http://www.newadvent.org/cathen/05711a.htm> accessed 03/12/03 'Exorcist'.

11 Ciruelo, *Treatise Reproving all Superstitions*, p. 267. It is important to note that exorcism as adjuration relates to the literal meaning of the word 'exorcise', 'to place on oath'. See D.P. Walter, *Unclean Spirits: possession and exorcism in France and England in the late sixteenth and early seventeenth centuries*, (London: Scolar Press, 1981), p. 6, citing the findings of David Mark Jones, 'Exorcism Before the Reformation: the problems of saying one thing and meaning another', (M.A. Thesis, University of Virginia, 1978).

12 Ciruelo, *Treatise Reproving all Superstitions*, p. 266.

13 Matt. 8.29; Mark 1.24–5; Mark 5.7; Luke 4.34, 41; Luke 8.28.

14 Peter Brown, *Relics and Social Status in the Age of Gregory of Tours* (Reading: University of Reading, 1977), p. 13.

15 A similar view of witchcraft beliefs is elaborated by Walter Stephens, *Demon Lovers: witchcraft, sex and crisis of belief* (Chicago, Ill. and London: University of Chicago Press, 2002).

16 Caesarius von Heisterbach, *The Dialogue on Miracles*, 2 vols, trans. H. von E. Scott and C. Swinton Bland, with an introduction by G.G. Coulton (London: Routledge, 1929), pp. 339–40.

17 The work is 'La tenture de St Etienne', held at Musée du Moyen Age Cluny, Paris, <http://www.musee-moyenage.fr/homes/home_id20754_u1l2.htm> accessed 03/12/03. I thank Katie McConnel for pointing this image out to me.

18 Jacobus de Voragine, *The Golden Legend: readings on the saints*, trans. William Granger Ryan (Princeton, N.J.: Princeton University Press, 1993), vol. 2, p. 42.

19 Ciruelo, *Treatise Reproving all Superstitions*, p. 267. Ciruelo also inveighed against exorcists who claimed a specialist role, when, he said, their powers were no greater than those of any other priest (p. 276).

20 Castañega, 'Treatise on superstition', p. 312.

21 Castañega, 'Treatise on superstition', p. 317.

22 Castañega, 'Treatise on superstition', p. 318.

23 Caesarius of Heisterbach, *The Dialogue on Miracles*, p. 332.

24 Caesarius of Heisterbach, *The Dialogue on Miracles*, p. 359.

25 See also Graham H. Twelftree, *Jesus the Exorcist: a contribution to the study of the historical Jesus* (Tübingen: J.C.B. Mohr (Paul Siebeck), 1993), pp. 98–113.

26 Krämer and Sprenger, *Malleus Maleficarum*, part II, qn 2, ch. 6, pp. 181–2. The 'exorcism' of places to rid them of infestation lies on a continuum with other forms of Catholic blessing and conjuration, and with exorcism of the possessed.

27 Ciruelo, *Treatise Reproving all Superstitions*, p. 270.

28 Desiderius Erasmus, "Exorcism", in *Ten Colloquies*, trans. Craig R. Thompson (New York: Bobbs-Merrill 1957), p. 40.

29 Castañega, 'Treatise on superstition', p. 318. J.A. Jungmann cites the popularity of the Gospel of St John in liturgy and para-liturgy in *The Mass of the Roman Rite*, revised edn, trans. F.A. Brunner (New York: Benziger, 1959) pp. 543–44.

30 Castañega, 'Treatise on superstition', p. 318.

31 See Charles Zika, 'The Devil's hoodwink: seeing and believing in the world of sixteenth-century witchcraft', in Charles Zika (ed.), *No Gods Except Me: orthodoxy and religious practice in Europe, 1200–1600* (Melbourne: Melbourne University History Monographs, no. 14 (1991), 152–98), at p. 188.

32 Another great defender of exorcism was the Jesuit Louis Richeome, also a 'devout humanist'. Jonathan L. Pearl, *The Crime of Crimes: demonology and politics in France, 1560–1620* (Waterloo, Ontario: Wilfred Laurier University Press, 1999), p. 72.

2 'Into the realm of the senses'

1 Jean Boulaese, *Le Thresor et entiere histoire de la triomphante victoire du corps de Dieu sur l'esprit maling Beelzebub, obtenüe a Laon l'an mil cinq cens soixante six* (Paris: Nicolas Chesneau, 1578). This 'treasury', the principal source for the case, reproduces several of the printed accounts and attestations, by Jean Boulaese and others. There is one series of folios, up to fol. 40, which is followed by pages. The contents pages are found at fols 23v to 26v. Modern accounts are: D. P. Walker, *Unclean Spirits: Possession and exorcism in France and England in the late sixteenth and early seventeenth centuries* (London: Scolar Press, 1981) pp. 19–28; Irena Backus, *Le Miracle de Laon: le déraisonnable, le raisonnable, l'apocalyptique et le politique dans les récits du miracle de Laon, (1566–1578)* (Paris: Vrin, 1994), an exhaustive study which emphasises the importance of this case for intellectual history; it details all the relevant manuscripts and printed sources for this case at pp. 197–204; Denis Crouzet, 'A woman and the Devil: possession and exorcism in sixteenth-century France', trans. Michael Wolfe, in Michael Wolfe (ed.), *Changing Identities in Early Modern France*, with a foreword by Natalie Zemon Davis (Durham: Duke University Press, 1997), 191–215; and Moshe Sluhovsky, 'A divine apparition or demonic possession? Female agency and church authority in demonic possession in sixteenth-century France', *Sixteenth Century Journal*, vol. 27, no. 4 (1996), 1039–55.

2 Jonathan L. Pearl, *The Crime of Crimes: demonology and politics in France, 1560–1620* (Waterloo, Ontario: Wilfred Laurier University Press, 1999), ch. 3.

3 Jean Boulaese, *Labregee histoire du grand miracle par Nostre Seigneur Jesus Christ en la Saincte Hostie du Sacrement de l'Autel, faict à Laon 1566* (reprinted in Boulaese, *Thresor*), p. 2.

4 Boulaese, *Labregee histoire*, p. 2.

5 Boulaese, *Labregee histoire*, p. 2.

6 Boulaese, *Labregee histoire*, p. 3.

7 See Gabriella Zarri, 'Purgatorio "particolare" e ritorno dei morti tra riforma e controriforma: l'area italiana', *Quaderni Storici*, vol. 17, no. 2 (1982), pp. 466–97, at pp. 488–9; Nancy Caciola, 'Spirits seeking bodies: death, possession and communal memory in the middle ages', in Bruce Gordon and Peter Marshall (eds), *The Place of the Dead: death and remembrance in late medieval and early modern Europe* (Cambridge

and New York: Cambridge University Press, 2000), 66–86; Jean-Claude Schmitt, *Ghosts in the Middle Ages: the living and the dead in medieval society*, trans. Teresa Lavender Fagan (Chicago, Ill.: University of Chicago Press, 1998), pp. 116–21; David Lederer, 'Living with the dead: ghosts in early modern Bavaria', in Kathryn A. Edwards (ed.), *Witches, Werewolves and Wandering Spirits: traditional belief and folklore in early modern Europe*, in *Sixteenth-century Essays and Studies*, vol. 62 (Kirksville: Truman State University Press, 2002), 25–54; also Jean Bodin, *De la demonomanie des sorciers*, rev. edn (Paris: Jacques Du Puy, 1587), fol. 184r; Martín Del Rio, *Disquisitionum magicarum libri sex* (Louvain: Gérard Rivière, 1599–1600), Lib. VI 'Anacephalaeosis', p. 334.

8   Gabriella Zarri, 'Purgatorio "particolare"', pp. 488–9.
9   Boulaese, *Labregee histoire*, p. 3.
10 Boulaese, *Thresor*, p. 64.
11 Irena Backus, *Le Miracle de Laon: le déraisonnable, le raisonnable, l'apocalyptique et le politique*, p. 15.
12 Boulaese, *Labregee histoire*, p. 3.
13 Graham H. Twelftree, *Jesus the Exorcist: a contribution to the study of the historical Jesus* (Tübingen, Germany: J.C.B. Mohr (Paul Siebeck), 1993), passim.
14 See for example Caesarius of Heisterbach, citing Gennadius, in *The Dialogue on Miracles*, 2 vols, trans. H. von E. Scott and C. Swinton Bland, with an introduction by G.G. Coulton (London: Routledge, 1929), p. 335.
15 [Jean Boulaese], *Le Miracle de Laon en Lannoys*, [facsimile in] A.H. Chaubard (ed.) (Lyon: Sauvegarde Historique, 1955), p. 5.
16 Pierre Crespet, *Deux Livres de la hayne de Sathan et malins esprits contre l'homme, & de l'homme contre eux* (Paris: Guillaume de la Noue, 1590), fol. 206v.
17 See, for example, [Pierre Maignart], *Traicté des marques des possedez, et la preuve de la veritable possession des religieuses de Louviers, par P.M. Esc., D. en M* (Rouen: Charles Osmont, 1644), p. 14. Maignart observes that 'Latin authors' do not make a great distinction between the two. Indeed, Latin texts seem to refer only to 'obsession'. See Barbara Newman, 'Possessed by the spirit: devout women, demoniacs, and the apostolic life in the thirteenth century', *Speculum*, no. 73 (1998), pp. 733–70. Thanks are due to Sabina Flanagan for sharing with me her views on the medieval understandings of possession and obsession.
18 Jean Fraikin, 'Un cas de sorcellerie à la fin du XVIe siècle: l'affaire du moine sorcier de Stavelot', *Tradition wallone: revue annuelle de la Commission Royale Belge de Folklore, Mélanges Albert Doppagne*, no. 4, (1987), 251–335.
19 See, for example, Fraikin, 'Un cas de sorcellerie', pp. 321–3.
20 Caesarius von Heisterbach, *The Dialogue on Miracles*, p. 335.
21 Cf. Mark 9:26.
22 Francesco Maria Guazzo, *Compendium Maleficarum: the Montague Summers edition* (1608), trans. E.A. Ashwin (New York: Dover, 1988), pp. 167–9.
23 Congnard, *Histoire de Marthe Brossier pretendue possedee tiree du Latin de Messire Jacques August. de Thou, President au Parlement de Paris. Avec quelques remarques et considerations generales sur cette Matiere, tirées pour la plus part aussi du Latin de Bartholomaeus Perdulcis celebre Medecin de la Faculté de Paris* (Rouen: Jacques Herault, 1652), p. 31.
24 A later report of Obry becoming blind then miraculously cured failed to attract the publicity of the original miracle. See Denis Crouzet, 'A woman and the Devil', p. 210.
25 Jean Boulaese, *Le Manuel de l'admirable victoire du corps de Dieu sur l'esprit maling Beelzebub, obtenuë à Laon 1566*, in Boulaese, *Thresor*, p. 72.
26 Boulaese, *Manuel*, p. 72.
27 See Pearl, *The Crime of Crimes*, and Crouzet, 'A woman and the Devil', pp. 196–7.
28 Backus, *Le Miracle de Laon: le déraisonnable, le raisonnable, l'apocalyptique et le politique*, p. 15.

29 Backus, *Le Miracle de Laon: le déraisonnable, le raisonnable, l'apocalyptique et le politique*, p. 15.

30 Boulaese, *Thresor*, fol. 29v. Edward Muir, *Ritual in Early Modern Europe* (Cambridge and New York: Cambridge University Press, 1997), p. 21. Though not strictly possessed, the catechumen was held to be in the devil's snare, until entering the Christian community through the sacrament of baptism.

31 [Boulaese], *Le Miracle de Laon en Lannoys*, p. 6.

32 [Boulaese], *Le Miracle de Laon en Lannoys*, p. 6.

33 [Boulaese], *Le Miracle de Laon en Lannoys*, p. 6.

34 Backus, *Le Miracle de Laon: le déraisonnable, le raisonnable, l'apocalyptique et le politique*, p. 16.

35 Boulaese, *Thresor*, pp. 118–31; Mark 5:1–20.

36 'Declaration des lettres de l'Alphabet', key to the contemporary engraving by Thomas Belot, showing the miracle action by action, in Chaubard edition of [Boulaese], *Miracle de Laon en Lannoys* (unpaginated). Elsewhere Beelzebub is referred to by his more common identifier, the 'Lord of the Flies', *Thresor*, 30v.

37 Crouzet, 'A woman and the Devil', p. 196.

38 Jean Bodin, *De la demonomanie des sorciers*, fols 84r, 175v. I thank Jürgen Beyer for pointing out this case to me.

39 [Boulaese], *Le Miracle de Laon en Lannoys*, p. 6.

40 H.C. Erik Midelfort, 'The Devil and the German people: reflections on the popularity of demon possession in sixteenth-century Germany', *Articles on Witchcraft, Magic and Demonology*, vol. 9, 'Possession and Exorcism', edited and with an introduction by Brian P. Levack (New York and London: Garland, 1992), 113–33, at p. 127.

41 Backus, *Le Miracle de Laon: le déraisonnable, le raisonnable, l'apocalyptique et le politique*, p. 18.

42 Recall here that the devil can correctly identify divine things, but that it is also typical for him to distort them, however slightly, in this case as signal of his rebellion, but often to mislead the faithful.

43 'Declaration des lettres de l'Alphabet'.

44 Walker, *Unclean Spirits*, p. 28.

45 Midelfort, 'The Devil and the German people', p. 118; Guillaume Postel, *De Summopere*, critical edition, translation and notes by Irena Backus (Geneva: Droz, 1995), p. xiii.

46 [Boulaese], *Le Miracle de Laon en Lannoys*, p. 6.

47 [Boulaese], *Le Miracle de Laon en Lannoys*, p. 6.

48 Guillaume Postel criticised both Huguenots and Catholics for their cruelty. *De Summopere* fols 22–3; Backus, *Le Miracle de Laon: le déraisonnable, le raisonnable, l'apocalyptique et le politique*, p. 42.

49 [Boulaese], *Le Miracle de Laon en Lannoys*, p. 7.

50 Backus, *Le Miracle de Laon: le déraisonnable, le raisonnable, l'apocalyptique et le politique*, p. 18.

51 Crespet, *Deux Livres de la hayne de Sathan*, (Paris: Guillaume de la Noue, 1590), fol. 211r.

52 Backus, *Le Miracle de Laon: le déraisonnable, le raisonnable, l'apocalyptique et le politique*, p. 17.

53 Crouzet, 'A woman and the Devil', pp. 209–10.

54 Walker, *Unclean Spirits*, p. 26.

55 Obry (or her 'demons') accused 'some women' of witchcraft, and said a gypsy woman had bewitched her (Walker, *Unclean Spirits*, p. 26; Boulaese, *Thresor*, p. 82), and her demon revealed that 'he' was there because her mother had cursed Obry some years before, after she carelessly allowed a rosary given her by her mother to be stolen. Crouzet, 'A woman and the Devil', p. 196.

56 Boulaese, *Thresor*, fol. 32r.

57 Backus, *Le Miracle de Laon: le déraisonnable, le raisonnable, l'apocalyptique et le politique*, p. 18.
58 Backus, *Le Miracle de Laon: le déraisonnable, le raisonnable, l'apocalyptique et le politique*, p. 19.
59 [Boulaese], *Le Miracle de Laon en Lannoys*, p. 8. Boulaese's large account provides lists of names of witnesses, identified by where they stood in the cathedral for the miracle; for example, 'near the image of Our Lady, adjacent to the scaffold', Boulaese, *Thresor*, p. 355.
60 Postel, *De Summopere*, fol. 17v. .
61 Walker, *Unclean Spirits*, p. 21.
62 Backus, *Le Miracle de Laon: le déraisonnable, le raisonnable, l'apocalyptique et le politique*, p. 20.
63 Crouzet, 'A woman and the Devil', p. 210.
64 Backus, *Le Miracle de Laon: le déraisonnable, le raisonnable, l'apocalyptique et le politique*, pp. 11–14; Walker, *Unclean Spirits*, pp. 20–1; cf. Postel, *De Summopere*.
65 Barthélemy Faye, *Energumenicus* (Paris: Sebastian Nivelle, 1571). The word 'energumene' is another word for demoniac.
66 See, for example, Pierre le Loyer, *Discours et histoires des spectres, visions et apparitions des esprits, anges, demons et ames, se monstrans visibles aux hommes* (Paris: Nicolas Buon, 1605), p. 244; Pierre Boaistuau, *Histoires prodigieuses extraictes de plusieurs fameux auteurs grecs at latins* (Paris: C. Macé, 1575), fols 109–23; Noel Taillepied, *Psichologie ou traité de l'apparition des esprits* (Paris: Guillaume Bichon, 1588), p. 306; 'Confession Catholique de Sieur de Sancy', in *Recueil de diverses pieces servant a l'histoire de Henry III* (Cologne: Pierre du Marteau, 1666), p. 351; Simon Goulart, *Le Troisième et quatrième du Thresor des histoires admirables et memorable de nostre temps* (Cologne: Samuel Crespin, 1614), p. 546; Louis Richeome, *Trois discours pour la religion catholique: des miracles, des saincts et des images* (Bordeaux: S. Millanges, 1598), pp. 199, 203; Bodin, *De la demonomanie des sorciers*, fols. 172r, 176v, 183r; Del Rio, *Disquisitionum magicarum*, p. 253.
67 Boulaese, *Thresor*, fol. 21v.
68 Boulaese, *Thresor*, fol. 21r. See Richard H. Popkin, *The History of Scepticism from Erasmus to Descartes*, rev. edn (New York: Harper and Row, 1968), for the views of Montaigne on the value of the senses, pp. 51–3.
69 'Declaration des lettres de l'Alphabet'.
70 [Boulaese], *Le Miracle de Laon en Lannoys*, p. 5.
71 Denis Crouzet has also pointed out that the spiritual significance of the exorcisms must be understood by reference to the times in the annual liturgical calendar in which they took place. Crouzet, 'A woman and the Devil', *passim*.
72 Pearl identifies all promoters of exorcism in this period as a 'zealot fringe'. Pearl, *The Crime of Crimes*, p. 57. The zeal is amply attested, however its 'fringe' status is possibly more open to debate.
73 Mack P. Holt, *The French Wars of Religion, 1562–1629* (Cambridge, New York and Melbourne: Cambridge University Press, 1995), pp. 122, 127; Robin Briggs, *Early Modern France, 1560–1715* (Oxford and New York: Oxford University Press, 1977), pp. 24–6.
74 I thank Alfred Soman for this clarifying observation.
75 See Crouzet, 'A woman and the Devil', p. 211; see also Barbara B. Diefendorf, *Beneath the Cross: Catholics and Huguenots in sixteenth-century Paris* (New York: Oxford University Press, 1991).
76 I stress here printed records, as print seems to be a fair criterion for polemical uses. However, there may be many accounts of public – and possibly polemical – exorcisms stored in archives. William Monter, for example, has recently discovered a major group possession case from Lorraine: 'The Catholic Salem; or, How the Devil

destroyed a saint's parish (Mattaincourt 1627–31)' (paper presented at Witchcraft in Context, University of York, 11–13 April 2002). Thanks are due to Professor Monter for making the paper available to me.

77 Natalie Zemon Davis, 'The sacred and the body social in sixteenth-century Lyon', *Past & Present*, no. 90 (1981), pp. 40–70, at p. 65; Jean Benedicti, *La Triomphante victoire de la vierge Marie, sur sept malins esprits, finalement chassés du corps d'une femme, dans l'Eglise des Cordeliers de Lyon* (Lyon: Pierre Rigaud, 1611).

78 On Soissons, 1582: Walker, *Unclean Spirits*, pp. 28–33, Charles Blendecq, *Cinq Histoires admirables, esquelles est monstré comme miraculeusement par la vertu et puissance du S. sacrement de l'autel a esté chassé Beelzebub*, Paris: G. Chaudière, 1582 and Gervasius Tornacensis, *Divina quatuor energumenorum liberation* (Paris: G. Chaudière, 1583); on Rouergue, 1597, Richeome, *Trois discours*, pp. 199–201, and Henri Weber, 'L'exorcisme à la fin du XVIe siècle, instrument de la contre-reforme et spectacle baroque', *Nouvelle Revue du XVIe Siècle*, no. 1 (1983), 79–101, at pp. 94–5; on Annonay, 1581, Claude Caron, *L'antechrist demasque* (Tournon: Guillaume Linocier, 1589), pp. 56–89. I thank Stuart Clark for kindly sending me this text.

79 Crespet, *Deux Livres de la hayne de Sathan*, fol. 211r.

80 Pierre-Victor Palma Cayet, *Chronologie novenaire, contenant l'histoire de la guerre sous le règne du très-chrestien Roy de France et de Navarre, Henri IV (1589–1598)*, in Michaud and Poujoulat (eds), *Nouvelle collection des mémoires rélatifs à l'histoire de France*, vol. 12 (Paris: Didier, 1857), pp. 310–17; *Procès verbal fait pour délivrer une fille possédée par le malin esprit à Louviers (1591)*, published after the original manuscript at the Bibliothèque Nationale by Armand Bénet. Introduction by B. du Moray, Bibliothèque Diabolique, no. 2 (Paris: Bureaux du Progrès Médical, 1883); Anita M. Walker and Edmund H. Dickerman, 'The haunted girl: possession, witchcraft and healing in sixteenth-century Louviers', *Proceedings of the Annual Meeting of the Western Society for French History*, vol. 23 (1996), 207–18.

81 [François Buisseret], *Histoire admirable et veritable des choses advenues a l'endroict d'une Religieuse professe du convent des Soeurs noires, de la ville de Mons en Hainaut, natifve de Sore sur Sambre, aagee de vingt cinq ans, possedee du maling esprit, & depuis delivree* (Paris: Claude de Monstre-oeil, 1586).

82 Blendecq, *Cinq Histoires admirables* and Caron, *L'Antechrist demasque* (cited in note 78).

83 One manuscript account of a long series of public exorcisms on a young boy, in a case of witchcraft, seems singular in having no polemic focus. Nicole Jacques-Chaquin and Maxime Préaud, *Les Sorciers du Carroi de Marlou: un procès de sorcellerie en Berry, 1582–1583* (Grenoble: Jérôme Millon, 1996).

84 Pierre Pigray, *Epitome des preceptes de Medecine et Chirurgie. avec ample declaration des remedes propres aux malades* (Lyon: S. Rigaud, 1616), pp. 453–6.

85 [Michel Marescot], *A true discourse, upon the matter of Martha Brossier of Romorantin, pretended to be possessed by a devill*, trans. Abraham Hartwel (London: John Wolfe, 1599), p. 38.

86 Benedicti, *Triomphante Victoire*, pp. 73–4.

87 Stuart Clark argues that these cases need to be seen more in their own terms (notably eschatological terms) and less as reducible to their function. Stuart Clark, *Thinking with Demons: the idea of witchcraft in early modern Europe* (Oxford: Oxford University Press, 1997), p. 392.

88 *Histoire de la naissance, progres, et decadence de l'heresie de ce siecle* (Arras: R. Maudhuy, 1611), p. 204. See also his *L'Anti-Christ et l'Anti-papesse*, 3rd edition, (Paris: A. L'Angelier, 1607), in which Raemond argues (pp. 477–87) that heretics are unable to perform exorcisms, including 'poor Luther' who failed in an attempt to do so.

89 Richeome, *Trois discours*, pp. 203–4.

90 Richeome aligned the behaviour of demons directly with the effects of Catholic

devotional apparatus: 'They show by their howling, shaking, and terrible counten-ances, that they inflict on this miserable body, that they feel the virtue of our relics, Agnus Dei, blessed grains, the sign of the Cross, and other ceremonies and spiritual arms of the Church, with which they are combated', Richeome, *Trois discours*, p. 201.

91 The *Thesaurus exorcismorum atque conjurationum terribilium* (Cologne: Lazar Zetzner, 1626), contained Maximilian Eynatten, *Manuale Exorcismorum*; Girolamo Menghi, *Flagellum Daemonum* and *Fustis Daemonum*; Valerio Polidoro, *Practicae Exorcistarum and Dispersio Daemonum* and Zacaria Visconti, *Complementum Artis Exorcistica*. Cf. *Rituale Romanum Pauli V [1614] Pontificis Maximi jussu editum* (Paris: Impensis Societatis Typographicae Librorum Officii Ecclesiastici, 1665). Mary R. O'Neil lists the manuals published in late sixteenth- and seventeenth-century Italy, 'Discerning superstition: popular errors and orthodox response in late sixteenth-century Italy', Ph.D. dissertation, Stanford University, Calif., 1982, p. 297.

92 See, for example, Ruth Martin, *Witchcraft and the Inquisition in Venice, 1550–1650* (Oxford: Basil Blackwell, 1989), p. 181.

93 *Rituale Romanum Pauli V Pontificis Maximi*, p. 412. Thanks are due to Jenny Ferber for this translation.

94 [Jean-Joseph Surin], *A relation of the devill Balam's departure out of the body of the Mother-Prioresse of the Ursuline nuns of Loudun Faithfully translated out of the French copie, with some observations for the better illustration of the pageant*, (London: R. B[adger], 1636), unpaginated title page of hostile English commentator's 'Observations' [translation of *Relation de la sortie du demon Balam du corps de la Mere prieure des Ursulines de Loudun*].

95 David Gentilcore, *From Bishop to Witch: the system of the sacred in early modern Terra d'Otranto* (Manchester and New York: Manchester University Press, 1992), pp. 7, 13, 105, 107, 110.

96 Del Rio, *Disquisitionum magicarum* Lib. VI 'Anacephalaeosis', p. 334.

3 Marthe Brossier

1 Mack P. Holt, *The French Wars of Religion, 1562–1629* (Cambridge, New York and Melbourne: Cambridge University Press, 1995), chapters 5 and 6; Robin Briggs, *Early Modern France, 1560–1715* (Oxford and New York: Oxford University Press, 1977), pp. 24–32. Crouzet notes that the League itself was portrayed as an enchantress who rendered France like one possessed, and that royal authority was the perceived means to 'exorcise' the country. Denis Crouzet, *Les guerriers de Dieu: la violence au temps des troubles de religion*, 2 vols (Seyssel: Champ Vallon, 1990), vol. 1, pp. 216–25.

2 Pierre de l'Estoile, *Journal de l'Estoile pour la règne de Henri IV, 1, 1589–1600* (1732), edited by Louis-Raymond Lefèvre (Paris: Gallimard, 1948), p. 567.

3 Even the fact that an imprisoned, accused peasant witch appears to have had the support of a literate sponsor gives us a hint of the seriousness with which the case was treated. Bibliothèque Nationale, Paris, Manuscripts fonds français 18453 (hereafter BN Mss fds fs), fols 2r, 68v. This manuscript source of 106 folios contains materials written both for and against the possession. Most items are eighteenth-century copies. Other major sources are the works by l'Estoile, *Journal*; [Michel Marescot], *Discours veritable sur le faict de Marthe Brossier de Romorantin, pretendue demoniaque* (Paris: Mamert Patisson, 1599), translated as *A true discourse, upon the matter of Martha Brossier of Romorantin, pretended to be possessed by a devill*, by Abraham Hartwel (London: John Wolfe, 1599), the English edition being cited here; [Pierre de Bérulle], 'Léon d'Alexis', *Traicté des energumenes, Suivy d'un discours sur la possession de Marthe Brossier: contre les calomnies d'un medecin de Paris*, (Troyes: no publisher, 1599); and Jacques-Auguste de Thou, *Historiarum sui temporis, 5*, translated in Congnard, *Histoire de Marthe Brossier pretendue possedee tiree du Latin de Messire Jacques August. de Thou,*

President au Parlement de Paris. Avec quelques remarques et considerations generales sur cette Matiere, tirées pour la plus part aussi du Latin de Bartholomaeus Perdulcis celebre Medecin de la Faculté de Paris. Le tout pour servir d'appendice & de plus ample éclarcissement au sujet d'un livre intitulé La Pieté affligée ou Discours Historique & Theoligique de la possession des Religieuses dictes de Sainte Elizabeth de Louviers &c (Rouen: Jacques Herault, 1652), (hereafter de Thou, in Congnard, *Histoire*), pp. 1–16; and Pierre-Victor Palma Cayet, *Chronologie septenaire contenant l'histoire de la paix entre les roys de France et d'Espagne*, in Michaud and Poujoulat (eds), *Nouvelle collection des mémoires pour servir à l'histoire de France*, series 1, vol. 12, part 2 (Paris: Éditeur du Commentaire Analytique du Code Civil, 1838), pp. 61–2. The best modern account is Anita M. Walker and Edmund H. Dickerman, '"A woman under the influence": a case of alleged possession in sixteenth-century France', *Sixteenth Century Journal*, vol. 22, no. 3 (1991), 534–54, a sensitive study of the subjectivity of Brossier. See also Robert Mandrou, *Magistrats et sorciers en France au XVIIe siècle: une analyse de psychologie historique* (1968) (Paris: Seuil, 1980), pp. 163–79; D.P. Walker, *Unclean Spirits: possession and exorcism in France and England in the late sixteenth and early seventeenth centuries* (London: Scolar Press, 1981), pp. 33–42; and an earlier version of the present chapter, 'The demonic possession of Marthe Brossier, France, 1598–1600', in Charles Zika (ed.), *No Gods Except Me: orthodoxy and religious practice in Europe, 1200–1600*, Melbourne: Melbourne University History Monographs, no. 14 (1991), 59–83.

4 BN Mss fds fs 18453, fol. 3v.
5 BN Mss fds fs 18453, fols 3v–4v, and 103r. Walker and Dickerman suggest that Brossier's assuming a masculine identity pre-figured her later and relatively more honourable guise as a male demon. 'A woman under the influence', p. 548.
6 BN Mss fds fs 18453, fol. 41v.
7 BN Mdss fds fs 18453, fol. 12r. This expression appears to have taken on currency as a description of frenzy, presumably in the decades following Obry's exorcism. A 1589 book on the death of Henri III captions an image of a grieving courtier, saying he was 'doing the demoniac'. Denis Pallier, *Recherches sur l'imprimerie à Paris pendant la Ligue (1585–1594)* (Geneva: Droz, 1975), ill. 5.
8 BN Mss fds fs 18453, fols 11v–12r. Marescot reported that Brossier had the book about Obry with her when imprisoned in the Châtelet, but that it was taken from her. [Marescot], *A True discourse*, p. 24. This somewhat poignant detail also suggests Brossier could read.
9 Walker and Dickerman, 'A woman under the influence', p. 551.
10 BN Mss fds fs 18453, fol. 64r. The seventeenth-century Italian exorcist, Giovan Battista Chiesa, also collected testimonials of his expertise, in order to present them, as he said, 'before any judge, ecclesiastical or secular'. Giovanni Levi, *Inheriting Power: the story of an exorcist*, trans. Lydia Cochrane (Chicago, Ill.: Chicago University Press, 1988), p. 13.
11 BN Mss fds fs 18453, fol. 5v.
12 BN Mss fds fs 18453, fol. 8v. On communications with purgatory, see Wolfgang Behringer, *Shaman of Oberstdorf: Chonrad Stoeckhlin and the phantoms of the night*, trans. H.C. Erik Midelfort, (Charlottesville: University Press of Virginia, 1998).
13 BN Mss fds fs 18453, fols 6r–9r
14 BN Mss fds fs 18453, fol. 68r.
15 De Thou in Congnard, *Histoire*, p. 1.
16 She speaks of 'all that they have earned' BN Mss fds fs 18453, fol. 9r. This is an accusation which would only be valid if their fraud could be established, which it cannot. We are constrained, I think, to accept that it is possible they acted in good faith, and that people gave alms as a good work, out of piety and pity for Brossier.
17 BN Mss fds fs 18453, fol. 7r. (See also l'Estoile, *Journal*, p. 567: l'Estoile also makes

another tantalising reference here to Brossier and her mother: 'the mother was even suspected of meddling with sorcery and the daughter with romance'.)

18 BN Mss fds fs 18453, fol. 7r. Of another of her exorcists, a canon in Cléry, Brossier was supposed to have said that he had 'the spirit of St John of Damascus'. fol. 7v.

19 Stephen Greenblatt, 'Exorcism into Art', *Representations*, no. 12, Fall (1985), 15–23; and 'Loudun and London', *Critical Inquiry*, vol. 12, no. 2 (1986), 326–46.

20 BN Mss fds fs 18453, fols 65v–66r. I thank Ian Robertson and Charles Zika for their translation of the Latin texts.

21 BN Mss fds fs 18453, fol. 69r.

22 BN Mss fds fs 18453, fol. 9v.

23 BN Mss fds fs 18453, fol. 9r–v.

24 BN Mss fds fs 18453, fol. 63r–v.

25 BN Mss fds fs 18453, fols 66v–67r.

26 BN Mss fds fs 18453, fol. 64v.

27 BN Mss fds fs 18453, fol. 16v.

28 [Marescot], *A true discourse*, p. 32. Thanks are due to Jenny Ferber for help with this interpretation.

29 [Marescot], *A true discourse*, p. 32. Marescot provided the recipe for the fumigant, as if this quite licit means of exorcism were self-evidently ridiculous (p. 33).

30 BN Mss fds fs 18453, fol. 11r.

31 [Marescot], *A true discourse*, p. 31.

32 BN Mss fds fs 18453, fol. 69r–v.

33 BN Mss fds fs 18453, fol. 69v.

34 BN Mss fds fs 18453, fol. 73r. See also Stuart Clark, *Thinking with Demons: the idea of witchcraft in early modern Europe*, (Oxford: Oxford University Press, 1997), ch. 39.

35 BN Mss fds fs 18453, fol. 73v.

36 BN Mss fds fs 18453, fol. 73v.

37 BN Mss fds fs 18453, fols 73v–74v.

38 BN Mss fds fs 18453, fols 63r–64v.

39 BN Mss fds fs 18453, fol. 64v.

40 BN Mss fds fs 18453, fol. 64v.

41 BN Mss fds fs 18453 fols 86r and 90r

42 BN Mss fds fs 18453, fols 79v–80r.

43 BN Mss fds fs 18453, fol. 80r–v.

44 BN Mss fds fs 18453, fol. 82r.

45 [Marescot], *A true discourse*, pp. 30–1. Anne Chevriou also attested that Bishop Miron presented two pieces of bread, one consecrated and one unconsecrated, to Brossier, which Brossier appeared successfully to distinguish. Chevriou urged the bishop of Paris to see this as the result Brossier's experience of such tests, and her earlier reading of the story of Nicole Obry. BN Mss fds fs 18453, fol. 11r–v. De Thou's account has her failing such a test outright. De Thou, in Congnard, *Histoire*, p. 2.

46 L'Estoile, *Journal*, p. 548.

47 L'Estoile, *Journal*, p. 555.

48 L'Estoile, *Journal*, p. 556.

49 L'Estoile, *Journal*, p. 566.

50 L'Estoile, *Journal*, p. 565.

51 I follow here Denis Crouzet's observation about the timing of events surrounding the Miracle of Laon: he argues that such dramas are more comprehensible when understood by reference to the dates on the Catholic liturgical calendar on which they occurred, such spiritual 'hot-spots' as the Easter cycle and saints' days. See his 'A woman and the Devil: possession and exorcism in sixteenth-century France', trans. Michael Wolfe, in Michael Wolfe (ed.), *Changing Identities in Early Modern France*,

with a foreword by Natalie Zemon Davis (Durham, N.C.: Duke University Press, 1997), 191–215, *passim*.

52 L'Estoile, *Journal*, p. 567–8; [Marescot], *A true discourse*, p. 9.

53 De Thou, in Congnard, *Histoire*, p. 2.

54 Henri Weber, 'L'exorcisme à la fin du XVIe siècle, instrument de la contre-reforme et spectacle baroque', *Nouvelle Revue du XVIe Siècle*, 1983, no. 1, 79–101, p. 85.

55 On the sociability of this early seventeenth-century mysticism, see John Cruickshank, 'The Acarie Circle', in *Seventeenth-Century French Studies*, vol. 16, (1994), 48–58.

56 L'Estoile, *Journal*, p. 567.

57 De Thou, in Congnard, *Histoire*, p. 3.

58 The doctors were Marescot, Ellain, Hautin, Riolan and Duret; l'Estoile, *Journal*, p. 568.

59 Pro-Brossier physicians nonetheless reported that she was able to respond to questions put to her in Greek and English. l'Estoile, *Journal*, p. 570.

60 [Marescot], *A true discourse*, p. 4.

61 [Marescot], *A true discourse*, p. 4.

62 [Marescot], *A true discourse*, p. 4.

63 [Marescot], *A true discourse*, p. 5.

64 Caesarius von Heisterbach, *The Dialogue on Miracles*, 2 vols, trans. H. von E. Scott and C. Swinton Bland, with an introduction by G.G. Coulton (London: Routledge, 1929), p. 333.

65 Jean-Joseph Surin famously 'caught' a state of possession from Jeanne des Anges (Michel de Certeau, *The Possession at Loudun* (1970), trans. Michael B. Smith, with a foreword by Stephen Greenblatt (Chicago, Ill. and London: University of Chicago Press, 2000), pp. 206–7), and one of the Capuchin exorcists at Loudun, Fr Tranquille, also seems to have suffered some kind of breakdown, and died (Mandrou, *Magistrats et sorciers*, p. 273).

66 It seems likely, nonetheless, that many of those diagnosed as possessed were suffering from something, if only a kind of collective delirium. A modern association of possession with different forms of mental illness, such as post-traumatic conditions, does not seem out of order, but for historical cases, it raises complex and ultimately unresolvable questions about the limits of retrospective diagnosis.

67 [Marescot], *A true discourse*, p. 5.

68 [Marescot], *A true discourse*, pp. 5 and 8.

69 [Marescot], *A true discourse*, p. 19. On the attitudes and procedures of the Parlement, see Alfred Soman, *Sorcellerie et justice criminelle: le Parlement de Paris (16e–18e siècles)* (Hampshire and Brookfield: Varorium, 1992).

70 [Marescot], *A true discourse*, pp. 5–6.

71 [Marescot], *A true discourse*, p. 6.

72 [Marescot], *A true discourse*, p. 6.

73 [Marescot], *A true discourse*, p. 6.

74 [Marescot], *A true discourse*, pp. 6–7.

75 [Marescot], *A true discourse*, p. 7.

76 [Marescot], *A true discourse*, p. 7.

77 [Marescot], *A true discourse*, p. 7.

78 [Marescot], *A true discourse*, p. 7.

79 [Marescot], *A true discourse*, p. 7. Presumably Marescot was singling out the most highly educated members of the congregation, but he also translated the text into French for his readers.

80 [Marescot], *A true discourse*, p. 11.

81 [Marescot], *A true discourse*, p. 8.

82 [Marescot], *A true discourse*, p. 8.

83 [Marescot], *A true discourse*, p. 8.

84 [Marescot], *A true discourse*, p. 8. See Jean Fernel, *De Abditis rerum causis Libri Duo* (Paris: Christian Wechel, 1548), bk 2, ch. 16, pp. 222–3.

85 [Marescot], *A true discourse*, p. 8.

86 [Marescot], *A true discourse*, p. 9. The *arrêt* may be found in BN Mss NAF 9938, 'Registres du Conseil du Parlement commençant 6 mars, 1599', fols. 109v–110r; BN Mss fds fs 16359, fol. 539; Archives Nationales U329 'Addition au registre du Parlement', 3 avril, 1599 and AN U24, fol. 10r–v, (an excerpt of which may be found in Mandrou, *Magistrats et sorciers*, p. 167).

87 [Marescot], *A true discourse*, p. 9. The report by the commission of 3 April and by the previous commission of 1 April are located in the BN Mss fds fs 17324, fols. 105r–107v and 103r–104r respectively; [Marescot], *A true discourse*, (pp. 13–17) contains the 3 April report and Mandrou, *Magistrats et sorciers*, contains an excerpt from the 1 April report, pp. 173–4.

88 BN Mss NAF 9938, fol. 110r.

89 BN Mss NAF 9938, fol. 110r; [Marescot], *A true discourse*, p. 9.

90 [Marescot], *A true discourse*, pp. 9–10.

91 [Marescot], *A true discourse*, pp. 9–10, 35; De Thou in Congnard, *Histoire*, p. 9 One of the doctors was the king's *premier médecin*, Jean Ribit de la Rivière, who wrote sceptically of possession in a letter to his Huguenot friend Agrippa d'Aubigné. Aubigné chided him for his disbelief and cited in response a number of irrefutable cases of possession. Hugh Trevor-Roper, 'The Sieur de la Rivière, Paracelsian physician of Henri IV', in Allen G. Debus (ed.), *Science, Medicine and Society in the Renaissance: essays to honour Walter Pagel*, 2 vols (London: Heinemann, 1972), vol. 2, 227–50, at pp. 228, 238, 243–4. I thank Stuart Clark for this reference.

92 The *arrêt* of 24 May 1599, may be found at BN fds Colbert, 500, t. 1, fol. 75 and is reprinted in [Marescot], *A true discourse*, pp. 34–7. Anne Chevriou was finally exonerated of the charge of witchcraft in 1605. My thanks are due to Alfred Soman for this information.

93 De Thou in Congnard, *Histoire*, p.11.

94 AN U 329, 'Addition au Registre du Parlement', 5 April 1599 (not paginated).

95 The Parlement obliged the priests to the extent of undertaking to suppress the books. AN U 329, 'Addition au Registre du Parlement', 5 April, 1599 (not paginated).

96 De Thou, in Congnard, *Histoire*, pp. 9–10.

97 De Thou, in Congnard, *Histoire*, p. 10.

98 De Thou, in Congnard, *Histoire*, pp. 10–11. Cf. Ubald d'Alençon, 'Une page de l'histoire de Paris: le Parlement et les immunités religieuse en 1599: le P. Brûlart', *Études franciscaines* (1903), 608–12. (This reference was kindly provided by Barbara Diefendorf, as part of a dissertation report.) 'In coena Domini' was a bull promulgated by the pope each Maundy Thursday which was frequently opposed by secular authorities because its claims for papal authority were seen to be excessive. Its publication was illegal in Gallican France, traditionally resistant to the forces of Rome. The bull referred to in this case was probably that of Gregory XIII in 1583, whose list of classes of person to be excommunicated included those who subject ecclesiastics to lay courts. *Catholic Encyclopedia*, eds C.G. Herbermann *et al.* (New York: Appleton, 1910), vol. 7, p. 717.

99 De Thou in Congnard, *Histoire*, pp. 9–11.

100 *Renaissance Dialectic and Renaissance Piety: Benet of Canfield's Rule* of Perfection, a translation and study by Kent Emery Jr., Medieval and Renaissance Texts and Studies, no. 50 (Binghamton, New York, 1987), p. 19.

101 De Thou, in Congnard, *Histoire*, p. 10.

102 [Marescot], *A true discourse*, p. 11.

103 [Marescot], *A true discourse*, p. 2.

104 [Marescot], *A true discourse*, p. 3.

105 [Marescot], *A true discourse*, p. 3.

106 [Marescot], *A true discourse*, p. 22. On the link between exorcism and theatre, see Stephen Greenblatt, 'Exorcism into art'.

107 [Marescot], *A true discourse*, p. 2.

108 He nonetheless did not shrink from engaging in polemic slanging to equal Marescot, a move which led D.P. Walker to describe the *Discours* as an 'astonishingly feeble' work (*Unclean Spirits*, p. 40). Such an assessment is possibly true from a scholarly point of view, however, Bérulle fulfilled his brief as an author of polemic, at least enough to make him seek the shelter of anonymity. Perhaps his scholarly reputation was also in the back of his mind in making such a choice. His seventeenth-century admirers appear to have fallen into step: for whatever reason, the *Discours* is not included in the first collection of his 'complete works', while the *Traicté* is. (*Oeuvres complètes du Cardinal de Bérulle, Reproduction de l'edition Princeps (1644)*, t. 1 (Montsoult: Maison d'Institution de l'Oratoire, 1962). There is a new edition which contains both works: *Oeuvres complétes* (8 vols) (Paris: Oratoire de Jésus/Éditions de Cerf, 1997), vol. 2, 'Courts traités', pp. 67–170.

109 [Bérulle], *Discours*, pp. 47–8.

110 Jean Dagens, *Bérulle et les origines de le restauration catholique (1575–1611)* (Bruges: Desclée de Brouwer, 1952), p. 150.

111 As cited in note 3. Hereafter, [Bérulle], *Traicté* and *Discours* respectively: the two works are separately paginated, the *Traicté* using folios, the *Discours* pages. On the title page of the *Discours*, 'sur la possession' is substituted with 'de la possession'.

112 Dagens, *Bérulle et les origines de le restauration catholique*, p. 153.

113 For a more detailed account of the works, particularly for their place in contemporary theology and in the oeuvre of Bérulle, see Dagens, *Bérulle et les origines de le restauration catholique*, pp. 150–65.

114 [Bérulle], *Traicté*, fols 12r–13r.

115 [Bérulle], *Traicté*, fols 20r; 37v; 41v.

116 [Bérulle], *Traicté*, fol. 22r.

117 [Bérulle] *Traicté*, fol. 38v. The notable idea of a parallel between possession and the Incarnation arose in other cases. Jean-Joseph Surin is said to have believed that he was possessed 'by the Word Incarnate as much as by the demon' (Certeau, *The Possession at Loudun*, p. 212) and an exorcist at Chinon claimed that the possession of the women there was as real as the presence of Christ 'sous les accidens de pain et vin'. Mandrou, *Magistrats et sorciers*, p. 254. As noted in Chapter 8, the demoniac mystic Marie des Vallées spoke of God promising her he would align her will to His so closely that He would 'leave no more of her than in a consecrated host', Bibliothèque Mazarine, Paris, Manuscript 3177, p. 77.

118 [Bérulle], *Traicté*, fol. 54r.

119 [Bérulle], *Traicté*, fols. 54r–v.

120 [Bérulle], *Discours*, p. 41.

121 [Bérulle], *Discours*, p. 52.

122 [Bérulle], *Discours*, pp. 19–20.

123 [Bérulle], *Discours*, p. 21.

124 [Bérulle], *Traicté*, fols 80v–81r.

125 [Bérulle], *Traicté*, fol. 46r–v.

126 Mary R. O'Neil, 'Discerning superstition: popular errors and orthodox response in late sixteenth-century Italy', Ph.D. dissertation, Stanford University, Calif., 1982 p. 365; [Bérulle], *Discours*, p. 56.

127 [Bérulle], *Discours*, p. 56. The analogy occurs at the very end of the *Discours* and seems to end in the middle of a sentence. The paraphrase is my understanding of these words: 'Et en un mesme homme, se trouvant comme deux sortes d'Estats & de

Républiques, dont l'une a ses mouvements fondés en la nature & ses réglemens establis en la structure & composition du corps humain, et l'autre en la volonté de l'homme & et en l'inclination'.

128 [Bérulle], *Discours*, p. 44.

129 [Bérulle], *Discours*, p. 48.

130 Henri Bremond, *Histoire littéraire du sentiment religieux en France depuis la fin des guerres de religion jusqu'à nos jours*, 11 vols (Paris: Librairie Bloud et Gay, 1933), II, pp. 128–31; Mandrou, *Magistrats et sorciers*, pp. 77, 198. (Joseph d'Orléans, *La Vie du Pere Pierre Coton* (Paris: Estienne Michallet, 1688, p. 88). During the Brossier saga Coton as a Jesuit was not present in Paris. Yet by 1604 the Jesuits were finding their way back into royal favour and Coton was an influential figure in the royal household. He was also later involved in the major possession case of Elisabeth de Ranfaing.

131 Joseph d'Orléans, *La Vie du Pere Pierre Coton*, p. 87.

132 Coton also raised hackles when he asked the demon if James I would convert to Catholicism. Jacques-Auguste de Thou, *Histoire universelle de Jacques-Auguste de Thou, depuis 1543 jusqu'en 1607* (Le Haye: P. Gosse & J. Neaulme, 1740), vol. 5, pp. 717–19. I thank Albrecht Burkardt for this reference.

133 Robert Bireley, *The Re-fashioning of Catholicism, 1450–1700: a reassessment of the Counter Reformation* (Basingstoke: Macmillan; New York: St Martin's Press, 1999), p. 2.

134 BN Mss NAF 9938, fols 145r–146v contains an *arrêt* of 30 December 1599, which attempted to curtail Brossier's renewed activities; also found in BN Mss fds Dupuy, no. 379, fol. 147. See also de Thou, in Congnard, *Histoire*, pp. 11–12.

135 De Thou, in Congnard, *Histoire*, p. 12.

136 Letter from Cardinal d'Ossat to the king, 19 April 1600, letter no. 211, *Lettres de illustrissime et reverendissime Cardinal D'Ossat, Eveque de Bayeaux. Au Roy Henry Le Grand et a Monsieur de Villeroy. Depuis l'annee M.D.XCIV jusques a l'annee MDCIII. Derniere edition, revue et augmentee* (Paris: Joseph Bouillerot, 1624), pp. 413 and 417. See BN Mss NAF 9938, fols 145r–146v (*arrêt* of 30 December, 1599) and AN U 24, fol. 32r (*arrêt* of 31 March, 1600).

137 Letter from Cardinal d'Ossat to the king, 19 April, 1600, letter no. 211, *Lettres de Cardinal D'Ossat*, p. 412.

138 The Jesuits were still active in southern France, as the Parlements of Bordeaux and Toulouse had not followed the example of Paris. See A. Latreille, E. Delaruelle and J.-R. Palanque, *Histoire du Catholicisme en France*, vol. 1, (Paris: Éditions spes, 1960), p. 268.

139 De Thou, in Congnard, *Histoire*, pp. 14–15.

140 Letter from Cardinal d'Ossat to the king, 19 April 1600, letter no. 211, *Lettres de Cardinal D'Ossat*, pp. 416–17.

141 De Thou, in Congnard, *Histoire*, p. 15.

142 Palma Cayet, *Chronologie septenaire*, p. 126. The phrasing of Palma Cayet is ambiguous, referring to Brossier's presence in Milan 'jusques à present', which appears to mean up to 1600, under which year the entry is made, but which might mean 1604, the last year of his chronology.

143 Denis Crouzet, 'A woman and the Devil', p. 196.

144 De Thou in Congnard, *Histoire*, pp. 8–9.

4 Priestcraft and witchcraft

1 Mary R. O'Neil, ' "Sacerdote ovvero strione": Ecclesiatical and superstitious remedies in sixteenth-century Italy', in Steven L. Kaplan (ed.), *Understanding Popular Culture* (Berlin: Mouton, 1984), pp. 53–83. On the phenomenon of witch-priests see Pierre de

Lancre, *Tableau de l'inconstance des mauvais anges et démons où il est amplement traité des sorciers et de la sorcellerie* (1612), with a critical introduction and notes by Nicole Jacques-Chaquin, Collection Palimpseste (Paris: Aubier, 1982), Book 5, Discours II.

2 For the pre-reformation era, see Charles Zika, 'Hosts, processions and pilgrimages: controlling the sacred in fifteenth-century Germany', *Past and Present*, no. 118, February (1988), 25–64.

3 Jean Delumeau, *Catholicism between Luther and Voltaire: a new view of the Counter-Reformation* (1971), trans. Jeremy Moiser, with an introduction by John Bossy (London: Burns and Oates, 1977) pp. 13–15.

4 For Protestant reformers' disputes, see Bodo Nischan, 'The exorcism controversy and baptism in the late reformation', *Sixteenth Century Journal*, vol. 18, no. 1 (1987), 31–51 at pp. 33–4.

5 Gallicans are traditionally distinguished from Ultramontanes: church personnel who take support and directives from across the Alps, that is, from Rome.

6 On Mother Françoise de La Croix, see Chapter 6. On Agen, see Gregory Hanlon and Geoffrey Snow, 'Exorcisme et cosmologie tridentine: trois cas agenais en 1619', *Revue de la Bibliothèque Nationale*, vol. 28, Summer (1988), 12–27. At Auxonne in 1665, Barbe Buvée, an older nun and former superior of another convent, was accused by her sister nuns of being a witch. See Robert Mandrou, *Magistrats et sorciers en France au XVIIe siècle: une analyse de psychologie historique* (1968) (Paris: Seuil, 1980), pp. 404–22. The physician Charles Poirot was executed following accusations made by the possessed widow, Elisabeth de Ranfaing. (The territory in which this occurred – the Duchy of Lorraine – was not part of France in 1622.)

7 See R.W. Scribner, 'Ritual and popular religion in Catholic Germany at the time of the Reformation', *Journal of Ecclesiastical History*, no. 35 (1984), 47–77, at pp. 69–71. The word 'sacramental' used as an adjective does not necessarily refer to 'sacramental' as a noun, which distinguishes rites and observances known as sacramentals from the seven sacraments.

8 Mary R. O'Neil, 'Discerning superstition: popular errors and orthodox response in late sixteenth century Italy', Ph.D. dissertation (Stanford University, Calif., 1981), p. 357.

9 Lyndal Roper, 'Exorcism and the theology of the body', in *Oedipus and the Devil: witchcraft, sexuality and religion in early modern Europe* (London: Routledge, 1994), 171–98, at p. 178.

10 Peter Burke, 'How to be a Counter-Reformation saint', in Kaspar von Greyerz (ed.), *Religion and Society in Early Modern Europe (1500–1800)* (London: Allen & Unwin, 1984), 45–55. It should be noted that a pure priest was theologically no more likely to be able to effect exorcism – a decision in God's hands – but the view that he might was nonetheless implied in practice. On this general point, see Paschal Boland, *The Concept of Discretio Spirituum in John Gerson's 'De Probatione Spirituum' and 'De Distinctione Verarum Visionum A Falsis'*, Washington: The Catholic University of America Press, 1959, pp. 85–6.

11 Joseph d'Orléans, *La Vie du Pere Pierre Coton* (Paris: Estienne Michallet, 1688), p. 87.

12 Bibliothèque Nationale, Paris, Manuscrits fonds français 18453, fols 66v–67r.

13 *Rituale Romanum Pauli V Pontificis Maximi jussu editum* (Paris: Impensis Societatis Typographicae Librorum Officii Ecclesiastici, 1665), p. 409. Thanks are due to Jenny Ferber for this translation.

14 O'Neil, 'Discerning superstition', pp. 313, 356–7.

15 [Michel Marescot], *A true discourse, upon the matter of Martha Brossier of Romorantin, pretended to be possessed by a devill*, trans. Abraham Hartwel (London: John Wolfe, 1599).

16 O'Neil, 'Discerning superstition', pp. 357–60. Ironically, no one did more to promote the virtues of exorcism than Menghi. Yet he couched his arguments in terms of the need for restraint, precisely in order to sustain the currency of sacred power.

17 Sanson Birette, *Refutation de l'erreur du Vulgaire, touchant les responses des diables exorcizez* (Rouen: Jacques Besongne, 1618), unpaginated dedicatory epistle to the Bishop of Coutances. Birette cited the ritual of the diocese of Coutances which he said limited the interrogation of demons to questions regarding the number of demons in the possessed, why the person was possessed and when the possession began (pp. 112–13). Even these limitations clearly left room for eliciting information about witchcraft.

18 Jean Benedicti, *La Triomphante victoire de la vierge Marie, sur sept malins esprits, finalement chassés du corps d'une femme, dans l'Eglise des Cordeliers de Lyon* (Lyon: Pierre Rigaud, 1611), p. 99.

19 *Thesaurus exorcismorum atque conjurationum terribilium, potentissimorum, efficacissimorum cum Practica probatissima: quibus spiritus maligni, daemones maleficiaque omnia de Corporibus humanis obsessis, tanquam Flagellis, Fustibusque Fugantur, expelluntur, doctrinus refertissimus atq, uberrimus: Ad maximam Exorcistarum commoditatem nunc ultimo plenariè in lucem editus & recusus: Cujus Authores, ut & singuli tractatus sequente pagellâ consignati, inveniuntur* (Cologne: Lazar Zetzner, 1626). The Latin title for such an arresting image of exorcism exposes neatly the desire to prevent access to the formulae of exorcisms risked by publishing in the vernacular, while seeking to appeal to a taste for excitement among educated exorcists. Thanks are due to Jenny Ferber for help with this translation.

20 O'Neil, 'Discerning superstition', pp. 333–4. Sanson Birette listed bishops, priests, deacons, sub-deacons and exorcists as those qualified to perform exorcisms, *Refutation*, pp. 104–5.

21 François Humier, *Discours theologiques, sur l'Histoire de Magdeleine Bavent, Religieuse Hospitaliere du Monastere de Louviers en Normandie* (Niort: Philippes Bureau, 1659), pp. 38–9.

22 Humier, *Discours*, p. 39. Exorcism is the second of seven so-called minor priestly orders, whose particular functions were suppressed by the Catholic church in 1972.

23 *Disquisitionum magicarum libri sex* (Louvain: Gérard Rivière, 1599–1600), Lib. VI, 'Anacephalaeosis', p. 333.

5 The trial of Louis Gaufridy

1 Gaufridy was convicted of 'rapt [kidnapping], séduction, impiété, magie, sorceleries, & autres abominations'. *Arrest de la Cour de Parlement de Provence, portant condamnation contre Messire Louis Gaufridi, originaire du lieu de Beau-vezer lès Colmaret, Prestre beneficié en l'Eglise des Accoules de la ville de Marseille: Convaincu de Magie, & autres crimes abominables du dernier Avril, mil six cens onze* (Aix-en-Provence: Jean Tholozan, 1611), p. 3. Manuscript copies of the trial proceedings are found in Bibliothèque Nationale, Paris, Manuscrits, fonds français (hereafter BN Mss fds fs) 23851 (132ff) and 23852 (496 pp.). These two collections are largely identical, however, Ms. 23852 contains a transcript of Gaufridy's interrogation and torture on 30 April 1611, the day of his execution, (pp. 240–4), and a record of the trial for witchcraft of Madeleine Demandols in 1653 (pp. 245–496). The Bibliothèque Municipale, Méjanes, holds an extract from the trial records: 'Audition de dem.lle Magdeleine de Demandols', Ms. 1632 (1497) pièce 32. See also: Bibliothèque Municipale Troyes, Ms. 316 (paraphrases of the confessions and *arrêt* of Gaufridy). The other principal sources for the case are *Confession faicte par Messire Louys Gaufridi Prestre en l'Eglise des Accoules de Marseille, Prince des Magiciens, depuis Constantinople jusques à Paris. A deux Peres Capuchins du couvent d'Aix, la veille de Paques, Le onzieme Avril mil six cens onze* (Aix: Jean Tholozan, 1611), and Sébastien Michaelis, *Histoire admirable de la possession et conversion d'une penitente, Seduite par un magicien, la faisant Sorciere & Princesse des Sorciers au pays de Provence, conduite à la S. Baume pour y estre exorcizee l'an M. DC. X.*

au mois de Novembre, soubs l'authorité du R. P. F. Sebastien Michaelis . . . Ensemble la Pneumalogie ou Discours du susdit P. Michaelis (Paris: Charles Chastellain, 1613). This chapter uses an English translation, *The Admirable Historie of the Possession and Conversion of a Penitent woman. Seduced by a magician that made her to become a Witch . . . Whereunto is annexed a Pneumology, or Discourse of Spirits.* trans. W.B. (London: William Aspley, 1613). See also François de Rosset, 'De l'horrible & espouventable sorcellerie de Louys Goffredy, prestre de Marseille', in *Histoires tragiques de nostre temps* (Rouen: Jean-Baptiste Behourt, 1632), 32–67. Modern accounts of the case have been written by Robert Mandrou, *Magistrats et sorciers en France au XVIIe siècle: une analyse de psychologie historique* (1968) (Paris: Seuil, 1980), pp. 198–210; Anita M. Walker and Edmund H. Dickerman, 'A notorious woman: possession, witchcraft and sexuality in seventeenth-century Provence', *Historical Reflections*, vol. 27, no. 1 (2001), 1–26 and Michelle Marshman, 'Exorcism as empowerment: a new idiom', *Journal of Religious History* (Great Britain), vol. 23, no. 3 (1999), 265–81. Stuart Clark has interpreted the case for its significance regarding fears of the Antichrist, as part of an argument for the importance of eschatology in possession cases. *Thinking with Demons: the idea of witchcraft in early modern Europe* (Oxford: Oxford University Press, 1997), ch. 28; Cf. the early research of Jean Lorédan, *Un grand procès de sorcellerie au XVIIe siècle: l'abbé Gaufridy et Madeleine de Demandolx, 1600–1670: d'après des documents inédits* (Paris: Perrin, 1912).

2 Clifford J. Ronan 'Lucan and the self-incised voids of *Julius Caesar*', *Comparative Drama*, vol. 22, no. 3, Fall (1988), 215–26) argues that 'the civil wound, is deeper than any foreigner could make' (p. 219).

3 Elizabeth Rapley, *The Dévotes: women and church in seventeenth-century France* (Montreal: McGill-Queens University Press, 1990), p. 48.

4 Rapley, *Dévotes*, pp. 48–51.

5 Marie de Chantal Gueudré, *Histoire de l'ordre des Ursulines en France*, 3 vols (Paris: Éditions St-Paul, 1957), vol. 1, pp. 201–16.

6 [Johann Weyer], *Witches, Devils and Doctors in the Renaissance: Johann Weyer, De praestigiis daemonum*, general editor, George Mora, Medieval and Renaissance Texts and Studies, no. 73 (New York: Binghamton, 1991), pp. 166–8. Several other cases of convent possession – most of them involving witchcraft accusations – had also arisen prior to the Aix outbreak, three of them prior to the 1552 Kentorp case: at Cambrai (1491); Lyons (1526) and Wertet (1550). Rossell Hope Robbins, *The Encyclopedia of Witchcraft and Demonology* (London: Peter Nevill, 1959), pp. 393–4.

7 Ruth Martin, *Witchcraft and the Inquisition in Venice, 1550–1650* (Oxford: Basil Blackwell, 1989), p. 207. See also Giovanna Paolin, *Lo spazio del silenzio: monacazioni forzate, clausura e proposte di vita religiosa femminile nell'età moderna*, Centro Studi Storici Menocchio Montereale Valcellina (Pordenone: Edizione Biblioteca dell'Immagine, 1996), 55–75 and Albrecht Burkardt, 'Les déboires d'une vocation: un cas d'obsession démoniaque chez les Visitandines parisiennes au debut des années 1620', in Bernard Dompnier (ed.), *Visitation et Visitandines aux XVIIe et XVIIIe siècles* (St-Étienne: Publications Université de St-Étienne, 2001), 417–39.

8 Michaelis, 'The Summarie of the History of the Magician burned at Aix, in the yeare 1611, the last of Aprill', in *Admirable Historie*, (hereafter 'Summarie') unpaginated.

9 Michaelis, *Admirable Historie*, 'Summarie'.

10 Léopold Willaert, *Après le Concile de Trente: la restauration Catholique, 1563–1648*, vol. 18 in A. Fliche and V. Martin (eds), *Histoire de l'église depuis les origines jusqu'à nos jours* (Paris: Bloud et Gay, 1960), p. 151.

11 *Pneumalogie* is a misprint of *Pneumologie* in the French edition

12 See note 1.

13 Michaelis, *Admirable Historie*, p. 139.

14 Michaelis, *Admirable Historie*, pp. 143, 166, 171, 176–83, 205–8.

15 Michaelis, *Admirable Historie*, p. 34. Cf. a similar assertion by nuns at Louviers that their possession would redound to the glory of their house. Antoine Laugeois, *L'Innocence opprimée; ou Défense de Mathurin Picard, curé de Mesnil-Jourdain . . . Ouvrage qui n'a jamais été imprimé et extrait sur l'original par M. Chemin curé de Tourneville* [1652], p. 45.

16 Michaelis, *Admirable Historie*, p. 23.

17 Michaelis, *Admirable Historie*, p. 82.

18 Michaelis, *Admirable Historie*, p. 261. Michaelis refers to five nuns at the house being possessed (p. 366).

19 Michaelis, *Admirable Historie*, pp. 83, 296, 304–5; BN Mss fds fs 23851, fols 8r, 18v; BN Mss fds fs 16359, fol. 599r.

20 Michaelis, *Admirable Historie*, p. 365.

21 Michel de Certeau has said in reference to the anticipated death of the priest Urbain Grandier at Loudun in 1634 that the very idea of a death underwrites all other undertakings, providing a system of value and a sense of narrative. Michel de Certeau, *The Possession at Loudun* (1970), trans. Michael B. Smith, with a foreword by Stephen Greenblatt (Chicago and London: University of Chicago Press, 2000), p. 52.

22 Michaelis, *Admirable Historie*, pp. 26, 103, 149, 160–1.

23 Michaelis, *Admirable Historie*, p. 289. The position of Fr d'Ambruc was ambivalent: his allegiances appeared to have shifted rapidly, possibly out of obedience to his superior Michaelis (cf. p. 201).

24 Michaelis, *Admirable Historie*, p. 308. It is not clear why these records might have been seen as a possible impediment to the case against Gaufridy: possibly they implicated Demandols too strongly in Gaufridy's witchcraft, threatening the subsequent construction of her role as his victim. And the fact that Michaelis had them seized from Domptius suggests their contents, which make up the first half of Michaelis's book, may well have been censored.

25 Michaelis informed his readers that he later returned the papers to Domptius. Michaelis, *Admirable Historie*, p. 309.

26 Jules Michelet cited the desire of Domptius to promote Capeau, and Michaelis's greater interest in Demandols as the basis for their divergence. See *Satanism and Witchcraft: a study in medieval superstition* [*La Sorcière*, 1862], trans. A.R. Allinson, (London: Arco, 1958), pp. 179–81.

27 Michaelis, *Admirable Historie*, p. 92.

28 Michaelis, *Admirable Historie*, p. 93.

29 Michaelis, *Admirable Historie*, p. 94.

30 Michaelis, *Admirable Historie*, pp. 201, 304. 'Some priests of the doctrine were tempted to forsake their vocation because of these possessions, and grew factious at the last against their very superiour [Father Romillon]' p. 140.

31 Michaelis, *Admirable Historie*, p. 130.

32 Michaelis, *Admirable Historie*, pp. 303 (paginated as 301), 304.

33 Michaelis, *Admirable Historie*, p. 317.

34 Michaelis, *Admirable Historie*, p. 287.

35 Michaelis, *Admirable Historie*, pp. 287, 307.

36 Michaelis, *Admirable Historie*, p. 292.

37 Michaelis, *Admirable Historie*, p. 293.

38 Michaelis, *Admirable Historie*, p. 288.

39 Michaelis, *Admirable Historie*, pp. 296–7; BN Mss fds fs 23851, fol. 31v; fol. 32r.

40 It was also alleged that Gaufridy had threatened the order of the Priests of the Doctrine, who governed the Ursulines at Aix; 'Summarie'.

41 Stephen Haliczer, *Sexuality in the Confessional: a sacrament profaned* (New York and Oxford: Oxford University Press, 1996).

42 Michaelis, *Admirable Historie*, p. 358.
43 James Farr, *Authority and Sexuality in Early Modern Burgundy* (Oxford and New York: Oxford University Press, 1995).
44 BN Mss fds fs 23851, fol. 12r.
45 Michaelis, *Admirable Historie*, p. 307.
46 BN Mss fds fs 23851, fols 6r–11v.
47 BN Mss fds fs 23851, fol. 12r.
48 Michaelis, *Admirable Historie*, p. 303, paginated as p. 301.
49 Michaelis, *Admirable Historie*, p. 308, marginal note.
50 See M. Viller *et al.*, *Dictionnaire de spiritualité, ascétique et mystique: doctrine et histoire* (Paris: Beauchesne, 1937–1995), vol. 3, cols 1854–7.
51 Michaelis, *Admirable Historie*, p. 369.
52 Michaelis, *Admirable Historie*, pp. 370, 372.
53 Other members of the Parlement and Commissioners, including Messrs Séguiran, Thomassin and Rabache, joined the proceedings at different stages. When the vicar-general Garandeau died in early April 1611, he was replaced by the new vicar-general at Aix, Joseph Pellicot.
54 BN Mss fds fs 23851, fols 12r–117r.
55 The Premier Président of the Parlement, Guillaume Du Vair, offered Demandols immunity on 17 February 1611. Michaelis, *Admirable Historie*, p. 370.
56 Jean Bodin, *De la demonomanie des sorciers*, rev. edn (Paris: Jacques du Puys, 1587), fol. 82r. An abridged English translation of this book is *On the Demon-mania of Witches*, trans. Randy A. Scott, abridged and with an introduction by Jonathan L. Pearl (Toronto: Centre for Reformation and Renaissance Studies, 1995).
57 Nicolas Rémy, *Demonolatry* (1595), trans. E. Allen Ashwin, edited and introduced by Montague Summers (Secaucus, N.J.: University Books, 1974), pp. 35–6.
58 *Disquisitionum magicarum libri sex* (Louvain: Gérard Rivière, 1599–1600), Lib VI, 'Anacephalaeosis', p. 334.
59 From 'Lettre de dom Vincent Longuespée, abbé de Loos-les-Lille, à dom Justo Valenti, secrétaire du procureur général de l'ordre de Cîteaux à Rome [3 May 1616]', in Alain Lottin, 'Sorcellerie, possessions diaboliques et crise conventuelle', in *L'Histoire des faits de la sorcellerie*, Publications de Centre de Recherches d'Histoire Religieuse et d'Histoire des Idées, 8, Angers: Presses de l'Université d'Angers, 1985, 111–132, appended Document 3, pp. 129–30.
60 In his 1585 *Pneumology, or Discourse of Spirits*, pp. 62–3; 91–3; appended to the *Admirable Historie*.
61 In England, the translation of Michaelis's *Histoire* was made, at least ostensibly, with the purpose of using it against itself, as anti-Catholic propaganda. Its preface states that the book was published in order to demonstrate that popery is 'a rotten house . . . growne so ruinous, not only in our estimation, but in the judgement of the chiefe professors and maintainers of the same, that they are driven to support the whole building and frame thereof, with the testimonie of Sathan, the father of lies'. Michaelis, *Admirable Historie*, unpaginated section, 'To the Reader' (English edition only). Note: The English edition of Michaelis's book contains two sections entitled 'To The Reader', the first being a preface for English readers, the second a translation from the French 'Au Lecteur'. Both are unpaginated. Unless otherwise stated, citations hereafter will refer to the section translated from the French edition. It is important to note, however, that both D.P. Walker and Stephen Greenblatt suggested independently that this introduction to the book of Michaelis is most likely a disclaimer inserted by recusant Catholics to disguise their real purpose in publishing a powerful piece of Catholic propaganda. See D.P. Walker, *Unclean Spirits: possession and exorcism in France and England in the late sixteenth and early seventeenth centuries* (London: Scolar Press, 1981), p. 108 and Stephen Greenblatt, 'Shakespeare and the Exorcists', in

Shakespearean Negotiations: the circulation of social energy in Renaissance England (Berkeley and Los Angeles: University of California Press, 1988), 94–128, at p. 188 (Notes).

62 Michaelis, *Admirable Historie*, unpaginated section 'To the Reader'.

63 The work cited is Jean Lorini, *In Acta Apostolorum Commentaria* (Lyon: H. Cardon, 1609), ch. 16.

64 Michaelis, *Admirable Historie*, second doubt, unpaginated section 'The Doubts'.

65 Michaelis, *Admirable Historie*, unpaginated section 'To the Reader'.

66 This supposition could be compared to that of the Franciscan exorcist Jean Benedicti, who describes, conversely, getting confirmation of what a possessed woman said by exorcising her demons, because the demons were more likely to tell the truth than their victim. Jean Benedicti, *La Triomphante victoire de la vierge Marie, sur sept malins esprits, finalement chassées du corps d'une femme, dans l'Eglise des Cordeliers de Lyon* (Lyon: Pierre Rigaud, 1611), p. 28.

67 BN Mss fds fs 23851 fol. 7r.

68 BN Mss fds fs 23851, fol. 17r. Demandols at one point refused for two weeks to participate in any exorcisms where there were strangers present, following the 'filthy gestures' that the demon Asmodeus had been making her perform. Michaelis, *Admirable Historie*, p. 317.

69 BN Mss fds fs 23851, fol. 17r.

70 BN Mss fds fs 23851, fol. 17v.

71 BN Mss fds fs 23851, fol. 19r.

72 BN Mss fds fs 23851, fols 65r–66r.

73 BN Mss fds fs 23851, fols 8r, 16v, 17r.

74 BN Mss fds fs 23851, fol. 19r.

75 BN Mss fds fs 23851, fols 65r–66r.

76 Michaelis, *Admirable Historie*, p. 379. Bodin was wary of the claim that possession could be caused by an outsider but nonetheless conceded that, with God's permission, it was possible. Bodin, *Demonomanie*, fols 179v–180r.

77 Anita M. Walker and Edmund H. Dickerman, 'Magdeleine Des Aymards: demonism or child abuse in early modern France?', *Psychohistory Review*, vol. 24, no. 3 (1996), 239–64.

78 Michaelis, *Admirable Historie*, p. 378.

79 Joseph Levy-Valensi, *La médecine et les médecins français au XVIIe siècle* (Paris: J.-B. Baillère et fils, 1933), p. 297; Jacques Fontaine, *Discours des marques des sorciers et de la reelle possession que le diable prend sur le corps des hommes. Sur le subject du procez de l'abominable & detestable Sorcier Louys Gaufridy, Prestre beneficié en l'Eglise Parrochiale des Accoules de Marseille, qui n'agueres a esté executé a Aix par Arrest de la Cour de Parlement de Provence* (Paris: Denis Langlois, 1611).

80 On the importance of the will, see Per Sörlin, 'The Blåkulla story: absurdity and rationality', trans. A. Cochrane, *Arv*, no. 53, (1997), 131–52 p. 134.

81 Michaelis, *Admirable Historie*, p. 378.

82 Michaelis, *Admirable Historie*, p. 388.

83 BN Mss fds fs 23852, p. 201. For a discussion of this power, see Henri Boguet, *An Examen of Witches*, [*Discours execrable des sorciers*, 1602 edn], trans. E. Allen Ashwin, ed. Montague Summers (London: John Rodker, 1929), Chapter 25. A seventeenth-century manuscript in the Bibliothèque Inguimbertine at Carpentras compares the confession of Gaufridy with chapters in Boguet, and draws attention to a correlation on this point. Bibliothèque Inguimbertine, Ms 2113, pp. 817–47, at p. 826. Many crimes to which Gaufridy confessed find correlations in Boguet, suggesting that Boguet's book may even have been used as a basis for interrogations of Gaufridy and Demandols. The practice of breathing on babies undergoing baptismal exorcism is what earned the early Christians the epithet of 'hissing Christians'. David Mark Jones,

'Exorcism before the Reformation: the problems of saying one thing and meaning another', MA thesis (University of Virginia, 1978), p. 40.

84 *Confession*, p. 3.

85 *Confession*, p. 10. According to Madeleine Demandols, the 'mas' or 'masques' were the lower order of the assembly, whose duty it was to dig up graves and kill children to provide the materials to make charms. The male and female witches were described as 'de mediocre qualité, comme bourgeois, marchand': their job was to make and distribute evil charms. The magicians were 'gentilhommes', whose office it was to do as much harm by blasphemy as they could and to oversee the distribution of the charms. BN Mss fds fs 23851, fol. 65v.

86 *Confession*, pp. 3–13. A longer manuscript version of the confession contains 120 confessions by Gaufridy. BN Mss fds Dupuy, 673, fols 172–7.

87 *Confession*, pp. 3–4. Cf. BN Mss fds fs 23852, p. 201, where a variant of the confession refers to the 'valeurs et fruits' of the sacraments.

88 *Confession*, p. 4.

89 BN Mss fds fs 23851, fols 110r–114v. Gaufridy also attempted to retract his confessions on 17 April but was immediately judged guilty on the 18th. BN Mss fds fs 23851, fols 115r–17r.

90 BN Mss fds fs 16359, (fols 599–601), at fol. 600r–v; also cited by Mandrou, *Magistrats et sorciers*, p. 203.

91 BN Mss fds fs 16359, fol. 600r.

92 BN Mss fds fs 23851, fols 115r–17r.

93 BN Mss fds fs 23851, fol. 117r.

94 BN Mss fds fs 23851, fol. 132r.

95 BN Mss fds fs 16359, fol. 601r.

96 Michaelis, *Admirable Historie*, p. 417.

97 Michaelis, *Admirable Historie*, p. 416.

98 Michaelis, *Admirable Historie*, pp. 416–17.

99 Cf. Walker and Dickerman, 'A notorious woman'.

100 BN Mss fds fs 23852, pp. 245–496.

101 Michaelis, *Admirable Historie*, 'Summarie'; my italics.

102 *Confession*, p. 3.

103 Michaelis, *Admirable Historie*, p. 99.

104 *Le Mercure françois* depicted the trial as 'strange', vol. 2, 1611–12, p. 18.

105 Michaelis, *Admirable Historie*, 'To the Reader'.

106 Michaelis, *Admirable Historie*, 'To the Reader'.

107 Alain Lottin, *Lille: Citadelle de la Contre-Réforme? (1598–1668)* (Dunkerque: Westhoek-Edition, 1984), 170–86, pp. 176–7.

108 On a later case, which involved papal scepticism, see Rainer Decker, 'Die Haltung der römischen Inquisition gegenüber Hexenglauben und Exorzismus am Beispiel der Teufelaustreibungen in Paderborn 1657', in Sönke Lorenz and Dieter Bauer (eds), *Das Ende der Hexenverfolgung* (Stuttgart: Franz Steiner Verlag, 1995), 97–115.

109 Jean Orcibal, *Les origines du Jansenisme* (Paris: J. Vrin, 1947), vol. 2, p. 144.

110 On Loudun, see Chapter 8; on Louviers, see Chapter 6. On Auxonne, 1658–65, see Mandrou, *Magistrats et sorciers*, pp. 204–22. On Agen, 1619, see Gregory Hanlon and Geoffrey Snow, 'Exorcisme et cosmologie tridentine: trois cas agenais en 1619', in *Revue de la Bibliothèque Nationale*, vol. 28, Summer (1988), 12–27. I thank Alfred Soman for this valuable reference. On Agen, see also I. Sylvius, *Miracles des diables chassez, a Bonencontre, & Garresou* (Montauban: Denis Haultin, 1620) and the anonymous *Les conjurations faites a un demon possedant le corps d'une grande Dame* (Paris: Isaac Mesnier, 1619). Sanson Birette wrote that Michaelis's book was also used to support an argument in favour of giving credence to demons in a case in

Normandy. *Refutation de l'erreur du Vulgaire, touchant les responses des diables exorcizez* (Rouen: Jacques Besongne, 1618), pp. 212–15.

111 Jonathan L. Pearl, *The Crime of Crimes: demonology and politics in France, 1560–1620* (Waterloo, Ontario: Wilfred Laurier University Press, 1999), introduction.

112 Birette, *Refutation*, p. 4.

113 Birette, *Refutation*, unpaginated dedication.

114 Birette, *Refutation*, pp. 112–13.

115 Jean Le Normant, *Histoire veritable et memorable de ce qui c'est passé sous l'exorcisme de trois filles possedées és païs de Flandre: en la descouverte & confession de Marie de Sains, soy disant Princesse de la Magie; & Simone Dourlet Complice, & autres*, vol. 2: *De la vocation des magiciens et magiciennes par le ministre des demons*, 2 vols (Paris: Nicolas Buon, 1623), p. 347.

116 *Censura facultatis theologiae parisiensis* (Paris: Claude Griset, [1623]), Bibliothèque Nationale, Paris, Manuscrits fonds Dupuy 641, 167r–170r at fols 168v–169r. My thanks are due to Constant Mews for translating and helping me to interpret this document. Le Normant responded to the censure with a remonstrance, published in pamphlet form, which was written in January 1623, when he had first heard that there were plans to censure the book. See *Remonstrances du Sieur de Chiremont à Messieurs de Sorbonne* (n.p.: no printer, [1623]).

117 It is not possible to tell whether the approbation given by the Faculty theologians is for the Latin edition only or for the Latin and the French editions. The royal privilege issued on 8 October 1622 refers specifically to both.

118 BN Mss fds Dupuy 641, fols 169r–170r.

119 The Faculty's passivity in this case, as Mandrou suggested, appears to have been out of deference to Richelieu, whose support of the possessions at Loudun was well known. Mandrou, *Magistrats et sorciers*, p. 323. The text of the response of the Faculty to the Loudun case may be found in Certeau, *The Possession at Loudun*, pp. 138–40. This response did not refer to the truthfulness of the speech by the 'devils' but instead affirmed that the physical signs of possession in Jeanne des Anges and Claire de Sazilly conformed to those of genuine possession.

120 Michaelis, *Histoire admirable*, approbation found at the end of the section 'Au Lecteur'.

121 Birette, *Refutation*, unpaginated 'Approbation des Docteurs de Sorbosne'. André Du Val also provided Birette with a separate letter of support. (*Refutation*, unpaginated 'Advis de Monsieur du Val'.)

122 Michaelis, *Admirable Historie*, 'To the Reader'; Birette wrote that Michaelis had written 'en qualité d'Historiographe', *Refutation*, p. 214.

123 Birette, *Refutation*, p. 5.

124 Cf. Mary R. O'Neil, '"Sacerdote ovvero strione": ecclesiastical and superstitious remedies in sixteenth-century Italy', in Steven L. Kaplan (ed.), *Understanding Popular Culture* (Berlin: Mouton, 1984), 53–83.

125 *The Life and Death of Lewis Gaufredy: A Priest of the Church of the Accoules in Marseilles in France . . . whose horrible life being made manifest, hee was Arraigned and Condemned by the Court of the Parliament of Aix in Province, to be burnt alive, which was performed the last day of Aprill, 1611. . . . Translated and faithfully collected out of two French Copies* (London: R. Redmer, 1612), unnumbered fourth page.

126 Michaelis, *Admirable Historie*, pp. 30, 31.

127 *Correspondance du Pierre de Bérulle*, edited by Jean Dagens, vol. 3, 1625–29 (Paris: Desclée de Brouwer, 1939), undated letter, pp. 613–14.

128 See *Advis de Messieurs Du Val, Gamache & Ysambert Docteurs de Sorbonne, donné en l'annee 1620. Sur un faict avenu en Lorraine* (n.p.: no printer, [1620]) (BN Mss fds Dupuy 641, fols 171r–172r.)

6 Fighting fire with fire?

1 The major twentieth-century studies of this case are: Daniel Vidal, *Critique de la raison mystique: Bénoît de Canfield, possession et dépossession au XVIIe siècle* (Grenoble: Jérôme Millon, 1990), (Vidal cited as a co-author Christiane Guignes, who had declined to be named as such) and Robert Mandrou, *Magistrats et sorciers en France au XVIIe siècle: une analyse de psychologie historique* (1968) (Paris: Seuil, 1980), pp. 219–26, 284–96. Vidal develops a complex and suggestive argument for the existence of structural homologies between the representational system of the financial world in Paris – many of whose members were adepts of the new mysticism – the structures of Canfield's theology, and the demonology of Louviers. Ultimately a meditation upon the linguistic fabric of social practices, Vidal's analysis leaves room for a more open-ended consideration of the possessions at Louviers, which traces the day-to-day negotiation of authority affecting the progress of the case. I gratefully acknowledge the help of the staff at the Bibliothèque Municipale in Rouen.

2 Indeed, the symbiotic relationship of exorcists to possessed women in many ways paralleled that of spiritual directors to penitents, and in a number of instances, exorcists continued as spiritual directors of the possessed after the woman's possession had ended. The most notable were Jeanne des Anges at Loudun and her exorcist, Jean-Joseph Surin, and Elisabeth de Ranfaing at Nancy, with the Jesuit Nicholas Viardin.

3 Jean Mauzaize (Raoul de Sceaux), *Le rôle et l'action des Capucins de la Province de Paris dans la France religieuse du XVIIème siècle*, 3 vols (Paris: H. Champion, 1978), pp. 905–8; Jean Mauzaize (Raoul de Sceaux), *Histoire des Frères Mineurs Capucins de la Province de Paris (1601–1660)*, 2 vols (Blois: Éditions Notre Dame de la Trinité, 1965), vol. 2, p. 20.

4 *Le Mercure françois*, vol. 9 (1622–24), pp. 355–70. The publication of the edict, a year before Richelieu's return to power as *premier ministre*, coincided with a new anti-Spanish stance in his policies. See also Mauzaize, *Le rôle et l'action*, p. 916.

5 Archange Ripaut, *Abomination des abominations des fausses devotions de ce tems* (Paris: Claude Cramoisy, 1632); Sophie Houdard, 'Des fausses saintes aux spirituelles à la mode: les signes suspects de la mystique', *Dix-Septième Siècle*, vol. 50, no. 3 (1998), 417–32.

6 Mauzaize, *Le rôle et l'action*, pp. 912–17.

7 See Mauzaize, *Le rôle et l'action*, pp. 902–34, for an account of illuminism in the context of the history of the Capuchin order.

8 Mauzaize, *Le rôle et l'action*, p. 927.

9 Mauzaize, *Histoire des Capucins*, vol. 2, p. 21.

10 '[Elles] sèment et espandent les dictes erreurs et pernicieuses opinions èz âmes des personnes simples, tenans assemblées dans les maisons particulières ou elles font lectures et interprétation de certains livres, sur lesquels elles fondent leurs malicieuses persuasions'. This is probably a reference to Madeleine de Flers and her followers. Mauzaize, *Histoire des Capucins*, p. 175, quoting BN Mss fds fs 2760, fol. 391. Sister Candide, a Cistercian nun at Maubisson, became (in the words of Jean Orcibal) 'as if obsessed' under the influence of the controversial mystic nun. She had on several occasions been examined by theologians who suspected her of illuminist practices. Sister Candide said de Flers was herself possessed, and, indicating a belief that possession was akin to witchcraft, she said that during de Flers' residency at Maubisson, she had caused seven nuns at the convent to become possessed. One of these women was said to have killed herself. It is reported that in order to escape the sway of de Flers, Candide required several months under the spiritual direction of the Abbé Saint-Cyran to be delivered of her obsession. Jean Orcibal, *Les origines du Jansensime*, 5 vols (Paris: J. Vrin, 1947), vol. 2 pp. 412–14. Cf. Henri Bremond, *Histoire littéraire du*

sentiment religieux en France depuis la fin des guerres de religion jusqu'à nos jours, 11 vols (Paris: Librairie Bloud et Gay, 1933), vol. 11, pp. 140–47. The early mystically inclined nuns of Port-Royal were similarly said to have been witches. Alexander Sedgwick, 'The nuns of Port-Royal: a study in female spirituality in seventeenth-century France', in Lynda L. Coon, Katherine J. Haldane and Elisabeth W. Sommer (eds), *That Gentle Strength. Historical Perspectives on Women in Christianity* (Charlottesville and London: University Press of Virginia, 1990), 176–89, at p. 182.

11 'Que s'assemblans hommes & femmes en maisons particulières, & la disnans & soupans, & à la fin de ce se joignent charnellement, ils disent qu'en cela ils ne pechent, pource qu'ils ne les cherchent pas', *Le Mercure françois*, vol. 9 (1622–24), p. 364.

12 Mauzaize, *Le rôle et l'action*, p. 908.

13 [Fr Pin], *Vie de la Venerable Mere Françoise de La Croix, institutrice des Religieuses Hospitalieres de la Charité de Notre-Dame, Ordre de S. Augustin* (Paris: Jacques Barrois, 1745), p. 23.

14 [Pin], *Françoise de La Croix*, p. 20.

15 Lucien Barbe, 'Histoire du couvent de Saint Louis et de Sainte Elizabeth de Louviers et de la possession des religieuses de ce monastère', *Bulletin de la Société d'études diverses de l'arondissement de Louviers*, vol. 5 (1898) (Louviers: Eugene Izambert, 1899), 103–434, at p. 116; [Pin], *Françoise de La Croix*, pp. 24, 34.

16 [Pin], *Françoise de La Croix*, p. 30.

17 [Pin], *Françoise de La Croix*, p. 31.

18 Barbe, 'Histoire', pp. 123 and 189.

19 [Pin], *Françoise de La Croix*, p. 34.

20 Esprit Du Bosroger, *La Pieté affligée ou discours historique & Theologique de la Possession des Religieuses dittes de Saincte Elizabeth de Louviers* (Rouen: Jean le Boulenger, 1652), pp. 47–8; Antoine Laugeois, *L'innocence opprimée; ou Défense de Mathurin Picard, curé de Mesnil-Jourdain . . . Ouvrage qui n'a jamais été imprimé et extrait sur l'original par M. Chemin curé de Tourneville* [1652], pp. 40–3. Both sources are, for different reasons, hostile to Pierre David.

21 See *Renaissance Dialectic and Renaissance Piety: Benet of Canfield's Rule of Perfection*, a translation and study by Kent Emery Jr. (Binghamton, New York: Medieval and Renaissance Texts and Studies, no. 50, 1987).

22 Mauzaize, *Le rôle et l'action*, p. 919. See also Louis Cognet, *La spiritualité moderne: l'essor, 1500–1650* (Paris: Aubier, 1966), pp. 485–95; [Agnès Arnauld], *Le Chapelet secret du tres-sainct Sacrement*, published together with the condemnation by the Paris Faculty of 18 June 1633, *Censure des Docteurs de Sorbonne* (n.p.: no publisher, [1633]).

23 *Recit veritable de ce qui s'est fait & passé à Louviers touchant les Religieuses possedées Extraict d'une Lettre escrite de Louviers à un Evesque* (Paris: François Beauplet, 1643), p. 2. This anonymous title will be cited hereafter as *Recit veritable*.

24 Barbe, 'Histoire', p. 121. Father Pin, the biographer of Mother Françoise, suggested, however, that letters written by her to the convent's superiors at the time of the possession, which criticised the possessed nuns, may have been at the root of the accusations of witchcraft levelled at her. *Françoise de La Croix*, p. 125.

25 Picard said to Dufour: 'j'ai le coeur serré . . . je suis tellement occupé a ôter à ces Filles les damnables maximes des adamites qu'elles disent avoir apprises de David'. Laugeois, *L'Innocence opprimée*, p. 41. It appears that David's techniques – whatever they entailed – did not appeal to all the nuns who came to the convent in Louviers. Laugeois, whose principal purpose in writing was to defend the memories of Picard and Boullé, mentioned a woman who came to the convent during the period when David was director, but left quickly. He reported that she said that David made 'vilaines demandes' of her at the grille, and that he had caused the other nuns to assume 'postures effroyables' in the chapel. These events led her to leave the convent

and pursue a life of chastity and devotion in the world. *L'Innocence opprimée*, pp. 32–3.

26 Laugeois, *L'Innocence opprimée*, pp. 42–3.

27 'plus de soixante petits livres qui traitoient de la vue de Dieu'. *L'Innocence opprimée*, pp. 42–4. Picard was himself the author of uncontroversial moral treatises: *L'Arsenac de l'ame d'ou elle tire trois sortes d'armes pour triompher plainement de ses communs ennemis, savoir, du jeusne, de l'aumosne, de l'oraison* (Rouen: L. Du Mesnil, 1626), and *Le Fouet des Paillards, ou Juste punition des voluptueux et charnels, conforme aux arrests divins & humains* (Rouen: E. Vereul, 1628). François Péricard held the bishopric of Evreux from 1613 until his death in July 1646. He was an enthusiastic supporter of new religious houses. M.H. Fisquet, *La France pontificale: histoire chronologique et biographique des archevêques & evêques de tous les diocèses de France* (Paris: Repos, 1865), p. 64.

28 Du Bosroger, *La Pieté affligée*, p. 54.

29 Laugeois, *L'Innocence opprimée*, p. 47.

30 Picard's will states that he wanted to be buried there because he spent so much of his time with the nuns and had been strongly edified by their piety and devotion. 'Testament de Mathurin Picard': reproduced in Barbe, 'Histoire', p. 295.

31 [Charles Desmarets and Madeleine Bavent], *Histoire de Magdelaine Bavent, Religieuse du Monastere de Saint Loüis de Louviers . . . Ensemble l'Interrogatoire de Magdelaine Bavent. De plus l'Arrest donné contre Mathurin Picard, Thomas Boullé & ladite Bavent, tous convaincus du Crime de magie, l'un brulé vif & l'autre mort* (Paris: [Jacques Le Gentil], 1652), p. 42. The Summers translation of this is quite unsatisfactory: *The Confessions of Madeleine Bavent*, trans. Montague Summers (London: The Fortune Press, [1933]).

32 *Sentences et arrests servans a la justification de la calomnieuse accusation faite contre Soeur Françoise de la Croix cy-devant superieure des religieuses & convent des Hospitalieres de la Charité Nostre-Dame, proche la Place Royale* (Paris: Veuve J. Guillemot, 1654), p. 7.

33 *Recit veritable*, p. 5.

34 [Desmarets and Bavent], *Histoire de Magdelaine Bavent*, p. 43. Mary O'Neil noted that Menghi allowed for the possibility of 'devout persons' without priestly office performing exorcisms. 'Discerning superstition: popular errors and orthodox response in late sixteenth-century Italy', Ph.D. Dissertation (Stanford University, 1981), p. 336.

35 *Sentences et arrests*, pp. 6–9; 'Copie en forme de Recueil De ce qui se fait de jour en jour dans le Monastere des filles Relligieuzes Saint Louis dont la pluspart sont folles, maleficiez & tourmentez des Diables. En ceste année 1643', hereafter 'Copie', in *Recueil de pièces sur les possessions des religieuses de Louviers*, (Rouen: Léon Deshays, 1879) (Bibliothèque Municipale, Rouen, I.479^d), p. 4. (The exhumation is referred to in this source as having been carried out on 6 March.) The 'Copie' and another text, 'Pièces détachées extraites du manuscrit HF No. 34 de la Bibliothèque Sainte-Geneviève formant suite à la pièce précédente ("Copie en forme de Recueil" [hereafter cited as 'Pièces'])' are excerpts from a substantial manuscript collection, now housed in the Bibliothèque Sainte-Geneviève, Ms 666, (formerly Ms H.F. no. 34, possibly renumbered by a wag). It contains 120 original *procès-verbaux* of exorcisms from 1643 to 1645. This manuscript was not used by Mandrou or Vidal in their studies of the case.

36 *Recit veritable*, p. 6. Exhumations of this type were rare, though not unknown. Jeanne Ferté found the story of an exhumation of the body of an eremite, carried out in Rueil around 1640. As the prior-curé of Nanterre departed from the mountainside where he had just inhumed Frère François, an eremite of Mont-Valérian, the curé of Rueil, came up the mountain from the other side, with a crowd of people, including twelve pages belonging to Cardinal Richelieu, and proceeded to exhume and then re-bury the brother's body. *La vie religieuse dans les campagnes parisiennes, 1622–1695* (Paris: J. Vrin, 1962), p. 137.

37 *Sentences et arrests*, p. 9.
38 Du Bosroger, *La Pieté affligée*, p. 383. Another promoter of the exorcisms, the anonymous author of the *Recit veritable*, said that one of the reasons Péricard was obliged to seek help from Paris was that 'sa réputation pouvoit estre altérée parmi les personnes qui n'auroient pas eu une assez grande connoissance de son procedé'. *Recit veritable*, p. 6.
39 *Sentences et arrests*, p. 8.
40 Bibliothèque de l'institut, Fonds Godefroy, ms. 273, fol. 10; *Sentences et arrests*, p.10.
41 *Recit veritable*, p. 6; *Sentences et arrests*, p. 9; 'Copie', p. 4.
42 In this trial, the reputation of the Parlement of Rouen for harshness in cases of witchcraft appears to have been overshadowed by a desire to act against an ecclesiastical verdict of witchcraft.
43 Roland Mousnier, *Peasant Uprisings in Seventeenth-century France, Russia and China* (London: Allen & Unwin, 1971), pp. 87–113.
44 'personnes de prélature ou de dignité Ecclesiastique'. Bibliothèque de l'Institut, Fonds Godefroy, ms. 273, fol. 10.
45 *Recit veritable*, p. 7.
46 Grenoble: Jérôme Millon, 1993. Jean-Joseph Surin, *Correspondance*, ed. and annotated by Michel de Certeau, (Bibliothèque européenne) (Paris: Desclée de Brouwer, 1966), p. 470.
47 *Attestation de Messieurs les Commissaires envoyez par sa Majesté pour prendre connoissance, avec Monseigneur l'Evesque d'Evreux, de l'estat des Religieuses qui paroissent agitées au Monastere de Saint Louys & Sainte Elizabeth de Louviers*, (n.p., no printer [1643]), p. 2.
48 *Attestation de Messieurs*, pp. 2–4.
49 *Recit veritable*, pp. 7–8; *Attestation de Messieurs*, pp. 2, 4.
50 According to Barbe, Anne Barré was received into the convent in 1633. 'Histoire', p. 189. However, the *Histoire de Magdelaine Bavent* (p. 42) refers to Barré having entered in 1642, not long before Picard's death. The anonymous *Recit veritable*, also lists her as a novice (p. 7).
51 *Recit veritable*, pp. 7–8.
52 *Sentences et arrests*, p. 10.
53 The original is housed at the Bibliothèque Mazarine, Ms 2214, fol. 111v. It is reproduced in Jules Garinet, *Histoire de la magie en France* (Paris: Foulon, 1818), p. 328, and in Du Bosroger, *La Pieté affligée*, p. 359.
54 Yet there is a crucial difference. Urbain Grandier was a high-profile public figure with powerful patrons. Not so Madeleine Bavent and Thomas Boullé. And while Françoise de La Croix's connections appear to have kept her from the worse extremes of a witch trial, she was nonetheless degraded in the process of being exonerated.
55 *Attestation de Messieurs*, p. 1; *Sentences et arrests*, p. 27.
56 *Recit veritable*, pp. 3–4.
57 A. Garreau, *Claude Bernard: le pauvre prêtre, parisien du Faubourg Saint-Germain* (Paris: Éditions du Cèdre, 1965).
58 Thomas Le Gauffre, *Recit veritable De ce qui s'est fait & passé aux Exorcismes de plusieurs Religieuses de la ville de Louviers, en presence de Monsieur le Penitencier d'Evreux, & Monsieur le Gauffre* (Paris: Gervais Alliot, 1643), p. 36.
59 Bibliothèque Nationale, Paris, Mss fds fs 18695, fol. 189r–v.
60 *Recit veritable*, pp. 1–2.
61 *Recit veritable*, p. 1.
62 Du Bosroger, *La Pieté affligée*, pp. 105, 108; BSG Ms 666, fol. 1 and 'Pièces', pp. 18–19, 23.
63 'nostre vénérable assemblée'; 'ces hauts & admirables exercices & perfections'; 'très-saints et adorables fondemens de perfection', 'hauts & sublimes exercises'. 'Explication

du testament de David' and 'Explication du testament de Picard' in [Desmarets and Bavent], *Histoire de Magdelaine Bavent*, second pagination run, p. 30.

64 Françoise de La Croix (called sometimes 'La Petite Mère' or 'La Nonnette') was implicated in the case late in 1643. See 'Copie', p. 14; BSG Ms 666, fol. 102. Clear allegations of witchcraft did not emerge until 1644. [Pin], *Françoise de La Croix*, p. 128.

65 See BSG Ms 666.

66 'Copie', pp. 9–10.

67 'Copie', p. 21.

68 See BSG Mss 666, throughout.

69 'Pièces', p. 11.

70 'Copie', p. 5.

71 'Copie', p. 12.

72 'Copie', p. 6; *Sentences et arrests*, p. 8.

73 '[I]l fauct une puissance extraordinaire de Dieu pour conserver cette chienne de maison.' 'Pièces', pp. 9–10.

74 'La nuict daprès que la pierre fondamentale fust cimentée, tous les Sorciers y vinrent & y donnèrent leurs bénédictions, & ce jour la mesme nous en firent feste à nostre sabath & voulions avoir icy toujours une Sorcière & par tous les Convents de cet Ordre, & il debvoit naistre lEntechrist d'une Abesse & dun Evesque.' 'Pièces', p. 12.

75 Jean Le Breton, *La Deffense de la verité. Touchant la possession des religieuses de Louviers*, (Évreux: Nicolas Hamillon, 1643) (facsimile in *Recueil de pièces sur les possessions des religieuses de Louviers* (Rouen: Léon Deshays, 1879), pp. 9–10.

76 [Pierre Yvelin], *Examen de la possession des religieuses de Louviers*, (Paris: no publisher, 1643), p. 12.

77 'Copie', pp. 12–13.

78 Le Gauffre, *Recit veritable de ce qui s'est fait & passé aux exorcismes*, p. 24.

79 'Copie', p. 22.

80 See, for example, 'Pièces', pp. 16–17; 'Copie', pp. 7–8, 23; BSG Ms 666, fols 78v, 84–88.

81 *Sentences et arrests*, p. 11.

82 'Interrogatoire', in [Desmarets and Bavent], *Histoire de Magdelaine Bavent*, (second pagination), pp. 5, 14, 20; 'Pièces', pp. 26–7.

83 An anonymous observer wrote: 'elle me dist quelle estoit encor si hors delle mesme quelle navoit point de mémoire davoir faict de pareille promesse au diable'. 'Pièces', p. 27.

84 Pierre de Langle, *Procès verbal de Mr le Penitentier d'Evreux de ce qui luy est arrivé dans la prison, interrogeant et consolant Magdeleine Bavent, Magicienne à une heureus Conversion & repentance* (Paris: François Beauplet, 1643).

85 *Sentences et arrests*, p. 11.

86 Bibliothèque de L'Arsenal Ms 5416, pp. 1204, 1241, 1264–96, 1315, 1340–1.

87 *Arrest de la Cour de Parlement de Roüen contre Mathurin Picard & Thomas Boullé deuëment attains & convaincus des crimes de Magie, Sortilege, Sacrileges, Impietez & cas abominables commis contre la Majesté divine, & autres mentionnez au Procez* (Rouen: David Du Petit Val et Jean Viret; Orléans: Gabriel Frémont, 1647), p. 6; *Sentences et arrests*, p. 11; Du Bosroger, *La Pieté affligée*, pp. 431–8 (paginated as 431–28).

88 See also Mandrou, *Magistrats et sorciers*, p. 225.

89 *Arrest de la Cour*, p. 7.

90 *Arrest de la Cour*, pp. 7–8.

91 *Arrest de la Cour*, p. 8. Lucien Barbe noted, however, that the actual dispersal was inconclusive and that within a few years the convent had re-formed. 'Histoire', p. 157.

92 *Arrest de la Cour*, p. 8.

93 Laugeois, *L'Innocence opprimée*, pp. 76–83.

94 'une entreprise manifeste contre la Jurisdiction de Monsieur l'Archevesque de Paris, à

laquelle elle [Françoise de La Croix] est entièrement sujette'. *Sentences et arrests*, p. 3. It might be noted that Bishop Péricard died in July 1646: thus the possessions lost their most influential supporter.

95 *Sentences et arrests*, pp. 3–6. The second intervention, on 21 June 1647, gave attribution of the case to the Parlement of Paris and forbad any other judges to consider it.

96 *Sentences et arrests*, pp. 17–18.

97 *Sentences et arrests*, pp. 18–25; [Pin], *Françoise de La Croix*, p. 154; Du Saussay was also a papal protonotary, and *officiel* of the archepiscopal court. For his role in the investigation of illuminism in Picardy in the 1630s, see Mauzaize, *Le rôle et l'action*, p. 927.

98 *Sentences et arrests*, p. 22; [Pin], *Françoise de La Croix*, pp. 156–57.

99 (Paris: Jean Du Crocq, 1652). Hereafter cited as *Advis*.

100 It is possible that if Mazarin had suppressed news of the case, it may have been to hide his own early support of the pursuit of the case by Péricard.

101 *Advis*, p. 4.

102 *Advis*, pp. 4–5.

103 The two-page pamphlet begins with the words: 'Ce qui donnera beaucoup de connoissances & de lumières à Mr. le Lieutenant Criminel pour le jugement de la petite Mere . . .'. No title page, no printer, no date (cited hereafter as 'Ce qui donnera'). This work is also included in *Recueil de pièces* (see note 35) at pp. 37–8.

104 'Ce qui donnera', p. 2.

105 'actions naturelles & surnaturelles, tant des extases, que des enlevemens de corps pratiquez par la Petite Mère dés [sic] son enfance'. 'Ce qui donnera', pp. 1–2.

106 *Sentences et arrests*, p. 22.

107 *Sentences et arrests*, pp. 24–9.

108 [Desmarets and Bavent], *Histoire de Magdelaine Bavent*, pp. 5–6. The printer Jacques Le Gentil wrote a dedicatory epistle to the Duchess of Orléans. The *Histoire* saw three editions, however, and the second and third editions suppressed the dedicatory epistle, the name of Desmarets and that of the printer. And where the first two editions contained extracts from the 1647 proceedings concerning Françoise de La Croix, the third saw them removed and replaced by the 'Interrogatoire' of Bavent. Lemonnyer suggested that the Duchess of Orléans may have been displeased by the association of her name with the lurid content of the confession. *Histoire de Madeleine Bavent religieuse du monastère de Saint-Louis de Louviers par le R.-P. Desmarets. Réimpression textuelle sur l'édition rarissime de 1652 précédée d'une notice bio-bibliographique et suivie de plusiers pièces supplémentaires* (Rouen: J. Lemonnyer, 1878), pp. xxiii–xxvi.

109 [Desmarets and Bavent], *Histoire de Magdelaine Bavent*, p. 8.

110 [Desmarets and Bavent], *Histoire de Magdelaine Bavent*, p. 8.

111 'Il disoit, qu'il falloit faire mourir le péché par le péché, pour rentrer en innocence, & ressembler à nos premiers parents, qui estoient sans aucune honte de leur nudité devant leur premiere coulpe.' [Desmarets and Bavent], *Histoire de Magdelaine Bavent*, p. 9.

112 [Desmarets and Bavent], *Histoire de Magdelaine Bavent*, pp. 9–10.

113 [Desmarets and Bavent], *Histoire de Magdelaine Bavent*, p. 11. Finding this piece of paper – which in other accounts was said to contain the 'testaments' of David and Picard – was one of the principal quests of the exorcisms.

114 [Desmarets and Bavent], *Histoire de Magdelaine Bavent*, pp. 12–13.

115 [Desmarets and Bavent], *Histoire de Magdelaine Bavent*, p. 15.

116 [Desmarets and Bavent], *Histoire de Magdelaine Bavent*, p. 15.

117 [Desmarets and Bavent], *Histoire de Magdelaine Bavent*, pp. 18, 21, 22, 26, 36, 39, 41.

118 [Desmarets and Bavent], *Histoire de Magdelaine Bavent*, p. 13.

119   Vidal, *Critique*, p. 189.
120   Du Bosroger, *La Pieté affligée*, pp. 36, 53. Du Bosroger conceded that some of the nuns did not reject the teachings of David as early as they might have. *La Pieté affligée*, p. 36.
121   Sister Marie Thenart had not been among the possessed. Barbe, 'Histoire', p. 202; Vidal, *Critique*, p. 189. Cf. also Du Bosroger, *La Pieté affligée*, p. 18.
122   Du Bosroger, *La Pieté affligée*, p. 35.
123   Du Bosroger, *La Pieté affligée*, p. 43.
124   Michel de Certeau, *La possession de Loudun* (1970), Collection Archives (Paris: Gallimard/Julliard, 1980), p. 68. I cite the French here, in preference to using the English translation's term 'body language'. Michel de Certeau, *The Possession at Loudun* (1970), trans. Michael B. Smith, with a foreword by Stephen Greenblatt (Chicago and London: University of Chicago Press, 2000), p. 44.
125   Du Bosroger, *La Pieté affligée*, pp. 43–4.
126   Du Bosroger, *La Pieté affligée*, pp. 46–7.
127   Du Bosroger, *La Pieté affligée*, p. 48.
128   On the association of illuminism with austerity, see Jean Orcibal, *Les origines du Jansenisme* (Paris: J. Vrin, 1947), vol. 2, p. 411.
129   Du Bosroger, *La Pieté affligée*, p. 76.
130   Du Bosroger, *La Pieté affligée*, p. 52.
131   Du Bosroger, *La Pieté affligée*, p. 53.
132   Du Bosroger, *La Pieté affligée*, pp. 49–50.
133   Du Bosroger, *La Pieté affligée*, pp. 50–1.
134   Du Bosroger, *La Pieté affligée*, p. 51.
135   Du Bosroger, *La Pieté affligée*, p. 51. A key text in this movement, which the nuns were also alleged to have read, was *La Theologie germanicque, Livret auquel est traicté comment il faut dépouiller le vieil homme, & vestir le nouveau* (Anvers: Christofle Plantin, 1558); in a modern edition *Theologia Germanica*, in Vergilius Ferm (ed.), *Classics of Protestantism* (London: Peter Owen, 1959), pp. 3–38.
136   Du Bosroger, *La Pieté affligée*, pp. 51–2.
137   See Andrew Cambers, 'Ritual Reading: Edward Fairfax's *Daemonologia* and the power of the book in possession cases in early modern England', ch. 3 in 'Print, manuscript, and godly cultures in the north of England, c. 1600–1650', University of York, D.Phil. thesis, 2003. I thank the author for this reference, following the presentation of an excerpt at the conference 'Witchcraft in Context', University of York, April, 2002
138   'Des faux spirituels, & du moyen de discerner entre la vraye & la fausse Spiritualité', Du Bosroger, *La Pieté affligée*, p. 68.
139   Du Bosroger, *La Pieté affligée*, p. 68.
140   Du Bosroger, *La Pieté affligée*, p. 70.
141   Du Bosroger, *La Pieté affligée*, p. 71.
142   Du Bosroger, *La Pieté affligée*, p. 71.
143   Du Bosroger, *La Pieté affligée*, p. 74. This example may also refer to Madeleine de Flers. I have found no reference to allegations of her having performed the Mass, however.
144   See Mauzaize, *Histoire des Capucins*, vol. 2, p. 175, concerning the women illuminists in Picardy. Du Bosroger also referred to a 'Beata' named Julia in Naples in 1615 who was said to have led several woman and girls into heresy. Du Bosroger, *La Pieté affligée*, p. 75.
145   Laugeois, *L'Innocence opprimée*, p. 43.
146   Du Bosroger, *La Pieté affligée*, pp. 48–9. Cf: Anon, *La perle évangélique* (1602), edited by Daniel Vidal, Grenoble: Jérôme Millon, 1997. I have been unable to identify 'The treasure hidden in the field'.

147   Du Bosroger, *La Pieté affligée*, p. 49.

7   Ecstasy, possession, witchcraft

1   E. William Monter, *Witchcraft in France and Switzerland: the borderlands during the Reformation* (Ithaca, N.Y.: Cornell University Press, 1976), p. 60.

2   Alison Weber, 'Between ecstasy and exorcism: religious negotiation in sixteenth-century Spain', *Journal of Medieval and Renaissance Studies*, vol. 23, no. 2, Spring (1993), 221–34; R. Po-Chia Hsia, *The World of Catholic Renewal, 1540–1770* (Cambridge, UK; New York: Cambridge University Press, 1998), ch. 9, 'Holy women, beatas, demoniacs'.

3   Mark 9:26–7.

4   H.C. Erik Midelfort, 'The Devil and the German people: reflections on the popularity of demon possession in sixteenth-century Germany', in *Articles on Witchcraft, Magic and Demonology*, vol. 9, 'Possession and Exorcism', ed. and with an introduction by Brian P. Levack (New York and London: Garland, 1992), 113–33, pp. 125–6.

5   Pierre Crespet, *Deux Livres de la hayne de Sathan et malins esprits contre l'homme, & de l'homme contre eux* (Paris: Guillaume de la Noue, 1590), fol. 209v.

6   Sanson Birette, *Refutation de l'erreur du Vulgaire, touchant les responses des diables exorcizez* (Rouen: Jacques Besongne, 1618), p. 31.

7   Birette, *Refutation*, pp. 30–81.

8   Pardoux's words were translated and annotated in Congnard, *Histoire de Marthe Brossier pretendue possedee tiree du Latin de Messire Jacques August. de Thou, President au Parlement de Paris* (Rouen: Jacques Herault, 1652), p. 23. The original text is *De Morbis animi* (Lyon: Rigaud, 1649), pp. 30–8.

9   Cf. [Pierre Maignart], *Traicté des marques des possedez, et la preuve de la véritable Possession des Religieuses de Louviers* (Rouen: Charles Osmont, 1644), p. 6; Crespet, *De la hayne de Sathan*, fol. 206r. Congnard, a medical doctor, was apparently unaware of this possibility: referring to the 'ecclesiastical censures', he noted, 'These are the words of Pardoux'. Congnard, *Histoire de Marthe Brossier*, p. 23. Jean Bodin suggested that this might be understood as excommunication. *De la demonomanie des sorciers*, rev. edn (Paris: Jacques du Puys, 1587), fol. 175r.

10   Birette, *Refutation*, p. 246; on parents' curses, pp. 31–40.

11   Pardoux in Congnard, *Histoire de Marthe Brossier*, pp. 22–3.

12   [François Buisseret], *Histoire admirable et veritable des choses advenues a l'endroict d'une Religieuse professe du convent des Soeurs noires, de la ville de Mons en Hainaut, natifve de Sore sur Sambre, aagee de vingt cinq ans, possedee du maling esprit, & depuis delivree* (Paris: Claude de Monstre-oeil, 1586), fol. 12r–v; 32r.

13   Grudius wrote a passage ('Le Discours de l'expulsion d'un autre malin esprit') in Jean Benedicti, *La Triomphante victoire de la vierge Marie, sur sept malins esprits, finalemant chassées du corps d'une femme, dans l'Eglise des Cordeliers de Lyon* (Lyon: Pierre Rigaud, 1611), pp. 70–1.

14   *Brièfve intelligence de l'opinion de trois Docteurs de Sorbonne & du livre du P. Birette. touchant les Diables Exorcisez*, part of (Fr) Tranquille, *Véritable relation des justes procedures observées au faict de la possession des Ursulines de Loudun. Et au procez d'Urbain Grandier* (La Flèche: George Griveau, 1634), pp. 50–80, at p. 68.

15   Henri Boguet, *An Examen of Witches*, trans. E. Allen Ashwin, ed. Montague Summers (London: John Rodker, 1929), pp. 13–14.

16   See Jacques Le Brun, 'Mutations de la notion de martyre au XVIIe siècle d'après les biographies spirituelles féminines', in Jacques Marx (ed.) *Sainteté et martyre dans les religions du livre* (Brussels: Institut d'Études des Réligions et de la Laïcité, 1989), pp. 77–96.

17   See Gillian T.W. Ahlgren, 'Negotiating sanctity: holy women in sixteenth-century Spain', *Church History*, vol. 64, no. 3 (1995), 373–88.

18 *Disquisitionum magicarum libri sex* (Louvain: Gérard Rivière, 1599–1600), lib. II, q. 25, p. 239. Here Del Rio appears to have followed Bodin, *Demonomanie*, fol. 101v.

19 *Disquisitionum magicarum*, lib. II, q. 25, p. 239; Bodin, *Demonomanie*, fol. 119r. See also Ahlgren, 'Negotiating sanctity', pp. 382–3.

20 André Duval, *La Vie admirable de soeur Marie de l'Incarnation religieuse converse en l'ordre de nostre Dame du mont Carmel, appellée au monde la Damoiselle Acarie* (Douay: Baltazar Bellère, 1621), pp. 122–32; Germain Habert, *La Vie du Cardinal Berulle instituteur et premier Supérieur Général de la Congrégation de l'Oratoire de Jesus-Christ nostre Seigneur* (Paris: Veuve Jean Camusat et Pierre le Petit, 1646), pp. 95–7.

21 Duval, *Vie admirable*, pp. 123–4.

22 Duval, *Vie admirable*, pp. 122, 131.

23 Duval, *Vie admirable*, p. 125.

24 Duval, *Vie admirable*, p. 127.

25 Duval, *Vie admirable*, p. 130.

26 Habert, *Vie de Bérulle*, p. 97. Habert's simile recalls the passage of Hermes Trismegistus in the *Asclepius*, concerning idols which were animated by magic. Frances A. Yates, *Giordano Bruno and the Hermetic Tradition* (London: Routledge and Kegan Paul, 1964), pp. 9, 37. I thank Charles Zika for this observation.

27 Habert, *Vie de Bérulle*, p. 97. I associate the absence in this case of any mention of the possibility that Tavernier was a witch with the fact that she had had support from members of the Parisian elite. The potential to undermine their authority by such an accusation would have been great and the will to do so was not there.

28 [Buisseret], *Histoire admirable et veritable*, fol. 12v.

29 [Buisseret], *Histoire admirable et veritable*, fol. 12v.

30 [Buisseret], *Histoire admirable et veritable*, fol 13r.

31 [Buisseret], *Histoire admirable et veritable*, fol. 15r.

32 [Buisseret], *Histoire admirable et veritable*, fol. 15r–v.

33 [Buisseret], *Histoire admirable et veritable*, fol. 15v.

34 See: J.-M. Sallmann, 'Théories et pratiques du discernement des esprits', in *Visions indiennes, visions baroques: les métissages de l'inconscient* (Paris: PUF, 1992), 91–116; Christian Renoux, 'Discerner la sainteté des mystiques: quelques exemples italiens de l'âge baroque', in *Rives nord-méditerranéennes*, 2e série, 3, 1999, 19–28; Paschal Boland, *The Concept of* Discretio Spirituum *in John Gerson's 'De Probatione Spirituum' and 'De Distinctione Verarum Visionum A Falsis'* (Washington: The Catholic University of America Press, 1959).

35 Cited in William Christian Jr., 'Provoked religious weeping in early modern Spain', in J. Davis (ed.), *Religious Organization and Religious Experience*, Association of Social Anthropologists Monograph no. 21 (London: Academic Press, 1982), pp. 97–114, at p. 103, citing Loyola, *Obras Completas* I, (Madrid: Biblioteca de Autores Cristianos, 1947). Cf. also Crespet, *De la hayne de Sathan*, fols 198v–199r.

36 [Buisseret], *Histoire admirable et veritable*, fol. 19r.

37 St Teresa of Avila, *Collected Works*, trans. Kieran Kavanagh and Otilio Rodriguez, vol. 3 (Washington: ICS Publications), 1985, p. 141.

38 Duval, *Vie admirable*, p. 561.

39 Duval, *Vie admirable*, p. 122.

40 Duval, *Vie admirable*, p. 131.

41 Claude Pithoys, *La Descouverture des faux possedez*, (Châlons: Germain Nobily, 1621), reproduced in *A Seventeenth-century Exposure of Superstition: Select texts of Claude Pithoys (1587–1676)*, with an introduction and notes by P.J.S. Whitmore (The Hague: Nijhoff, International Archives of the History of Ideas, no. 49, 1972), p. 53 (modern editor's pagination). The value of the Whitmore edition is in its relative accessibility in modern libraries, rather than in its commentaries. The best full-length account of the Ranfaing case remains Étienne Delcambre and Jean Lhermitte, *Un cas énigmatique*

de possession diabolique en Lorraine au XVIIe siècle: Élisabeth de Ranfaing, l'énergumène de Nancy (Nancy: Societé d'Archéologie Lorraine, 1956).

42   Pithoys, *La Descouverture des faux possedez*, p. 63.

43   Robert Mandrou, *Magistrats et sorciers en France au XVIIe siècle: une analyse de psychologie historique* (1968) (Paris: Seuil, 1980), p. 249.

44   Mandrou, *Magistrats et sorciers*, p. 251.

45   Sébastien Michaelis, *The Admirable Historie of the Possession and Conversion of a Penitent woman. Seduced by a magician that made her to become a Witch . . . Whereunto is annexed a Pneumology, or Discourse of Spirits*, trans. W.B. (London: William Aspley, 1613), pp. 416–17. Bibliothèque Nationale, Paris, Manuscrits fonds français, 23852, pp. 245–496. See also Anita M. Walker and Edmund H. Dickerman, 'A notorious woman: possession, witchcraft and sexuality in seventeenth-century Provence', *Historical Reflections*, vol. 27, no. 1 (2001), 1–26.

46   *Advis de Messieurs Du Val, Gamache & Ysambert Docteurs de Sorbonne, donné en l'annee 1620. sur un faict avenu en Lorraine*, n.p., no printer, [1620], Bibliothèque Nationale, Paris, Manuscrits, fonds Dupuy 641, 171r–172r, at fol. 172r.

47   BN Mss fds fs 23851, fols 7r, 17r.

48   BN Mss fds fs 18695, fol. 167r. A Dominican was also permitted to touch the nun (fol. 167v).

49   'Relation de M. Hédelin, abbé d'Aubignac, touchant les possédées de Loudun au mois de septembre 1637', in Robert Mandrou, (ed.) *Possession et sorcellerie au XVIIe siècle: Textes inédits* (Paris: Fayard, 1979), p. 180.

50   *Brièfve Intelligence*, p. 76.

8 'God's witches'

1   The term is from Gabriella Zarri, *Le sante vive: cultura e religiosità femminile nella prima età moderna* (Turin: Rosenberg and Sellier, 1990), p. 12.

2   Lucetta Scaraffia and Gabriella Zarri (eds), *Women and Faith: Catholic religious life in Italy from late antiquity to the present* (Cambridge, Massachusetts and London: Harvard University Press, 1999), Introduction, p. 4.

3   For a discussion of the many forms of martyrdom to which female devotees turned in this period, see Jacques Le Brun, 'Mutations de la notion de martyre au XVIIe siècle d'après les biographies spirituelles féminines', in Jacques Marx (ed.), *Sainteté et martyre dans les religions du livre* (Brussels: Institut d'Études des Religions et de la Laïcité, 1989), pp. 77–96. See also James R. Farr, *Authority and Sexuality in Early Modern Burgundy* (1550–1730), (Oxford and New York: Oxford University Press, 1995).

4   See Zarri, *Le sante vive*.

5   The literature on these developments for Spain and Italy is vast. Some important monographs are: Alison Weber, *Teresa of Avila and the Rhetoric of Femininity* (Princeton, N.J.: Princeton University Press, 1990); Richard L. Kagan, *Lucrecia's Dreams: politics and prophecy in sixteenth-century Spain* (Berkeley, Calif.: University of California Press, 1990); Jodi Bilinkoff, *The Avila of Saint Teresa: religious reform in a sixteenth-century city* (Ithaca, N.Y.: Cornell University Press, 1989) and Gillian T.W. Ahlgren, *Teresa of Avila and the Politics of Sanctity* (Ithaca, N.Y. and London: Cornell University Press, 1996). See bibliography for further items. For France: Sophie Houdard, 'Des fausses saintes aux spirituelles à la mode: les signes suspects de la mystique', *Dix-Septième Siècle*, vol. 50, no. 3 (1998) 417–32; Alexander Sedgwick, 'The nuns of Port-Royal: a study in female spirituality in seventeenth-century France', and Thomas Head, 'The religion of the "Femmelettes": ideals and experience among women in fifteenth- and sixteenth-century France' in Lynda L. Coon, Katherine J. Haldane and Elisabeth W. Sommer (eds), *That Gentle Strength. Historical perspectives on women in Christianity*, (Charlottesville and London: University Press of Virginia,

1990), 176–89 and 149–75 respectively. See note 182, however, for recent French theories of mystical psychology.

6 Sanson Birette referred to possession as the action of a 'spiritual substance which seems to dislodge the soul'. *Refutation de l'erreur du Vulgaire, touchant les responses des diables exorcizez* (Rouen: Jacques Besongne, 1618), p. 21.

7 Jeanne des Anges, *Autobiographie* (reprint of 1886 edition), followed by Michel de Certeau, 'Jeanne des Anges' (Grenoble: Jérôme Millon, 1990), 304–44.

8 D. P. Walker, *Unclean Spirits: possession and exorcism in France and England in the late sixteenth and early seventeenth centuries* (London: Scolar Press, 1981), p. 72; cf. Stuart Clark, *Thinking with Demons: the idea of witchcraft in early modern Europe* (Oxford: Oxford University Press, 1997) Part One.

9 Parts of chapter 8 appeared in 'Possession sanctified: the case of Marie des Vallées', in Jürgen Beyer, Albrecht Burkardt, Fred van Lieburg and Marc Wingens, (eds), *Confessional Sanctity, (c.1550–c.1800)*, (Veröffentlichungen Des Instituts Für Europäische Geschichte Mainz, Abteilung Abendländische Religionsgeschichte, Beiheft 51, Herausgegeben von Gerhard May), (Mainz: Verlag Philipp von Zabern, 2003), 259–70. Reproduced by kind permission.

10 Le P. Costil, 'Annales de la Congregation de Jesus et Marie' (1722), manuscript (Eudist Archives, Paris), p. 48.

11 Jean Eudes, 'Vie Admirable de Marie des Vallées et des choses admirables qui se sont passées en elle', fol. 4v–5r. This text is referred to as the 'Quebec manuscript' (hereafter referred to as MS Q), a partial rendering of a longer biography, or hagiography, of Vallées by Eudes, the original of which is lost. The manuscript is held in the Eudist Archives in Paris. I gratefully acknowledge the generosity of the archivist P. Joseph Racapé, who permitted me to consult the work, and provided much assistance with other aspects of this research.

12 MS Q, fol 6r.

13 Bibliothèque Mazarine, Paris, Manuscript 3177 (hereafter BM MS 3177), p. 4. (This is known as the 'Manuscrit Renty', or 'Memoire d'une admirable conduite de Dieu sur une âme particulière appelée Marie des Coutances'). Historians are divided as to the extent of the contribution of Jean Eudes and Gaston de Renty to this text; however it appears that Renty wrote the first section and the remainder is from the writings of Eudes. Cf. Raymond Triboulet, *Gaston de Renty, 1611–1649, un homme de ce monde, un homme de Dieu* (Paris: Beauchesne, 1991), p. 333; Paul Milcent, *Saint Jean Eudes: un artisan du renouveau chrétien au XVIIe siècle* (Paris: Cerf, 1992), p. 152. Cf. Gaston Jean-Baptiste de Renty, *Correspondance*, texte établi et annoté par Raymond Triboulet (Bibliothèque Européenne) (Paris: Desclée de Brouwer, 1978).

14 MS Q, fol. 6v.

15 BM MS 3177, p. 5.

16 Bibliothèque Nationale, Paris, Manuscrits, Fonds français (hereafter BN Mss fds fs.) 11950, p. 4; Jean Eudes 'Abrégé de la vie et de l'état de Marie des Vallées', MS 68, Bibliothèque Municipale Jacques Prévert, Cherbourg (hereafter MS Cherbourg), fol. 3v. My thanks are due to Mme Jacqueline Vastel at the Bibliothèque Municipale Jacques-Prévert, Cherbourg, for kindly supplying this material. The date of the Cherbourg MS is uncertain Paul Milcent, ('Marie des Vallées' in M. Viller *et al.*, (eds), *Dictionnaire de spiritualité, ascétique et mystique: doctrine et histoire* (Paris: Beauchesne, 1937–1995), vol. 16, 207–12, at p. 212) and the Abbé of Montmartin, Lelièvre, in a 1920 note on its cover, dated it at 1653, whereas Charles du Chesnay says it was written in 1674 ('Quelques questions relatives à Marie des Vallées', *Notre Vie*, 49, jan.–fév., 1956, pp. 7–14, at p. 10.)

17 BM MS 3177, pp. 1–2.

18 On this tension, see H.C. Erik Midelfort, 'The Devil and the German people: reflections on the popularity of demon possession in sixteenth-century Germany', in

Articles on Witchcraft, Magic and Demonology, vol. 9, 'Possession and Exorcism', (ed.) and with an introduction by Brian P. Levack (New York and London: Garland, 1992), 113–33 at p. 127.

19 See Le Brun, 'Mutations de la notion de martyre'.

20 [Charles Dufour], Lettre à un docteur de Sorbonne sur le sujet de plusieurs Écrits composez de la vie & de l'état de Marie des Valées, du Diocese de Coutances (n.p.: no publisher, 1674), p. 2.

21 MS Q, fols 7v–8r. Cf. also BM MS 3177, p. 5.

22 MS Cherbourg, fol. 3v.

23 Paul Milcent, Saint Jean Eudes, p. 153.

24 MS Cherbourg, fol. 4r; MS Q fol. 7r.

25 MS Q, fol. 7r.

26 MS Q, fol.10v.

27 The Premier Président of the Parlement of Aix, Guillaume Du Vair, offered Demandols immunity on 17 February 1611. Sébastien Michaelis, The Admirable Historie of the Possession and Conversion of a Penitent woman. Seduced by a magician that made her to become a Witch . . . Whereunto is annexed a Pneumology, or Discourse of Spirits, trans. W.B. (London: William Aspley, 1613), p. 370.

28 MS Q, fol. 10v; BM MS 3177, p. 109.

29 MS Q, fol. 11v.

30 MS Q, fol. 12r.

31 MS Cherbourg, fol. 5r.

32 MS Cherbourg, 4r.

33 MS Q, fols 17r, 39r–40r

34 MS Q, fol. 39r.

35 MS Q, fol. 39v.

36 MS Q, fol. 39r; Milcent, Saint Jean Eudes, p. 154.

37 BM MS 3177, pp. 22–3.

38 BN Mss fds fs., 11950, 23; BM MS 3177, p. 96.

39 [Dufour], Lettre à un docteur, p. 6.

40 MS Q, fols 16v–17r..

41 MS Cherbourg, fol. 7r.

42 MS Q, 18r.

43 MS Q, 18r.

44 See Irena Backus, Le Miracle de Laon: le déraisonnable, le raisonnable, l'apocalyptique et le politique dans les récits du miracle de Laon (1566–1578) (Paris: Vrin, 1994), pp. 11–24 and Denis Crouzet, 'A woman and the Devil: possession and exorcism in sixteenth-century France', trans. Michael Wolfe, in Michael Wolfe (ed.), Changing Identities in Early Modern France, with a foreword by Natalie Zemon Davis (Durham: Duke University Press, 1997), 191–215.

45 MS Cherbourg, 8v. Coton reassured Vallées in person when she had doubts about the source of her inspirations, saying, somewhat enigmatically, if they are the result of trickery, it is 'good trickery'. BM MS 3177, p. 248. Joseph d'Orléans, La Vie du Pere Pierre Coton (Paris: Estienne Michallet, 1688), pp. 87–91. Coton also wrote a letter of support for Elisabeth de Ranfaing. Étienne Delcambre, and Jean Lhermitte, Un cas énigmatique de possession diabolique en Lorraine au XVIIe siècle: Élisabeth de Ranfaing, l'énergumène de Nancy (Nancy: Societé d'Archéoligie Lorraine, 1956), pp. 126–7.

46 MS Q, fol. 28r–v; BM MS 3177, p. 99.

47 MS Q, fol. 24r–v.

48 MS Cherbourg, fol. 14r.

49 BN Mss fds fs., 11949, 'Extraicts des procez verbaux Informations etc touchant ce qui regarde Marie des Vallées', p. 66.

50 MS Q, fol. 34r.

51   MS Q, fol. 9v.

52   Ranfaing's possession ended in 1626, after more than six years of exorcisms, and she went on to establish a new Lorraine- and France-wide religious order, Notre Dame du Refuge, beginning in Nancy, in 1629. She also became the so-called 'spiritual mother' of a secret confraternity, known as the 'Médaillistes'. Delcambre and Lhermitte, *Un cas énigmatique*, p. 138. Ranfaing and Jeanne des Anges had in common the fact that each woman only attained a reputation as a mystic as her possession waned. Cf. Michel de Certeau, *The Possession at Loudun* (1970), trans. Michael B. Smith, with a foreword by Stephen Greenblatt (Chicago and London: University of Chicago Press, 2000), pp. 213–26.

53   BM MS 3177, p. 95.

54   BN Mss fds fs. 11944, fol. 325r.

55   BM MS 3177, pp. 29, 35.

56   BM MS 3177, p. 76.

57   BM MS 3177, p. 243.

58   BM MS 3177, p. 131.

59   BM MS 3177, p. 78.

60   BM MS 3177, pp. 24, 29.

61   James Farr, *Authority and Sexuality in Early Modern Burgundy*; Robin Briggs, *Communities of Belief: cultural and social tension in early modern France* (Oxford: Clarendon Press, 1989), ch. 6.

62   The Jesuit Barthélemy Jacquinot was involved with both Ranfaing and Jeanne – suspecting one and approving the other.

63   Milcent, *Saint Jean Eudes*, p. 191.

64   Witchcraft historians are beginning to enter into the previously taboo territory of motivation – including the motivations of those with institutional power – in their attempts to plumb witchcraft belief. See Walter Stephens, *Demon Lovers: witchcraft, sex and crisis of belief* (Chicago and London: University of Chicago Press, 2002), pp. 311, 345. For psychologies at the local level, see Robin Briggs, *Witches and Neighbours: the social and cultural context of European witchcraft* (London: Fontana Press, 1996).

65   Triboulet, *Gaston de Renty*, p. 343.

66   BM MS 3177, p. 77.

67   Costil, 'Annales de la Congregation de Jesus et Marie', p. 622.

68   Émile Dermenghem, *La Vie admirable et les révélations de Marie des Vallées* (Paris: Plon-Nourrit, 1926), p. 54.

69   BN Mss fds fs, 11949, p. 37.

70   BN Mss fds fs, 11949, p. 37.

71   BN Mss fds fs, 11949, p. 72.

72   BN Mss fds fs, 11949, p. 55.

73   [Charles Dufour] *Factum pour la deffense de l'autheur de la lettre a un Docteur pour respondre aux objections & invectives D.P. Eudes ou de ses amis*, (held in BN Mss Fds fr., 14562), p. 45. (The book has a handwritten title page and is also found at the Bibliothèque de Pont-Audemer with the telling title: 'Factum concerant la magie et les sortilèges de Marie des Vallées'. My thanks are due to Mme E. Carbonneaux at the Bibliothèque Municipale, Pont-Audemer, for kindly supplying this material.)

74   BM Ms 3177, p. 243.

75   BN Mss fds fs, 14563, fol. 4v.

76   [Charles Dufour] *Brieve réponse à un écrit que l'on fait courir contre la 'lettre à un Docteur'* (contained in the collection BN Mss fds fs., 14562), p. 8.

77   Ms Cherbourg, fol. 33v.

78   Letter to M. Trochu, almoner to Mgr de Ligny, the Bishop of Meaux, 2 January 1675, in Jean Eudes, *Oeuvres Complètes* (Paris: R. Haton, 1905–1909), vol. XI, p. 112. I am

grateful to Professor William Monter, who informs me he has found no reference to the arrest of Vallées in records of Norman witch trials, but that this does not mean it did not take place.

79   'Copie du document presenté en Cour de Rome pour la cause de Père Eudes', 21 December 1869, copied by Fr Ange le Doré (a copy of Ms Q, held at the Eudist Archives, Paris).

80   Cf. Milcent, 'Marie des Vallées'.

81   Other twentieth-century accounts of the case may be found in Michel Carmona, *Les diables de Loudun* (Paris: Fayard, 1988); Robert Mandrou, *Magistrats et sorciers en France au XVIIe siècle: une analyse de psychologie historique* (1968) (Paris: Seuil, 1980), pp. 210–19; Henri Bremond, *Histoire littéraire du sentiment religieux en France depuis la fin des guerres de religion jusqu'à nos jours*, 11 vols (Paris: Librairie Bloud et Gay, 1933), vol. 5, pp. 178–251. Popularising accounts include: Aldous Huxley, *The Devils of Loudun* (1952) (London: Panther Books, 1977); Robert Rapley, *A Case of Witchcraft: the trial of Urbain Grandier* (Montreal and Kingston: McGill-Queens University Press, 1998). Michel de Certeau lists fictional and theatrical adaptations of the case, *The Possession at Loudun*, p. 6 and in unpaginated illustrations.

82   Assembled together, the bibliographical data in Carmona, *Les diables de Loudun*; Mandrou, *Magistrats et sorciers*; Certeau, *The Possession at Loudun*, and Jean-Joseph Surin, *Correspondance*, compiled, edited and annotated by Michel de Certeau, Bibliothèque européenne (Paris: Desclée de Brouwer, 1966), provide the full range of materials concerning this case. See also Moshe Sluhovsky, 'The devil in the convent', *American Historical Review*, vol. 107, no. 5, (2002), 1378–411, which appeared when the present book was in production.

83   Three publications appeared before the death of Grandier in August 1634, 21 more in 1634, 16 in 1635, and 14 between 1636 and 1638. Certeau, *The Possession at Loudun*, pp. 188–9. This book provides extensive excerpts of materials from Loudun, with commentaries relating to language, subjectivity, politics, the Jesuit mystic Surin, theatre, the body and the importance of smell. The present chapter revisits just one aspect of this case, by using the autobiography of Jeanne des Anges, and a selection of manuscripts (addressed in passing by Certeau), to test the parameters of female authority in Catholicism.

84   Certeau, *The Possession at Loudun*, p. 225. See also Certeau's essay, 'Jeanne des Anges'.

85   Jeanne was also asked on several occasions to become the superior of other houses. Certeau, *The Possession at Loudun*, p. 226.

86   See his *Histoire abrégée de la possession des Ursulines de Loudun, et des peines du Père Surin* (Paris: Bureau de l'Association Catholique du Sacré-Coeur, 1828), p. 97.

87   Certeau, *The Possession at Loudun*, pp. 221–4; Jeanne des Anges, *Autobiographie*, p. 70.

88   Certeau, *The Possession at Loudun*, pp. 59–64; Mandrou, *Magistrats et sorciers*, p. 211. Grandier's 'Traicté du coelibat' was not printed but appears to have circulated in manuscript. Grandier had not been a spiritual director to the nuns at Loudun.

89   Jeanne des Anges, *Autobiographie*, pp. 76–7.

90   [Nicolas Aubin], *The Cheats and Illusions of Romish Priests and Exorcists. Discover'd in the History of the Devils of Loudun: Being an account of the Pretended Possession of the Ursuline nuns and of the Condemnation and Punishment of Urban Grandier a parson of the same Town* (London: W. Turner and R. Bassett, 1703), p. 4; Certeau, *The Possession at Loudun*, pp. 13–14.

91   Certeau, *The Possession at Loudun*, p. 19.

92   Certeau, *The Possession at Loudun*, pp. 90–93.

93   'Relation de M. Hédelin, Abbé d'Aubignac, touchant les possedés de Loudun au mois du septembre 1637', in Robert Mandrou (ed.) *Possession et sorcellerie au XVIIe siècle: Textes inédits* (Paris: Fayard, 1979), p. 145.

94   Mandrou, *Magistrats et sorciers*, p. 211; Certeau, *The Possession at Loudun*, Ch. 7.

95   Mandrou, *Magistrats et sorciers*, p. 212; Certeau, *The Possession at Loudun*, pp. 68–9; 74–5.
96   Mandrou, *Magistrats et sorciers*, p. 212; Certeau, *The Possession at Loudun*, pp. 67–8.
97   Mandrou, *Magistrats et sorciers*, p. 213; Certeau, *The Possession at Loudun*, ch. 7.
98   Jeanne des Anges, *Autobiographie*, pp. 72–6.
99   Certeau, *The Possession at Loudun*, ch. 11.
100 *Extraict des Registres de la Commission ordonnée par le Roy. Pour le Procez criminel fait a l'encontre de Maistre Urbain Grandier & ses complices* (Poitiers: J. Thoreau, 1634), p. 25.
101 Certeau, 'Jeanne des Anges', pp. 320–1.
102 Certeau, *The Possession at Loudun*, pp. 199–200.
103 Certeau, *The Possession at Loudun*, p. 204.
104 Certeau, 'Jeanne des Anges', p. 321.
105 Jeanne des Anges, *Autobiographie*, p. 129.
106 Jeanne des Anges, *Autobiographie*, p. 112.
107 Jeanne des Anges, *Autobiographie*, p. 148.
108 *Relation veritable de ce qui s'est passé aux Exorcismes des Religieuses Ursulines possédées de Loudun, en la presence de Monsieur Frere unique du Roy* (Paris: Jean Martin, 1635), p. 22. See also Certeau, *The Possession at Loudun*, pp. 199–200.
109 Jeanne des Anges, *Autobiographie*, p. 112.
110 Jeanne des Anges, *Autobiographie*, p. 112.
111 Jeanne des Anges, *Autobiographie*, p. 154. The Jesuit superior-general expressed the wish that Jesuit exorcists would expel the demons and not dally with them. Certeau, *The Possession at Loudun*, p. 215. However, the fact that for around four years Jesuit superiors continually, if reluctantly, renewed the commission for members of the order to exorcise at Loudun, indicates a commitment to the possessions which should not be underestimated.
112 *A relation of the devill Balams departure out of the body of the Mother-Prioresse of the Ursuline Nuns of Loudun* (London: R.B[adger], 1636), fol 1r–v.
113 Jeanne des Anges, *Autobiographie*, p. 137; cf. Midelfort, 'German people', p. 127.
114 Certeau, *The Possession at Loudun*, pp. 199–200.
115 Jeanne des Anges, *Autobiographie*, p. 112.
116 Jeanne des Anges, *Autobiographie*, p. 155.
117 Jeanne des Anges, *Autobiographie*, p. 155.
118 Jeanne des Anges, *Autobiographie*, pp. 156–7.
119 Jeanne des Anges, *Autobiographie*, pp. 158–9.
120 Jeanne des Anges, *Autobiographie*, p.159.
121 Certeau, 'Jeanne des Anges', p. 326.
122 Jeanne des Anges, *Autobiographie*, pp. 177–85.
123 Jeanne des Anges, *Autobiographie*, p. 183.
124 Jeanne des Anges, *Autobiographie*, p. 184.
125 Jeanne des Anges, *Autobiographie*, p. 185. The second miracle occurred in 1639. Certeau, 'Jeanne des Anges', p. 326.
126 Certeau, *The Possession at Loudun*, p. 215.
127 Jeanne des Anges, *Autobiographie*, p. 186.
128 Certeau, *The Possession at Loudun*, p. 215.
129 Certeau, *The Possession at Loudun*, pp. 217–19; Jeanne des Anges, *Autobiographie*, pp. 191, 193–4, 230.
130 Jeanne des Anges, *Autobiographie*, pp. 230–1.
131 Jeanne des Anges, *Autobiographie*, p. 203.
132 Jeanne des Anges, *Autobiographie*, pp. 200–16.
133 Jeanne des Anges, *Autobiographie*, p. 217.
134 Jeanne des Anges, *Autobiographie*, p. 221.

135 Jeanne des Anges, *Autobiographie*, pp. 208, 221.

136 Jeanne des Anges, *Autobiographie*, p. 224.

137 Certeau, 'Jeanne des Anges', p. 335.

138 See Surin, *Correspondance, passim*.

139 Certeau, 'Jeanne des Anges', p. 335. A selection from these letters is reproduced as an appendix to Jeanne des Anges, *Autobiographie*, pp. 235–89.

140 Certeau, in Surin, *Correspondance*, p. 468. See also Ferdinand Cavallera, 'L'autobiographie de Jeanne des Anges d'aprés des documents inédits' (1928), in Jeanne des Anges, *Autobiographie*, pp. 291–300, at p. 293.

141 Certeau, *The Possession at Loudun*, p. 223.

142 The autobiography remained in manuscript and was not published until 1886.

143 Jeanne des Anges, *Autobiographie*, p. 193 and *passim*.

144 Surin, *Correspondance*, p. 1506.

145 Jeanne des Anges, *Autobiographie*, pp. 288–9. Jeanne also had visions of the dead in purgatory, who confessed their sins and told Jeanne to seek the prayers of their relatives. Certeau, 'Jeanne des Anges', pp. 339–40.

146 Jeanne des Anges, *Autobiographie*, p. 242. The authority of a guardian angel might also be seen as the less controversial equivalent to a prophesying demon.

147 Jeanne des Anges, *Autobiographie*, p. 237.

148 Jeanne des Anges, *Autobiographie*, p. 282.

149 *La Gloire de S. Ursule*, Valenciennes: Jean Bouche, pp. 329–38. The author was cited as 'Père de le Cie de Jésus'. Jeanne's name is suppressed, because the author does not know if she is still alive. Cf. Certeau, in Surin, *Correspondance*, p. 1506.

150 Certeau, 'Jeanne des Anges', p. 339.

151 Certeau, 'Jeanne des Anges', p. 341.

152 'La vie de la vénérable Mère Jeanne des Anges . . . recueillie de ses propres écrits, et des mémoires des Révérends pères Seurin et Saint-Jure, jésuittes, et de ceux de nostre vénérable soeur du Houx', 2 vols, 1039 pp. This seventeenth-century collection was stored at the Visitation Archives at Grand Fougeray until 1978. Since then it has been housed at the archive of the Visitation in Mayenne. A nineteenth-century manuscript, 'Vie de la Mère Jeanne des Anges religieuse ursuline de Loudun', which contains material similar to that in the collection at Mayenne, formerly held at the Jesuit archives in Toulouse, is now housed at the Jesuit archives at Vanves. My thanks are due to the Sister Archivist, Thérèse-Édith Barré, at Mayenne, and to Father Robert Bonfils, archivist at Vanves, for their generous assistance in locating these collections and making them accessible for use.

153 See Certeau, 'Jeanne des Anges', pp. 325–6, for references to other cases involving claims of divine intervention in which Jeanne was involved.

154 Jeanne-Marie Pinczon Du Houx (1616–77) was widowed in 1645, and later entered the second Visitandine convent at Rennes.

155 'La Vie de la vénérable Mère Jeanne des Anges', p. 720.

156 The young woman is referred to as a 'fille', the epithet applied to any unmarried woman. Her age is not given, nor is her name.

157 Louis Chatellier, *The Europe of the Devout: the Catholic Reformation and the formation of a new society*, trans. Jean Birrell (Cambridge: Cambridge University Press, 1989), p. 71. The manuscript does not mention de Meur by name; see Certeau, 'Jeanne des Anges', p. 325.

158 'La Vie de la vénérable Mère Jeanne des Anges', p. 720.

159 'La Vie de la vénérable Mère Jeanne des Anges', p. 720.

160 'La Vie de la vénérable Mère Jeanne des Anges', pp. 720–1.

161 'La Vie de la vénérable Mère Jeanne des Anges', p. 721.

162 'La Vie de la vénérable Mère Jeanne des Anges', p. 721.

163 'La Vie de la vénérable Mère Jeanne des Anges', p. 721.

164 'La Vie de la vénérable Mère Jeanne des Anges', p. 722.
165 'La Vie de la vénérable Mère Jeanne des Anges', p. 722.
166 'La Vie de la vénérable Mère Jeanne des Anges', p. 722.
167 'La Vie de la vénérable Mère Jeanne des Anges', p. 723.
168 'La Vie de la vénérable Mère Jeanne des Anges', p. 723
169 'La Vie de la vénérable Mère Jeanne des Anges', pp. 723–4.
170 'La Vie de la vénérable Mère Jeanne des Anges', p. 724.
171 'La Vie de la vénérable Mère Jeanne des Anges', p. 725.
172 'La Vie de la vénérable Mère Jeanne des Anges', pp. 725–6.
173 'La Vie de la vénérable Mère Jeanne des Anges', p. 726.
174 'La Vie de la vénérable Mère Jeanne des Anges', p. 726.
175 'La Vie de la vénérable Mère Jeanne des Anges', p. 863.
176 'La Vie de la vénérable Mère Jeanne des Anges', p. 863.
177 'La Vie de la vénérable Mère Jeanne des Anges', p. 866. These accusations appear to have been drafted in the context of complaints by some of the nuns about her temperament and an indisposition to prayer.
178 'La Vie de la vénérable Mère Jeanne des Anges', p. 864.
179 'La Vie de la vénérable Mère Jeanne des Anges', p. 866.
180 'La Vie de la vénérable Mère Jeanne des Anges', p. 866.
181 'La Vie de la vénérable Mère Jeanne des Anges', p. 867.
182 Certeau added: 'Not by chance is the possessed body essentially female; behind the scenes a relation between masculine discourse and its feminine alteration is acted out'. 'Discourse disturbed: the sorceror's speech', in *The Writing of History* (1975), trans. Tom Conley (New York: Columbia University Press, 1988), 245–68, p. 245. See also Luce Irigaray, 'La Mystérique', in *Speculum of the Other Woman* (1974), trans. Gillian C. Gill (Ithaca, N.Y.: Cornell University Press, 1985), 191–202; Hélène Cixous and Catherine Clément, *The Newly Born Woman*, trans. Betsy Wing, Theory and History of Literature, no. 24 (Manchester: Manchester University Press, 1986).
183 Certeau, 'Discourse disturbed', p. 248.
184 'Discourse disturbed', p. 254. An apparent late seventeenth-century text (date uncertain, possibly 1686), which I take to be a satire of accounts of possession, found in the Bibliothèque Sainte-Geneviève, has its source of humour simply in the narration of a man's experience of his own possession, using the language usually found in the accounts of outsiders: 'Tous les médecins disoient qu'ils n'avoient jamais veu une telle maladie que la mienne, je commençay à mettre fois une épingle sur mon lict, et aussytot je fis plus de cent tours avec mes mains alentour et plusieurs autres choses que je faisois de tout mon corps contre ma volonté, ce qui fit conclure à tous mes Médecins que j'estois possédé, mais quelqu'uns n'osoient me le dire, toutefois Mr Guenauet dit, Si nous croyons aux possédés il sembleroit que Mr le seroit; car je vous asseure que tous ceux qui ont esté à Loudun et Louviers n'ont jamais fait de postures pareilles à celles que nous venons de veoir, je rompois mon lict jy tournois comme une boulle sans estre estourdy, quelquefois je sautois couché tout de mon long jusques au fond du lict . . . [E]n mesme temps je me leva en haut sur les pieds en me faisant faire des grimaces furieuses.' 'Recit véritable de tout ce qui s'est passé en une maladie qui ma duré depuis le 11e novembre 1649 jusques en l'année 1655, et dont les plus habiles medecins de Paris nont pût avoir la connaissance, et a la fin s'est trouvé que c'étoit possession du démon ce que l'on voira par la suitte de ce discours'. BSG Ms 1033 T. f in–fol. 1, 85ff., fols. 3v–7r.
185 Michaelis, *The Admirable historie*, unpaginated 'Summarie'.
186 Stuart Clark, *Thinking with Demons: the idea of witchcraft in early modern Europe* (Oxford: Oxford University Press, 1997), pp. 134–8.

Conclusion

1   That is why the titles of two books, *Jesus the Exorcist* (by Graeme H. Twelftree, Tübingen, Germany: J.C.B. Mohr/Paul Siebeck, 1993) and the earlier *Jesus the Magician* (by Morton Smith, San Francisco, Calif.: Harper & Row, 1978) work as apparent oxymorons: they invoke a controversial version of Christianity.
2   'Comforting the afflicted', <http://more.abcnews.go.com/sections/world/dailynews/vatican000911.html>, accessed 17 December, 2000.

Selected bibliography

This is not an exhaustive bibliography of demonic possession, nor of possession in France. It lists all published works cited in this book, with the addition of a number of further readings, including materials for other European possession studies. The bibliographical information in Mandrou, *Magistrats et sorciers*; Certeau, *The Possession at Loudun*; Carmona, *Les diables de Loudun*, and Yve-Plessis, *Essai d'une bibliographie française*, together with newer material here, provides the bulk of research materials for France. Manuscripts used in this book are cited in the relevant chapters only.

Works written before 1750

Advis de Messieurs Du Val, Gamache & Ysambert Docteurs de Sorbonne, donné en l'annee 1620. sur un faict avenu en Lorraine, n.p.: no publisher [1620].

Advis horrible et epouvantable pour detruire le Cardinal Mazarin, avec les puissans moyens de le faire hayr au Roy, & à ceux qui le tiennent près de sa personne, Paris: Jean du Crocq, 1652.

[Arnauld, Agnès], *Le Chapelet secret du tres-sainct Sacrement*, [including] *Censure des Docteurs de Sorbonne*, n.p.: no publisher [1633].

Arrest de la Cour de Parlement de Provence, portant condamnation contre Messire Louis Gaufridi, Aix-en-Provence: Jean Tholozan, 1611.

Arrest de la Cour de Parlement de Roüen contre Mathurin Picard & Thomas Boullé deuëment attains & convaincus des crimes de Magie, Sortilege, Sacrileges, Impietez & cas abominables commis contre la Majesté divine, & autres mentionnez au Procez, Rouen: David du Petit Val et Jean Viret; Orléans: Gabriel Frémont, 1647.

Attestation de Messieurs les Commissaires envoyez par sa Majesté pour prendre connoissance, avec Monseigneur l'Evesque d'Evreux, de l'estat des Religieuses qui paroissent agitées au Monastere de Saint Louys & Sainte Elizabeth de Louviers, n.p.: no publisher [1643].

Aubigné, Agrippa d', *Oeuvres complètes*, Geneva: Slatkine Reprints, 1967.

[Aubin, Nicolas], *The Cheats and Illusions of Romish Priests and Exorcists. Discover'd in the History of the Devils of Loudun: Being an account of the Pretended Possession of the Ursuline nuns and of the Condemnation and Punishment of Urban Grandier a parson of the same Town*. London: W. Turner and R. Bassett, 1703.

Benedicti, Jean, *La Triomphante victoire de la vierge Marie, sur sept malins esprits, finalemant chassées du corps d'une femme, dans l'Eglise des Cordeliers de Lyon*, Lyon: Pierre Rigaud, 1611.

[Benet of Canfield], *Renaissance Dialectic and Renaissance Piety: Benet of Canfield's Rule of*

Perfection, a translation and study by Kent Emery Jr., Binghamton, N.Y.: Medieval and Renaissance Texts and Studies, 50, 1987.

Bérulle, Pierre de, *Oeuvres complètes du Cardinal de Bérulle, Reproduction de l'edition Princeps (1644)*, t. 1, Montsoult: Maison d'Institution de l'Oratoire, 1962.

——, *Oeuvres complètes*, 8 vols, Paris: Oratoire de Jésus/Éditions de Cerf, 1997.

——, *Correspondance du Pierre de Bérulle*, ed. Jean Dagens, vol. 3, 1625–29, Paris: Desclée de Brouwer, 1939.

——, 'Léon d'Alexis', *Traicté des energumenes, Suivy d'un discours sur la possession de Marthe Brossier: contre les calomnies d'un medecin de Paris*, Troyes: no publisher, 1599.

Birette, Sanson, *Refutation de l'erreur du Vulgaire, touchant les responses des diables exorcizez*, Rouen: Jacques Besongne, 1618.

Blendecq, Charles, *Cinq Histoires admirables, esquelles est monstré comme miraculeusement par la vertu et puissance du S. sacrement de l'autel a esté chassé Beelzebub*, Paris: G. Chaudière, 1582.

Boaistuau, Pierre, *Histoires prodigieuses extraictes de plusieurs fameux auteur grecs at latins*, Paris: C. Macé, 1575.

Bodin, Jean, *De la demonomanie des sorciers*, rev. edn, Paris: Jacques du Puys, 1587.

——, *On the Demon-mania of witches*, trans. Randy A. Scott, abridged and with an introduction by Jonathan L. Pearl, Toronto: Centre for Reformation and Renaissance Studies, 1995.

Boguet, Henri, *An Examen of Witches* [*Discours execrable des sorciers*, 1602 edn], trans. E. Allen Ashwin, ed. Montague Summers, London: John Rodker, 1929.

Boulaese, Jean, *L'Abbregee histoire du grand miracle par nostre Sauveur & Seigneur Jesus-Christ en la saincte Hostie du Sacrement de l'Autel, faict à Laon 1566*, Paris: Thomas Belot, 1573.

——, *Le Manuel de l'admirable victoire du corps de Dieu sur l'esprit maling Beelzebub obtenue à Laon, 1566*, Liège: H. Houins, 1598.

——, *Le Miracle de Laon en Lannoys*, ed. A.H. Chaubard, Lyon: Sauvegarde Historique, 1955.

——, *Le Thresor et entiere histoire de la triomphante victoire du corps de Dieu sur l'esprit maling Beelzebub, obtenuë a Laon l'an mil cinq cens soixante six*, Paris: Nicolas Chesneau, 1578.

Briefve intelligence de l'opinion de trois Docteurs de Sorbonne & du livre du P. Birette. touchant les Diables Exorcisez, in (Fr) Tranquille, *Veritable relation des justes procedures observees au faict de la possession des Ursulines de Loudun. Et au procez d'Urbain Grandier*, La Flèche: George Griveau, 1634, 50–80.

[Buisseret, François], *Histoire admirable et veritable des choses advenues a l'endroict d'une Religieuse professe du convent des Soeurs noires, de la ville de Mons en Hainaut, natifve de Sore sur Sambre, aagee de vingt cinq ans, possedee du maling esprit, & depuis delivree*, Paris: Claude de Monstre-oeil, 1586.

Caesarius von Heisterbach, *The Dialogue on Miracles*, 2 vols, trans. H. von E. Scott and C. Swinton Bland, introduction by G.G. Coulton, London: Routledge, 1929.

Canons and Decrees of the Council of Trent, original text with an English translation by H.J. Schroeder, Rockford, Ill.: Tan Books, 1978.

Caron, Claude, *L'Antechrist demasque*, Tournon: Guillaume Linocier, 1589.

Castañega, Martin de Darst, David, H. 'Witchcraft in Spain: the Testimony of Martin De Castañega's Treatise on Superstition and Witchcraft (1520)', *Proceedings of the American Philosophical Society*, 1979, vol. 123, no. 5, 298–322.

'Ce qui donnera beaucoup de connoissance & de lumiere à Mr le Lieutenant Criminel pour le jugement de la petite Mere Françoise, Superieure des Religieuses de la Place Royale', n.p.: no printer [1647?].

Censura facultatis Theologiae Parisiensis Libri Latino & Gallico Idiomate conscripti, cujus Titulus est. Vera ac Memorabilis Historia de tribus Energumenis in partibus Belgij, &c. Cum tribus Appendicibus: 1. De Mirabilibus hujus Operis 2. De conformitate ipsius ad Scripturas, &c. 3. De potestate Ecclesiastica super Daemones &c. *Edita in lucem diligentia Joannis le Normant, &c*, Paris: Claude Griset, [1623].

Ciruelo, Pedro, *Pedro Ciruelo's* A Treatise Reproving all Superstitions and Forms of Witchcraft: Very Necessary and Useful for all Good Christians Zealous for Their Salvation (c. 1530), trans. Eugene A. Maio and D'Orsay W. Pearson, annotated and with an introduction by D'Orsay W. Pearson, Cranbury, New Jersey and London: Associated University Presses, 1977.

'Confession Catholique de Sieur de Sancy', in *Recueil de diverses pieces servant a l'histoire de Henry III*, Cologne: Pierre du Marteau, 1666.

Confession faicte par Messire Louys Gaufridi Prestre en l'Eglise des Accoules de Marseille, Prince des Magiciens, depuis Constantinople jusques à Paris. A deux Peres Capuchins du couvent d'Aix, la veille de Paques, le onzieme Avril mil six cens onze, Aix: Jean Tholozan, 1611.

The Confessions of Madeleine Bavent, trans. Montague Summers, London: The Fortune Press, [1933].

Congnard, *Histoire de Marthe Brossier pretendue possedee tiree du Latin de Messire Jacques August. de Thou, President au Parlement de Paris. Avec quelques remarques et considerations generales sur cette Matiere, tirées pour la plus part aussi du Latin de Bartholomaeus Perdulcis celebre Medecin de la Faculté de Paris. Le tout pour servir d'appendice & de plus ample éclarcissement au sujet d'un liure intitulé* La Pieté affligée ou Discours Historique & Theoligique de la possession des Religieuses dictes de Sainte Elizabeth de Louviers &c, Rouen: Jacques Herault, 1652.

Les Conjurations faites a un demon possedant le corps d'une grande Dame, Paris: Isaac Mesnier, 1619.

'Copie en forme de Recueil De ce qui se fait de jour en jour dans le Monastere des filles Relligieuzes Saint Louis dont la pluspart sont folles, maleficiez & tourmentez des Diables. En ceste Année 1643', in *Recueil de pièces sur les possessions des religieuses de Louviers*, Rouen: Léon Deshays, 1879.

Coton, Pierre, *Intérieure occupation d'une âme dévote*, 2nd edn, Paris: C. Chappelet, 1609.

Crespet, Pierre, *Deux Livres de la hayne de Sathan et malins esprits contre l'homme, & de l'homme contre eux*, Paris: Guillaume de la Noue, 1590.

Del Rio, Martín, *Disquisitionum magicarum libri sex*, Louvain: Gérard Rivière, 1599–1600.

——, *Martin Del Rio: investigations into magic*, ed. and trans. by P.G. Maxwell-Stuart, Manchester; New York: Manchester University Press, 2000.

——, *Les Controverses et recherches magiques*, (abridged) trans. André du Chesne, Paris: Jean Petit-Pas, 1611.

La Demonomanie de Lodun. Qui montre la veritable possesion des Religieuses Ursulines, et autres seculieres, La Flèche: George Griveau, 1634.

[Desmarets, Charles and Madeleine Bavent]. *Histoire de Madeleine Bavent du monastère de Saint-Louis de Louviers par le R.-P. Desmarets. Réimpression textuelle sur l'édition rarissime de 1652 précédée d'une notice bio-bibliographique et suivie de plusieurs pièces supplémentaires*, Rouen: J. Lemonnyer, 1878.

[Desmarets, Charles and Madeleine Bavent], *Histoire de Magdelaine Bavent, Religieuse du*

Monastere de Saint Loüis de Louviers . . . Ensemble l'Interrogatoire de Magdelaine Bavent. De plus l'Arrest donné contre Mathurin Picard, Thomas Boullé & ladite Bavent, tous convaincus du Crime de magie, l'un brulé vif & l'autre mort, Paris: [Jacques Le Gentil], 1652.

Le Diable exorcisé ou Mazarin chassé de France, Paris: no publisher, 1651.

Discussion Sommaire d'un livret intitulé Le Chapelet Secret du Tres-sainct Sacrement; *Et de ce qui a esté escrit pour en defendre la doctrine*, Paris: no publisher, 1635.

Du Bosroger, Esprit, *La Pieté affligee ou discours historique & Theologique de la Possession des Religieuses dittes de Saincte Elizabeth de Louviers*, Rouen: Jean le Boulenger, 1652.

[Dufour, Charles] *Brieve réponse à un écrit que l'on fait courir contre la 'lettre à un Docteur'*, n.p.: no publisher, [c. 1675] (contained in BN Mss fds fs, 14562).

——, *Factum pour la deffense de l'autheur de la lettre a un Docteur pour respondre aux objections & invectives D.P. Eudes ou de ses amis*, n.p.: no publisher, [c. 1674].

——, *Lettre à un docteur de Sorbonne sur le sujet de plusieurs Écrits composez de la vie & de l'état de Marie des Valées, du Diocese de Coutances*, n.p.: no publisher, [c. 1675].

Duval, André, *La Vie admirable de soeur Marie de l'Incarnation religieuse converse en l'ordre de nostre Dame du mont Carmel, appellée au monde la Damoiselle Acarie*, Douay: Baltazar Bellère, 1621.

Erasmus, (Desiderius), *Ten Colloquies*, trans. Craig R. Thompson, New York: Bobbs-Merrill, 1957.

Eudes, (St) Jean, *Oeuvres complètes*, Paris: Beaucheshe, 1905–9.

Exorcisme du D. Mazarin, dans lequel il est conjuré par le Parlement et le Clergé, a sortir du corps de l'Estat, n.p.: no publisher, 1649.

Extraict des Registres de la Commission ordonnée par le Roy. Pour le Procex criminel fait a l'encontre de Maistre Urbain Grandier & ses complices, Poitiers: J. Thoreau, 1634.

L'Exorciste de la Reyne, faisant voir: Que la Reyne est possedée par le Mazarin [sic] et que ses inclinations sont esclaves sous la tyrannie de ce lutin de cour, n.p.: no publisher, 1652.

Factum pour Maistre Urbain Grandier, prestre curé de l'Eglise St. Pierre du Marché de Loudun et l'un des chanoines en l'Eglise sainct Croix dudit lieu, n.p.: no publisher, [1634].

Faye, Barthélemy, *Energumenicus*, Paris: Sebastian Nivelle, 1571.

Fernel, Jean, *De Abditis rerum causis Libri Duo*, Paris: Christian Wechel, 1548.

Fontaine, Jacques, *Discours des marques des sorciers et de la reelle possession que le diable prend sur le corps des hommes*, Paris: Denis Langlois, 1611.

Goulart, Simon, *Le Troisième et quatrième du Thresor des histoires admirables et memorable de nostre temps*, Cologne: Samuel Crespin, 1614.

Guazzo, Francesco Maria, *Compendium Maleficarum: the Montague Summers edition* (1608), trans. E.A. Ashwin, New York: Dover, 1988.

Habert, Germain, *La Vie du Cardinal de Berulle instituteur et premier Superieur General de la Congregation de l'Oratoire de Jesus-Christ nostre Seigneur*, Paris: Veuve Jean Camusat and Pierre le Petit, 1646.

Histoire prodigieuse nouvellement arrivee à Paris. D'une jeune fille agitee d'un Esprit Fantastique & invisible, Paris: Veuve Ducarroy, 1625.

Histoire veritable arrivee de nostre temps en la ville de Beauvais touchant les conjurations et exorcismes faicts à Denise de la Caille, possedée du Diable, avec les actes et procez verbaux faicts sur les lieux par le commandement de M. l'Evesque, histoire non moins profitable que prodigieuse, remplie d'admirables et estranges effets des Démons, Paris: Pierre Billaine, 1623.

Humier, François, *Discours theologiques, sur l'Histoire de Magdeleine Bavent, Religieuse Hospitaliere du Monastere de Louviers en Normandie*, Niort: Philippes Bureau, 1659.

Jugement de Nosseigneurs les Commissaires nommez par le Roy, au fait des personnes Religieuses, et autres possedées du malin esprit, à Aussonne, Paris: André Soubrion, 1662.

Jeanne des Anges, *Autobiographie d'une hystérique possédée*, annotated and published by Gabriel Legué and Gilles de la Tourette, Collection Bourneville 5, Paris: Bureaux du Progrès Médical, 1886.

——, *Autobiographie* (reprint of 1886 edn), followed by 'Jeanne des Anges' by Michel de Certeau, Grenoble: Jérôme Millon, 1990.

Krämer, Heinrich (Institoris), and James Sprenger, *Malleus Maleficarum*, trans. with introductions, bibliography and notes by Rev. Montague Summers, New York: Dover, 1971.

Lancre, Pierre de, *Tableau de l'inconstance des mauvais anges et démons où il est amplement traité des sorciers et de la sorcellerie* (1612), critical introduction and notes by Nicole Jacques-Chaquin, Collection Palimpseste, Paris: Aubier, 1982.

Langle, Pierre de, *Procès verbal de Mr le Penitentier d'Evreux, de ce qui luy est arrivé dans la prison, interrogeant et consolant Magdeleine Bavent, Magicienne à une heureuse Conversion & repentance*, Paris: François Beauplet, 1643.

Laugeois, Antoine, *L'Innocence opprimée; ou Défense de Mathurin Picard, curé de Mesnil-Jourdain . . . Ouvrage qui n'a jamais été imprimé et extrait sur l'original par M. Chemin curé de Tourneville*, [1652; microfilm collection *Witchcraft in Europe and America*, Reading, England: Primary Source Media, reel 60, no. 556].

Le Breton, Jean, *La Deffense de la verité. Touchant la possession des religieuses de Louviers*, Evreux: Nicolas Hamillon, 1643 (facsimile in *Recueil de pièces sur les possessions des religieuses de Louviers*, Rouen: Léon Deshays, 1879).

Le Gauffre, Thomas, *La Vie de Claude Bernard, dit Le Pauvre Prestre*, no place: Claude Sonnis & Denis Bechet, 1642.

——, *Recit veritable De ce qui s'est fait & passé aux Exorcismes de plusieurs Religieuses de la ville de Louviers, en presence de Monsieur le Penitencier d'Evreux, & Monsieur le Gauffre*, Paris: Gervais Alliot, 1643.

——, *Recit veritable, Contenant ce qui s'est fait & passé aux Exorcismes de plusieurs Religieuses de la ville de Louuiers, en presence de Monsieur le Penitencier d'Evreux, & de Monsieur le Gauffre*, Paris: Laurens Fouquoyre, 1643.

——, *Testament du feu Reverend Pere Thomas Le Gaufre, vivant Conseiller du Roy, Maistre en sa Chambre des Comptes à Paris, Prestre Successeur du bien heureux Pere Bernard*, Paris: Martin le Prest, 1646.

Le Normant, Jean, *De l'Exorcisme au Roy Tres-chrestien Louis Le Juste*, n.p.: no publisher, 1619.

——, *Histoire veritable et memorable de ce qui c'est passé sous l'exorcisme de trois filles possedées és päis de Flandre: en la descouverte & confession de Marie de Sains, soy disant Princesse de la Magie; & Simone Dourlet Complice, & autres*, vol. 2: *De la vocation des magiciens et magiciennes par le ministre des demons*, 2 vols, Paris: Nicolas Buon, 1623.

——, *Remonstrances du Sieur de Chiremont à Messieurs de Sorbonne*, n.p.: no publisher, [1623].

[Le Picard, Mathurin], *L'Arsenac de l'ame d'ou elle tire trois sortes d'Armes pour triompher plainement de ses communs Ennemis, savoir, Du jeusne, De l'Aumosne, de l'oraison*, Rouen: L. du Mesnil, 1626.

——, *Le Fouet des Paillairds, ou Juste punition des voluptueux et charnels, conforme aux arrests divins & humains*, Rouen: E. Vereul, 1628.

Lemnius, Levinus, *Les Occultes merveilles et secretz de nature*, Paris: G. du Pré, 1574.

[Lempèrière, Jean] *Censure de l'Examen de la possession des religieuses de Louviers*, Rouen: no publisher, 1643.

——, *Response à l'apologie de l'examen du Sieur Yvelin, Sur la possession des Religieuses de Saint Louys de Louviers*, Rouen: no publisher, 1644.

L'Estoile, Pierre de, *Journal de l'Estoile pour la règne de Henri IV, 1, 1589–1600* (1732), ed. Louis-Raymond Lefèvre, Paris: Gallimard, 1948.

Lettres de illustrissime et reverendissime Cardinal D'Ossat, Eveque de Bayeaux. Au Roy Henry Le Grand et a Monsieur de Villeroy. Depuis l'annee M.D.XCIV jusques a l'annee MDCIII. Derniere edition, revue et augmentee, Paris: Joseph Bouillerot, 1624.

The Life and Death of Lewis Gaufredy: A Priest of the Church of the Accoules in Marseilles in France . . . whose horrible life being made manifest, hee was Arraigned and Condemned by the Court of Parliament of Aix in Province, to be burnt alive, which was performed the last day of Aprill, 1611. . . . Translated and faithfully collected out of two French Copies, London: R. Redmer, 1612.

Le Loyer, Pierre, *Discours et histoires des spectres, visions et apparitions des esprits, anges, demons et ames, se monstrans visibles aux hommes*, Paris: Nicolas Buon, 1605.

Lorini, Jean, *In Acta Apostolorum Commentaria*, Lyon: H. Cardon, 1609.

Lough, J. and D.E.L. Crane, 'Thomas Killigrew and the possessed nuns of Loudun: the text of a letter of 1635', *Durham University Journal*, 1986, vol. 78, no. 2, 259–68.

Maignart, Pierre, *Lettre adressée a Monsieur D.L.V. Medecin du Roy, et Doyen de la Faculté de Paris. Sur l'apologie du Sieur Yvelin, Medecin*, n.p.: no publisher, [1644] (facsimile in *Recueil de pièces sur les possessions des religieuses de Louviers*, Rouen: Léon Deshays, 1879).

——, *Response a l'examen de la Possession des Religieuses de Louviers, a Monsieur Levilin*, Evreux: Jean de la Vigne, 1643.

——, *Traicté des marques des possedez, et la preuve de la veritable possession des religieuses de Louviers, par P.M. Esc., D. en M*, Rouen: Charles Osmont, 1644.

Mandrou, Robert (ed.), *Possession et sorcellerie au XVIIe siècle: Textes inédits*, Paris: Fayard, 1979.

[Marescot, Michel], *A True discourse, upon the matter of Martha Brossier of Romorantin, pretended to be possessed by a devill*, trans. Abraham Hartwel, London: John Wolfe, 1599.

——, *Discours veritable sur le faict de Marthe Brossier de Romorantin, pretendue demoniaque*, Paris: Mamert Patisson, 1599.

Menghi, Girolamo, *Compendio dell'arte essorcistica, et possibilita delle mirabili, et stupende operationi delli Demoni, et dei Malefici. Con li rimedii opportuni alle infirmità maleficiali*, Bologna: Giovanni Rossi, 1582.

——, *Flagellum daemonum*, Bologna: Giovanni Rossi, 1589.

Le Mercure françois, vol. 2, 1611–12; vol. 9, 1622–24.

Michaelis, Sébastien, *The Admirable Historie of the Possession and Conversion of a Penitent woman. Seduced by a magician that made her to become a Witch . . . Whereunto is annexed a Pneumology, or Discourse of spirits*, trans. W.B., London: William Aspley, 1613.

——, *Histoire admirable de la possession et conversion d'une penitente, Seduite par un magicien, la faisant Sorciere & Princesse des Sorciers au pays de Provence, conduite à la S. Baume pour y estre exorcizee l'an M. DC. X. au mois de Novembre, soubs l'authorité du R. P. F. Sebastien Michaelis . . . Ensemble la Pneumalogie ou Discours du susdit P. Michaelis*, Paris: Charles Chastellain, 1613.

Montaigne, Michel de, *Journal de voyage en Italie par la Suisse et l'Allemagne en 1580 et 1581*, ed. Charles Dédéyan, Paris: Société les Belles Lettres, 1946.

L'Ombre d'Urbain Grandier de Loudun. Sa rencontre et conference avec Gaufridy en l'autre monde, n.p.; no publisher, 1634.

Orléans, Joseph d', *La Vie du Pere Pierre Coton*, Paris: Estienne Michallet, 1688.

Pacheco, Andres, *Edict d'Espagne contre la detestable Secte des Illuminez. Eslevez és Archevesché de Seville & Evesché de Cadiz*, n.p.: no publisher, 1623.

Palma Cayet, Pierre-Victor, *Chronologie novenaire, contenant l'histoire de la guerre sous le règne du très-chrestien Roy de France et de Navarre, Henri IV (1589–1598)*, in Michaud and Poujoulat (eds), *Nouvelle Collection des Mémoires rélatifs à l'Histoire de France*, vol. 12, Paris: Didier, 1857.

——, *Chronologie septenaire contenant l'histoire de la paix entre les roys de France et d'Espagne*, in Michaud and Poujoulat (eds), *Nouvelle collection des mémoires pour servir à l'histoire de France*, series 1, vol. 12, part 2, Paris: Éditeur du Commentaire Analytique du Code Civil, 1838.

Pardoux, Barthélemy, *De Morbis animi*, Lyon: Rigaud, 1649.

'Père de la Cie de Jésus', *La Gloire de S. Ursule*, Valenciennes: Jean Bouche, 1656.

La perle évangelique (1602), ed. Daniel Vidal, Grenoble: Jérôme Millon, 1997.

Pichard, Rémy, *Admirable Vertu des Saints Exorcismes sur les Princes d'enfer possédant réellement Vertueuse Demoiselle Elisabeth de Ranfaing avec Ses justifications contre les ignorances et les calomnies de F. Claude Pithoys Minime*, Nancy: Sébastian Philippe, 1622.

'Pièces détachées extraites du manuscrit H.F. no. 34 de la Bibliothèque Ste Geneviève, formant suite à la pièce précédente ('Copie en forme de Recueil')', in *Recueil de pièces sur les possessions des religieuses de Louviers*, Rouen: Léon Deshays, 1879.

Pigray, Pierre, *Epitome des Preceptes de Medecine et Chirurgie. Avec ample declaration des remedes propres aux malades*, Lyon: S. Rigaud, 1616.

Pin, [Father], *Vie de la Venerable Mere Françoise de la Croix, institutrice des Religieuses Hospitalieres de la Charité de Notre-Dame, Ordre de S. Augustin*, Paris: Jacques Barrois, 1745.

Pithoys, Claude, *A Seventeenth-century Exposure of Superstition: select texts of Claude Pithoys (1587–1676)*, introduction and notes by P.J.S. Whitmore, The Hague: Nijhoff, International Archives of the History of Ideas, no. 49, 1972.

——, *La Descouverture des faux possedez*, Châlons: Germain Nobily, 1621.

Postel, Guillaume, *De Summopere*, critical edn, trans. and notes by Irena Backus, Geneva: Droz, 1995.

Procès verbal fait pour délivrer une fille possédée par le malin esprit à Louviers (1591), published after the original manuscript at the Bibliothèque Nationale by Armand Bénet, with an introduction by B. du Moray, Bibliothèque Diabolique, no. 2, Paris: Bureaux du Progrès Médical, 1883.

Raemond, Florimond de, *Histoire de la naissance, progres, et decadence de l'heresie de ce siècle*, Paris, 1605, Arras: R. Maudhuy, 1611.

——, *L'Anti-Christ et l'Anti-papesse*, 3rd edition, Paris: A. L'Angelier, 1607.

Recit veritable de ce qui s'est fait & passé à Louviers touchant les Religieuses possedées Extraict d'une Lettre escrite de Louviers à un Evesque, Paris: François Beauplet, 1643.

Relation de la Sortie du demon Balam du corps de la Mere Prieure, des Urselines de Loudun. Et ses espouventables mouvemens & contorsions en l'Exorcisme, Paris: Jean Martin, 1635.

Relation veritable de ce qui s'est passé aux Exorcismes des Religieuses Ursulines possédées de Loudun, en la presence de Monsieur Frere unique du Roy, Paris: Jean Martin, 1635.

Rémy, Nicholas, *Demonolatry (1595)*, trans. E. Allen Ashwin, ed. and with an introduction by Montague Summers, Secaucus, N.J.: University Books, 1974.

Renty, Gaston Jean-Baptiste de, *Correspondance*, texte établi et annoté par Raymond Triboulet, (Bibliothèque Européenne) Paris: Desclée de Brouwer, 1978.

——, *Correspondance*, texte établi et annoté par Raymond Triboulet, (Bibliothèque européenne) Paris: Desclée de Brouwer, 1978.

Richeome, Louis, *Trois discours pour la religion catholique: des miracles, des saincts et des images*, Bordeaux: S. Millanges, 1598.

Ripaut, Archange, *Abomination des abominations des fausses devotions de ce tems*, Paris: Claude Cramoisy, 1632.

Rituale Romanum Pauli V Pontificis Maximi jussu editum, Paris: Impensis Societatis Typographicae Librorum Officii Ecclesiastici, 1665.

Rosset, François de, 'De l'horrible & espouventable sorcellerie de Louys Goffredy, prestre de Marseille', in *Histoires tragiques de nostre temps*, Rouen: Jean-Baptiste Behourt, 1632, 32–67.

St Teresa of Avila, *Collected Works*, trans. Kieran Kavanagh and Otilio Rodriguez, 3 vols, Washington D.C.: ICS Publications, 1976–1985.

[Surin, Jean-Joseph], *A relation of the devill Balams departure out of the body of the Mother-Prioresse of the Ursuline nuns of Loudun Faithfully translated out of the French copie, with some observations for the better illustration of the pageant*, English. London: R. B[adger], 1636.

Surin, Jean-Joseph, *Correspondance*, compiled, annotated and edited by Michel de Certeau, Bibliothèque européenne, Paris: Desclée de Brouwer, 1966.

——, *Histoire abrégée de la possession des Ursulines de Loudun, et des peines du Père Surin*, Paris: Bureau de l'Association Catholique du Sacré-Coeur, 1828.

Surin, Jean-Joseph, *Triomphe de l'amour divin*, Grenoble: Jérôme Millon, 1993.

Sylvius, I, *Miracles des diables chassez, a Bonencontre, & Garresou*, Montauban: Denis Haultin, 1620.

Taillepied, Noel, *Psichologie ou traité de l'apparition des esprits*, Paris: Guillaume Bichon, 1588.

Theologia Germanica, in Vergilius Ferm (ed.), *Classics of Protestantism*, London: Peter Owen, 1959, 3–38.

La Theologie germanicque, Livret auquel est traicté Comment il faut dépouiller le vieil homme, & vestir le nouveau, Anvers: Christofle Plantin, 1558.

Thesaurus exorcismorum atque conjurationum terribilium, potentissimorum, efficacissimorum cum Practica probatissima, Cologne: Lazar Zetzner, 1626.

Thou, Jacques-Auguste de, *Histoire universelle de Jacques-Auguste de Thou, depuis 1543 jusqu'en 1607*, La Haye: P. Gosse & J. Neaulme, 1733.

Thyraeus, Petrus, *De daemoniacis. Liber unus in quo daemonum obsidentium conditio; obsessorum hominum status; rationes item & modi, quibus ab obsessis damones exiguntur, discutiuntur & explicantur*, Ex Officina Mater, Cologne: Cholini, Sumptibus Gosuini Cholini, 1594.

——, *Demoniaci, Hoc est: De obsessis a spiritibus daemoniorum hominibus, liber unus*, Lyons: Jehan Pillehotte, 1603.

Tornacensis, Gervasius, *Divina quatuor energumenorum liberation*, Paris: G. Chaudière, 1583.

Tranquille, (Father), *Briefve intelligence de l'opinion de trois Docteurs de Sorbonne & du livre du P. Birette. touchant les Diables Exorcisez*, in his *Veritable relation des justes procedures observees au faict de la possession des Ursulines de Loudun. Et au procez d'Urbain Grandier*, La Flèche: George Griveau, 1634.

——, *Veritable relation des justes procedures observees au faict de la possession des Ursulines de Loudun. Et au procez d'Urbain Grandier*, La Flèche: George Griveau, 1634.

Voragine, Jacobus de, *The Golden Legend: readings on the saints*, trans. William Granger Ryan, Princeton, N.J.: Princeton University Press, 1993.

Weyer, Johan, *Witches, Devils and Doctors in the Renaissance: Johann Weyer*, De praestigiis daemonum, general editor, George Mora, Binghamton, N.Y.: Medieval and Renaissance Texts and Studies, 73, 1991.

[Yvelin, Pierre], *Apologie pour l'autheur de l'Examen de la possession des Religieuses de Louviers. A Messieurs l'Emperiere & Magnart Medecins à Roüen*, Rouen: no publisher, 1643.

——, *Examen de la possession des religieuses de Louviers*, Paris: no publisher, 1643.

Works written after 1750

Adam, Antoine, *Grandeur and Illusion: French literature and society, 1600–1715*, trans. Herbert Tint, Harmondsworth: Penguin, 1974.

Ahlgren, Gillian T.W., 'Negotiating sanctity: holy women in sixteenth-century Spain', *Church History*, 1995, vol. 64, no. 3, 373–88.

——, *Teresa of Avila and the Politics of Sanctity*, Ithaca, N.Y. and London: Cornell University Press, 1996.

Alençon, Ubald d', 'Une page de l'histoire de Paris: le Parlement et les immunités religieuse en 1599: le P. Brûlart', *Études franciscaines*, 1903, 608–12.

Angenendt, A., 'Der Taufexorzismus und seine Kritik in der Theologie des 12. Und 13. Jahrhunderts', *Miscellanea mediaevalia*, 1977, no. 11, 388–409.

Anglo, Sydney, 'Melancholy and witchcraft: the debate between Wier, Bodin and Scot', in A. Gerlo (ed.) *Folie et déraison à la Renaissance*, Travaux de l'Institut pour l'étude de la Renaissance et de l'Humanisme, Université de Bruxelles, Brussels: Éditions de l'Université de Bruxelles, 1976, 209–22.

Azouvi, François, 'Possession, révélation et rationalité médicale au début du XVIIe siècle', *Revue des Sciences Philosophiques et Théologiques*, 1980, no. 64, 355–62.

Backus, Irena, 'Le Miracle de Laon comme moyen de conversion violente. Le cas de Wilhelm van der Linden, évêque de Roermond, et de Johannes Campanus', *Bulletin de la Societé de l'Histoire du Protestantisme français*, 1995, vol. 141, no. 3, 303–21.

——, *Le Miracle de Laon: le déraisonnable, le raisonnable, l'apocalyptique et le politique dans les récits du miracle de Laon (1566–1578)*, Paris: Vrin, 1994.

Barbe, Lucien, 'Histoire du couvent de Saint Louis et de Sainte Elizabeth de Louviers et de la possession des religieuses de ce monastère', *Bulletin de la Société d'études diverses de l'arondissement de Louviers*, 1898, vol. 5, Louviers: Eugene Izambert, 1899, 103–434.

Bée, Michel, 'La possession des filles de Landes-sur-Ajon', *Annales de Normandie*, 1982, vol. 1, special no. 1, 21–37.

Behringer, Wolfgang, *Shaman of Oberstdorf: Chonrad Stoeckhlin and the phantoms of the night*, trans. H.C. Erik Midelfort, Charlottesville: University Press of Virginia, 1998.

Bilinkoff, Jodi, *The Avila of Saint Teresa: religious reform in a sixteenth-century city*, Ithaca, N.Y.: Cornell University Press, 1989.

——, 'A Spanish prophetess and her patrons: the case of Maria de Santo Domingo', *Sixteenth Century Journal*, 1992, vol. 23, Spring, 21–34.

——, 'Confessors, penitents, and the construction of identity in early modern Avila', in Barbara Diefendorf and Carla Hesse (eds), *Culture and Identity in Early Modern Europe:*

essays in honor of Natalie Zemon Davis, Ann Arbor, Mich: University of Michigan Press, 1993, 83–100.

Bireley, Robert, *The Refashioning of Catholicism, 1450–1700: a reassessment of the Counter Reformation*, Basingstoke: Macmillan; New York: St. Martin's Press, 1999.

Bossy, John, 'The Counter Reformation and the people of Catholic Europe', *Past and Present*, 1970, no. 47, 51–70.

——, *Christianity in the West, 1400–1700*, Oxford: Oxford University Press, 1985.

——, *The English Catholic Community, 1570–1850*, London: Darton, Longman and Todd, 1975.

Boulay, D., *Vie du vénérable Jean Eudes*, Paris: R. Haton, 1905–09.

Bremond, Henri, *Histoire littéraire du sentiment religieux en France depuis la fin des guerres de religion jusqu'à nos jours*, 11 vols, Paris: Librairie Bloud et Gay, 1933.

Briggs, Robin, *Communities of Belief: cultural and social tension in early modern France*, Oxford: Clarendon, 1989.

——, *Early Modern France, 1560–1715*, Oxford: Oxford University Press, 1977.

——, *Witches and Neighbours: the social and cultural context of European witchcraft*, London: Fontana Press, 1996.

Brown, Judith C., *Immodest Acts: the life of a lesbian nun in Renaissance Italy*, Oxford: Oxford University Press, 1986.

Brown, Peter, *Relics and Social Status in the Age of Gregory of Tours*, Reading: University of Reading, 1977.

Brun, Isabelle, 'La possession diabolique aux XVIe–XVIIe siècles: le cas de Nicole de Vervins', MA thesis, 1992, Université de Lyon II.

Bruno de Jésus-Marie, *La Belle Acarie: bienheureuse Marie de l'Incarnation*, Paris: Desclée de Brouwer, 1942.

Burkardt, Albrecht, 'A false saint living in Cologne in the 1620s: the case of Sophia Agnes von Langenberg', in Marijke Gijswit-Hofstra, Hilary Marland and Hans de Waardt (eds), *Illness and Healing Alternatives in Western Europe*, Routledge Social History of Medicine Series, London: Routledge, 1997, 80–97.

——, 'Les déboires d'une vocation: un cas d'obsession démoniaque chez les Visitandines parisiennes au début des années 1620', in Bernard Dompnier (ed.), *Visitation et Visitandines aux XVIIe et XVIIIe siècles*, St-Étienne: Publications Université de St-Étienne, 2001, 417–39.

Burke, Peter, 'How to be a Counter-Reformation Saint', in Kaspar von Greyerz (ed.), *Religion and Society in Early Modern Europe (1500–1800)*, London: Allen & Unwin, 1984, 45–55.

Caciola, Nancy, *Discerning spirits: divine and demonic possession in the Middle Ages*, Ithaca, New York: Cornell University Press, 2003.

——, 'Spirits seeking bodies: death, possession and communal memory in the middle ages', in Bruce Gordon and Peter Marshall (eds), *The Place of the Dead: death and remembrance in late medieval and early modern Europe*, Cambridge and New York: Cambridge University Press, 2000, 66–86.

Cambers, Andrew, 'Print, manuscript, and godly cultures in the north of England, c. 1600–1650', University of York, D.Phil. thesis, 2003.

Carmona, Michel, *Les diables de Loudun*, Paris: Fayard, 1988.

Catholic Encyclopedia, <http://www.newadvent.org/cathen/>, accessed 3 December 2003.

Catholic Encyclopedia, C.G. Herbermann *et al.* (eds), New York: Appleton, 1910.

Cavallera, Ferdinand, 'L'Autobiographie de Jeanne des Anges d'après des documents inédits' (1928), in Jeanne des Anges, Autobiographie (reprint of 1886 edition), Grenoble: Jérôme Millon, 1990, 291–300.

Céard, Jean, 'Folie et démonologie au XVIe siècle', in A. Gerlo (ed.), Folie et déraison à la Renaissance, Travaux de l'Institut pour l'étude de la Renaissance et de l'Humanisme, Université de Bruxelles, Brussels: Éditions de l'Université de Bruxelles, 1976, 129–47.

Certeau, Michel de, 'Discourse disturbed: the sorcerer's speech', in The Writing of History (1975), trans. Tom Conley, New York: Columbia University Press, 1988, 245–68.

——, 'Jeanne des Anges' (1966), in Jeanne des Anges, Autobiographie (reprint of 1886 edition), Grenoble: Jérôme Millon, 1990, 301–47.

——, The Mystic Fable: Volume One, The Sixteenth and Seventeenth Centuries, trans. Michael B. Smith, Chicago and London: University of Chicago Press, 1992.

——, 'Mystique au XVIIe siècle', in L'homme devant Dieu. Mélanges offerts au Père Henri de Lubac, vol. 2, Paris: Aubier, 1964, 267–91.

——, The Possession at Loudun, trans. Michael B. Smith, with a foreword by Stephen Greenblatt, Chicago, Ill.: University of Chicago Press, 2000.

——, La Possession de Loudun (1970), Collection Archives, Paris: Gallimard/Julliard, 1980.

Cervantes, Fernando, 'The devils of Querétaro: scepticism and credulity in late seventeenth-century Mexico', Past and Present, 1991, no. 130, 51–69.

——, The Devil in the New World: the impact of diabolism in New Spain, New Haven, Conn. and London: Yale University Press, 1994.

Cervo, Diane M. (ed.), Witchcraft in Europe and America: guide to the microfilm collection, Woodbridge, Connecticut: Research Publications, 1983.

Chajes, J.H., 'Judgments sweetened: possession and exorcism in early modern Jewish culture', Journal of Early Modern History, 1997, vol. 1, no. 2, 124–69.

Chalendard, Marie, La promotion de la femme à l'aposolat, 1540–1650, Paris: Alsatia, 1950.

Chartier, Roger, The Cultural Uses of Print in Early Modern France, trans. Lydia G. Cochrane, Princeton, New Jersey: Princeton University Press, 1987.

Chatellier, Louis, The Europe of the Devout: the Catholic Reformation and the formation of a new society, trans. Jean Birrell, Cambridge: Cambridge University Press, 1989.

Christian, William Jr., Apparitions in Late Medieval and Renaissance Spain, Princeton, N.J.: Princeton University Press, 1981.

——, 'Provoked religious weeping in early modern Spain', in J. Davis (ed.), Religious Organization and Religious Experience, Association of Social Anthropologists, London: Academic Press, 1982, Monograph no. 21, 97–114.

Cixous, Hélène and Catherine Clément, The Newly Born Woman, trans. Betsy Wing, Theory and History of Literature, 24, Manchester: Manchester University Press, 1986.

Clark, Stuart, '"The Demoniacke World": possession, exorcism and eschatology in early modern Europe', Bulletin of the Society for the Social History of Medicine, 1987, no. 41, 12–15.

——, 'Inversion, misrule and the meaning of witchcraft', Past and Present, 1980, no. 87, 98–127.

——, Thinking with demons: the idea of witchcraft in early modern Europe, Oxford: Oxford University Press, 1997.

Cognet, Louis, La spiritualité moderne: l'essor, 1500–1650, Paris: Aubier, 1966.

'Comforting the afflicted', <http://more.abcnews.go.com/sections/world/dailynews/vatican 000911.html>, accessed 17 December, 2000

Cooper-Forst, Julianne Siudowski, 'To rend and teare the bodies of men: theology and the body in demonic possession; France, England, and Puritan America, 1150–1700', Ph.D. thesis, University of New Hampshire, 1992.

Corlieu, Auguste, *L'ancienne faculté de médecine de Paris*, Paris: A. Delahaye, 1877.

Crouzet, Denis, 'A woman and the Devil: possession and exorcism in sixteenth-century France', trans. Michael Wolfe, in Michael Wolfe (ed.), *Changing Identities in Early Modern France*, with a foreword by Natalie Zemon Davis, Durham, N.C.: Duke University Press, 1997, 191–215.

——, *Les guerriers de Dieu: la violence au temps des troubles de religion*, 2 vols Seyssel: Champ Vallon, 1990.

Cruickshank, John, 'The Acarie Circle', in *Seventeenth-Century French Studies*, 1994, vol. 16, 48–58.

Cunningham, Carleton, 'The Devil and religious controversies of sixteenth-century France', in *Essays in History* (published under the auspices of The Corcoran Department of History, University of Virginia, Charlottesville), vol. 35, 1993, 33–47.

Cupples, Cynthia Jean, 'Âmes d'élite: visionaries and politics in France from the Holy Catholic League to the reign of Louis XIV', Ph.D. Thesis, Princeton University, 1999, Ann Arbor, Michigan: UMI Dissertation Services, 2003.

Dagens, Jean, *Bérulle et les origines de la restauration catholique (1575–1611)*, Bruges: Desclée de Brouwer, 1952.

——, *Bibliographie chronologique de la littérature de la spiritualité et ses sources (1501–1610)*, Bruges: Desclée de Brouwer, 1952.

Davis, Natalie Zemon, *Society and Culture in Early Modern France: eight essays*, London: Duckworth, 1975.

——, 'The sacred and the body social in sixteenth-century Lyon', *Past & Present*, 1981, no. 90, 40–70.

Decker, Rainer, 'Die Haltung der römischen Inquisition gegenüber Hexenglauben und Exorzismus am Beispiel der Teufelaustreibungen in Paderborn 1657', in Sönke Lorenz and Dieter Bauer (eds), *Das Ende der Hexenverfolgung*, Stuttgart: Franz Steiner Verlag, 1995, 97–115.

Delcambre, Etienne and Jean Lhermitte, *Un cas énigmatique de possession diabolique en Lorraine au XVIIe siècle: Elisabeth de Ranfaing, l'énergumène de Nancy*, Nancy: Societé d'Archéoligie Lorraine, 1956.

Delumeau, Jean, 'Les Réformateurs et la superstition', in *Actes du Colloque l'Amiral de Coligny et son temps (Paris 24–28 octobre 1972)*, Paris: Societé de l'Histoire du Protestantisme français, 1974, 451–87.

——, *Catholicism between Luther and Voltaire: a new view of the Counter-Reformation* (1971), trans. Jeremy Moiser, with an introduction by John Bossy, London: Burns and Oates, 1977.

Deregnaucourt, Gilles and Didier Poton, *La vie religieuse en France aux XVIe, XVIIe, XVIIIe siècles*, Paris: Ophrys, 1994.

Dermenghem, Émile, *La vie admirable et les révélations de Marie des Vallées*, Paris: Plon-Nourrit et Cie, 1926.

Dessi, Cristina, 'Medicina e possessione demoniaca nel seicento francese. Pierre Yvelin e le possedute di Louviers', in *Cultura Populare e Cultura dotta nel seicento, Atti del Convegno di Studio di Genova (23–25 novembre, 1982)*, Milano: Franco Angeli, 1983, 190–98.

——, 'Un dibattito medico-filosofico su stregoneria e possessione demoniaca: il caso Gaufridy a Aix (1611)', in A. Cadeddu, G. Nonnoi and C. Dessi, *Questioni di Storia del*

Pensiero filosofico e scientifico, Annalo della Facoltà di Magistero dell'Università degli Studi di Cagliari, Quaderno 28, Cagliari: Istituto di Filosofico, 1987, 103–60.

Dibon, Paul, *Essai historique sur Louviers*, Rouen: Nicétas Périaux, 1836.

Dictionnnaire d'histoire et de géographie ecclésiastiques, Alfred Baudrillart et al. (eds), Paris: Le Touzey et Ané, 1912–.

Diefendorf, Barbara B., *Beneath the Cross: Catholics and Huguenots in sixteenth-century Paris*, Oxford and New York: Oxford University Press, 1991.

Du Bois, Louis, *Recherches archéologiques historiques biographiques et littéraires sur la Normandie*, Paris: Dumoulin, 1843.

Du Chesnay, Charles, 'Quelques questions relatives à Marie des Vallées', *Notre Vie*, 1956, no. 49, jan.–fév., 7–14.

Emery, Kent Jr., 'Mysticism and the coincidence of opposites in sixteenth- and seventeenth-century France', *Journal of the History of Ideas*, 1984, vol. 45, no. 1, 3–23.

Ernst, Cécile, *Teufelaustreibungen: die praxis der Katholischen Kirche im 16. und 17. Jahrhundert*, Bern: Huber, 1972.

Farr, James, *Authority and Sexuality in Early Modern Burgundy*, Oxford and New York: Oxford University Press, 1995.

Fèbvre, Lucien, 'Aspects méconnus d'un renouveau religieux en France entre 1590 et 1620', *Annales: Economies, Sociétés, Civilisations*, 1958, vol. 13, no. 4, 639–50.

Ferber, Sarah, 'The demonic possession of Marthe Brossier, France, 1598–1600', in Charles Zika (ed.), *No Gods Except Me: orthodoxy and religious practice in Europe, 1200–1600*, Melbourne: Melbourne University History Monographs, 1991, no. 14, 59–83.

——, 'Le sabbath et son double', in Nicole Jacques-Chaquin and Maxime Préaud (eds), *Le Sabbat des sorciers en Europe, XVe–XVIIIe siècle*, Grenoble: Jerôme Millon, 1993, 101–09.

Ferber, Sarah and Howe, Adrian, 'The man who mistook his wife for a devil: exorcism, expertise and secularisation in a late twentieth-century Australian criminal court', in Hans de Waardt, Jürgen Michael Schmidt and Dieter Bauer (eds), in co-operation with Sönke Lorenz and H.C. Erik Midelfort, *Dämonische Besessenheit. Zur Interpretation eines kulturhistorischen Phänomens/Demonic Possession. Interpretations of a historico-cultural Phenomenon* (Hexenforschung 9), Bielefeld: Verlag für Regionalgeschichte, 2003, 299–312.

Ferté, Jeanne, *La vie religieuse dans les campagnes parisiennes, 1622–1695*, Paris: J. Vrin, 1962.

Fisquet, M.H., *La France pontificale. Histoire chronologique et biographique des archévêques et évêques de tous les diocèses de France*, 16 vols, Paris: E. Repos, 1866.

Floquet, Amable, *Histoire du Parlement de Normandie*, 7 vols, Rouen: E. Frère, 1840–42.

Fraikin, Jean, 'Un cas de sorcellerie à la fin du XVIe siècle: l'affaire du moine sorcier de Stavelot', in *Tradition Wallone: Revue Annuelle de la Commission Royale Belge de Folklore, Mélanges Albert Doppagne*, 1987, no. 4, 251–335.

Freud, Sigmund, 'A seventeenth-century demonological neurosis', *The Standard Edition of the Complete Psychological Works*, ed. James Strachey, vol. 19, London: Hogarth, 1961, 69–105.

Garinet, Jules, *Histoire de la magie en France*, Paris: Foulon, 1818.

Garnier, Samuel, *Barbe Buvée . . . et la prétendue possession des Ursulines d'Auxonne (1658–1663), Etude historique et médicale d'après des manuscrits de la Bibliothèque Nationale et des archives de l'ancienne province de Bourgogne*, Préface de M. le Dr

Bourneville, Bibliothèque Diabolique Bourneville, no. 7, Paris: Bureaux du Progrès Médical, 1895.

Garreau, A., *Claude Bernard: le pauvre prêtre, parisien du Faubourg Saint-Germain*, Paris: Éditions du Cèdre, 1965.

Garrett, Clarke, 'Witches, werewolves and Henri Boguet', *Western Society for French History: Proceedings*, 1976, vol. 4, 126–34.

Geertz, Clifford, *The Interpretation of Cultures*, New York: Basic Books, 1973.

Gentilcore, David, 'The church, the devil and the healing activities of living saints in the Kingdom of Naples after the Council of Trent', in Ole Peter Grell and Andrew Cunningham (eds), *Medicine and the Reformation*, London: Routledge, 1993, 134–55.

——, *From Bishop to Witch: the system of the sacred in early modern Terra d'Otranto*, Manchester and New York: Manchester University Press, 1992.

——, *Healers and Healing in Early Modern Italy*, Manchester and New York: Manchester University Press, 1998.

Ginzburg, Carlo, *Ecstasies: deciphering the witches' sabbath*, trans. Raymond Rosenthal, London: Hutchinson Radius, 1990.

Golden, Richard M., *The Godly Rebellion: Parisian Curés and the Religious Fronde, 1652–1662*, Chapel Hill, N.C.: University of North Carolina Press, 1981.

Greenblatt, Stephen, 'Exorcism into art', *Representations*, 1985, vol. 12, Fall, 15–23.

——, 'Loudun and London', *Critical Inquiry*, 1986, vol. 12, no. 2, 326–46.

——, 'Shakespeare and the exorcists', in *Shakespearean Negotiations: the circulation of social energy in Renaissance England*, Berkeley and Los Angeles: University of California Press, 1988, 94–128.

Gueudré, Marie de Chantal, *Histoire de l'ordre des Ursulines en France*, 3 vols, Paris: Éditions St-Paul, 1957.

Haliczer, Stephen, *Sexuality in the Confessional: a sacrament profaned*, New York; Oxford: Oxford University Press, 1996.

Hanlon, Gregory and Geoffrey Snow, 'Exorcisme et cosmologie tridentine: trois cas agenais en 1619', *Revue de la Bibliothèque Nationale*, 1988, vol. 28, Summer, 12–27.

Hannah, Barbara, *Possession and Exorcism: polarities of the psyche*, Zurich: C.G. Jung Institute, 1955.

Hanotaux, Gabriel and Le Duc de la Force, *Histoire du Cardinal de Richelieu*, in *La politique intérieure du Cardinal*, vol. 4, Paris: Société de l'Histoire Nationale, 1935.

Harbage, Alfred, *Thomas Killigrew, Cavalier Dramatist*, New York: Benjamin Blom, 1930.

Head, Thomas, 'The religion of the "Femmelettes": ideals and experience among women in fifteenth- and sixteenth-century France', in Lynda L. Coon, Katherine J. Haldane and Elisabeth W. Sommer (eds), *That Gentle Strength: historical perspectives on women in Christianity*, Charlottesville and London: University Press of Virginia, 1990, 149–75.

Holt, Mack P., *The French Wars of Religion, 1562–1629*, Cambridge, New York and Melbourne: Cambridge University Press, 1995.

Houdard, Sophie, 'Des fausses saintes aux spirituelles à la mode: les signes suspects de la mystique', *Dix-Septième Siècle*, 1998, vol. 50, no. 3, 417–32.

——, (ed.), *Les sciences du diable: quatre discours sur la sorcellerie, XVe–XVIIe siècle*, Paris: Les Éditions du Cerf, 1992.

Hsia, R. Po-Chia, *The World of Catholic Renewal, 1540–1770*, Cambridge and New York: Cambridge University Press.

Huxley, Aldous, *The Devils of Loudun* (1952), London: Panther Books, 1977.

Irigaray, Luce, 'La Mystérique', in *Speculum of the Other Woman* (1974), trans. Gillian C. Gill, Ithaca, N.Y.: Cornell University Press, 1985, 191–202.

Irigaray, Luce, *Divine Women*, trans. Stephen Muecke, Local Consumption Occasional Paper, 1986, no. 8.

Jacques-Chaquin, Nicole and Maxime Préaud (eds), *Le Sabbat des sorciers, XVe–XVIIIe siècles*, Grenoble: Jérôme Millon, 1993.

——, *Les Sorciers du carroi de Marlou: un procès de sorcellerie en Berry, 1582–1583*, Grenoble: Jérôme Millon, 1996.

Jacques-Chaquin, Nicole (ed.), *La Sorcellerie* (1978), 2nd edn, in series *Les Cahiers de Fontenay*, no. 11/12, Paris: École Normale Supérieure de Fontenay-St Cloud, 1992.

Jones, David Mark, 'Exorcism before the Reformation: the problems of saying one thing and meaning another', MA thesis, University of Virginia, 1978.

Jouhaud, Christian, *Les Mazarinades: la Fronde des mots*, Paris: Aubier, collection historique, 1985.

Jungmann, J.A., *The Mass of the Roman Rite*, revised edn, trans. F. A. Brunner, New York: Benziger, 1959.

Kagan, Richard L., *Lucrecia's Dreams: politics and prophecy in sixteenth-century Spain*, Berkeley, Calif.: University of California Press, 1990.

Kieckhefer, Richard, *Unquiet Souls: the fourteenth-century saints and their religious milieu*, Chicago, Ill.: University of Chicago Press, 1984.

Kreiser, Robert B., 'The devils of Toulon: demonic possession and religious politics in eighteenth-century Provence', in Richard M. Golden (ed.), *Church, State and Society under the Bourbon Kings of France*, Lawrence, Kansas: Coronada Press, 1982, 173–221.

Kuntz, Marion Leathers, 'Angela da Foligno: a paradigm of Venetian spirituality in the sixteenth century', in Clare M. Murphy, Henri Gibaud and Mario A. di Cesare (eds), *Miscellanea Moreana: essays for Germain Marc'hadour*, Moreana 100, Binghamton, N.Y.: *Medieval and Renaissance Texts and Studies*, vol. 26, 1989, 449–64.

Larner, Christina, *Enemies of God: the witch-hunt in Scotland*, Oxford: Basil Blackwell, 1981.

Latreille, A., E. Delaruelle and J.-R. Palanque, *Histoire du Catholicisme en France*, vol. 2, *Sous les rois très chrétiens*, Paris: Éditions Spes, 1960.

Lavenia, Vincenzo, '"Cauda tu seras pendu": lotta politica ed esorcismo nel Piemonte di Vittorio Amedeo I (1634)', *Studi storici*, 1996, vol. 73, no. 2, 541–91.

Le Brun, Charles, *Marie des Vallées et le culte public du coeur de Jésus: Réponse à M. Émile Dermenghem*, Paris: Librairie P. Lethielleur, 1926.

Le Brun, Jacques, 'La fête du coeur de Jésus et l'actualité de son temps', *Vie Eudiste*, 1972, vol. 3, septembre, 36–48.

——, 'Mutations de la notion de martyre au XVIIe siècle d'après les biographies spirituelles féminines', in Jacques Marx (ed.), *Sainteté et martyre dans les religions du livre*, Brussels: Institut d'Études des Religions et de la Laicité, 1989, 77–96.

Le Brun, François, 'The two reformations: communal devotion and personal piety', in *A History of Private Life*, Volume III, *Passions of the Renaissance*, trans. Arthur Goldhammer, ed. Roger Chartier, Cambridge, Mass.: Harvard University Press, [1989].

Le Tenneur, René, *Magie, sorcellerie et fantastique en Normandie, dès premiers hommes à nos jours*, Coutances: Éditions OCEP, 1979.

Lea, Henry Charles, *Materials Towards a History of Witchcraft*, arranged and edited by

Arthur C. Howland, with an introduction by George Lincoln Burr, 3 vols, New York and London: Thomas Yoseloff, 1957.

Leblond, V., *Denise de la Caille, la Possédée de Beauvais: Ses crises de possession démoniaque; scènes d'exorcismes et de conjurations (1612–1613)*, Paris: Société française d'imprimerie et de librairie, 1908.

——, *Notes pour servir à l'histoire des possessions démoniaques*, Paris: Société Française d'Imprimerie et de Librairie, 1910.

Lederer, David , 'Living with the dead: ghosts in early modern Bavaria', in Kathryn A. Edwards (ed.), *Witches, Werewolves and Wandering Spirits: traditional belief and folklore in early modern Europe*, in *Sixteenth-century essays and Studies*, vol. 62, Kirksville: Truman State University Press, 2002, 25–54.

Lehoux, Françoise, *Le cadre de vie des médecins parisiens aux XVIe et XVIIe siècles*, Paris: A. and J. Picard, 1976.

Levack, Brian P., *The Witch-hunt in Early Modern Europe*, 2nd edn, London, New York: Longman, 1995.

Levi, Giovanni, *Inheriting Power: the story of an exorcist*, trans. Lydia G. Cochrane, Chicago, Ill.: University of Chicago Press, 1988.

Lévy-Valensi, Joseph, *La médecine et les médecins français au XVIIe siècle*, Paris: J.-B. Baillère et fils, 1933.

Lorédan, Jean, *Un grand procès de sorcellerie au XVIIe siècle: l'abbé Gaufridy et Madeleine de Demandolx, 1600–1670: d'après des documents inédits*, Paris: Perrin, 1912.

Lottin, Alain, 'Sorcellerie, possessions diaboliques et crise conventuelle', in *L'Histoire des faits de la sorcellerie*, Publications de Centre de Recherches d'Histoire Religieuse et d'Histoire des Idées, 8, Angers: Presses de l'Université d'Angers, 1985, 111–32.

——, *Lille: citadelle de la Contre-Réforme? (1598–1668)*, Dunkerque: Westhoek-Edition, 1984.

Lussana, Fiamma, 'Rivolta e misticismo nei chiostri femminili del seicento', *Studi Storici*, 1987, vol. 28, no. 1, 243–60.

MacDonald, Michael (ed.), *Witchcraft and Hysteria in Elizabethan London: Edward Jorden and the Mary Glover case*, with an introduction by Michael MacDonald, London and New York: Tavistock/Routledge, 1991.

Mandrou, Robert, *Magistrats et sorciers en France au XVIIe siècle: une analyse de psychologie historique* (1968), Paris: Seuil, 1980.

Marshman, Michelle, 'Exorcism as empowerment: a new idiom', *Journal of Religious History* (Great Britain), 1999, vol. 23, no. 3, 265–81.

Martin, Henri-Jean and Roger Chartier, *Histoire de l'édition française*, 4 vols, Paris: Promodis, 1982–86.

Martin, Henri-Jean, *Livre, pouvoirs et société à Paris au XVIIe siècle, 1598–1701*, 2 vols, Geneva: Droz, Geneva, 1969.

Martin, Ruth, *Witchcraft and the Inquisition in Venice, 1550–1650*, Oxford: Basil Blackwell, 1989.

Mauzaize, Jean, (Raoul de Sceaux), *Histoire des Frères Mineurs Capucins de la Province de Paris (1601–1660)*, 2 vols, Blois: Éditions Notre Dame de la Trinité, 1965.

Mauzaize, Jean, (Raoul de Sceaux), *Le rôle et l'action des Capucins de la Province de Paris dans la France religieuse du XVIIème siècle*, 3 vols, Paris: H. Champion, 1978.

Michelet, Jules, *Satanism and Witchcraft: a study in medieval superstition* (*La Sorcière*, 1862), trans. A.R. Allinson, London: Arco, 1958.

Midelfort, H.C. Erik, 'The Devil and the German people: reflections on the popularity of demon possession in sixteenth-century Germany', in *Articles on Witchcraft, Magic and Demonology*, vol. 9, 'Possession and Exorcism', edited and with an introduction by Brian P. Levack, New York and London: Garland, 1992, 113–33.

——, 'Madness and the problems of psychological history in the sixteenth century', *Sixteenth Century Journal*, 1981, vol. 12, no.1, 5–12.

Milcent, Paul, *Saint Jean Eudes: Un artisan du renouveau chrétien au XVIIe siècle*, Paris: Cerf, 1992.

——, 'Marie des Vallées' in M. Viller *et al.*, *Dictionnaire de spiritualité, ascétique et mystique: doctrine et histoire*. Paris: Beauchesne, 1937–95, vol. 16, 207–12.

Minvielle, Edmond, *La médecine au temps d'Henri IV*, Paris: Baillère et fils, 1904.

Monter, E. William, *Witchcraft in France and Switzerland: the borderlands during the Reformation*, Ithaca, N.Y.: Cornell University Press, 1976.

——, 'The Catholic Salem: or, How the Devil destroyed a saint's parish (Mattaincourt 1627–31)', (paper presented at Witchcraft in Context, University of York, 11–13 April, 2002)

Mousnier, Roland, *Peasant Uprisings in Seventeenth-century France, Russia and China* (1967), London: Allen & Unwin, 1971.

Muir, Edward, *Ritual in Early Modern Europe*, Cambridge and New York: Cambridge University Press, 1997.

Mullett, Michael A., *The Catholic Reformation*, London: Routledge, 1999.

Musée National du Moyen Âge web-site, <http://www.musee-moyenage.fr/homes.home_id20754_u1l2.htm>, accessed 3 December 2003.

Newman, Barbara, 'Possessed by the spirit: devout women, demoniacs, and the apostolic life in the thirteenth century', *Speculum*, 1998, no. 73, 733–70.

Niccoli, Ottavia, 'Esorcismi ed esorcisti tra cinque e seicento', *Societa e Storià*, 1986, no. 9, vol. 32, 409–18.

Nischan, Bodo, 'The exorcism controversy and baptism in the late Reformation', *Sixteenth Century Journal*, 1987, vol. 18, no. 1, 31–51.

Oesterreich, Traugott Konstantin, *Possession, Demoniacal and Other: among primitive races, in antiquity, the middle ages and modern times*, London: Kegan Paul, 1930.

O'Neil, Mary R., '"Sacerdote ovvero strione": ecclesiatical and superstitious remedies in sixteenth-century Italy', in Steven L. Kaplan (ed.), *Understanding Popular Culture*, Berlin: Mouton, 1984, 53–83.

——, 'Discerning superstition: popular errors and orthodox response in late sixteenth-century Italy', Ph.D. dissertation, Stanford University, Calif., 1982.

Orcibal, Jean, *Les origines du Jansenisme*, 5 vols, Paris: J. Vrin, 1947.

——, *Saint-Cyran et le Jansenisme*, Séries Maîtres Spirituels, Paris: Éditions du Seuil, 1961.

Pallier, Denis, *Recherches sur l'imprimerie à Paris pendant la Ligue (1585–1594)*, Geneva: Droz, 1975.

Paolin, Giovanna, *Lo spazio del silenzio: monacazioni forzate, clausura e proposte di vita religiosa femminile nell'età moderna*, Centro Studi Storici Menocchio Montereale Valcellina, Pordenone: Edizione Biblioteca dell'Immagine, 1996.

Pearl, Jonathan L., *The Crime of Crimes: demonology and politics in France, 1560–1620*, Waterloo, Ontario: Wilfred Laurier University Press, 1999.

Petrocchi, Massimo, *Esorcismi e Magia nel'Italia del cinquecento e del seicento*, Naples: Libreria Scientifica Editrice, 1957.

Pfister, Christian, *L'énergumène de Nancy, Elisabeth de Ranfaing et le couvent du Refuge*, Nancy: Berger-Levrault, 1901.

Pócs, Éva, *Between the Living and the Dead: a perspective on witches and seers in the early modern age*, translated by Szilvia Rédey and Michael Webb, Budapest: Central European University Press; Ithaca, N.Y.: Distributed in the U.S. by Cornell University Press Services, 1999.

Popkin, Richard H., *The History of Scepticism from Erasmus to Descartes*, rev. edn, New York: Harper and Row, 1968.

Porter, Roy 'Witchcraft and magic in Enlightenment, romantic and liberal thought', in Marijke Gijswijt-Hofstra, Brian P. Levack and Roy Porter, *The Athlone History of Witchcraft and Magic in Europe: The eighteenth and nineteenth centuries*, v. 5, general editors, Bengt Ankarloo and Stuart Clark, London: Athlone Press, 1999, 191–282.

Prat, J. M. *Recherches historiques et critiques sur la Compagnie de Jésus en France du temps du Père Coton*, 6 vols, Lyon: Briday, 1876.

Ramsey, Ann W., *Liturgy, Politics, and Salvation: the Catholic League in Paris and the nature of Catholic reform, 1540–1630*, Rochester, N.Y.: University of Rochester Press, 1999.

Rapley, Elizabeth, *The Dévotes: women and church in seventeenth-century France*, Montreal: McGill-Queens University Press, 1990.

——, *A Social History of the Cloister: daily life in the teaching monasteries of the Old Regime*, Montreal and Kingston; London; Ithaca, N.Y.: McGill-Queen's University Press, 2001.

Rapley, Robert, *A Case of Witchcraft: the trial of Urbain Grandier*, Montreal and Kingston: McGill-Queens University Press, 1998.

Renoux, Christian, 'Discerner la sainteté des mystiques: quelques exemples italiens de l'âge baroque', *Rives nord-méditerranéennes*, 2e série, 1999, no. 3, 19–28.

Robbins, Rossell Hope, *The Encyclopedia of Witchcraft and Demonology*, London: Peter Nevill, 1959.

Romano, Franca, *Guaritrici, veggenti, esorcisti: aspetti magici e religiosi della cultura delle classi popolari nella diocese di Brescia*, Rome: Gangemi Editore, 1987.

Romeo, Giovanni, *Inquisitori, esorcisti e streghe nell'Italia della Controriforma*, Florence: Sansoni Editore, 1990.

Ronan, Clifford J., 'Lucan and the self-incised voids of *Julius Caesar*', *Comparative Drama*, 1988, vol. 22, no. 3, 215–26.

Roper, Lyndal, *Oedipus and the Devil: witchcraft, sexuality and religion in early modern Europe*, London: Routledge, 1994.

Rousset, Jean, *L'Intérieur et l'extérieur: essais sur la poésie et sur le théâtre au XVIIe siècle*, Paris: J. Corti, 1968.

Rubin, Miri, *Corpus Christi: the Eucharist in late medieval culture*, Cambridge: Cambridge University Press, 1991.

Sallmann, J.-M., 'Théories et pratiques du discernement des esprits', in *Visions indiennes, visions baroques: les métissages de l'inconscient*, Paris: PUF, 1992, 91–116.

Sauzet, Robert, 'Sorcellerie et possession en Touraine et Berry aux XVIe–XVIIe siècles', *Annales de Bretagne et des pays de l'ouest*, 1994, vol. 101, no. 3, 69–83.

Sauzet, Robert and Elisabeth Laborie, *Du christianisme flamboyant à l'aube des Lumières: XIV–XVIIIe siècles*, vol. 2 in Jacques le Goff and René Raymond (eds), *Histoire de la France religieuse*, Paris: Seuil, 1988.

Scaraffia, Lucetta and Gabriella Zarri (eds), *Women and Faith: Catholic religious life in Italy from late antiquity to the present*, Cambridge, Mass. and London: Harvard University Press, 1999.

Schmitt, Jean-Claude, *Ghosts in the Middle Ages: the living and the dead in medieval society*, trans. Teresa Lavender Fagan, Chicago, Ill.: University of Chicago Press, 1998.

Scribner, R.W. 'Ritual and popular religion in Catholic Germany at the time of the Reformation', *Journal of Ecclesiastical History*, 1984, vol. 35, no. 1, January, 47–77.

Sedgwick, Alexander, *Jansenism in Seventeenth-Century France: voices from the wilderness*, Charlottesville, Va.: University Press of Virginia, 1977.

——, 'The nuns of Port-Royal: a study in female spirituality in seventeenth-century France', in Lynda L. Coon, Katherine J. Haldane and Elisabeth W. Sommer (eds), *That Gentle Strength. Historical Perspectives on Women in Christianity*, Charlottesville, Va. and London: University Press of Virginia, 1990, 176–89.

Séguin, Jean-Pierre, *L'Information en France avant la périodique: 517 canards imprimés entre 1529 et 1631*, Paris: Maissonneuve, 1964.

Sharpe, James, *The Bewitching of Anne Gunter: a horrible and true story of football, witchcraft, murder, and the King of England*, London: Profile Books, 1999.

Sluhovsky, Moshe, 'A divine apparition or demonic possession?: female agency and church authority in demonic possession in sixteenth-century France', *Sixteenth Century Journal*, 1996, vol. 27, no. 4, 1039–55.

——, 'The devil in the convent', *American Historical Review*, 2002, vol. 107, no. 5, 1378–411.

Smith, Morton, *Jesus the Magician*, San Francisco: Harper & Row, 1978.

Soman, Alfred, *Sorcellerie et justice criminelle: le Parlement de Paris (16e–18e siècles)*, Hampshire and Brookfield: Varorium, 1992.

Sorlin, Per, 'The Blåkulla story: absurdity and rationality', trans. Alastair Cochrane, *Arv*, 1997, no. 53, 131–52.

Stephens, Walter, *Demon Lovers: witchcraft, sex and crisis of belief*, Chicago and London: University of Chicago Press, 2002.

Taveneaux, René, *Le Catholicisme dans la France Classique, 1610–1715*, 2 vols, Paris: Société d'Édition d'Enseignement Supérieur, 1980.

Thomas, Keith, *Religion and the Decline of Magic*, Harmondsworth: Penguin, 1973.

Thompson, William M., (ed.) *Bérulle and the French School: selected writings*, New York; Mahwah, N.J.: Paulist Press, 1989.

Tolosana, Carmelo Lisón, *Demonios y Exorcismos en los Siglos de Oro*, in *La España Mental*, vol. 1, Madrid: Akal, 1990.

Toorn, Karel van der, Bob Becking, Pieter W. van der Horst (eds), *Dictionary of Deities and Demons in the Bible*, Leiden, E.J. Brill, 1995.

Trevor-Roper, Hugh, 'The Sieur de la Rivière, paracelsian physician of Henri IV', in Allen G. Debus (ed.), *Science, Medicine and Society in the Renaissance: Essays to Honor Walter Pagel*, 2 vols, London: Heinemann, 1972, vol. 227–50.

Trexler, Richard, 'Ritual behavior in Renaissance Florence: the setting', *Medievalia et Humanistica, Studies in Medieval and Renaissance Culture*, N.S.4, 1973, 125–44.

Triboulet, Raymond, *Gaston de Renty, 1611–1649, un homme de ce monde, un homme de Dieu*, Paris: Beauchesne, 1991.

Twelftree, Graham H., *Jesus the Exorcist: a contribution to the study of the historical Jesus*, Tübingen, Germany: J.C.B. Mohr (Paul Siebeck), 1993.

Venard, Marc, 'Le démon controversiste', in Michel Peronnet (ed.), *La Controverse religieuse (XVIe–XIXe siècles)*, 2 vols, Montpellier: Université Paul Valéry, 1980, vol. 2 45–60.

Vidal, Daniel, *Critique de la raison mystique: Bénoît de Canfield, possession et dépossession au XVIIIe siècle*, Grenoble: Jérôme Millon, 1990.

Viguerie, Jean de, *Notre Dame des Ardilliers à Saumur: le pèlerinage de Loire*, Paris: O.E.I.L, 1986.

Viller, M., et al., Dictionnaire de spiritualité, ascétique et mystique: doctrine et histoire. Paris: Beauchesne, 1937–95.

Walker, Anita M. and Edmund H. Dickerman, 'A notorious woman: possession, witchcraft and sexuality in seventeenth-century Provence', Historical Reflections, 2001, vol. 27, no. 1, 1–26.

——, '"A woman under the influence": a case of alleged possession in sixteenth-century France', Sixteenth Century Journal, 1991, vol. 22, no. 3, 534–54.

——, 'The haunted girl: possession, witchcraft and healing in sixteenth-century Louviers', Proceedings of the Annual Meeting of the Western Society for French History, 1996, 23, 207–18.

——, 'Magdeleine Des Aymards: demonism or child abuse in early modern France?', Psychohistory Review, 1996, vol. 24, no. 3, 239–64.

Walker, D. P., Spiritual and Demonic Magic: from Ficino to Campanella, London: Warburg Institute, 1958.

——, Unclean Spirits: possession and exorcism in France and England in the late sixteenth and early seventeenth centuries, London: Scolar Press, 1981.

Weber, Alison, 'Between ecstasy and exorcism: religious negotiation in sixteenth-century Spain', Journal of Medieval and Renaissance Studies, 1993, vol. 23, no. 2, 221–34.

——, 'Demonizing ecstasy: Alonso de la Fuente and the Alumbrados of Extremadura', in Robert Boenig (ed.), The Mystical Gesture: essays on medieval and early modern spiritual culture in honor of Mary C. Giles, Brookfield, Vt: Ashgate Press, 2000, 147–65.

——, 'Spiritual administration: gender and discernment in the Carmelite reform', Sixteenth Century Journal, 2000, vol. 31, no. 1, 123–46.

——, Teresa of Avila and the Rhetoric of Femininity, Princeton, N.J.: Princeton University Press, 1990.

Weber, Henri, 'L'exorcisme à la fin du XVIe siècle, instrument de la contre-reforme et spectacle baroque', Nouvelle revue du XVIe siècle, 1983, no. 1, 79–101.

Wessley, Stephen, 'The thirteenth-century Guglielmites: salvation through women', in Derek Baker (ed.), Medieval Women, Oxford: Ecclesiastical History Society/Basil Blackwell, 1978, 289–303.

Willaert, Léopold, Après le Concile de Trente: la restauration Catholique, 1563–1648, vol. 18 in A. Fliche and V. Martin (eds), Histoire de l'église depuis les origines jusqu'à nos jours, Paris: Bloud et Gay, 1960.

Yates, Frances A., Giordano Bruno and the Hermetic Tradition, London: Routledge and Kegan Paul, 1964.

Yve-Plessis, Robert-Charles, Essai d'une bibliographie française méthodique et raisonnée de la sorcellerie et de la possession démoniaque (1900), Nieuwkoop: de Graf, 1971.

Zarri, Gabriella, Le sante vive: cultura e religiosità femminile nella prima età moderna, Turin: Rosenberg and Sellier, 1990.

——, 'Purgatorio "particolare" e ritorno dei morti tra riforma e controriforma: l'area italiana', Quaderni Storici, 1982, vol. 17, no. 2, 466–97.

Zika, Charles, 'The devil's hoodwink: seeing and believing in the world of sixteenth-century Witchcraft', in Charles Zika (ed.), No Gods Except Me: orthodoxy and religious practice in Europe, 1200–1600, Melbourne: Melbourne University History Monographs, 1991, no. 14, 152–98.

——, Exorcising our demons: magic, witchcraft, and visual culture in early modern Europe, Leiden and Boston: Brill, 2003.

——, 'Fears of flying: representations of witchcraft and sexuality in early sixteenth-century Germany', *Australian Journal of Art*, 1989/1990, vol. 8, 19–47.

——, 'Hosts, processions and pilgrimages: controlling the sacred in fifteenth-century Germany', *Past and Present*, 1988, no. 118, February, 25–64.

Index